全国专门用途英语(ESP)规划教材

法 律 英 语
Legal　English

孙国平　编著

苏州大学出版社

图书在版编目(CIP)数据

法律英语/孙国平编著. —苏州:苏州大学出版社,2015.8
全国专门用途英语(ESP)规划教材
ISBN 978-7-5672-1428-6

Ⅰ.①法… Ⅱ.①孙… Ⅲ.①法律-英语-教材 Ⅳ.①H31

中国版本图书馆 CIP 数据核字(2015)第 193771 号

书　　名：	法律英语 Legal English
作　　者：	孙国平　编著
责任编辑：	汤定军
策　　划：	汤定军
装帧设计：	刘　俊
出版发行：	苏州大学出版社(Soochow University Press)
社　　址：	苏州市十梓街1号　邮编:215006
印　　刷：	苏州市正林印刷有限公司
网　　址：	www.sudapress.com
E - mail：	tangdingjun@suda.edu.cn
邮购热线：	0512-67480030
销售热线：	0512-65225020
开　　本：	787mm×960mm　1/16　印张:20　字数:389 千
版　　次：	2015 年 8 月第 1 版
印　　次：	2015 年 8 月第 1 次印刷
书　　号：	ISBN 978-7-5672-1428-6
定　　价：	49.00 元

凡购本社图书发现印装错误,请与本社联系调换。服务热线:0512-65225020

前言

苏州大学王健法学院作为"南东吴"之传人,身处东南沿海的改革开放前沿苏州。苏州外资企业众多,涉外法律实务需求旺盛。往昔东吴大学毕业生的特色之一便是其对比较法的深刻体悟、强劲的法律外文能力、实务导向的法律教育,这些使他们能够轻松应对各种涉外和国际法律业务。现在我国推行"走出去"战略,大量企业需要通晓中国法律与投资国法律加之英文熟练的高端法律人才,对法律英文操作能力要求甚高。

法律作为经世致用之学科要求法科毕业生必须具备较高的法律从业能力,其中包括熟练的法律英文操作能力。国内目前的法律英语教材大多侧重于知识(knowledge)的传授而忽略技能(skill)的培养,这对于娴熟的法律英文能力培养目标的达成殊为不利,因为学生毕业后有些将从事涉外法律业务,他们需要在法律英文的听、说、读、写、译、辩等方面做好储备,具备良好的口头表达能力、商务谈判能力、法律翻译能力、法律文书撰写能力以及法律辩护能力。编者根据自己学习和运用法律英语的体会结合近年来讲授法律英语的经验,将相关讲义整编成册,期望通过本课程的带动,为我院毕业生未来的从业之路夯实法律英文基础。

本教材注重实际能力的培养,兼顾知识灌输,侧重案例运用,以期使学生熟稔掌握英美法国家法律人员必须掌握的法律数据库(如 westlaw.com & lexisnexis.com 等),以及如何进行法律翻译、如何阅读英美法案例(how to read cases)、如何分析这些案例(analysis)、如何撰写案例摘要与法律意见书(case briefs and memos)、如何进行法庭辩论(argument)等内容。本教材基本上按照搜(research)—读(reading)—析(analysis)—写(writing)—辩(argument)脉络对法科学生需具备的几项能力进行培养。

学生万子锐、陈丽、刘禹、戚小乐、施骏、杨柳等承担了相关内容的文字输入工作,在此谨表谢忱。今年恰逢苏州大学法学院百年华诞,谨以此教材作为献礼以示致敬。感谢责编汤定军先生专业和辛苦的工作。编者才疏学浅,错讹之处还请大方之家多加指正,以便日后修订。

编者
2015 年 7 月

Contents

Chapter 1 Main Features of Legal English / 1

1. 准确（Precise or Exact） / 1
2. 拘谨（Formal） / 2
3. 费解（Tough） / 3
4. 模糊（Amiguous） / 8
5. 冗长（Lengthy） / 9
6. 保守（Conservative） / 11

Chapter 2 Typical Sentence Structures in Legal English Translation 13

1. otherwise / 15
2. subject to / 19
3. without prejudice to / 20
4. 引导法律英语条件句的连接词 / 21
5. for the purpose(s) of / 33
6. not with standing / 36
7. save …/except (for) / 37
8. in respect of / 38
9. purport / 41

Chapter 3 Archaic Adverbs and Model Verbs in Legal Documents 45

1. 英语法律文书中的古旧副词 / 45
2. 英语法律文书中的情态动词 / 52

Chapter 4 How to Deal with *Number* and *Time* in Legal Documents 66

1. 数(Number) / 66
2. 时间(Time) / 73

Chapter 5 How to Read a Case 83

1. 为什么要阅读案例　　　　　　　／ 83
2. 案例汇编与案例结构　　　　　　／ 85
3. 案例典型结构　　　　　　　　　／ 99

Chapter 6 Case Briefings 106

1. 如何做研究性案例摘要　　　　　／ 106
2. 课堂案例摘要　　　　　　　　　／ 108

Chapter 7 Neutral Analysis—the Office Memo 115

1. "Legal Memo" 简介　　　　　　　／ 115
2. "memo" 写作一般注意事项　　　　／ 116
3. "Office Memo" 的特点　　　　　　／ 118
4. "Office Memo" 的结构　　　　　　／ 119

Chapter 8 Structuring Legal Writing: The CRuPAC Formula 138

1. Introduction　　　　　　　　　　／ 138
2. Using CRuPAC　　　　　　　　　／ 139
3. A Final Note on the CRuPAC Formula　／ 145

Chapter 9 Identifying and Synthesizing Rules 147

1. Introducion　　　　　　　　　　／ 147
2. Types of Rules　　　　　　　　　／ 148
3. Hierarchy of Authority　　　　　　／ 149
4. Finding the Rule　　　　　　　　／ 151
5. Synthesizing Rules　　　　　　　／ 152

Chapter 10 Approaching a Case and Developing a Core Theory 156

1. Facts in Context　　　　　　　　／ 156
2. Develeping a Core Theory　　　　／ 158

Chapter 11 How to Write an External Memo—a Brief 165

1. Introduction　　　　　　　　　　／ 165

2. Parts of a Brief / 168
3. Sample Briefs: *Bell-Wesley v. O'Toole* / 182

Chapter 12 Introduction to Oral Argument 184

1. Preparing for Oral Argument / 185
2. Organizing the Oral Argument / 189
3. Questions by the Court / 194
4. Presenting the Oral Argument / 198
5. How to End Gracefully and Persuasively / 201

Appendix A History of Soochow University Law School / 202
Appendix B Jessup Materials / 240
Appendix C Sample Predictive Memorandum / 271
Appendix D Sample Record / 279
Appendix E Sample Appellant Brief / 290
Appendix F Sample Appellee Brief / 300
Bibliography / 309

Chapter 1　Main Features of Legal English

▶ 1. 准确（Precise or Exact）

正常情况下,起草法律文件时,用词造句务必十分精准(with great exactness),因为一旦笔者的思想、观点、企图落实成文字,即成为法庭判断是非的重要依据。尽管实践中还存在推测意图原则(principle of presumed intent),但其不占主导地位,书面文字仍然是法官解释法律文件的唯一依据。

实务中由于对法律文件文字理解不一,常有纠纷出现。

> The Charter required that directors "shall be elected on a vote of the stockholders representing not less than two-thirds of outstanding capital stock of the corporation".

甲方理解成:被选上董事的人需三分之二的股东投票赞成(a candidate to be elected needs the votes of two-thirds of the stockholders)

乙方则认为:选董事时须有三分之二的股东出席(two-thirds of the stockholders must be present at the meeting at which the election is held)

What's the judge's opinion?

一个阿肯色州的美国人临终前写了一个遗嘱,遗嘱写道:

> The remainder of the testator's property should be "divided equally between all of our nephews and nieces on my wife's side and my niece".

问题出在对"between"一词的理解上。立遗嘱人的妻子一方的外甥和外甥女加在一起共有22个人。这句话是指立遗嘱人的一半遗产归其妻子一方的22个外甥和外甥女,另一半归其本人一方的外甥女？还是指将遗产在双方的外甥、外甥女中平均分配呢？

为达准确之目的，常使用下列方法：

- 使用专门术语（下文有述）。
- 重复使用具有绝对含义的词汇，如 all、none、perpetuity、never、unavoidable。
- 使用具有绝对限制含义的短语，如 and no more（仅此而已），shall not constitute a waiver（不构成对权利的放弃），shall not be deemed a consent（不应视为同意）等此类表达方式。
- 使用含义宽泛的短语，如 including but not limited to（包括但不限于），or other similar or dissimilar cause（或其他类似或非类似的原因），shall not be deemed to limit（不应视为限制），without prejudice（不得损害）等。
- 使用详细的告知条款，如 on deposit in the United States mail registered and postage prepaid（在美国邮寄挂号函件，邮资预付）。
- 使用特别定义条款，如 words in the singular include the plural and vice versa（单数形式的词汇包括复数，反之亦然）等表达方式。
- 反复详细定义法律文件、事实情况、限制性条件、适用条件、例外情形、权利要求、表达不满（grievances）等。

> To all to whom these presents shall come or may come—Greeting: Know ye that I, _____, of _____, for and in consideration of _____ Dollars, to me in hand paid by _____, do by these presents for myself, my heirs, executors, and administrators, remise, release and forever discharge _____ of _____, his heirs, executors, and administrators, of and from any and all manner of action or actions, cause and causes of action, suit, debts, dues, sums of money, accounts, reckonings, bonds, bills, specialties, covenants, contracts, controversies, agreements, promises, trespasses, damages, judgments, claims, and demands whatsoever, in law or equity, which against him I have had, now have, or which my heirs, executors, or administrators, hereafter can, shall, or may have, for or by reason of any matter, cause, or thing whatsoever, from the beginning of the world to the day of the date of these presents, excepting a claim as to _____. In witness whereof, etc.

▶ **2. 拘谨（Formal）**

造成法律英语的拘谨而非大众化，原因多多，或出于传统的职业习惯，或出于显示自己与众不同的才华,或出于维护自己的职业尊严和职业利益圈,这些造成了人们常常使用与众不同的词或表达方法。例如,通常情况下,我们说"come here",而律师往往就用"approach the bench";我们说"He has become a judge",而法律界常用"He is on the bench";我们说"trust each other",而法学工作者常用"repose in one another"。凡此等等,请看下面的对照表:

通常用法	法学界用法
law teacher	law don
refer	advert
tell	advise
inform	apprise
begin or start	commence
show	demonstrate
building	edifice
bring about	effectuate
use	employ
unfriendly	inimical
work	employment
follow	ensue
for the same reason	by the same token

律师的此种做法招来各界的批评。美国诸多有关学者著书立说,在报刊上撰文要求法律界进行文字改革,呼吁他们"能用小字时不用大字"、"能用短字时不用长字"、"尽量用平实语言(plain English)"。

▶ **3. 费解(Tough)**

造成法律英语难学、难懂的原因还有以下几个方面:
(1) 经常使用常用词汇的不常用含义

常用词汇	不常用含义
action	a lawsuit (either civil or criminal)

alien	to transfer property to another
assigns	person to whom a right or property is assigned
avoid	to make void
bill	a draft law
brief	a written statement submitted to a court
charge	a form of security
clean hands	without dishonest motives (as in, "to have clean hands")
color	apparent legal right (as in, "under color of law")
consideration	the main cause for a contract
counterpart	a duplicate of a document
covenant	to make a binding promise
cover	to purchase goods to replace those not delivered because of a breach of contract
damages	the compensation sought for a loss
demise	to lease
depose	to state under oath
demur	not to agree
discovery	disclosure of information by the opposing party in a law suit
distress	the seizure of goods as security for an obligation
draft	an order for payment of money
draw	to sign a draft
endorsement	the signing of one's name on the back of a document
equitable	relating to equity as opposed to law
finding	determination
garnish	to obtain satisfaction of a debt from a third party rather than from the debtor directly
hand	signature
honor	to pay or accept
instrument	a formal legal document
interest	a right or claim to property
issue	living descendants
majority	legal age (as in, "to reach majority")
master	an employer
motion	a formal request to a court to seek an order or rule
note	a written promise to pay a debt

of course	as a matter of right (as in, "as a matter of course")
paper	an instrument evidencing a financial obligation
party	a person engaged in a transaction; a litigant in a lawsuit
plead	to file pleadings
pray	request for relief addressed to a court
prejudice	a detriment to legal rights (as in, "without prejudice")
prescription	the acquisition of a right over a long period
presents	this formal legal documents (as in, "by these presents")
provided	upon condition (word used to create a proviso)
purchase	to acquire title to land by means other than descent
remove	to transfer to another court
said	mentioned above
save	to except
security	collateral
serve	to deliver legal papers
show	to make clear by evidence
specialty	a contract under seal
tender	an offer of money
tenement	estate in land
utter	to put something counterfeit into circulation
virtue	authority or reason (as in, "by virtue of")
waive	to relinquish

（2）经常使用古英语和中世纪英语词汇

古英语（old English）指公元450—1100年间流行的英语；中古英语（middle English）指公元1100—1500年之间常用的英语。

古英语和中世纪英语词汇	现代英文含义
aforesaid	mentioned above; referred to previously
hereafter	from now on; at some future time
hereby	by this document; by these very words
herein	in this thing (such as a document, section, or matter)
hereinabove	in the above thing (such as a provision or document, clause)
hereinafter	later in this document;
hereof	of this thing (such as a provision or document)

pursuant to	in compliance with; in accordance with; under
thence	from that place; from that time
thereafter	afterward; later
therein	in that place or time
thereto	to that place, thing, issue, or the like
whereas	while by contrast; although
whereby	by which; through which; in accordance with which
whereof	of what; of which; of whom
whilst	during

（3）经常使用拉丁语词汇

在英国，人们把拉丁文看成是一个人深造的基础（the basis for advanced learning），对法科学生尤其如此。

拉丁词汇	英文含义
ab initio	from the beginning
ad hoc	for this purpose
ad litem	for the lawsuit
alibi	elsewhere (a defense that the accused was elsewhere when the offense was committed)
amicus curiae	friend of the court
bona fide	good faith
caveat emptor	let the buyer beware
ex parte	from one side
in re	in the matter of
inter alia	among others
prima facie	at first appearance
respondeat superior	let the superior answer (the employer is liable for the acts of his employees)
quorum	of whom (the minimum number of people required for a meeting)
scienter	having knowledge
situs	location
stare decisis	to stand by the decided matters (precedents must be followed)
sui generis	of its own kind
ultra vires	beyond the power

mutatis mutandis	all necessary changes having been made
versus	against

（4）使用古法语及法律法语中的词汇

法律语言常使用一般词汇表中不会有的古法语及法律法语，或称"盎格鲁诺曼语"（Anglo Norman）词汇。

古法语词汇	含义相当的英语
action	lawsuit
alien	transfer (property)
assigns	assignees (those to whom something has been assigned)
champerty	offense of financing a lawsuit in exchange for a portion of the proceeds
chance-medley	sudden quarrel or right
chose in action	a thing in action, a right to recover a debt
color	reason, pretext
coverture	status and rights of a wife arising from marriage
delict	wrong, offense
demise	grant, lease, death
issue	progeny
laches	neglect to assert a right or claim
lien	an encumbrance on property for the payment of debt
malfeasance	wrongdoing
nonfeasance	not doing, inaction
parol	oral
petty	small, minor
save	except
seisin	possession of real property
specialty	a contract under seal
style	name
suffer	permit
tort	a wrong or injury
remise	to give up

（5）专门术语的使用

- agency
- domicile
- certiorari
- discovery
- consideration
- double jeopardy

- easement
- jurisdiction in personam
- specific performance
- verdict
- recision
- ex parte
- jurisdiction in rem
- statue of limitation
- will
- variance
- intestate
- principal
- surety
- recuse

(6)"行话"(argot)的使用

"行话"是普遍适用于某一团体(如律师团体)的特定词汇或短语。

- abet
- adhesion contract
- circumstantial evidence
- grandfather clause
- issue of law
- negotiate instrument
- rescind
- accessory
- adverse possession
- foreclosure
- insider trading
- latent defect
- plea bargain
- without prejudice
- accomplice
- cause of action
- forum-shopping
- issue of fact
- legal fiction
- promissory estoppel

(7)经常使用官样文章用语

- Before me, the undersigned, a notary public
- By virtue of the authority vested in me
- From the beginning of the world to the date hereof
- In witness of these things
- In witness, this instrument is executed as of the day and year first written above
- In witness whereof I have hereunto set my hand and caused the seal of … to be affixed
- Know all people by these presents
- To whom it may concern

▶ 4. 模糊(Ambiguous)

法律人士常用模糊语言,或出于不愿明确地表达自己的立场与观点,或出于表示礼貌和对他人的尊重,或为不至于将自己的手脚捆住,诸如此等,视情况而定。

> Unless this account is paid within the next ten days, it will be necessary to take appropriate action.

本句中的"take appropriate action"是"start legal proceedings","bring suit",还是别的,不清楚。此外,常见的词或短语还有:adequate, all reasonable means, due care, due process, improper, reasonable care/man/speed, satisfactory, serious misconduct, undue influence 等。

▶ 5. 冗长（Lengthy）

法律英语多冗长，一旦遇见，不必方寸大乱，忍耐与专注乃是必备条件，先细读数遍，理出主句来。

> If the Vendor fails to apply for and obtain any necessary extension of time for completing the Development under Sub-Clause（2）and fails to complete the Development by the expiry date of the Building Covenant Period, the Purchase shall be entitled unless the completion of the sale and purchase herein has taken place, in addition to any other remedy that he may have, to give the Vendor notice in writing in that behalf to rescind this Agreement and upon service of such notice, this Agreement shall be rescinded within 7 days thereafter and the Vendor shall repay to the Purchaser all amounts paid by the Purchase hereunder together with interest thereon at the rate of 2% per annum above the prime rate specified by Hong Kong and Shanghai Banking Corporation Limited from time to time the date or dates on which such amounts were paid to the date of repayment, the repayment of such amounts and interest to be in full and final settlement of all claims by the Purchaser against the Vendor hereunder.

Mellinkoff 所说的"赘言"（tautology），即通过使用双式词（doublets）、对句（couplets）以及三联词（triplets）的表达方式反复地表达一个意思或使用同义词。那么为何法律语言显得冗长？对此存在多种解释。

（1）在英语发展过程中，经常出现两种或多种语言并存的情况。与英语有最密切联系的语言是拉丁语和法语，而拉丁语实际上在法律语言中处于一种权威性的地位。在法律语言中，拉丁语垄断了13世纪和14世纪两个世纪，此后拉丁语依然作为法律的书面语言被使用着。甚至在法律法语的使用最为盛行的14世纪、15世纪，拉丁语依旧在法律语言中被广泛地使用。在14世纪，法语成为英国法律的通用语言，并一直作为法律语言被使用至15世纪的末期。

源自拉丁语	古英语
doner	giver
homicide	manslaughter
testify	witness
testament	will

此外还有：

- able（古法语）and willing（古英语）
- acknowledge（古英语）and confess（古法语）
- act（法语或拉丁语）and deed（古英语）
- bills（古法语）and notes（古英语）
- breaking（古英语）and entering（法语）
- conjecture（中古法语或拉丁语）and surmise（中古法语）
- deem（古英语）and consider（古法语）
- depose（古法语）and say（古英语）
- encumbrance（古法语）or burdens（古英语）

在这些语意重复的词语中，一些是为了进一步阐明词义，一些是为了强调，而另一些则是为了符合当时使用两种语言的习惯。

（2）语意重复的做法另外是出于头韵的考虑（the power of alliteration）。"alliteration"是通过重复使用一个语音（一般来说是辅音）以使赘言式的语意重复保留在法律语言之中，如：

- aid and abet
- to have and to hold
- part and parcel
- safe and sound
- remise, release and forever quit claim
- rest, residue and remainder

（3）大量使用近义词，如：

- able and willing
- annul and set aside
- authorize and empower

- construed and interpreted
- covenant and agree
- duties and obligations
- each and every
- final and conclusive
- in lieu of and in place of
- right, title, and interest

（4）16世纪证据法的发展在一定程度上造成了法律语言的冗长。由于当事人被禁止以证人的身份出庭，为了在诉讼中保护自己，他们都希望能够向法庭提交一份内容翔实的长篇书面诉状，这样会有助于其从自身的立场出发来阐明案件的情况。

当然还有其他一些原因，如答辩状由拉丁文翻译而来，就似中文的古文被译成现代文一般，总是显得比古文啰唆冗长。

简文	冗长
annul	annul and set aside
remove	entirely and completely remove
will	last will and testament
void	totally null and void
without hindrance	without let or hindrance

为表述"当事人各方因已接受对价而同意"，下例中用了四行文字：

> Now, therefore, in consideration of the premises, and the representations, warranties, covenants and undertakings of the parties hereinafter set forth, and for other good and valuable considerations, the parties agree among themselves as follows ...

此处"good consideration"意思是"consideration that is valid under the law"。

▶ 6. 保守（Conservative）

法律语言的保守产生于公式化的语言，即在语言中使用某些公式。Mellinkoff 曾对最早的英国法进行过研究。他认为，口头传统是造成法律语言对宗教仪式般系统阐述依赖的主要因素，如盎格鲁-撒克逊的誓言必须依赖形式的重复才能得到其他任何词语不会产生的效果。在文盲充斥的社会里，只有逐字重复才能确保重要的观点得以继续存在。若词句以一种愉悦听觉的形式出现,保留和重复就会变得容易。语言被赋予韵律之后就会变得容易传播。盎格鲁-撒克逊的法律采用了当时头韵和节律的形式才使古英语保留在一般的誓言之中。如下列一澳洲法庭提供的宣誓词范本,适合刑事程序:

> I ... do solemnly, sincerely and truly affirm and declare that the evidence which I shall give to the court and jury sworn between our Sovereign Lady the Queen and the prisoner at the bar shall be the truth, the whole truth and nothing but the truth.
>
> When you are taken an affirmation as a witness in a civil trial, you will be asked to say:
>
> I ... do solemnly, sincerely and truly affirm and declare that the evidence which I shall give to the court touching the matter in question between the two parties shall be the truth, the whole truth and nothing but the truth.

此外,法律语言的保守还表现在对先例(precedent)的引用上。

Chapter 2
Typical Sentence Structures in Legal English Translation

法律翻译有一个非常重要的原则,即要在法律文书中保持法律术语、习语及相同句式结构译文的同一性和一致性,不能随意使用不同形态的同义词或近义词表达相同的法律概念,也不能让同样的句式结构存在多种不同形式的翻译表述。法律英译为了维护同一概念、内涵或事物在法律上始终同一,以免引起歧义,词语一经选定就必须前后统一,在翻译中只要认准并用准某词语,就不要避讳反复使用。此即法律英译同一律原则。

Henry Weihofen 在其《法律文体》一书中曾告诫英语法律起草工作者:Don't be afraid to repeat the right word! 其所以这样,旨在保证法律文字的准确:Exactness often demands repeating the same term to express the same idea. Where that is true, never be afraid of using the same word over and over again. Many more sentences are spoiled by trying to avoid repetition than by repetition.

据研究,我国《民法通则》中"法律规定"的动词"规定",就被英译者反复地更换译名,如"stipulate"(Art. 72),"specify"(Art. 52),"prescribe"(Art. 64),"require"(Art. 65)和"provide"(Art. 107)。这自然违反了同一律,会使法律概念混淆,使读者不必要地去揣测不同词语之差别,从而影响法律的精确度。

■ 原文

For the purpose of this Part—
(a) an instrument is false if it purports to have been—
(i) made in the form in which it is made by a person who did not in fact make it that form;
(ii) made in the form in which it is made on the authority of a person who did not in fact authorize its making in that form;

（ⅲ）made in terms in which it is made by a person who did not in fact make it in those terms；

（ⅳ）made in terms in which it is made on the authority of a person who did not in fact authorize its making on those terms；

（ⅴ）altered in any respect by a person who did not in fact alter it in that respect；

（ⅵ）altered in any respect on the authority of any person who did not in fact authorize its alteration in that respect；

（ⅶ）…

■ 译文

就本部分而言——

（a）任何文书如有下列情况，即属虚假——

（ⅰ）该文书是以某种式样制成，并看来是由某人以该式样制成，但事实上该人并未以该式样制造该文书；

（ⅱ）该文书是以某种式样制成，并看来是经某人授权以该式样制造，但事实上该人并未授权以该式样制造该文书；

（ⅲ）该文书是按某些条款制造，但事实上该人并未按该等条款制造该文书；

（ⅳ）该文书是按某些条款制成，并看来是经某人授权按该等条款制造，但事实上该人并未授权按该等条款制造该文书；

（ⅴ）该文书看来曾由某人在某些方面予以更改，但事实上该人并未在该方面予以更改；

（ⅵ）该文书看来是经某人授权在某方面予以更改，但事实上该人并未授权在该方面予以更改；

（ⅶ）……

从上例中可看出，在正式程度很高的法律文件中，无论是在原文还是在翻译中，所用的词汇及句型的重复率都非常高，如"instrument"译成"文书"、"made"译成"制成"、"a person"译成"某人"，在整个条款中皆保持一致。虽然以上词汇均有若干种甚至数十种的不同译法，句型也可五花八门，而有所创新和变化也许会使条文读起来不那么刻板、单调，但法律文献的写作及翻译须恪守译名同一律要求，不允许有此种变化。

法律英语中存在一些特别的句式、句型和短语，此类句式、句型和短语是法律英语神秘化、象牙塔化的主要原因，它们实际上是法律文件常用的连接词，其在法律文书中的频繁出现，使普通读者对法律文书望而生畏。在此挑选一些法律英语中使用频率较高的句式、句型、短语连接词加以介绍。

▶ 1. otherwise

"otherwise"有多种含义和不同搭配用法。在英文里,"otherwise"的释义为：under other circumstances（以其他形式/在其他情况下）, in another manner/differently（其他方式；别样；以另外方式）, in other respects（其他方面；除此之外）。

在法律英语中,"otherwise"通常跟"unless"引导的从句（让步状语从句）连用或放在连词"or"之后使用。还有一种用法是跟"than"一起,通常用来否定句子的主语。

> In this Ordinance, <u>unless the context otherwise requires</u>, "state" means a territory or group of territories having its own law of nationality.
>
> 在本条例中,<u>除文意另有所指外</u>,"国家"指拥有本身国籍法的领域或一组领域。

"unless the context otherwise requires"这一结构在法律的释义部分最为常见,汉译一般译成"除……另有……外"。根据此类条例的上下文,"otherwise"的意思是"不同地",用来修饰"unless"从句中的动词"requires"。被动语态中,"otherwise"通常放在主语与动词之间或放在被动句的助动词"be"与分词形式之间。汉语中的译法与主动语态相同。

> <u>Unless in any enactment it is otherwise provided</u>, the period of imprisonment, which may be imposed by a magistrate exercising summary jurisdiction, in respect of the non-payment of any sum of money adjudged to be paid by a conviction, whether it be a fine or in respect of the property the subject of the offence, or in respect of the injury done by the offender, or in respect of the default of a sufficient distress to satisfy any such sum, shall be such period as, in the opinion of the magistrate, will satisfy the justice of the case, but shall not exceed in any case the maximum fixed by the following scale ...
>
> <u>除成文法另有规定外</u>,对于因不缴付根据定罪裁定须缴付的款项（不论是罚款或就作为犯罪主体的财物而须缴付的款项）,或因犯罪者所造成的损害,或因无足够扣押物以抵偿此等款项,则行使简易程序审判权的裁判官可判处其认为就案情而言是符合公正原则的监禁刑期,但无论如何不得超过下表所定的最长刑期……

> A notice under subsection (1) shall, <u>unless it otherwise provides</u>, apply to the income from any property specified therein as it applies to the property itself.
>
> 根据第(1)款发出的通知书,<u>除其中另有订定外</u>,亦适用于通知书内指明的财产的收入,一如适用于该项财产本身。

被动语态中的"otherwise"结构常简写成"unless otherwise + V(p/pp)"形式。

> Unless otherwise stipulated in L/C, the expression "shipment" used in stipulating an earliest and/or latest shipment date will be understood to include the expression "loading on board", "dispatch" and "taking in charge".
>
> 除信用证另有规定外,用于规定最早(或最迟)装运期的"装运"一词应理解为包括"装船"、"发运"和"接受监管"。

> Unless otherwise specified herein, neither Party may transfer its capital contribution to any third party.
>
> 除非本合同另有规定,任何一方均不得向任何第三方转让其出资。

需要指出的是,"unless otherwise"比"if not"和"otherwise"正式,在汉语中无一成不变的"对等词",根据上下文应有不同的译法。

"otherwise"用在正式文体中,其基本意思是"另外"。而"or otherwise"是一固定短语,意思是:① 或相反,或其反面,如:the attractive ness or otherwise of a suit of clothes; It was necessary to discover the truth or otherwise of these statements。② 用别的方法,通过别的途径;出现相反的情况,如:Fine or otherwise, we shall have to go; We insure against all damage, accidental or otherwise。

但在法律文件中,有人认为,若"otherwise"与"or"连用,其意思与起连接作用的连词"or"之前的短语相同。

> If two or more persons are defendants to a claim, as partners or otherwise, a process may be served on any of them and an award may be obtained and execution issued against any person so served notwithstanding that any other persons jointly liable may not have been served or been a party or may not be within the jurisdiction of the Board.
>
> 如有2名或以上的人以合伙人或其他身份而属同一诉讼的被告人,传票可送达其中任何一人,而判定该收件人败诉的裁定可由原告获得,执行令亦可向该收件人进行,即使任何其他共同有责之人可能未获传票,或不属当事人,或不在仲裁处的管辖范围内,均无例外。

上例中,"otherwise"的语法作用与介词短语"as partners"完全相同,两者语法功能虽然相同,但意思还是取"不同、相反或别的(方式、方法、手段、身份等)"。

> Any person who by threats, persuasion or otherwise induces a witness or a party not to give evidence in any hearing before the Board commits an offence.
>
> 任何人藉恐吓、怂恿或以其他手段诱使证人或一方当事人不在仲裁处聆讯中作证,即属犯罪。

Chapter 2　Typical Sentence Structures in Legal English Translation

在本句中,"otherwise"是一个副词,意为"以其他手段",用来修饰动词 induces。

> Where a court is satisfied in proceedings for an offence under subsection (1) (b) that, having regard to the closeness of his relationship to the accused and to other circumstances, there is reason to believe that any person was holding pecuniary resources or property in trust for <u>or otherwise</u> on behalf of the accused or acquired such resources or property as a gift from the accused, such resources or property shall, until the contrary is proved, be presumed to have been in the control of the accused.
>
> 在因第(1)(b)款所定罪行而进行的法律程序中,法庭经顾及任何人与被控人关系的密切程度及其他情况后,如有理由相信该人为被控人以信托形式持有或<u>以其他方式</u>代被控人持有金钱资源或财产,或因被控人的馈赠而获取该等金钱资源或财产,则在相反证明成立之前,该等金钱资源或财产须推定为由被控人控制。

> A person who disposes of <u>or otherwise</u> deals with any property specified in a notice under subsection (1) or a bank or deposit-taking company which pays any money to a person specified in a copy of a notice served on it under subsection (1A) <u>other than</u> in accordance with the consent of the Commissioner shall be guilty of an offence and shall be liable on conviction to a fine of $50,000 or the value of the property disposed of <u>or otherwise</u> dealt with, whichever is greater, and to imprisonment for 3 years.
>
> 任何人并非经由专员同意而将根据第(1)款所发通知书中指明的任何财产处置或<u>以其他方式</u>处理,或任何银行或接受存款公司并非经由专员同意而将款项付予据第(1A)款向其送达的通知书副本中指明的人,即属犯罪,一经定罪,可处罚款$50,000,或处以所处置或<u>以其他方式</u>处理的财产价值的罚款,两款额以较大者为准,并监禁3年。

在上面两例中,"otherwise"意为"in another way/manner","differently",均译成"以其他方式"。

此外,"otherwise"后跟上"than",可形成"otherwise than"结构,其作用相当于"unless",其中"otherwise"起方式状语作用,且一般只用在否定句中。

> No claim shall be recoverable hereunder if the benefit of the contract herein contained shall become vested in any other person or persons at law or in equity <u>otherwise than</u> by will or operation of law, unless the written consent of the Insurer thereto shall have first been obtained.
>
> 如果本单所含合约利益<u>不用遗嘱</u>或<u>不运用法律</u>的方式归于在普通法或衡平法上享有权益的其他任何人,就不能取得所索之赔偿,除非事先得到承保人对此的书面同意。

No will or any part thereof shall be revoked otherwise than—

(a) by marriage as provided by Section 13; or

(b) by another will executed in accordance with Section 5; or

(c) by a written revocation executed in the manner in which the will was executed; or

(d) by the burning, tearing or otherwise destroying of it by the testator, or by some person in his presence and by his direction, with the intention of revoking it.

除藉以下方式外，任何遗嘱的全部和任何部分均不得撤销——

(a) 根据第 13 条的规定因缔结婚姻而撤销；或

(b) 藉按照第 5 条签立的另一份遗嘱而撤销；或

(c) 藉依照签立遗嘱方式签立的遗嘱撤销书而撤销；或

(d) 由立遗嘱人或由其他人在立遗嘱人当面并依其指示将遗嘱烧毁、撕毁或以其他方法毁灭，而其意愿是撤销遗嘱。

No will or any part thereof, which is in any manner revoked, shall be revived otherwise than by the re-execution thereof or by a codicil executed in accordance with Section 5 and showing an intention to revive it.

遗嘱的全部或任何部分无论以任何方式撤销后，除非按照第 5 条重新签立或加入依第 5 条签立的遗嘱更改附件，并表明意愿是恢复遗嘱的效力，否则该遗嘱的全部或任何部分均不能恢复效力。

在以上三例中，"otherwise than"意思等同于"by other means than"或"unless"，词性仍为副词，通常译为"除了……之外"或"除非"。

★ "otherwise than"与"other than"的比较：二者词性结构相似，意思也十分相近，但用法很不相同。前者修饰的总是句子中的动词，后者可修饰名词。虽然在普通英语里，"other than"词性上仍然是副词，用来修饰动词，如：We can't collect the rent other than by suing the tenant，意思相当于"differently"（除非）。但在法律英语中，"other than"也常用来修饰名词，可译成"除……之外"、"非……"。

Any person guilty of an offence under this Part, other than an offence under Section 3, shall be liable—

(a) on conviction on indictment—

…

(b) on summary conviction—

…

除第 3 条所定罪行外，任何人犯了本部所定罪行，可遭处罚如下——

(a) 一经循公诉程序裁定——
……
(b) 一经循简易程序裁定——
……

Subject to this section, where an order is made under Section 12AA in respect of pecuniary resources or property held by a person <u>other than</u> the person convicted, that other person may, within 28 days after the date of making the order, appeal against the other of the Court of Appeal.

在符合本条规定下,凡法庭根据第12AA条对并非被定罪之人持有的金钱资源或财产做出命令,该人可在命令做出的日期后28天内就该命令向上诉法院提出上诉。

总之,"otherwise"是一个使用频率很高、用途相当广泛的法律英语用词,通常与置前的"unless"、"or"或置后的"than"连用。在所有例子中,"otherwise"都只起副词的作用。如上述各例所示,"otherwise"的结构在汉语里一般译成"除了……以外"或"以其他……方式"。至于何种译法更为合理,须依上下文及词语习惯搭配而定。

▶ **2. subject to**

该短语在法律英语中一般都跟"agreement"、"section"、"contract"等法律文件名或文件中的特定条款名配合使用,常译为"以……为条件"、"根据……规定"、"在符合……的情况下"、"除……另有规定外"、"在不抵触……下"等。

<u>Subject to this section</u>, an appeal shall be brought in such manner and shall be <u>subject to such conditions</u> as are prescribed by rules made under Subsection (5).

<u>在符合本条的规定下</u>,上诉须根据(5)款订立的规则内订明的方式提出,并须<u>受该规则所订明的条件规限</u>。

<u>Subject to</u> Subsection (2), there shall be payable and recoverable by way of rent of premises to which this Part applies such amount as may be agreed between the landlord and tenant …

<u>在符合第(2)款的规定下</u>,本部适用的处所的应缴付与可追收的租金须为业主与租客双方所可能议定的款额……

> This Contract is subject to the approval of the Examination and Approval Authority before the same may become effective.
>
> 本合同须经审批部门批准方能生效。

"subject"一词作名词时意思是"主题"、"臣民"等,作动词时意思是"使服从"和"使蒙受"。但这两种用法通常出现在普通英语中,一般不会造成理解困难和翻译上的疑惑。此处的"subject"为形容词,多用在法律英语中,其汉语译法较多,但核心意思大同小异。不管译成"以……为条件"、"根据……规定",还是"在符合……情况下"、"在……规限下",其中心意思都是"受制于"有关条款或须"依照"有关条款办事。翻译时可进行词性转换,将"subject"由形容词变为动词,可根据情况译为"适用"、"遵守"、"遵循"等,如:This credit is subject to UCP600;The parties to the contract are subject to Chinese laws。

▶ 3. without prejudice to

此连接短语的功能相当于普通英文中的"without affecting"。与"subject to"的句法结构相同,跟在"without prejudice to"之后的通常是一个指代某项法律条款的名词,但其对有关事物或条款的规限程度没有前者那么强硬。前者规限的程度是必须"符合"或"依照"有关条款或规定,后者指不要影响或损害其规限的事物。汉语中,其意思常译为"在不损害……的原则下"、"在不影响……的情况下"、"……不受影响"、"不妨碍……"等。

> Without prejudice to Section 24, the following shall be treated as properly executed …
>
> 在不影响第24条规定的原则下,以下的遗嘱须视为正式签立……

> If, upon the hearing of a claim, the claimant does not appear, the Board may strike out the claim, without prejudice, however, to the restoration of such claim by the Board, on the application of the claimant, on such terms as it may think just.
>
> 如原告不出庭聆讯,仲裁委可剔除该诉求,但此举对仲裁委在原告提出申请后,按其认为公正的条款恢复该诉求并无影响。

Without prejudice to your powers and discretions, we hereby authorize you or your agents to take any actions including but not limited to the following: ...

在贵行权力和任意决定权<u>不受影响的情况下</u>,本公司兹授权贵行或贵行代理采取包括但不限于下列的任何行动:……

Without prejudice to the rights of the Attorney General every complainant or informant shall be at liberty to conduct the complaint or information respectively and to have the witnesses examined and cross-examined by him or by counsel on his behalf.

在<u>不损害律政司权利的原则下</u>,每名申诉人或告发人可进行其申诉或告发,并亲自或由代表律师讯问及盘问证人。

由此可见,该连接短语指的是"对法定利益或要求无影响或无损害",通常译为"在不损害……的原则下"或"在……不受影响的情况下"。

▶ 4. 引导法律英语条件句的连接词

(1)"if"的引导与翻译

严格来讲,如果事件通常会发生,应该用 if 作为条件句的引导词。

If any Schedule Goods are found not to conform to the warranty requirement, the University may, in addition to any other remedies at law or in the Contract, return such Schedule Goods to the Contractor, at the Contractor's expense, for correction, replacement or credit, as the University may direct.

如果交付的表列货品与保证规定不符,大学除了寻求其他合法的或合约规定的补偿外,可将表列货品退还给承包商,由承包商根据大学可能做出的指示予以纠正、替换或记入贷方账户,退货费用则由承包商承担。

If you fail to pay the Tuition Fees (or any part of the Tuition Fees) within 14 days of the date when are due the University shall be entitled to charge interest at the rate of 3% per year above the base rate of the Bank of England from time to time on the amount of the Tuition Fees outstanding.

如果你在规定的到期期限的14天内未支付学费(或部分学费),大学有权按照高于英格兰银行不时规定的基本年利率的3%向你收取未付学费部分的利息。

> If your studies with the University are terminated as a result of disciplinary action taken against you in accordance with the disciplinary procedures of the University, this Agreement shall end automatically without the need for any notice, unless the University agrees otherwise in writing.
>
> 如果你由于大学根据其惩戒程序对你采取的惩戒行为而中止学业，本合约在无须通知的情况下自动终止，但若大学另有书面同意书则属例外。

> Therefore, in general, if a tenant is late in paying the rent for 15 days, the landlord is entitled to terminate the tenancy.
>
> 因此，一般而言，如果租客迟付租金超过15天，业主有权终止租约。

上述四例中的"情况"属贸易往来或日常生活中司空见惯之事。此类条件句的引导词一律用"if"，实属情理之中。"if"一般译成"如果"，且为体现法律语言的严谨或保守，一般不宜缩略成"如"，尤其在中央一级的或全国性的法律法规中极少使用（如该用"或者"的地方不用"或"；该用"应当"的地方不用"应"；该用"可以"的地方不用"可"等）。原文中用了"you"等来表示假设的法律主体，现代英语写作都提倡使用"you"和"we"拉近政府机构（法规制定者）和群众间的距离。虽然用"you"翻译避免了"he"或"she"，使译文更简洁，但在我国的立法中还没有这种格式，也无人试图这样翻译。

美国国家档案和记录管理局出版的写作手册 *Drafting Legal Documents* 中规定：如果只有一个"if"、一个"then"，则先说"if"，再说"then"。这样做的好处是，假如"if"表示"then"的适用对象，读者读完"if"后就知道是否需要往下读了。例如，对于 If you invested in Class A shares, then ……一句，如果读者不投资于A股，就不用读下去了。如果有一个"if"、数个"then"，则先说"if"，再把"then"以清单形式列举出来；如果只有一个"then"、几个"if"，则先说"then"，把"if"的内容以清单形式列举出来；如果有多个"if"、多个"then"，可能就需要把一个句子断为几个句子，分清哪个"if"对应哪个"then"，或者列表说明。清单式列举可使逻辑清楚，避免 and/or 引起的歧义，下面对这条规则（列举）的英语说明本身就体现了这一规则的用法：

When you list, use the following rules:

- Use parallel structure.
- List each item so that it makes a complete thought when reading with the introductory text.
- If the introductory language for the list is a complete sentence—
- End the introduction with a colon; *and*

- Make each item in the list a separate sentence.
- If the introductory language for the list is an incomplete sentence—
- End the introduction with a dash;
- End each item in the list except the last item with a semi-colon;
- After the semi-colon in the next-to-last item in the list, write "and" or "or" as appropriate; and
- End the last item in the list with a period.

据此规则，试比较下列译文有何不妥：

> 第十条　有下列情形之一的,婚姻无效：
> （一）重婚的；
> （二）有禁止结婚的亲属关系的；
> （三）婚前患有医学上认为不应当结婚的疾病,婚后尚未治愈的；
> （四）未到法定婚龄的。
> Article 10　Marriage shall be invalid under any of the following circumstances：
> （1）if one party commits bigamy；
> （2）if the man and the woman are relatives by blood up to the third degree of kinship；
> （3）if, before marriage, one party is suffering from a disease which is regarded by medical science as rendering a person unfit for marriage and, after marriage, a cure is not effected； and
> （4）if the legally marriageable age is not attained.

译文违反了列举的规则：List each item so that it makes a complete thought when reading with the introductory text. ("Marriage shall be invalid under any of the following circumstances"与"if one party commits bigamy"不构成完整的句子); and 用得不对,应当用 or。

改译：

> Article 10　A marriage is invalid if—
> （1）One party commits bigamy；
> （2）The two parties are blood relatives that may not be married under law；
> （3）Either party before marriage suffered from a disease considered by medical science as rendering a person unfit for marriage and that is not cured after marriage; or
> （4）Either party has not attained the legal age for marriage.

(2)"where"的引导与翻译

英语法律文本中存在着可以用"if"但却用"where"表达的情形,通常是由于撰写人希望文本在语体上更加正式,译成"那里"绝对为错。虽然二者并无本质上的差别,但"where"在译成中文时未必皆可译成"如果",其对应的中文主要是"凡"(香港用得多)、"……的"(内地用得多)。

> Where a defendant is fined and the same is not forthwith paid, the magistrate may order the defendant to be searched.
>
> 凡被告人被判处罚款,但没有随即缴付罚款,裁判官可命令搜查被告人。

用"where"替代"if"在我国英文版本的各类法律条文中随处可见。

> 前款规定的人员,索取他人财物或者非法收受他人财物,犯前款罪的,处五年以上十年以下有期徒刑,并处罚金。
>
> Where a person stated in the preceding paragraph extorts money and goods from others or illegally accepts money and goods from others to commit the aforementioned crime, he or she is to be sentenced to more than five years but not more than ten years of fixed-term imprisonment and a fine.

如果中文文本中含有"在该种情形之下,该人应当负有何种责任或应当给予何种奖惩"的条文,用"where"引导其中的条件句,既能恰到好处地表达原文的内涵,又能使句子符合法律文体的风格。

(3)"when"的引导与翻译

法律英语条文中的条件句如果含有时间上的寓意——即将来某一天可能会去做某事或会发生某事,通常可用"when"作引导词。

> When one Party removes and replaces any directors whom it has appointed, it shall give written notice to the other Parties, the former and newly appointed directors and the Joint Venture Company, and state the reasons therefor.
>
> 如果一方要撤换任何董事,应向其他各方及原任董事、新任董事和合营公司发出书面通知,并说明撤换情由。

> When a patent application is filed for an invention or utility model, relevant documents shall be submitted, including a written request, a specification and an abstract thereof, and a patent claim.
>
> 申请发明或者实用新型专利的,应当提交请求书、说明书及其摘要和权利要求书等文件。

由此可见,在英文法律条文中,遇到以"when"作为引导词的条件句时,要细心辨析,不能按普通英文那样一概将其译成"当……时";若能确定其所引导的是条件句,译成"如果……"、"凡……"、"……的"更为准确。

(4)"in case"和"in the event that"的引导和翻译

二者引导的条件句通常指不太可能或不容易发生的事件。

> In the event that any provision of this Agreement is declared invalid or void by statute or judicial decision, or when an appropriate administrative agency has issued a final decision, such action shall not invalidate the entire Agreement.
> 万一本合约的任何条款被法令或司法机构判定无效,或者有关的行政机构已经做出最终决定,整个合约不得因为此类诉讼而失效。

虽然这两个短语在普通文体的翻译中译意较多,如"如果"、"万一"、"一旦"、"若",但在法律文件中,则译成"万一"、"一旦"较为妥帖。

> In case the house burns down, we'll get the insurance money.
> 万一房子烧掉,我们会得到保险公司的赔偿。

需要注意的是,虽然这两个短语后跟的都是一个完整的从句,但就这两个短语结构而言,"in case"之后一定不可跟代词"that",再带出一个完整的从句,如果要引出一个从句,必须直接跟在"in case"之后;而"in the event that"这个短语的构成正好相反,其中"that"在较规范的法律文句中不可以省略。

★ 与"in case of","in the event of"的比较:"in case of","in the event of"与"in case","in the event that"不同之处是:这两个短语之后只跟名词,不跟从句。就翻译而言,二者相同。

> Always keep a bucket of water handy in case of fire.
> 附近常备一桶水,以防万一失火。

> In the event of emergency we may make off.
> 万一发生紧急情况,我们可以逃走。

> Notwithstanding anything to the contrary contained herein, PCBS may immediately take corrective action, including disconnection or discontinuance of any and all Services, or terminate this Agreement in the event of notice of possible violation by Customer of the TANGIBLES Acceptable Use.
> 尽管有与本合约中内容相反的情形,但万一发现客户可能违犯 TANGIBLES 准许使用条款的情况,PCBS 可立刻采取纠正措施,包括截断或中断所有服务,或终止本合约。

"in case"及"in case of"在美式英语里较常使用,而"in the event that"及"in the event of"在英式英语和美式英语中都广泛使用。

(5)"should"的引导与翻译

"should"引导的条件句指的是将"should"当作"if"放在条件从句的句首使用的句子。此类句子中"should"并无"应该"或"应当"的含义。它所表示的是一种语气较强的虚拟或假设状态,在销售合约中通常指天灾人祸。虽然天灾人祸随处可见、天天发生,但要让这类事件与某一特定合约中的当事人联系在一起,实属罕见,故将其译成"假如"或"万一"皆可。

> The Seller shall be liable for any dead freight or demurrage, should it happen that he has failed to have the commodity ready for loading after the carrying vessels has arrived at the port of shipment on time.
>
> 假如卖方在货船抵达后未能按期将货物运交装运港口,则卖方应承担由此而产生的任何空舱费或滞港费。

> Within the guarantee period, should the quality and/or the specifications of the goods be found not in conformity with the contracted stipulations or should the goods prove defective for any reasons, including latent defect or the use of unsuitable materials, the Buyer shall arrange for an inspection to be carried out by the Inspection Bureau and have the right to claim against the Seller on the strength of the inspection certificate issued by the Bureau.
>
> 在保证期限内,假如发现货物的质量和/或规格与本合同规定不符,或发现货物由于任何原因引起的缺陷,包括内在缺陷或使用不良原料所致的缺陷,买方应申请商检局检验,并有权根据商检证书向卖方索赔。

> Should either of the parties to the contract be prevented from executing contract by force majeure, such as earthquake, typhoon, flood, fire, war, etc., the prevented Party shall notify the other party by cable without any delay, and within 15 days thereafter provide the detailed information of the events.
>
> 合同任何一方,假如遇地震、台风、水灾、火灾、战争等不可抗力情况而不能履行合同时,应立即将该情况电报通知对方,并在事发后的15天内提供详情。

装货船已到码头而货物尚未备妥,货物品质在保证期内出问题,执行合同时碰到天灾人祸,这些事件发生的概率较低,所以英文文本一律用"should"引导出一个虚拟句子,译成中文时,以"假设"或"万一"对应"should"符合逻辑,成为一种通译。

此外，如前所述，"in the event that"引导的条件句本身就表示罕见、不常发生的情形，而且这个短语在条件句中还可以与同样表示"万一"情况的引导词"should"联用，以加强语气。

> In the event that the shipment should not be made within the time stipulated in the Contract, the Buyer shall have the right to make the purchase elsewhere and to charge the Seller for any loss incurred, unless the delay in shipment is due to unforeseeable causes beyond one's control, for which the Seller is not responsible.
>
> 万一装船未能在合同规定的时间内进行，除非造成装船延误属无法控制、无法预见的原因所致，则买方有权到其他地方另购货物，并要求卖方承担由此造成的损失。

同样，"should"也可以与前述的条件句最常用的引导词"if"联用，以表示一种不常发生或假设的情形。

> Arbitration. If a dispute should arise regarding this Agreement, the parties agree that all claims, disputes, controversies, differences or other matters in question arising out of this relationship shall be settled finally, completely and conclusively by arbitration in Houston, Taxas in accordance with the Commercial Arbitration Rules of the American Arbitration Association (the "Rules").
>
> 仲裁。假如由于本协议而发生分歧，各方同意所有由于这一关系而产生的索赔、分歧、纠纷、争执或其他有关事项，应在德州休斯敦根据美国仲裁协会的商业仲裁规则（简称"规则"）作最后、完全和终局的解决。

总之，"in the event that + subject + should + verb"以及"if + subject + should + verb"这两个条件句句式所传达的信息与仅仅将"should"置放句首的条件句没有太大区别，一概表示在现实中发生概率较低的虚拟状况或假设性的条件。但要注意的是，"should"在行使"if"功能时，其后所跟动词必须是动词的原型，如"Should a dispute arise …"；但如果用"if"，则动词"arise"之后必须加"s"，即"If a dispute arises …"。

（6） "provided that"和"providing that"的引导和翻译

"provided that"及"providing that"是最受现代英语摒弃的条件句引导词，在普通英语中与两个短语联用的 that 均可以省略，如：Provided (that) no objection is raised, we shall hold the meeting here, 其位置既可置于全句的句首，也可以置于句中，如：You were permitted into the hall for the film, provided you sat at the back.

在法律文书中，由于文体较正式，其中的"that"一般不可以省略。在词性上"provided"以及"providing"均为连词；在语法上两者功能一样，相当于"if"；并且均列入古旧词的系列，在现代英语中越来越少使用；凡法律条文中出现这两个短语的句子，一定是一个前提性的条件，一般译为"倘若"。

> Oxford University is happy to receive applications from students from any country in the world proving that they are studying for, or have already achieved, three A-Levels or other equivalent academic qualifications ... Providing that any specific subject requirements have been met, all A-Levels are approved for admissions purposes, with the exception of General Studies.
>
> 牛津大学很高兴收到来自世界各国学生的入学申请——倘若他们目前正在修习或已经取得三门高级程度课程证书或其他相同的学业资格……倘若他们已经达到特别科目的要求，除通识教育科之外的所有高级程度课程证书均准予作为入学资格评估。

> Provided that should the Purchaser or his nominee have entered into possession of the premises hereby agreed to be sold the Purchaser shall thereupon be deemed to have accepted the title of the Vendor and shall not be entitled to raise any requisition or objection in respect of any of the matters aforesaid.
>
> 倘若买主或其指定人已占有凭本合约出售的楼宇，买主将被认为已接受卖主的所有权，并无权在上述任何问题方面提出任何要求或反对意见。

无论在法律文本还是在普通文体中，"providing that"都比"provided that"更加常用。此外值得注意的是，"provided that"是法律文体中"但书"（proviso）的引导词。"但书"指的是文件中提出"资格、条件或限制"的一个条款（a clause in a document making a qualification, condition, or restriction）。如果能确定"provided that"引导的是一个"但书"，就不应译成"倘若"或"如果"，而应译成"但"或"但是"。

> Every broker, dealer or lender who ... shall forfeit to the owner of the goods the full value thereof:
>
> Provided that no such order shall bar any such broker, dealer or lender from recovering possession of such goods by action from the person into whose possession they may come by virtue of the magistrate's order, provided that such action is commenced within 6 months next after such order has been made.
>
> 每名被如此命令的经纪人、商人或贷款人，如……则须向物主偿付其全部价值：
>
> 但上述命令并不禁止有关经纪人、商人或贷款人向凭借裁判官命令获得管有此等财物的人士提出诉讼，以取回其管有权，只要此等诉讼是在该项命令做出后6个月内提起。

值得注意的是，当"provided that"作"但书"使用时，其之前的主句如果是单独成为一段的，该段通常以冒号（：）结尾（见上例）；但如果"provided"引导的"但书"与主句同属一段,则它与主句往往用分号(;)隔开。

在普通书面英文中,使用"provided that"肯定属于文风不良的语篇,"if"和"but"具有与"provided that"相同的功能。且事实上,"provided that"当"if"用的情况也不普遍,但作"但书"用的情形比比皆是。其主要原因是因为使用"provided that"可产生法律行业文书需要的风格。因为"if"与"but"是英语中普通得不能再普通的小词,很多从事律师行业的人士,鉴于长期偏见,认为在法律文书中使用此类小词,不能制作出具有庄重风格的法律文本,有损法律的威严。因此,在法律文书中,不少现代英语中已被废弃之词受到偏爱,常被滥用。这就是在诸多情形之下,完全可以用"if"和"but"表达的词,时常被"where","when","in case","in the event that","providing that","provided that"等词或短语所取代。更有甚者,尤其是不少从事法律文书写作的人士喜欢玩弄文字,喜欢在"但是"后面大做文章:写完一个条件之后,往往觉得意犹未尽或者需要再补充一点什么,同时又不想回过头来修改前文,故最佳的做法是来一段"但书"。有时,写作者甚至觉得"但书"比前述的条件更重要,于是他们更会花样翻新,在"但书"内再加上一些花色,如将该词大写,或再添一个"always"之类的强调词。

> The Covenantor hereby undertakes to procure that the Customer will comply with all the Customer's obligations to you, the beneficiaries of this deed, (jointly and severally) but should the Customer default in the payment when due of any payment or default in complying with any other obligation, the Covenantor will, without the need for any demand, make immediate payment or performance thereof as the case may be, at the place, in the funds and currency and/or in the manner required of the Customer and without any withholding or deduction whatsoever PROVIDED ALWAYS HOWEVER that no time for limitation of liability in respect of this Deed shall begin to run in favor of the Covenantor unless and until one or both of you shall have made demand on the Covenantor, and if more than one demand is made, then only from the date and to the extent of each demand respectively.
>
> 订约人兹承诺:保证客户将履行其对贵方——即本契约之共同或单独受益人——应尽之所有义务,但是假如客户未支付任何到期的款项或未能履行任何其他义务,订约人将在无须要求的情况下,在客户指定的地点、以所要求的款项及货币形式及/或付款方式,立即做出支付或履行本契约的义务(根据具体情况而定),所付款项不得有任何扣留和减少。但是,除非组成贵方之一公司或两公司已经向订约人提出要求,否则有关本契约之债务时效任何时候都不得按有利于订约人一方的方式开始计算;如果贵方向订约人提出一项以上的要求,则分别按每项要求提出的日期及具体状况开始计算债务时效。

(7)"any person who"的引导和翻译

在法律条例中,尤其在各地的刑法典及条例中,类似"any person who does ... shall be guilty of an offence"句型重复率相当高。"any person who"用来指称具备一定条件之人,并不似"whoever"那样可泛指所有的人。此外,"any person who"引导定语从句,后边可以带好几个并行成分的句子而读者读起来不感到吃力,这点也非"whoever"能比。在句法上,该句型有时会把主语和谓语用逗号分开,中间加插一个定语修饰词。

> Any person who, without lawful authority or reasonable excuse, while having dealings of any kind with any other public body, offers any advantage to any public servant employed by that public body, shall be guilty of an offence.
>
> 任何人与其他公共机构进行任何事务往来时,无合法授权或合理理由而向受雇于该公共机构的公职人员提供任何利益,即属犯罪。

> Any person convicted of an offence under this Ordinance shall, by reason of such conviction, be disqualified for a period of 10 years from the date of such conviction from ...
>
> 任何人被裁定犯了本条例所订罪行,须因该项定罪而由定罪日期起计10年期内丧失以下资格……

> Any person in respect of whom an order under Subsection (1) has been made who contravenes the order commits an offence and is liable to a fine of $50,000 and to imprisonment for 12 months.
>
> 受法庭根据第(1)款所做命令限制的人如违反该命令,即属犯罪,可处罚款$50,000及监禁12个月。

> Any person who has reached the level of a graduate from the faculty of medicine of a university or a polytechnic school and, under the guidance of a licensed doctor, worked on probation for at least one year in the medical treatment, disease-prevention or health care institution may take the examinations for the qualifications of an assistant doctor.
>
> 具有高校医学专科或者中等专业学校医学专业学历,在执业医师指导下,在医疗、预防、保健机构中试用期满一年的,可以参加执业助理医师资格考试。

该句型标准的谓语动词是"shall + do",但也可使用与第三人称配合的动词现在式,如该部分第3例中用"commits an offence"和"is liable to a fine of …",也可据句子实际使用其他情态动词,如该部分第4例中的"may"。此类句型尚有若干变种,如主语改为

"every person"或"a person",其译义不变,为"任何(人)"。

> Every person on whom a notice under Subsection (1) is served shall, notwithstanding the provisions of any other law to the contrary save only the provisions of Section 4 of the Inland Revenue Ordinance (Cap.112), comply with the terms of that notice within such time as may be specified therein or within such further time as the commissioner may, in his discretion, authorize, and any person on whom such a notice had been served, without reasonable excuse, neglects or fails so to comply shall be guilty of an offence and shall be liable on conviction to a fine of $20,000 and to imprisonment for 1 year.
>
> 任何人获送达根据第(1)款发出的通知书,则即使任何其他法律条文有相反规定,该人仍须在该通知书指明的时间内,或者在专员酌情授权延长时间内遵照该通知书办理,但受(税务条例)(第112章)第4条规定的情况除外;获送达该通知书的人如无合理理由疏忽遵照或不遵照该通知书办理,即属犯罪,一经定罪,可处罚款$20,000及监禁1年。

> Every person who is an employee at the commencement of the period during which the business or part thereof is closed down for the purpose specified in subsection (1), and who is not otherwise entitled to annual leave pay in respect of any day during that period, shall, as regards the period beginning on the appropriate day and ending on the day preceding the first day of the close down, be entitled to annual leave calculated in accordance with Subsection (4).
>
> 任何人如在因第(1)款所指明目的而停业或停止部分业务的期间开始时已成为雇员,而该人若非因该次停业则无权获得该段期间内任何一天的年假薪酬者,则就始于适用日而止于停业首天之前一天的期间,须有权享有按照第(4)款计算的年假。

> A person who willfully makes any false statement in answer to a notice under Subsection (1) shall be guilty of an offence and shall be liable to a fine of $20,000 and to imprisonment for 1 year.
>
> 任何人在回应根据第(1)款发出的通知书时故意做出虚假陈述,即属犯罪,可处罚款$20000及监禁1年。

> A person shall not, by reason only of his being an executor of a will, be incompetent to be admitted a witness to prove the execution of such will, or a witness to prove the validity or invalidity thereof.
>
> 任何人不会仅因为身为遗嘱执行人,而无资格接纳为见证人以证明遗嘱的签立,或证明该遗嘱具备或不具备效力。

> At the hearing of a complaint or information, <u>a party</u> may be represented by counsel; and an absent party so represented <u>shall be deemed</u> not to be absent.
> 在申诉或告发案聆讯时,<u>任何一方</u>均可由代表律师代表;某一方如有律师代表,即使缺席,亦不当作缺席。

由此可见,该句式无论是以"any person/party"开头还是以"every person/party","a person/a party"开头,皆可译成"任何人/任何一方"。该句式多用在刑典或刑法条例中,最受法律文书人士欢迎的标准英文表达为"any person who does sth., shall be guilty of an offence/commit an offence"。当然不同法律条例在不同时期由不同人士撰写,风格可能不一致,如表示"任何人做某事,即属犯罪"。另一标准表达是"any person who does …, is guilty of an offence/commits an offence"。当然该句套子实际上包含了"anyone who"开头的句型,也视为是该句型的变种,只是在实务中后者的出现频率没前者高,希望大家注意。

(8)"whoever"的引导与翻译

逻辑主语是行为者且比较短的句子,适合用"whoever"来引导,有包括一切人的含义,比较适用于翻译那种泛指一切人的句子。

> 具有下列条件之一的,可以参加执业医师资格考试。
> <u>Whoever</u> meets one of the following requirements may take the examinations for the qualifications of a licensed doctor.

> Article 115　<u>Whoever sets</u> fire, breaches dikes, causes explosions, and spreads poison; employs other dangerous means that lead to serious injuries or death; or causes public or private property major losses <u>is to be sentenced to not less than 10 years of fixed-term imprisonment</u>, life imprisonment, or death. <u>Whoever commits</u> the crimes in the preceding paragraph negligently <u>is to be sentenced to not less than three years to not more than seven years of fixed-term imprisonment</u>; or not more than three years of fixed-term imprisonment, or criminal detention, when circumstances are relatively minor.
> 第115条　放火、决水、爆炸、投毒或者以其他危险方法致人重伤、死亡或者使公私财产遭受重大损失的,<u>处十年以上有期徒刑</u>、无期徒刑或者死刑。过失犯前款罪的,<u>处三年以上七年以下有期徒刑</u>;情节较轻的,<u>处三年以下有期徒刑或者拘役</u>。

类似上面的句子在早期英文版的《中华人民共和国刑法》中比比皆是。该句型可简化为：Whoever does sth. is to be sentenced to years of fixed-term imprisonment, life imprisonment, or death。

从文法上看，句式结构完全正确，但并非以英语为母语国家的法律条文的典型表述形式，其出现频率并不高。

值得大家注意的是，法律文书中不用"those who"开头引导句子，因为此类句式比较口语化，与法律文书的文体要求不符，但"those who"在法律文体句子中间出现是有的，但不表示条件或隐藏条件。

还请注意，以 no one 引导的句子是没有的。有人统计过，英语使用"if"表示条件是最多的，其次是"any person who"（当然不限于 person），然后是"where"，"whoever"，还有其他如"in the event that"等。

总之，表示条件的几种主要句式列举如上，在汉译英时，汉语的"的"字结构包含了很多隐藏条件，需根据情况，考虑各句型的对应情形及其在法律英语中的接受度（出现频率的高低）采取不同处理方法，不能千篇一律。必要时需要找出主语，加以增补。

> If any person or unit stores, transports or treats urban house refuse against the provisions of this Law, he or it shall be punished in accordance with the relevant regulations of the State Council regarding environmental protection and urban environmental sanitation.
>
> 储存、运输、处置城市生活垃圾违反本法规定的，按照国务院关于环境保护和城市卫生的有关规定予以处罚。

▶ 5. for the purpose(s) of

这是法律英语中又一个常用连接短语。其中的"purpose"可以是复数，也可以是单数。普通英语中的对应译文是"为了……目的"，在我国中译英法律文献中的确不乏这样的译文。

有下列情形之一,以非法占有为目的,在签订、履行合同过程中,骗取对方当事人财物,数额较大的,处三年以下有期徒刑或者拘役,并处或者单处罚金……

Whoever, for the purpose of illegal possession, uses one of the following means during signing or executing a contract to obtain property and goods of the opposite party by fraud, and when the amount of money is relatively large, is to be sentenced to not more than three years of fixed-term imprisonment, criminal detention, and may in addition or exclusively be sentenced to a fine ...

但在大多数情形下,"purpose"一词并非一定要在句子中出现。

为保护计算机软件著作权人的利益,调整计算机软件在开发、传播和使用中发生的利益关系,鼓励计算机软件的开发与流通,促进计算机应用事业的发展,依照《中华人民共和国著作权法》的规定,制定本条例。

These Regulations are formulated in accordance with the provisions of the Copyright Law of the People's Republic of China for the purpose of protecting the rights and interests of copyrinht owner of computer software, of adjusting the interests arising from the development, dissemination and use of computer software, of encouraging the development and circulation of computer software, and of promoting the development of computer application.

但在原文为英文的法律文本中,以表达"为……目的"这层意思而使用"for the purpose of"的句子并不多见,译成"为……目的"的译例则更为罕见。专家建议用 for 替代短语"for the purpose of"。倘若需要明确表达"为了……(目的)"的意思,用不定式短语"in order to"则更好,不容易产生歧义。

为了保护发明创造专利权,鼓励发明创造,有利于发明创造的推广应用,促进科学技术的发展……特制定本法。

This Law is formulated in order to protect patent rights for invention-creations, encourage invention-creations and facilitate their popularization and application, promote the development of science and technology ...

反对使用"for the purpose of"的主要原因在于该短语在英文法律文件中的用法早已"变味",且此种"变味"的用法已到了约定俗成、不可逆转的程度,译法也显得匪夷所思。

> For the purpose of these presents, any default or omission of the agents, servants, workmen or licensees of the Tenant, shall be deemed to be the act default or omission of the Tenant.
>
> 基于这些通知,租户的代理人、佣人、工人或所许可者的任何行为、违约或疏忽,应被认为是租户的行为、违约或疏忽。

> For the purpose of the Landlord and the Tenant Ordinance and for the purpose of these presents, the rent in respect of the said premises shall be deemed to be in arrear if not paid in advance as stipulated by Clause 1 hereof.
>
> 基于租务条例并基于这些通知,有关该楼宇的租金,如果未照合约第一条规定的那样提前缴付,就应该被认为是拖欠。

当"purpose"以复数形式出现在法律篇章中且与某个具体的条例编号搭配在一起时,该短语的"目的性"更是丧失殆尽。

> For the purposes of Section 37, the Commissioner may, either by notice in writing served by registered post or by notice in the Gazette, require any employer or class of employers to send to him all or any records of sickness days in respect of any period not exceeding 2 years preceding the date of the notice.
>
> 为施行第37条,处长可藉挂号邮递方式送达通知书,或藉宪报公告,要求任何雇主或任何类别雇主向其呈交通知书或公告日期前两年内任何期间的全部或任何病假日记录。

> For the purposes of Subsection (1) of this section the attestation of a will by a person to whom or to whose spouse there is given or made any such disposition as is described in that subsection shall be disregarded if the will is duly executed without his attestation and without that of any other such person.
>
> 为第(1)款的施行,获得该款所述的处置的任何人或其配偶,如为遗嘱作见证,而该遗嘱没有其见证或任何其他此类人的见证亦已妥为签立,则该人所做的见证须不予理会。

> For the purposes of Subsection (2), "land" does not include incorporeal hereditament;
>
> 就第(2)款而言,"土地"(land)并不包括无体可继承产;

> For the purposes of Subsection (3) permission shall be in writing and—
>
> 就第(3)款而言,许可须为书面形式,并且——

同样在法律汉译英的实践中,一些译者也在努力尝试摆脱"为……目的"的传统语用桎梏,试看与"for the purpose of"对等的一些新颖译法:

> For the purpose of this Law, "invention-creation" means inventions, utility models and designs.
> 本法所称的发明创造是指发明、实用新型和外观设计。

> For the purpose of these Regulations, computer software (hereafter referred to as software) refers to computer programs and their related documentation.
> 本条例所称的计算机软件(简称软件,下同)是指计算机软件程序及其有关文件。

> For the purpose of this Agreement, "control" shall mean either the ownership of fifty percent (50%) or more of the ordinary share capital of the company carrying the right to vote at general meetings or the power to nominate a majority of the board of directors of the Company.
> 在本协议中,"控制"系指拥有在股东大会上有投票权的百分之五十(50%)或50%以上的公司普通股股本,或拥有任命公司董事会中多数董事的权力。

从上述各例中可以看出,该短语在法律文件中的翻译并非如一般人想象得那样简单,其最恰当的译法是"就……而言",其次是"为施行×××条",或"在……中"等。普通词典里的"为……目的"这一解释并不一定适合法律英语中的"for the purpose(s) of"。在绝大多数情况下,法律英语中"for the purpose(s) of"未必有真正的"目的性",但若"purpose"前面有一个修饰它的形容词时,如"for commercial purpose",此时"purposes"的"目的性"是非常明确的,在翻译时必须译成"为商业目的"。

▶ 6. notwithstanding

介词"notwithstanding"在普通英语中使用极为罕见,也可列入古旧废词的行列,但其在法律英语中的使用已经达到"司空见惯"的程度。其译法跟"although"、"though"、"even if"引导的状语从句没有太大分别,但比它们正式,基本上皆可译成"尽管……"、"即使……",表示一种让步。但该词所引导的并非是一个让步状语从句,因为在习惯用法中,该词之后只跟一个名词性短语。

> Notwithstanding any law or practice to the contrary, it shall be lawful for the court in any proceedings for an offence under Part II to comment on the failure of the accused to give evidence on oath.
> 即使任何法律或惯例有相反规定,在因第II部分所定罪行而进行的法律程序中,法庭可就被控人不宣誓作供一事加以评论。

Chapter 2　Typical Sentence Structures in Legal English Translation　‖　037

> <u>Notwithstanding</u> any other provision of the Contract, if the Contractor intends to claim any additional payment pursuant to any Clause of these Conditions or otherwise, he shall give notice of his intention to the Engineer, with a copy to the Employer, within 28 days after the event giving rise to the claim has first arisen.
>
> 尽管合同有其他规定，如果承包人根据合同条件的任何条款或其他有关规定企图索取任何追加付款的，他都应在引起索赔的事件首次发生后28天内，将其索赔意向通知工程师，同时将一份副本呈交业主。

> <u>Notwithstanding</u> the foregoing, a Party hereby waives its preemptive right in the case of any assignment of all or party of the other Party's registered capital to an affiliate of the other Party.
>
> 尽管有上述规定，如果一方将其全部或部分注册资本转让给一家关联公司，另一方则在此放弃其优先购买权。

虽然该词也可作连词使用，引导一个完整的让步状语从句，如：He is honest, notwithstanding he is poor.（他虽贫穷，却诚实）。但这种用法并非是法律英语中的典型用法，上述例句已充分说明了这一点。尽管由该词构成的短语在英译中时不构成问题，但在法律文书中译英实践中须特别小心，因为该词不作连词使用，不跟一个带主谓宾的句子。最典型的用法与"subject to"，"for the purpose(s) of"相似，后面跟的是"law"、"ordinance"或"section"，"subsection"，"clause"，"provision"之类的法律或法律条款、规定等的指代词，汉译几乎千篇一律："尽管有×××法例/条款的规定"。

▶ **7. save …/except (for)**

在普通现代英语中，"save"是一个妇孺皆知、人人会用的及物动词。但在法律英语中，它是一个与"except (for)"含义相同的介词。从词源上看，它是一个法文词，汉译为"除……外"。不管是"save"还是"except (for)"之后都可跟一个名词性短语，也可以跟一个从句或另一个介词短语。

> <u>Save</u> as is provided in this Ordinance, no claim within the jurisdiction of the Board shall be actionable in any court.
>
> 除非本条例另有规定，否则凡属仲裁处司法管辖权范围内的申索，不得在任何法庭进行诉讼。

> Save as is provided in this section, nothing in this Ordinance shall require the disclosure by a legal adviser of any privileged information, communication, book, document or other article.
>
> 除本条另有订定外,本条例并不要求法律顾问须披露任何有特权的资料、通讯、簿册、文件或其他物品。

> Save under and in accordance with the provisions of this section no action shall lie in any civil court against a magistrate for any act done in a manner over which by law he has no jurisdiction or in which he has exceeded his jurisdiction.
>
> 除根据及按照本条的条文外,不得就裁判官在一项其在法律上并无司法管辖权或超越其司法管辖权的事项上所做的任何作为,在民事法庭提起针对裁判官的诉讼。

由于法律翻译人员对"save"一词的用法可能不太熟悉,故中译英法律文本中很少使用该词。自然,普通英语中的习语"except"或"except for"便成了更常见的表达方式。

> 除本法第 255 条的规定外,保险标的发生全损,保险人支付全部保险金额的,取得对保险标的的全部权利;但是,在不足额保险的情况下,保险人按照保险金额与保险价值的比例取得对保险标的的部分权利。
>
> Except as stipulated in Article 255 of this Code, where a total loss occurs to the subject matter insured and the full insured amount is paid, the insurer shall acquire the full right to the subject matter insured. In the case of under-insurance, the insurer shall acquire the right to the subject matter insured in the proportion that the insured amount bears to the insured value.

事实上,"save/except as(is)provided/stipulated"可以用另一个法律上常用的结构取代,即"unless otherwise provided/stipulated",功能与其相同。

▶ 8. in respect of

在普通英语中,若要表达一个与某事物有关的概念,最常用的介词莫过于"regarding"或"concerning"。其他类似的表达还有"for"、"of"、"in connection with"、"in relation to"、"relating"、"pertaining to"、"with reference to"等。但在法律英语中,这些词或短语似乎都显得太普通,取而代之的则是"in respect of"。不过,由于该短语本身灵活性强、粘附性与词俱来,加之正式程度又高,故在法律英语中往往被过度使用甚至滥用,有时会使习惯普通英语的读者、译者颇感头痛:既难理解,也不好翻译,但只要知晓其最常用的替代词,对使用了该冷僻关联词的有关法律句子的理解和翻译皆有帮助。

> Unless in any enactment it is otherwise provided, the period of imprisonment, which may be imposed by a magistrate exercising summary jurisdiction, in respect of the non-payment of any sum of money adjudged to be paid by a conviction, whether it be a fine or in respect of the property the subject of the offence, or in respect of the injury done by the offender, or in respect of the default of a sufficient distress to satisfy any such sum, shall be such period as, in the opinion of the magistrate, will satisfy the justice of the case, but shall not exceed in any case the maximum fixed by the following scale …
>
> 除成文法另有规定外,对于因不缴付根据定罪裁定须缴付的款项(不论是罚款或就作为罪行主体的财物而须缴付的款项),或因犯罪者所造成的损害,或因无足够扣押物以抵偿此等款项而致拖欠付款,则行使简易程序审判权的裁判官可判处其认为就案情而言是符合公正原则的监禁刑期,但无论如何不得超过下表所定的最长刑期……

仅从此段,我们即可看出该短语在法律英语中出镜率很高,甚至到了滥用的地步。显然,其最典型的译法是"对于"。且在此例中,"对于"是"以一抵三",一个"对于"针对三个被修饰的主语(因……的款项/因……的损害/因……等款项)。其中第二个"in respect of"虽然未被明显译成任何对应词语,但其"有关"(即"有关罪行主体的财物的……")的含义还是相当清晰的。

> The Licensor shall conduct all legal proceedings in respect of any infringement or alleged infringement of the Licensed Trademarks and any claim or counterclaim brought or threatened to be brought in connection with the use or registration of the Licensed Trademarks and shall in its absolute discretion decide what to do.
>
> 对于受许可商标所受到的侵权或侵权指控,以及就受许可商标的使用或注册提出或拟将提出的索赔或反索赔,许可方应进行一切法律诉讼,并完全由其自行决定采取何种行动。

> If the Licensee becomes aware that any other person, firm or company alleged that any of the Licensed Trademarks is invalid or that use of the Licensed Trademarks infringes any rights of another party, the Licensee shall immediately give the Licensor in writing full particulars thereof and may make no disclosure of information or admission to any third party in respect thereof.
>
> 如果被许可方获悉任何其他人、商行或公司宣称受许可商标是无效的或受许可商标的使用侵犯了他方权利,应立即以书面形式将详细情况告知许可方,并不得向任何第三方披露有关此方面的资讯或对此做出承认。

上面最后一例是"in respect of"的一个变种。"thereof"相当于"of(the)information

or admission of the Licensed Trademarks' infringement of another party's rights"。此处的中文译文恰好是"in respect of"两个主要译法的总结：一个译成"有关"，一个译成"对（于）"。总之，其意思相当于"regarding"，但用法更为灵活，可以与一个包含"of"的古旧副词（thereof）结合使用。这一点是"concerning"、"regarding"或"with regard to"所不具备的。

> Where an employee is granted any period of annual leave, the employer shall pay him annual leave pay in respect of that period not later than the day on which he is next paid his pages after that period.
> 凡雇员获给予任何一段期间的年假，雇主最迟须于该段期间后的第一个发薪日付给该雇员该段期间的年假薪酬。

> For the purpose of the Landlord and the Tenant Ordinance and for the purpose of these presents the rent in respect of the said premises shall be deemed to be in arrear if not paid in advance as stipulated by Clause 1 hereof.
> 基于租务条例并基于这些通知，有关该楼宇的租金，如果未照合约第一条规定的那样提前缴付，就应该被认为是拖欠。

上面两例中，"in respect of"相当于介词"for"；在第一例中译为"的"，表示一种从属关系；在第2例中译为"有关……的"。总之，万变不离其宗，"in respect of"都表示与该词之后的名词的一种从属关系，须根据情况译为"对于……"或"有关……的"。

另一个与"in respect of"意义相同的短语"with respect to"也属正式用语，多用于法律、商业文书，相当于"concerning"（关于；就……而言）。

> This Agreement and all its appendices shall constitute the entire agreement between the Parties with respect to the subject matter set forth herein and supersede any and all previous oral and written discussions, negotiations, notices, memoranda, documents, contracts and communications between the Parties relating to such subject matter.
> 本协议及其附件构成双方就本协议规定的标的达成的完整协议，并取代双方先前与该标的有关的一切口头和书面的洽谈、谈判、通知、备忘录、文件、协议、合同和通讯。

> With respect to your enquiry, we enclose an explanatory leaflet.
> 关于你的询问，兹附上有关说明资料。

> The police informed him about his rights with respect to the forthcoming extradition.
> 警察在行将执行的引渡问题上就他的权利向他做了说明。

▶ 9. purport

作名词使用时,"purport"的意思为"意旨"、"目的",但这种用法并非法律上的用法。作为动词,"purport"的主要意思为"声称"、"据称"、"意指"或"看起来是",词义上与另一个英文词"allege"颇为相似(用法上大不相同)。该词的衍生词还有"purported","purporting","purportedly"等。该词在普通英语中的功用无足轻重,可以完全忽略。在以英语为母语的国家受过高等教育的普通人士一般都不会使用该词。然而在法律英语中,虽然其实际意义含糊,用途飘忽,但时常被滥用,故其在法律英语中也时常失去其实际意义。在权威的英汉双语法律版本中,通常找不到其相应的或对等的译文。

> For the purpose of this Part—
> (a) an instrument is false if it purports to have been—
> (i) made in the form in which it is made by a person who did not in fact make it that form;
> (ii) made in the form in which it is made on the authority of a person who did not in fact authorize its making in that form;
>
> 就本部而言——
> (a) 任何文书如有以下情况,即属虚假——
> (i) 该文书是以某种式样制成,并看来是由某人以该式样制成,但事实上该人并未以该式样制造该文书;
> (ii) 该文书是以某种式样制成,并看来是获某人授权以该式样制造,但事实上该人并未授权以该式样制造该文书;

如果要使译文达到完全忠实的程度,译文势必为:"(a) 如任何文书据称已被(i) 制成这么一种形式,即它看起来是由某人以该式样制成,但事实上该人并未以该式样制造该文书;(ii) ……即属虚假。"

如此译文,会使读者莫名其妙,且译文本身也有逻辑上的矛盾:既然制成这么一种形式不过是"据称的",事实上可能并非如此,那怎么可以被认定"即属虚假"呢?而在实际的译文中,"purports to have been"却被完全忽略。

> As to the drafts or acceptances under or purporting to be under the Credit, which are payable in US Dollars, we agree ...
>
> 对于本信用证项下的用美元支付的汇票或承兑汇票,我们同意……

> If at our special request the Credit is issued in transferable form, it is understood and agreed that you are under no duty to determine the proper identity of a (one) appearing in the draft or documents as transferee, nor shall you be charged with responsibility of any nature or character for the validity or correctness of any transfer or successive transfers, and payment by you to any purported transferee or transferees as determined by you hereby authorized and approved ...
>
> 如应我方特别要求,此信用证以可转让形式开立时,我们同意贵行不负担鉴定任何汇票或单据受让人身份的责任,贵行则无须负担任何性质的转让或连续转让的合法性或真实性的责任,在此特准许贵行支付给由贵行认定的任何受让人……

上述两例中的"purporting"和"purported"在译文中同样被完全忽略,如逐字对译,则可能会移意害义,造成逻辑上矛盾,实不可取,不译为上策。

> In absence of written instructions expressly to the contrary, we agree that you or any of your correspondents may receive and accept as "bills of lading" under the Credit, any document issued or purporting to be issued by or on behalf of any carrier, which acknowledges receipt of property for transportation, whatever the other specific provisions of such document(s) ...
>
> 如无相反的书面文件明确规定,我们同意贵行或贵行代理行接受任何承运人或其代理人签发或将签发的作为收到付运财物证明的本信用证下的提单,不论该单有无其他任何具体规定……

上面例句中"purporting to be issued"译为"将签发的",可能与原文意思较为吻合。由此可见,从上述例句中可以总结出"purport"及其变体翻译的一点规律,有时不译为好,有时则需根据原文实际情况加以翻译。

下段是对该词的翻译练习,请根据原文实际需要,看哪些可译,哪些可不译,并对原文文风加以品味,其目的何在,体验一下法律英语的特点:

> Should any purported ① obligation or liability of the Customer which, if valid or enforceable, would be the subject of this Deed be or become wholly or in part invalid or unenforceable against the Customer on any ground whatsoever, including any defect in or insufficiency or want of powers of the Customer, or irregular or improper purported ② exercise thereof, or breach or want of authority by any person purporting ③ to act on behalf of the Customer, or any legal limitation,

Chapter 2　Typical Sentence Structures in Legal English Translation　|| 043

> disability, mental or other incapacity, or any other fact or circumstance, whether or not known to you, or if, for any other reason whatsoever, the Customer is not or ceases to be legally liable to discharge any obligation or liability undertaken or <u>purported</u> ④ to be undertaken on the Customer's behalf, the Covenantor shall nevertheless be liable to you in respect of that obligation or liability or <u>purported</u> ⑤ obligation or liability as if the same were wholly valid and enforceable and the Covenantor were the principal debtor in respect thereof. You are not to be concerned to see or enquire into the powers of the Customer or its officers (if the Customer is a limited company), employees or agents <u>purporting</u> ⑥ to act on the Customer's behalf and the Covenantor agrees that you will thus rely on the acts <u>purported</u> ⑦ carried out on behalf of the Customer as being validly binding on the Customer so that the Covenantor is estopped from taking or raising any point or defense on such matter(s).

课后练习

1. 参考本章内容,将下列法律英文译成中文,特别注意画线部分短语的译法。

(1) Any Party may terminate this Contract prior to the expiration of the Joint Venture Term by delivery to the other Parties of a written notice of its intention to terminate under any of the following circumstances, or <u>as otherwise provided in this Contract or under law</u>.

(2) <u>Subject to</u> the provisions of Article 4, the carrier shall properly and carefully load, handle, stow, carry, keep, care for, and discharge the goods carried.

2. 请用 where 引导或用 then-if-if、清单式、if-if-then 改译本段文字。

夫妻对婚姻关系存续期间所得的财产约定归各自所有的,夫或妻一方对外所负的债务,第三人知道该约定的,以夫或妻一方所有的财产清偿。

If husband and wife agree, as is known to the third party, to separately possess their property acquired during their marriage [should be married] life, the debt owed by the husband or the wife to a third party, shall be paid off out of the property separately possessed by him or her.

3. 用 whoever 翻译下句。

《中华人民共和国刑法》第236条:"以暴力、胁迫或者其他手段强奸妇女的,处3年以上10年以下有期徒刑。"

4. 翻译下面各段,并注意画线单词或短语的用法。

(1) Notwithstanding the provisions of the preceding articles, a carrier, master or agent of the carrier and a shipper shall in regard to any particular goods be at liberty to enter into any agreement in any terms as to the responsibility and liability of the carrier for such goods, and as to the rights and immunities of the carrier in respect of such goods, or his obligation as to seaworthiness, so far as this stipulation is not contrary to public policy, or the care or diligence of his servants or agents in regard to the loading, handling, stowage, carriage, custody, care and discharge of the goods carried by sea, provided that in this case no bill of lading has been or shall be issued and that the terms agreed shall be embodied in a receipt which shall be a non-negotiable document and shall be marked as such.

(2) Save as provided herein and unless otherwise specified in writing, all Confidential Information must be returned to the disclosing Party or destroyed after the Party's need for it has expired.

(3) It is hereby expressly agreed that no servant or agent of the Carrier (including every independent contractor from time to time employed by the Carrier) shall in any circumstances whatsoever be under any liability whatsoever to the Shipper, Consignee or Owner of the goods or to any holder of this Bill of Lading for any loss, damage or delay of whatsoever kind arising directly or indirectly from any act, neglect or default on his part while acting in the course or in connection with his employment and, without prejudice to the generality of the foregoing provisions in this Clause, every exemption, limitation, condition and liberty herein contained and every right, exemption from liability, defence and immunity of whatsoever nature applicable to the Carrier or to which the Carrier is entitled hereunder shall also be available and shall extend to protect every such servant or agent of the Carrier acting as aforesaid and for the purpose of all the foregoing provisions of this Clause the Carrier is or shall be deemed to be acting as agents or trustee on behalf of and for the benefit of all persons who are or might be his servants or agents from time to time (including independent contractors as aforesaid) and all such persons shall to this extent be or be deemed to be parties to the contract in or evidenced by this Bill of Lading.

Chapter 3

Archaic Adverbs and Model Verbs in Legal Documents

▶ 1. 英语法律文书中的古旧副词

词根为 here，there 的古旧副词在法律文书中尤其是合约条文中广泛应用。所谓古旧副词，主要是以 here，there，where 为词根，然后与-after, -by, -in, -before, -of, -to, -under, -with, -about, -among, -around, -at, -for, -from, -on, -upon 等合成的副词，如：hereafter, hereby, herein, hereinafter, hereinbefore, hereof, hereto, hereunder, hereupon, herewith; thereafter, thereby, therefrom, therein, thereafter, thereinbefore, thereon, thereof, thereupon, therewith; whereas, whereby, wherein, whereon, etc.。这种使用现代英语中基本淘汰的古旧副词的现象在法律英语中源远流长，可追溯到公元 1100 年以前的古英语，其在英联邦国家的商业合约中更是历来如此(在美加的法律文书中其使用频率较低)，其意义和用法在现代英语中虽已属古旧行列，但在法律英语中仍较普遍。

> No failure or delay by either of you in exercising any right, power or privilege hereunder shall operate as a waiver thereof, nor shall any single or partial exercise preclude any other or further exercise thereof or the exercise of any other right, power or privilege. The remedies provided herein are not to be exclusive of any other remedy and each and every remedy shall be cumulative and in addition to every other remedy given hereunder or now or hereafter existing at law or in equity, by statute or otherwise.
>
> 贵方任何一家公司在行使本契约的权利、权力或特权时的失误或延误都不得被当作对该等权利、权力或特权的弃权；对任何该等权利、权力或特权的单独行使或部分行使并不排除其他的或将来的对该等权利、权力或特权的行使。本契约中规定之补救措施并不排除任何其他的补救措施，每一项补救措施应是累积的(附加的)，应视为对根据本契约项下规定之补救措施，或现在或本契约签订之后的普通法、衡平法、成文法或其他法律所赋予的每项其他补救措施之补充。

汉译英时准确适度地使用此类法律英语中的专门用语，往往能使行文简洁明了、含义准确无误，既能避免重复，又能准确表达原意，不出现歧义，使译文合乎法律文件的要求。

由于这些古旧副词基本上都是合成词，故在翻译时可采用"分拆＋合成＋还原"的方法处理，即将该副词拆散成两个原形词加以考虑，然后将其意思合成，再通过逻辑推理，将其原来省略而避免重复的内容加以还原成现代英语，得出符合上下文、能自圆其说的现代译文。

如上段中的"hereafter"，即将该词分拆成"here"及"after"，实际顺序是"after＋here"。而在合约文类中，"here"包括或含指的范围比较广泛，通常指整个合约，"here"经常系指"this Agreement"、"this Contract"、"this Deed"、"this Covenant"，etc.，视情况而定。"hereafter"可还原成"after this Agreement"、"after this Contract"、"after this Deed"，etc.，然后进行适当增词，译为"本契约（签订）之后"。但请注意，"hereafter"这个词有两种意思：hereafter =（1） henceforth（从此以后）;（2）at some future time（在将来某个时候）。存在这两种意思可能使该词引起歧义，如规定一项法律"effective hereafter"（随即生效），这个意思更准确的表述是"effective with the passage of this Act"（本法案于通过时生效）或"after the date this Act takes effect"（本法案生效之日后生效）。第（1）个含义是"hereafter"更常用的意思。

"hereinafter"意思是"in a part of this document that follows or later in the same Agreement, Contract, Deed, Covenant, etc."（在下文……，以下），一般与"to be referred to as"、"referred to as"、"referred to"、"called"等连用，以避免重复，如：The parties have stipulated that an exchange of telegrams hereinafter referred to constitutes the contract.（双方约定下文提到的交换电报使合同成立）。在美国，"hereinafter"一词通常被省略，因为人们认为它并没有使意思更明确，如人们一般说"later in this will"（本遗嘱下文）或"later in this paragraph"（本款下文）而不用"hereinafter"。

正是因为"hereafter"和"hereinafter"可能指某一款、某一文件或整个文件，而不清楚它们究竟指哪个，从而会引起歧义。美国倡议用英文起草法律文件时，要避免使用此类法律术语。

"hereunder"可分拆成"here"及"under"，实际顺序为"under＋here"。"hereunder"可还原成"under this Agreement"、"under this Contract"、"under this Deed"、"under this Covenant"，etc.，因此可译为"本契约项下"。依此类推，"hereby"可还原成"by means of (by reason of) this Agreement"、"by means of (by reason of) this Contract, Deed"、"by

Chapter 3 Archaic Adverbs and Model Verbs in Legal Documents

means of (by reason of) this Covenant",etc.,即可译为"根据本合约"、"特此"、"兹"等意,常用于法律文件、合同、协议书等正式文件的开头语,在条款中需要强调时也可用。"hereto"则表示"to this Agreement","to this Contract","to this Deed","to this Covenant",etc.(至此,对此)。同理像"herein"(此中,于此)、"hereof"(关于此点,在本文件中)等"here"与其他介词组成的复合词均可照此类推。

　　there-在合约文类中包含的范围往往较窄,通常指"该条款的"或该条款中、在该词之前刚刚提到过的那件事物,而不是"该合约的"。"thereof"可分拆为"there + of",实际顺序是"of + there"。本部分第1个例句中的两个"thereof"均为"of the right, power, or privilege under this Agreement",翻译时将其分拆成"thereof = of + there",相当于"waiver of any right, power or privilege under this Agreement"(对该权利、权力或特权的放弃)和"further exercise of any right, power or privilege under this Agreement"(对该权利、权力或特权的进一步行使)。由此可见,法律英语中"thereof"一词避免了一连串名词的多次重复,但是按汉语的表达方式,这些名词必须重复出现,没有什么词可以使之简化或取而代之。

　　同理,其他以"there"开头的副词皆可依此类推,如:therein = in that, in that particular context; in that respect, etc.,翻译为"在那里;在那点上,在那方面"。

　　All operations necessary for the execution and completion of the Works and the remedying of defects therein shall, so far as compliance with the requirements of the Contract permits, be carried on so as not to interfere unnecessarily or improperly with …

　　在合同许可的范围内,在工程施工、完工及缺陷维修过程中所必需的一切操作(施工),在进行时均应对下述方面遭受不必要和不恰当的……

　　句中 therein = in the Works(在工程中),the remedying of any defects therein 意为"修补工程中的缺陷"。

- thereafter: after that 此后

He was very ill as a child and was considered delicate thereafter.
他幼年多病,其后一向被认为弱不禁风。

- thereafter: after that illness

> The Contractor shall, during the execution of the Works and thereafter, provide all necessary superintendence as long as the Engineer may consider necessary for the proper fulfilling of the Contractor's obligations under the Contract.
>
> 只要工程师认为是为正确履行合同规定的承包人义务所必需时，承包人应在工程施工期间及其后提供一切必要的监督。

- thereafter: after the execution of the Works

during the execution of the Works and thereafter 意为"在工程施工期间及其后"。

> Should any Party be directly prevented from executing this Agreement or be delayed in performing this Agreement by any event of force majeure, such as earthquake, typhoon, flood, fire and war and other unforeseen events, the happening and consequences of which are unpreventable and unavoidable, the affected Party shall notify the other Parties without delay and, within 15 days thereafter, provide detailed information regarding the events of force majeure and sufficient proof thereof, explaining the reason for its inability to perform or the delay in the execution of all or part of this Agreement.

- thereto: to that 有关

> Instructions for the issuance of credits, the credits themselves, instructions for any amendments thereto and the amendments themselves shall be complete and precise.
>
> 开立信用证的指示、信用证本身、有关对信用证修改的指示及其修改书本身，必须完整、明确。

- any amendments thereto: any amendments to the credits

"thereto"有时与"with respect to"及"relating to"等词连用，形成变体形式"with respect thereto"、"relating thereto"等。

> In the event that such taxes, tariffs or duties are assessed against Consultant, Client shall reimburse Consultant for any such amounts paid by Consultant or, prior to the payment of such amounts by Consultant, provide Consultant with valid tax exemption certificates with respect thereto.
>
> 如果该等税收、关税或税项向顾问征收，则客户须偿还顾问缴纳的该等税款，或在顾问缴纳该等税款前，向顾问提供该等税款予以豁免的有效证明。

"with respect thereto"相当于"with respect to such amounts"（有关该等税款）。"valid tax exemption certificates with respect thereto"可译为"该等税款予以豁免的有效证明"。

Chapter 3 Archaic Adverbs and Model Verbs in Legal Documents

> All intellectual property rights subsisting in or used in connection with the Project, including all the documents and manuals relating thereto, and including all intellectual property rights owned by Party B prior to the execution of this Contract as well as all intellectual property rights acquired or created by Party B during the term of this Contract, are and shall remain the sole property of Party B and/or its possible licensor(s).
>
> 项目固有的或与项目相关使用的一切知识产权，包括有关知识产权的一切文件和手册，及包括乙方在本合同签署之前拥有的一切知识产权和乙方在本合同期间获得或创立的一切知识产权，现在是，以后仍然是乙方和/或其可能的许可人的独家财产。

"relating thereto"相当于"which relate to the intellectual property rights"（有关知识产权的）。

- therewith：with that 以此；此外

> Before submitting his Tender, the Contractor shall be deemed to have inspected and examined the Site and its surroundings and information available in connection therewith and to have satisfied himself (so far as is practicable, taking cost and time into consideration) as to: (a) the form and nature thereof, including the sub-surface conditions.

"in connection therewith"相当于"in connection with the Site and surroundings"（与工地和环境有关的资料）。"the form and nature thereof"相当于"the form and nature of the Site and surroundings"（工地和环境的形状及其性质）。

总之，以"there"词根合成的这类副词所指的事物范围通常比以"here"为词根的合成词所指更为狭窄、更为具体，通常不会指整个合约，而是指该有关条款中的某一个特定事件、时间等。在翻译时，是否一律将此类古旧副词译成对应的中文，须具体情况具体分析，有的非译不可，有的可以不译，要视情况灵活对待。

> Party A has full legal right, power and authority to execute and deliver this Contract and all of the agreements and documents referred to in this Contract to which Party A is a party and to observe and perform its obligations hereunder and thereunder.
>
> 甲方在法律上有充分的权利、权力和权限签署和交付本合同及本合同中提及的该方为一方的所有协议和文件，遵守并履行本合同及该等协议和文件规定的义务。

此例中的 here = this Contract, there = the agreements and documents，翻译时必须加以还原，译为"本合同"和"该等协议和文件"，即把这几个词重复译出。

> Associated items shall mean those associated items and services specified in Exhibit "C" which is attached hereto and made a part hereof.
> 附属项目是指 C 表中规定的附属及服务项目，C 表附属本协定且为本协定的一部分。

据上下文推测，本例中的 here = the Agreement ······须加以还原成"本协定"，不可省却。

> The Purchaser shall, upon receipt of Corporation's respective invoices therefor, pay to Corporation all amounts which become due by the Purchaser to Corporation hereunder, including without limitation an amount equal to the taxes and duties.
> 收到公司的各种发票后，买方必须立刻付给公司业已到期应付的所有款项，包括各种税收费用在内，不得有例外。

本例中的 there = respective invoices issued by the Corporation for the Purchaser。因发票是卖方（公司）为其销售的货物所出具的，人人皆知，故翻译时不必画蛇添足译为"收到公司为其出售的货物所出具的发票后"，故可省略不译。here = this Agreement。上下文中因"业已到期的应付的所有款项"已含"本合约下"之意，亦可略去不译，不会导致任何文意上的曲解或遗漏。

> If, after the signing of this Agreement, the Chinese government either at the State, provincial, municipal or local level adopts any new law, regulation, decree or rule, amends or repeals any provision of any law, regulation, decree or rule, or adopts any different interpretation or method of implementation of any law, regulation, decree or rule, which contravenes this Agreement or which materially and adversely affects a party's economic benefit under this Agreement, then upon written notice thereof from the affected party to the other Party ...
> 如果本协议签署之后，中国国家、省、市或地方政府通过任何新的法律、法规、法令或条例，修改或废除任何法律、法规、法令或条例的任何条款，或对任何法律、法规、法令或条例给予不同的解释或采取不同的实施办法，导致与本协议相冲突，或对一方在本协议项下的经济利益造成实质性的不利影响，受影响的一方经书面通知另一方后……

本例中的"thereof"在这里所表示的是前面的假设情况，并不涉及任何具体的法律、法规、法令或条例，在句子上下文意思清楚的情况下可以省略不译。

课后练习

1. 下面对中国合同法中的两句译得不是很到位，请尝试用古旧副词对其加以改造。

（1）第五条　当事人应当遵循公平原则确定各方的权利和义务。

Chapter 3 Archaic Adverbs and Model Verbs in Legal Documents

译文：Parties shall adhere to the principle of fairness in designating each party's rights and obligations. （用 thereto）

（2）第六条 当事人行使权利,履行义务应当遵循诚实信用的原则。

译文：Parties shall adhere to the principle of honesty and trust worthiness in exercising their rights and performing their obligations. （用 thereof）

2. 把下面的句子翻译成中文,注意古旧副词的处理。

（1）No claim shall be recoverable hereunder if the benefit of the contract herein contained shall become vested in any other person or persons at law or in equity otherwise than by will or operation of law, unless the written consent of the Insurer thereto shall have first been obtained.

（2）During the three months immediately preceding the expiration of the term hereby created the Landlord shall be at liberty to affix and maintain without interference on any external part of the said premises a notice stating that the premises are to be let and such information in connection therewith as the Landlord shall reasonably require.

（3）If any or more of the provisions contained in this Agreement or any document executed in connection herewith shall be invalid, illegal, or unenforceable in any respect under any applicable law, (i) the validity, legality and enforceability of the remaining provisions contained herein or therein shall not in any way be affected or impaired and shall remain in full force and effect …

（4）All notices, demands and other communications to be given hereunder shall be made by registered airmail, or cable or telex followed by a confirmation letter, to the parties at the addresses indicated above or at such addresses as are notified in writing by the parties. If either party has changed his address, such party shall give a written notice thereof to the other party. All notices, demands and other communications mentioned above shall be deemed to have been given or made at the date of their dispatch.

（5）Unless the notice of loss or damage and the general nature of such loss or damage be given in writing to the carrier or his agent at the port of discharge before or at the time of the removal of the goods into the custody of the person entitled to delivery thereof under the contract of carriage, or, if the loss or damage be not apparent, within three days, such removal shall be prima facie evidence of the delivery by the carrier of the goods as described in the bill of lading.

▶ 2. 英语法律文书中的情态动词

英语法律文书中主要的情态动词有：can/could，may/might，shall/should，will/would 和 must。但在法律英语中，主要情态词或使用频率最高的情态动词依次是 shall，may，must 和 should。

在法律或合同的起草中，情态动词的功能是：修饰某一个条款，使之正确反映起草者或制定者对条款表述可能含义的判断，或反映其对自己所说所写内容正确与否的判断。这些情态词表达出一系列不同的含义，"许可"、"义务"和"决心"可能是其中的三种，这三种皆与人们控制事件的能力有关。另外三种含义是"可能"、"必需"和"预期"，这三种则表示事件是在人们的控制能力之外，人们对可能发生事件的判断。

（1）情态动词"shall"的用法

① "shall"在非法律文件中的用法

"shall"在非法律文件中的用法，有四点值得注意：

● "shall"被用作表示预期和决心，但是这种用法很少见。在一般的口语和书面语中，用"will"表示预期和决心要普遍得多。但若在法律文件中表示"义务"的话，"shall"（而非 will）用得更为普遍。使用"shall"或"will"可以产生微妙的意思差别：

> You shall hear.（你应该听到）（其隐含意思是"我将会告诉你"）
> You will hear.（你将听到）（其隐含意思为"你将会从独立于我的意志之外的其他人那里听到它"）

> You shall be rewarded.（你应获奖赏）（意味着"我会注意让你获奖"）
> You will be rewarded.（你将获奖赏）（意味着"你将获奖，但这不依赖于我"）

由此可见，若有人告诉你说，"You will get a bonus this year"（你今年将得到一笔奖金）而非"You shall get a bonus this year"（你今年应得到一笔奖金），这其中暗含的意思就会有所不同。

● 每个情态动词都有歧义，能被用于表示至少两种不同的意思。

● 在情态动词的不同含义之间有一些显著的重叠区。在某些情况下，关于将来时的情况就难以区分预期、决心和义务，如在"I will see you tomorrow then"（那我明天将见你）中的"will"就既有预期又有决心的意思。

● 每个情态词不同含义之间的区分是渐进的，而非绝对的。

Chapter 3　Archaic Adverbs and Model Verbs in Legal Documents

"shall"的几种用法:
- "shall"表示预期(prediction)和决心(volition)

在非法律语言环境中,"shall"首先用来表示预期,但只是在主语为第一人称的句子中,如"According to the public opinion, I shall win this election."(根据民意测验,我将赢得此次选举)及"When shall we know the election result?"(我们何时将知道选举结果?)

"shall"可以表示决心,而且此种用法也是用在主语为第一人称的句子中,如"We shall support their ideas."(我们会支持他们的想法。)及"What shall we do tonight?"(今晚我们要做些什么?)

但"shall"在主语为第一人称的句子中表示预期和决心,在北美尤其在书面中用得不多,在英联邦国家的英文作品中较常使用。

"shall"可用于第一人称表示强烈的决心、意愿,这是"shall"一词的强调用法,含有誓约或承诺之意。例如,二战期间,日军占领菲律宾之后,麦克阿瑟(American Caesar)率军撤退之际曾说"I shall return"便是表示强烈决心的例子。

- "shall"在第二人称为单数时的用法——这是"shall"在《圣经》中的用法,富含强烈修辞色彩。例如,在《出埃及记》的第20.13章中的"十诫"之一"你不得(shalt not)杀人"(Thou shalt not kill)。又如,Thou shalt love thy neighbor as thy self.(你要像爱自己一样爱你的邻居)

- "shall"表示义务,如:You shall do exactly as I say.(你应当严格按我说的办)He shall be punished if he disobeys.(如果不遵守的话,它应当受到惩罚)。

② "shall"在法律起草中的使用及用法实例

"shall"在法律起草中的字面及隐含意思如何? 要解决四个问题:
- 在法律起草中为何要使用"shall"?
- 当法条中用了该词,其含义是什么? 是否指明某种预期(prediction)、决心(volition)、义务(obligation),抑或其他?
- 应当如何将其译成中文?
- 在合同起草中,是否也要用"shall"一词? 若是,该怎么使用?

早期立法者遵循罗马传统的立法体制,针对用于表达"义务"、"许可"和"禁止"概念的表达方式不用情态动词,不用"shall",而是使用其他一些一般化、抽象化的非人格化的立法风格,诸如"它是必需的"(it is obligatory)、"它是经授权的"(it is authorized)、"它是合法的"(it is lawful)、"它是被禁止的"(it is prohibited),其优点是非常清晰,避免了情态动词固有的歧义。

但此种传统风格之所以没有被采用,而是用了"shall"来起草法律,有其历史因素:一是 18 世纪末和 19 世纪初,两位立法起草学者 Jeremy Bentham 和 George Coode 反对传统风格,强烈反对将无生命的事物当作法律语句的主语,因此他们用情态动词而没有采用罗马式的抽象做法,强调个人的行为,而非一种静止或持续的状态。他们的思想使得立法起草更加规范化,同时也变得更加人格化、特定化和具体化。二是因为现代对标点符号的习惯用法产生出大量短句而非一个长句,这也弱化了制定条款的施为性作用(illocutionary force)。结果便使起草者感到在法律开头的单个制定条款不够权威,于是通过加上"shall"来增加各项规定的权威感。

"shall"在法律起草中的用法常会引起歧义,因在法律文本中很少使用"预期"这一含义,故其可能含有表示义务的意思,或者仅仅意味着修辞意义,且二者之间存在重叠区,"shall"在具体法律中用法究竟是完全表示义务,还是修辞性质,区别不是很清楚。"shall"被用于将来时中有一定道理。然而在法律起草里面"shall"一词并非用于表示将来时。因为习惯上法律是以恒定不变的状态(constantly speaking)而言的,其背后的理念便是:一部法律一旦生效,就假定在一段长时间内适用于任何一个时间点上,适用于许多年、数十年,也许是几个世纪。每当一个人观察那部法律时,那个人无论生活于何时,也无论是否生活在该法颁布的时期,都应该理解到法律是以现在时态表示的,在那一特定时刻适用于他。假如是用将来时态的话,法律就有可能被误解,以致观察法律的人可能会说:"哦,这法律不适用于我。它适用于将来的某一个时候,但不是对我。"故为避免误会,习惯上"shall"一词在法律上并不用于表示将来时,且将来时态一般也不用在法律里面。因此,"shall"一词在法律里的歧义性只是介于表示义务和修辞之间,并不暗指将来时。

但究竟如何区分其真正含义,是有一个判断标准的。总而言之,"shall"一词具有以下特征:它具有指示性施为性作用;在"义务"、"修辞"以及"将来"等含义之间,易生歧义;"shall"一词用以表达"义务"的含义时和中文"应"的用法相似。

若是要给主语施加义务,可用"shall",若非如此,与使用"is/are"或"will"相比,使用"shall"并未使句子获得额外的含义,则纯粹是修辞性用法。

> In General—Part I of Subchapter A of Chapter 75 of the Internal Revenue Code of 1986 (relating to crimes, other offenses, and forfeitures) is amended by adding after Section 7213 the following section ...

上述条款中提到,《国内税收法》被修订时,用了"is"一词而非"shall"。依据上述标

Chapter 3 Archaic Adverbs and Model Verbs in Legal Documents

准,这是有道理的,因为它仅仅描述一个事实:《国内税收法》被修订,并没有为任何人施加实际修订该法的义务,而只是说,"《国内税收法》被修订"。

> Federal Employees and other Persons. It shall be unlawful for ….

> State and Other Employees. It shall be unlawful for any person …

> Any violation of subsection (a) shall be punishable …

上述3例都用了"shall",但它们究竟是表示义务还是修辞性的,不是很清楚。有没有施加一项义务?若是,它又是施加给谁的?另外一种处理该问题的方法就是去设问"shall"一词是否增添了什么?若将其用"is"替用后,意思是否全然不同或改变?我们发现不是,因此与其说是义务,不如说是带有更多的修辞成分,甚至也许是完全是修辞性的。

> An officer or employee of the United States who is convicted of any violation of Subsection (a) shall in addition to any other punishment, be dismissed from office or discharged from employment.
> 合众国的官员或雇员如果被判触犯(a)款应被免除职务或解除雇佣关系。

本例中"shall"表示义务,因为这里的主语是一个人,并且有一个行为动词。但因为是用在被动语态中,所以有一点欺骗性。读者不清楚谁有权免职,是老板吗?但谁是老板?该人的老板不确定,所以"shall"在此处可能是代表义务,但是不能精确地知道承担义务的人是谁。

> The Secretary shall notify such taxpayer as soon as practicable of such inspection or disclosure.

这是一个完全用"shall"表示义务的很好的例子,因为存在作为主语的人,句子是主动语态,也存在一个要被采取的行为,很显然此处表达了一种意愿,那就是使部长担负做某事的义务。

由此可见,在法律起草中,"shall"一词通常只是在表示义务和修辞之间出现歧义。"shall"在法律中也被用于将来时态,如前所述,但通常不这么做。下面是一些不恰当地用"shall"表示将来时态的例子。

> If any person shall give notice, that person may appeal …
> 如果有人要发布通知……

> If any balance shall have been found to be due ...
>
> 假如已经发现任何余额要到期……

> A person who shall allow any animal to stray ... shall be guilty of ...
>
> 如果有人要放任动物走失,他将因……而被认定有罪。

不注意这种"法律以恒定状态而言"的习惯就会导致歧义——人们不清楚"shall"的用法是指预期、义务还是修辞。

下面是另一些关于"shall"可能有争议的用法的例子:

> An aggrieved party shall file an appeal within 30 days of entry of judgment.
>
> 受害方应在判决下达之日起30日内提出上诉。

这是一个所谓"虚假义务"的例子。受害方没有提出上诉的这项义务。但是如果他想这样做的话,那他就必须在30天内提出,否则就不会接受。

> A pleading shall be filed with the clerk.
>
> 诉状应向助理提出。

这意味着如果要提出一份诉状,必须向助理提出,否则就不会被接受。

> The certificate ... shall be conclusive evidence.
>
> 证书应是最终证据。

> No defect or irregularity ... shall vitiate any act done by him ...
>
> 瑕疵或不合规范不会贬损他所做的任何行为。

上述两句中的"shall"一词纯粹是修辞性的用法,与使用"is"或"will"相比,使用"shall"并未使句子获得额外的含义。

> The governor shall fill the vacancy from a list of three persons nominated by the commission.
>
> 州长应从委员会提名的3人名单中找人填补空缺。

这是否意味着州长应去找人填补空缺,并且应该从委员会提名的3个人中进行挑选?还是意味着州长并不一定要去填补空缺,但如果他要这样做的话,就只能指定一个由委员会提名的人?

> The General Manager shall be a member of the Board.
>
> 总经理应是董事会的一名成员。

这是否意味着必须从董事会成员中挑选总经理?或者总经理不必非得从董事会成

Chapter 3 Archaic Adverbs and Model Verbs in Legal Documents ‖ 057

员中进行挑选,但是其一旦被任命,就自动地兼任董事会成员?或总经理必须始终为董事会成员,而任职期间如果不再是董事会成员,他就自动地停止担任总经理职务?

> The Commissioner to be appointed shall be a resident of Canada.
> 将被任命的专员应是加拿大居民。

这是否意味着要从加拿大居民中进行选择,而不管他在被任命后选择居住何处?还是要求其在被任命为专员之后仍保持加拿大居民身份?对此可能有两种解释:一是"一个人没有资格被任命为专员,除非他是加拿大居民",另一则是"一个人没有资格被任命为专员或继续担任这一职务,除非他是加拿大居民"。

> The house shall be completely painted before the payment of $400 is due.
> Does this mean that the painter has assumed a duty to paint the house that is also a constructive condition of the owner's duty to pay $400—a bilateral contract? Or is this simply a unilateral offer the acceptance of which, by completely painting the house, triggers the owner's duty to pay—but itself not creating any duty on the painter's part to accept?

> The Mayor is empowered to appoint the Chief of Police who shall be a resident of the city.
> Does this merely describe the Mayor's pool of eligible appointees, limiting it to persons already living in the city, with the appointment of a non-resident going beyond the scope of his power? Or does it mean that although the eligible pool is unlimited, once appointed the Chief of Police has a duty to become a resident of the city?

由此可见,英美人自己都认为"shall"属于可能引起歧义的词,其用法有时令外国人束手无策,有人将其称作英语中最大的魔怪。无论外国法律还是中国法律英译均存在着严重滥用"shall"一词的情况,要尽量避免使用。美国简明英语行动和信息网出版的写作手册 Writing User-Friendly Documents 中专门对法律文件中"shall"等情态动词的用法做出说明:

Use "must" for obligation, "may" for permission, and "should" for preference. Use "may not" to convey prohibitions. Avoid the ambiguous "shall".

同理,在 Drafting Legal Documents 中,也对此加以说明:

- Use "must" instead of "shall"

shall	imposes an obligation to act, but may be confused with prediction of future action
will	predicts future action
must	imposes obligation, indicates a necessity to act
should	infers obligation, but not absolute necessity
may	indicates discretion to act
may not	indicates a prohibition

To impose a legal obligation, use "must". To predict future action, use "will".

DON'T SAY: The Governor shall approve it.

SAY: The Governor must approve it. [obligation]

OR: The Governor will approve it. [future action]

- Use the present tense

A regulation of continuing effect speaks as of the time you apply it, not as of the time you draft it or when it becomes effective. For this reason, you should draft regulations in the present tense. By drafting in the present tense, you avoid complicated and awkward verb forms.

DON'T SAY: The fine for driving without a license shall be $10.00.

SAY: The fine for driving without a license is $10.00.

下面结合汉英法律翻译实例,具体说明情态动词在法律英语中的用法。A 为修改前的说法,B 是修改后的说法。

A: Any oil or gas lessee who wishes to use timber for fuel in drilling operations *shall* file an application with the officer who issued the lease.

B: You *must* file an application to use the timber for fuel on your oil or gas lease. File the application with the office where you got your lease. [表示义务]

A: The applicant *shall* be notified by registered mail in all cases where the permit applied for is not granted, and *shall* be given 30 days within which to appeal such decision.

B: Our agency *will* notify you by registered mail if we reject your application. You *must* file an appeal of that decision within 30 days. [表示将来]

Chapter 3　Archaic Adverbs and Model Verbs in Legal Documents　‖　059

第八条　依法成立的合同,对当事人具有法律约束力。当事人应当按照约定履行自己的义务,不得擅自变更或者解除合同。

A: Article 8　As soon as a contract is established in accordance with the law, it *shall* be legally binding on the parties. The parties *shall* perform their respective obligations in accordance with the terms of the contract. Neither party may unilaterally modify or rescind the contract.

B: Article 8　A contract drawn up in accordance with the law *is* legally binding upon the parties. A party *must* perform its obligation in accordance with the contract, and may not arbitrarily modify or terminate the contract.

第七条　有下列情形之一的,禁止结婚:
(一)直系血亲和三代以内的旁系血亲;(二)患有医学上认为不应当结婚的疾病。

A: Article 7　No marriage *shall* be contracted under any of the following circumstances:
(1) if the man and the woman are lineal relatives by blood, or collateral relatives by blood up to the third degree of kinship; and
(2) if the man or the woman is suffering from any disease, which is regarded by medical science as rendering a person unfit for marriage.

B: Article 7　Marriage *is* prohibited if——
(1) The two parties are lineal relatives by blood, or collateral relatives by blood up to the third degree of kinship; or
(2) Any party suffers from a disease considered by medical science as making a person unfit for marriage.

如果像 A 译那样,用否定的表达方法,应该说"No marriage *may* be contracted …",而不是"*shall* be …"。

现在,在一些权威性双语法律条文里处理"shall"一词时,选词取向是很清楚的:凡中文版条文用"必须"之处,英文版不用"shall"来表达,而基本上是用"must";反之,英文版中出现的"shall",在中文条文中不用"必须",而是分别用"应"或"须"及其他形式来表达。

The Chief Executive of the Hong Kong Special Administrative Region must be a person of integrity, dedicated to his/her duties.
香港特别行政区行政长官必须廉洁奉公、尽忠职守。

Public servants serving in all government departments of the Hong Kong Special Administrative Region must be permanent residents of the Region ... Public servants must be dedicated to their duties and be responsible to the Government of the Hong Kong Special Administrative Region.

在香港特别行政区政府各部门任职的公务人员必须是香港特别行政区永久性居民……公务人员必须尽忠职守，对香港特别行政区政府负责。

任何单位或个人实施他人专利的，除本法第十四条规定的以外，都必须与专利权人订立书面实施许可合同，向专利权人支付专利使用费……专利权的所有单位或持有单位应当对职务发明创造的发明人或者设计人给予奖励。

Except as provided for in Article 14 of this law, any entity or individual exploiting the patent of another must conclude a written licensing contract with the patentee and pay the patentee a fee for the exploitation of its or his patent ... The entity owning or holding the patent right on a job-related invention-creation shall reward the inventor or designer.

当然，英文中的"shall"在中文文本中有时可以不译。较为典型的情形有：在法律及合约条文中，如主句含"have the right/power/jurisdiction/obligation of"，"be/hold responsible for（bear/take responsibility/cost for）"，"be obliged/liable/accountable to"，"be entitled to"，"have the option of"，"be at liberty to"，"be free to"，"be able to"等经常用来表示权利、责任和义务的动词短语，以及"be + predicative adjective"的动词短语，这些短语前面的"shall"一般不可把它译成"须"、"应当"、"应"等。

All Hong Kong residents shall be equal before the law.

香港居民在法律面前一律平等。

The homes and other premises of Hong Kong residents shall be inviolable. Arbitrary or unlawful search of, or intrusion into, a resident's home or other premises shall be prohibited.

香港居民的住宅和其他房屋不受侵犯。禁止任意或非法搜查、侵入居民的住宅和其他房屋。

The Board shall have such jurisdiction and powers as are conferred on it by this or any other Ordinance.

仲裁处有本条例或任何其他条例授予其司法管辖权及权力。

If the Buyers fail to provide such letter of credit in the Sellers' favor as prescribed above, the Sellers shall have the option of reselling the contracted goods for the account of the Buyers or delaying any shipment and/or canceling any orders at any time on the Buyers' account and risk.

如果买方未能向卖方提供上述规定之信用证,卖方有权选择把合约规定之货物转售或随时推迟付运和/或撤销任何订单,由此造成的损失和风险由买方承担。

The Landlord shall not be in any way responsible to the Tenant for any damage caused to the said premises or the contents thereof arising as a result of the negligence of any other tenant of the said building.

由于该大厦其他任何住户的过失而产生的对该楼宇或其里面东西的任何损坏,业主对租户不负任何责任。

Provided that should the Purchaser or his nominee have entered into possession of the premises hereby agreed to be sold, the Purchaser shall thereupon be deemed to have accepted the title of the Vendor and shall not be entitled to raise any requisition or objection in respect of any of the matters aforesaid.

倘若买主或其指定人已占有凭本合约出售的楼宇,买主将被认为已接受卖主的所有权,并无权在上述任何问题方面提出任何要求或反对意见。

The cost of and incidental to the preparation and registration of this Agreement shall be borne and paid by the Vender and the Purchaser jointly. In addition to this the Purchaser shall bear and pay all the cost of Messrs. & Co. Solicitors for services in connection with the sale and purchase of the said premises …

卖主和买主共同支付本合约草拟和登记的费用和有关附带费用。除此之外,买主还须负责支付某律师行与所述楼宇买卖有关的服务费……

(2) "may"的用法

① "may"三种含义及其判断手段

● "may"的三种含义:

"may"类似于"shall",具有三种含义:

* 当"may"用于法律起草时,它通常的含义是给予许可或者给予某人做某事的授权;

* "may"同样也有可能性的意思,具有"或许"(perhaps)或者"可能"(possibly)的含义;

*它还表示义务,并且在特定的上下文中,它可以等同于"shall",在普通法国家"may"可以被法庭作为"shall"来解释。

> If the tea is not obtainable at our limits, you may invest one-half of the whole proceeds in silk.
> 如果你无法在我们限定的价格之内购得茶叶,你应该将全部收益的一半投资于丝绸生意中。

法庭据此商业交易的所有事实和客观形势将"may"解释为"shall"之意。不过"may"的这种意义最可能发生在法律当中,而不是合同中。"may"通常表达的意思是"被授权"(is authorized)或者"可能"(possibly)。

- 判断"may"所要表达的意思,对其三种含义的判断有三个参照物:
  * 特定句子或段落当中使用"may"这个词的总的上下文环境;
  * 查阅文档,看看"might"这个单词是否作为"可能"(possibly)解释,而如果可能的话,按黄金法则,"may"这个单词将不会以"可能"(possibly)的意思出现;
  * 看"may"这个单词后面是否使用了"自由裁量权"(in his discretion)这样的语句。在此情形下,起草者正试图告诉读者,此处"may"的使用并不表示义务,亦即拥有这一授权的人并不被强制去行使授权,而是具有自由裁量权。

(3)"should","must"的用法

① "should"的使用

前文述及"*should* infers obligation, but not absolute necessity"有时表示道德上的义务(moral obligation),与"shall"表示法律规定的义务(legal obligation)有所不同,不能混用。翻译中宜将"shall"译为"应",而"should"则译为"应当"、"应该",以示区别。但"shall"有时也被译为"应当"之意,极易混淆,"应当"在法律文件中就是"必须";而婉转的"should"则意味着原该或最好如此这般(如果不如此这般,那只好算了),究竟应译为"shall"或者"should",须斟酌原文精神实质。

> 职工应当……从事劳动……
> A: All employees *should* do their work …
> B: All employees *shall* do their work …

> 单位应当……给予一定时间的产假
> A: A maternity leave of a fixed days *should* be given by the unit.
> B: A maternity leave of a fixed days *shall* be given by the unit.

> ……在劳动时间内进行产前检查,应当算作劳动时间。
> A: ... antenatal examination during the labor hours *should* be counted as labor time.
> B: ... time spent ... for prenatal exams during working hours *is* to be included in the work hours.

本例中虽有"应当"二字,但与"必须"以及"应当"与否毫不相干,只是客观地、平铺直叙地阐明了计算方法,故改译 is.

此外,在起草诸如正式的法律意见、咨询信函或为客户撰写一份备忘录之时,除非把从法律中直接引用过来的话放在引号之间,请不要对第三人称使用"shall"一词,在此种间接表述中宜用"should"。如有一份由当地律师写给美国律师的传真法律意见函,基本内容是对劳动标准法的描述。该份传真描述了该法律的规定,使用的是间接性陈述。其中写道:

> Based on the above provision, the Labor Commission had ruled that managers appointed by a company pursuant to the provisions of the Company Law shall not be considered "workers".
> 依据上述条款,劳工委员会有这样的规则,即公司根据公司法任命的管理人员不"应"被认为是"工人"。

此处不应当使用"shall"一词。写传真之人并非在命令收到传真之人做任何事情,并不是在施加任何义务,此份传真也并非法律。如果这份传真是作者在引用法律的话,可以使用"shall"一词,然而并不是引用法律,故应当使用"should"。

② "must"的使用
- 可用来表示义务。

> Every driver must observe the traffic regulations.
> 每一位驾驶者都必须遵守交通规则。

- 也可表示逻辑必要性。

> Each application must submit his application report by July 1.
> 每一个申请者务须在 7 月 1 日前递交申请报告。

在合同当中,"must"一词只被用来表示逻辑必要性,这样的做法是有意义的,并且以这样的用法来代替"shall"的"虚假义务"(false obligation)的使用也是有意义的。然而在某些合同当中,"must"一词有时也被用来替代"shall"以表示义务。"must"用以表示这层意思时,一般可译为"须"、"必须"、"务须"等。

(4) 情态动词用作施加禁止时的歧义
① 禁令中潜在的歧义
尽管上下文以及语言习惯通常会使意思得以澄清,伴随着否定词的情态动词仍然是潜在的产生歧义的因素。

• "A person may not do X"可解释为"某人不被允许做某事"(A person is not allowed to do X)或者"可能某人将不做某事"(Perhaps a person will not do X),这是因为"may"这个词所产生的歧义。

• "No person may do X"可解释为"没有人被允许做某事"(No person is allowed to do X)或者"也许没有人将做某事"(Perhaps no person will do X)。

• "A person shall not do X"可解释为"某人有义务不做某事"(A person has an obligation not to do X),但是也可表达"某人没有义务做某事"(A person has no obligation to do X)。

• "No person shall do X"可解释为"某人有义务不做某事"(A person has an obligation not to do X)或者"没有人有义务做某事"(No person has an obligation to do X)。

② 使用不同类型否定语的效果力度
下列例句中情态动词施加禁止的效果依次递减:

• It is not lawful for any person to do X.

这是最为有效的形式,有明确的主题和焦点,伴随着以主动形式表达的行为,否定词适用于什么很清楚。此种形式具有宣告性施为性作用,符合法律制定条款的宣告性施为性作用,但其不具备"shall"所拥有的指示性效力以及修辞方面的力量。由于起草者偏爱"shall"的上述特点,故此种句型不被采用。

• A person may not do X.

此句型在表达可能与允许上有潜在的歧义。这种形式具有宣告性施为性作用,符合法律制定条款的宣告性施为性作用。此句型有时被采用。

• No person may do X.

此句型在表达可能与允许上同样存在潜在的歧义。这种形式具有宣告性施为性作用,符合法律制定条款的宣告性施为性作用,但是不太具有情态动词的义务性含义,因为它指向"no person",此句型有时被采用。

• A person shall not do X.

此句型在表达否定对象上有潜在的歧义。该句型有时被采用。

Chapter 3 Archaic Adverbs and Model Verbs in Legal Documents

- No person shall do X.

该句型没有从情态动词"shall"的义务性含义上得到什么,因为它指向"no person"。

课后练习

1. 汉译英

(1) 一切法律、行政法规和地方性法规都不得同宪法相抵触。一切国家机关的武装力量、各政党和各社会团体、各企业事业组织都必须遵守宪法和法律。一切违反宪法和法律的行为,必须予以追究。

(2) 中华人民共和国公民必须遵守宪法和法律,保守国家秘密,爱护公共财产,遵守劳动纪律,遵守公共秩序,尊重社会公德。

2. 英译汉

(1) They shall have the freedom to travel and freedom of entry and exit. Unless restrained by law, Hong Kong residents who hold valid travel document shall be free to leave the Region without special authorization.

(2) Any party wishing to set a foreign bank should have the following qualifications:

(3) No one shall operate bus, tram or trolly bus passenger transport without a Qualification Certificate.

(4) No person may reside in the Free Trade Zone without permission of the Administrative Committee.

(5) Citizens shall enjoy the rights of life and death.

Chapter 4
How to Deal with *Number* and *Time* in Legal Documents

▶ **1. 数（Number）**

本部分讨论"数"的翻译过程中应注意的一些细节问题。

（1）法律文书中名词的单数和复数

The Fundamentals of Legal Drafting 一书的作者 Reed Dickson（美国法律起草的泰斗）认为，只要上下文允许，用单数形式比用复数形式好，因为如用复数，则不清楚谓语是分别适用于每一单项，还是一并适用于所有各项。

> The engineer shall sign releases for the stages set forth in Section 5.
> 工程师应为第 5 条规定的各阶段签署几份许可书。

应改译为：

> The engineer shall sign a release for each stage set forth in Section 5.
> 工程师应为第 5 条规定的每一阶段签署一份许可书。

除非要表达的意思是：

> The engineer shall sign releases for each stage set forth in Section 5.
> 工程师应为第 5 条规定的每一阶段签署几份许可书。
> The engineer shall sign releases, each of which will cover all the stages set forth in Section 5.
> 工程师应签署几份许可书，每一份许可书将涵盖第 5 条规定的所有阶段。

反之，使用复数易生歧义，如：

> The Secretary shall not award grants, or enter into contracts, in excess of $25,000 without the approval of the National Advisory Committee.
>
> 未经国家咨询委员会的批准,部长拨款或订立合同不得超过 25000 美元。

此处的 25000 美元的限额是对整个拨款总额的限制还是对每一笔拨款的限制？同理,这是对合同总体规模的限制还是对每一份合同的限制？抑或是要限制所有拨款和合同放在一起的数额？不清楚。该句用单数重新撰写,这些问题即可迎刃而解:

> The Secretary shall not award a grant, or enter into a contract, in excess of $25,000 without the approval of the National Advisory Committee.
>
> 未经国家咨询委员会的批准,部长拨一次款或订立一项合同不得超过 25000 美元。

重新起草的规定虽然用的是单数,但会被理解为适用于所有拨款和合同。又如"Any employee who …"这个短语所表示的意思与"Employees who …"是一样的,但它不会使读者或法庭把这句话错误地理解为:在覆盖任何雇员之前必须至少牵涉两个雇员,或者这只适用于雇员群体。法令适用于受其制约的每一个人,其起草也应适用于每一个人。单数并不是限制,不用复数是为了明晰；如果在某种特殊情况下,你有理由认为单数名词可能会被理解为不适用于你想覆盖的群体里每一个人,就用"each"或"every"代替"a","an"或"any"。

总之,无论是在法律起草或合同撰写中,只要意思允许,用单数名词,不用复数名词:

> A: The guard shall issue security badges to employees who work in Building D and Building E.
>
> B: The guard shall issue a security badge to each employee who works in Building D and each employee who works in Building E.

除非意思是:

> C: The guard shall issue a security badge to each employee who works in both Building D and Building E. (There are other possible meanings)

> 第四条 当事人依法享有自愿订立合同的权利,任何单位和个人不得非法干预。
>
> A: Article 4 The parties shall have the rights to be voluntary to enter into a contract in accordance with the law. No unit or individual may illegally interfere.
>
> B: Article 4 A party has the right to enter into a contract voluntarily in accordance with the law and no entity or individual may unlawfully interfere with such a right.

(2) 中英文互译中的单数和复数
① 中英文名词的单数和复数用法分析

中文对名词的单数和复数一般是不加区别的,而英文中的名词要严格区分单数和复数。用英文起草法律文件时，可以用单数避免歧义，然而总的来说，中文名词词语本身易有"数"的歧义。见下列中英文名词单数和复数的分析表。

中英文名词单数和复数分析建议

	单 数	单数/复数	复 数
中 文	在特殊情况下使用"一个"或"每个"	每个成员，类别全体	在特殊情况下使用"们"指人，或用"都"指人和东西
英 文	a = each member each = each member	each member, class jointly (exceptional use of "___(s)")	each member, class jointly

中译英时，建议使用英文的复数，因为复数形式两种意思都有；英译中时，若原文的含义是指复数，也许应该用中文单数/复数的形式，若原文的含义是指单数，可能在某些情况下可以使用中文的单数形式，不过那是很少有的。如下述中译英时用复数而不用单数的例子：

一份征税通知

国家税务局关于外国企业向境内转让无形资产取得收入征收营业税问题的通知（国税发〔1998〕4号）

各省、自治区、直辖市和计划单列市国家税务局、地方税务局：

关于在中国境内未设立机构的外国企业向中国境内转让无形资产取得收入是否征收营业税的问题，现明确如下：

根据《中华人民共和国营业税暂行条例》第一条和该条例实施细则第七条规定，在中国境内未设立机构的外国企业向中国境内转让无形资产取得收入应当征收营业税。

一九九八年一月十三日

Notice From the State Administration of Taxation Concerning the Levy of Business Tax on Income Derived From Transfers of Intangible Assets in China by Foreign Enterprises Guo-Shui-Fa〔1998〕No.4

The State Tax Bureau and Local Tax Bureau of Provinces, Autonomous Regions, Municipalities directly under the Central Government and Cities independently listed in the State Plan:

The issue of whether the income derived from transfers of intangible assets in China by foreign enterprises which do not have establishments in China is clarified as follows:

Pursuant to the provisions under Article 1 of the Provisional Rules of the People's Republic of China on Business Tax and Article 7 of the Detailed Rules for the Implementation of the Provisional Rules, business tax should be levied on the income derived from transfers of intangible assets in China by foreign enterprises which do not have establishments in China.

January 13, 1998

上述词语如"外国企业"、"无形资产"、"机构"等在中文文件中反复被提到,但并没有表明其为单数还是复数,而其对应的英文处理如"foreign enterprises"、"intangible assets"、"establishments"都用了复数,是因为英文的复数既可以指单数,即一个类别的个别成员,也可以指整个类别,因此使用复数保留了中文的歧义。另一方面英文法令解释推定中复数包含单数。

中译英时,要表示中文的歧义,用"(s)"也不失为一种办法,但是在英文里这种办法不如就用复数好,这种办法只宜在极个别情况下采用。

> The party receiving confidential information (Recipient) shall make use of the Discloser's confidential information only for the following purpose(s):
> 接受保密资料的一方("接收方")应只为下述一项或多项目的使用披露方的保密材料:

(3) 法律文书中"等"的表述和翻译

"等"一词用在一串名词的最后,有三种不同的意思:

- 表示列举没有完,也就是说事务清单里还会有别的事项但不再举例了,译成英文时用"etc.";
- 表示举例已完,清单中没有别的事项了。英文没有对应的词语,译文中也就无须另加词汇;
- "等"出现在一个总括性词语前面,在短语的最后,表示选择性列举。说了"等",然后用一个总括性词语,在英文里这相当于先说总括性词语和"such as"然后一个一个列举。

"等"在中译英和英译中时的一些基本规则:

① 中译英

中 文	位 置	意 思	译成英文
等	在一串名词最后	举例不尽	etc., and so on
等	在一串名词最后	列举已完	不译
等	在总括性词语之前 在一串名词之后	选择性列举	〔总括性词语〕such as

② 英译中

英　文	意　思	译成中文
etc., and so on	举例不尽	等
no specific words	列举已完	不译
〔superordinate〕such as	选择性举例	等〔总括性词语〕

（4）法律文书中"倍数"的表述和翻译

英语中"times"常常会引起歧义。

① "times more"含义的歧义，如"His income is four times more than it was last year."可理解为4倍也可理解为5倍，应该说"four times as much as"。

② "times more（or times larger, times stronger, times brighter, etc.）"的歧义，如"She has three times more money than he does."她有他三倍的钱。

"three times more than"既可指三倍又可指四倍，实为严重的意义不清；而"four times as much as"意为"……的四倍"，意义清楚。因此，我们建议不要用"times more"而用"times as much"以避免这种歧义。

③ 中文法律文书中倍数的表述

年份	产量的标志	English	中　文
1985	1 unit	1985 Production Volume	1985年的产量
1999	1 unit 1 unit 1 unit	3x as much as 1985 3x that of 1985	"……的三倍"
2000	1 unit 1 unit 1 unit 1 unit	3x greater than 1985 increased 3x over 1985 3x larger than 1985 (but can be ambiguous; sometimes understood as "3x as much as 1985")	……增加三倍 比……多三倍 比……大三倍 （但可能有歧义，有时被理解为"……的三倍"）

如上表所示，若1985年的产量为一个单位，1999年的产量就是三个单位，2000年是四个单位，那么用英文怎么表示1999年比1985年产量增加了多少？准确无误的说法应是：The 1999 production is "three times as much as 1985" or "three times that of 1985"。

总之，"times"这个词会产生歧义，在起草时用"as much as"或"… times such and such"，不要用"greater than"或"larger than"。如果中文或英文的原文就是有歧义的，那么中文或英文的译文也应该反映这种歧义。

Chapter 4　How to Deal with *Number* and *Time* in Legal Documents　‖　071

（5）实例分析

法律条文中出现的数量幅度大致可分为两种：数量的上限或下限、数量的上限和下限。

> 中外合资经营企业的投资总额在一千万美元以上至三千万美元（含三千万美元）的，其注册资本至少应占投资总额的五分之二。
>
> Where the total investment of a Sino-Foreign equity joint venture is between US $10 million and US $30 million (US $30 million inclusive), its registered capital shall be at least 40% of its total investment.

"between"作为口语用语还是可以接受的，但是在书面语中算入还是不算入起始和终止数字，答案是模棱两可的。有比其更好的选择，如"一千万以上"可以说"not less than US $10 million"，或者说"US $10 million or more"。此外，翻译"至"可以不用"to"而说"US $30 million or less"，故此句可改译为：When the total investment of a Sino-Foreign equity joint venture is US $10 million or more but US $30 million or less (including US $30 million).

> 外国（或地区）企业同一类整车产品不得在中国建立<u>两家以上</u>的合资、合作企业。
>
> A foreign enterprise may not establish <u>more than two</u> equity or cooperative joint ventures in China for the same category of assembled automobiles or motorcycles.

上面例子中将"两家以上"译成"more than two"，显然不符合《民法通则》第155条之规定：民法所称的"以上"、"以下"、"以内"、"届满"，包括本数；所称的"不满"、"以外"，不包括本数。"因此，改译为：A foreign enterprise may not establish <u>two or more</u> equity or cooperative joint ventures in China for the same category of assembled automobiles or motorcycles.

"between"短语是忌用的。Reed Dickerson 在其 *The Fundamentals of Legal Drafting* 一书中就曾告诫：

Ambiguities similar to those described above for period of time exist also for ages.

DON'Y SAY: between the ages of 17 and 45

SAY: 17 years old or older and under 45

Although the phrase "less than 46 years old" is clear (it means anyone who has not reached his 46th birthday). The phrase "more than 17 years old" is ambiguous because it is not clear whether a person becomes "more than 17" on the day after his 17th birthday or on his 18th birthday.

DON'T SAY: who is more than 17 years old

SAY: who has passed his 17th birthday

Unless you mean who is 18 years old or older

此段引文虽直接表明，有关年龄幅度之表达忌用"between"，但其也间接地指出了使用"between"之忌。关于用"between X and Z"（X 与 Z 均表示数量幅度之极限）而 X 与 Z 又是要包括在极限之内，Bryan A. Garner 在其 *A Dictionary of Modern Legal Usage* 一书中认为是这有问题的：

Between and Numbers. This may cause problems, if the numbers at either end of the spectrum are intended to be included. For example, if three petitioners and one respondent advance to Round Three from a bracket, then those four teams' names will be placed in a hat, and between one and three read from one to three only whole number between one and three.

这就是在直截了当地告诉我们，本例中"between … and …"须更正为"from … to …"。

当数量幅度不止一个而先后连续地出现于上下文时，往往会产生如下的错误：

吨位	每吨吨税（人民币）
50 吨以下	3 角
51 吨至 150 吨	3 角 5 分
tonnes	tonnage per ton（RMB）
below 50 tonnes	3 *jiao*
51 tonnes to 150 tonnes	3 *jiao* 5 *fen*

按原文 50 吨（和未满 50 吨一样）的吨税是人民币 3 角（每吨）；但是英语国家人士读了英语译文后，却对于 50 吨（不多也不少）一级的吨税税率究竟是多少感到迷茫了。因此，必须把"below 50 tonnes"更正为"50 tonnes or less"。此类英译错误属于"undistributed middle"（不周延的中项）歧义，是法律英译所必须防止的。

Chapter 4   How to Deal with *Number* and *Time* in Legal Documents   ‖ 073

> 外商投资者将其从企业分得的利润,再投资于本企业或其他外商投资企业,或举办新的外商投资企业,经营期不少于5年的,退还再投资部分已缴纳的企业所得税税款的40%。
> Foreign investors who reinvested their share of profits earned in their own enterprises, or in other foreign-invested enterprises, or in setting up new foreign-invested enterprises for a business period no less than five years shall be refunded forty percent of the enterprise income tax paid on the reinvested amount.

> 不少于1000万美元等值的自由兑换货币
> freely convertible currencies equivalent to no less than US $10 million

上面两译文皆属错译,其中"no less than"应改为"not less than"。请看关于"no less than"的说明:You can use no less than before an amount to indicate that you think the amount is surprisingly large (*Essential English Dictionary*)

由此可见,"not less than"是客观的、没有立法者主观感情色彩的,而"no less than"则有立法者的感情所在。众所周知,不能以感情代替政策,不能以感情代替法律,亦不能让法律受到感情的影响。

> 中华人民共和国主席、副主席每届任期同全国人民代表大会每届任期相同,连续任职不得超过两届。
> The term of office of the President and Vice President of the People's Republic of China is the same as that of the National People's Congress, and they shall serve no more than two consecutive terms.

> 香港特别行政区行政长官任期5年,可连任一次。
> The term of office of the Chief Executive of the Hong Kong Special Administrative Region shall be five years. He or she may serve for not more than two consecutive terms.

▶ 2. 时间(Time)

时间往往与法律中的期限有关,因此正确使用时间表述至关重要。

(1) day / clear day / calendar day / business day

① 根据 *Webster's Third New Int'l Dictionary*,"day"与法律相关的含义指 the hours or the daily recurring period established by usage or law for week,它也可以作"工作日"讲。澳州起草法律文书的权威 Piesse(*The Elements of Drafting* 的作者)认为"day"一词至少有三种含义：一是与黑夜对照的白天的意思；二是指连续 24 小时的时段（通常是从一个午夜到下一个午夜）；三是从任何时刻开始的 24 小时。法律或规范性文件的意图和上下文应当有助于理解所用的"day"一词应是哪种含义。

② calendar day：a consecutive 24-hour day running from midnight to midnight—also termed natural day. 这是一个可能引起歧义的术语，如下列合同的终止条款：

> Termination. Anything herein to the contrary notwithstanding, this Agreement may be terminated at any time by either Party for cause upon the giving of twenty-one (21) calendar days notice.
>
> 终止。不管本文有无任何相反的内容，任何一方都可因故提前二十一（21）个日历日发出通知终止本协议。

③ business day：a day that most institutions are open for business, usu. a day on which banks and major stock exchanges are open, excluding Saturdays and Sundays. 此义在中国一般与 working day 相同。

④ clear day：Piesse 认为，"clear day"（整日）是指一个在午夜开始的 24 小时时段。在 1 月 1 日后的整十天是指在 1 月 1 日与 2 日午夜开始到 1 月 11 日与 12 日午夜结束的时段。BLD 认为，One of many full, consecutive days between (1) the date when a period, measured in days, and begins (2) the date when an event that ends the period occurs. For example, if a statute or contract requires a party to give another party five clear days of notice of a hearing, and the hearing is scheduled to be held on the 31st day of the month, the party giving notice must do so by the 25th day of the month so that five full (clear) days elapse between but not including the 25th and 31st. 也就是说，如果在某个数目的整日时间里从事任何行为，计算时间就要把第一天和最后一天都排除在外。

普通法关于"day"的计算：

A：15 days from the date of commencement of risk（从风险开始之日起的十五天）

B：15 days from commencement of risk（从风险开始起的十五天）

A 与 B 的区别是：A 的 15 天从风险开始那天的午夜开始；B 的 15 天在那天风险开始的时间开始。区别的关键在于：如果不写上"date"这个词，行为时的那个钟点就成了开始的时间。因此，当以日计算期间时，如果由某一特定的事件引发开始计算日子，那个事件是在它发生的那个日子的某个钟点发生的。但是当计算日子的数目，或者草拟日子的计算时,一般不应该说"(那个事件)之后(多少)天",而应该说"(那个事件发生的)那天之后(多少)天",因为这样就使得终止日在那一天的午夜终止,而不是在与引发计算的那个事件发生的钟点相对应的时间终止。

(2) week / weekend

"week"一词有以下几种含义:

① "week"的一般含义

• 各种历法里七天一周期系列中的一个周期(one of a series of seven-day cycles used in various calendars);

• 任何连续的七天(any seven consecutive days);

• 每一个七天周期里正常的工作日、营业日或学校上课日系列(a series of regular working, business or school days during each seven-day period)。

使用"week"要注意其意思是"工作周"还是"七天"?

② 表示"从星期日到星期六"

就其法律含义,"a week"是指从星期日早晨开始到星期六夜里结束的一段时间。在英文国家里,星期日被确认为一周的第一天。中文"星期"事实上是用来表示从星期一开始的"工作周"。

③ 表示"七天"

a secular week(世俗周):一个连续七天的时段;a Biblical week(圣经周):一个从星期日到星期六的时段。该词在某一特定法律中的含义要依其用法和内容而定。

(3) month / calendar month / year

在普通法里,"month"这个词的意思是一个月,即28天,也称"lunar month"。现在它等同于日历月,除非表明有不同的意思。有关其计算的一般规则是,一件事情发生后的日历月时段从发生这件事情的当天午夜开始到下个月最后一天的午夜结束。"calendar month"也被解释为表示从一个公历月份的任何一天到下个月相应日子(如果有的话;如果没有,就到该月份的最后一天)的时间。就此而言,一个日历月是指时间的长度而不是一个特定的月份;它从起始那个月的那一天开始算起到下个月相同日子的前一天结束截止。

需要注意的是,应该避免以月计算时间,因为在英文(而非中文,中文很清楚)中存在问题,如果要表示一个期间且是用英文起草,就用"30 days"而不说"one month";用"60 days"而不说"two months"。

BLD 把"year"定义为:1. twelve calendar months beginning January 1 and ending

December 31—also termed *calendar year*; 2. a consecutive 365-day period beginning at any point; a span of twelve months。但是有关法律或合同的标注或语境可能改变其含义。

"month"和"year"都有另外一个定义,那就是不同时段的总和或一天一天累积到一个月或一年。如我们在服务合同或雇员合同里可能看到一条关于义务的规定,要求某人一年里在中国停留两个月。这是什么意思?是指全年零散累积,如一月停留三天、二月停留五天、三月停留六天等,还是集中居住60天?这需要在合同起草时加以明确。

(4) 法律文书中与时间有关的英语介词的用法

如上所述,表示时段的词(day, week, month, year)本来就有歧义,若再与也有歧义的介词用在一起则要更加小心,其关键问题是要注意:所提的日子是否包括在内?例如,"after"理解为不包括所提到的日子,"before"理解为不包括所提到的日子。

① 起草英文文本并将其译成中文

应避免使用带 * 号的词语,因其有歧义

英文	中文
1) after _____	_____后,_____以后
2) before _____	_____前
3) beginning _____ … ending _____	_____开始……_____终止
4) between _____ *	_____内
5) by _____ (inclusive)	_____以前
6) from _____ (inclusive) *	自_____(含_____)
7) from _____ (exclusive) *	自_____(不含_____)
8) on _____	于_____,在_____
9) through _____	至_____(含_____)
10) to _____ (exclusive) *	至_____(不含_____)
11) until _____ (inclusive) *	至_____(为止)
12) month	月
13) year	年
14) _____ or more	_____以上
15) _____ or less	_____以下
16) more than _____	超过_____
17) less than _____	低于_____

Chapter 4 How to Deal with *Number* and *Time* in Legal Documents

本组词语里需要注意的是 2）、5）、6）、7）、10）、11）、14）、15）。这些词语中的"以上"和"以下"是包括本数的。

② 将客户的英文文本译成中文

英文	中文
1）after _____	后，_____以后
2）before _____	_____前
3）between _____	_____内
4）by _____（if clearly exclusive）	_____以前 _____前
5）from _____（if clearly inclusive, if clearly exclusive）	自_____ 自_____（含） 自_____（不含）
6）on _____	于_____，在_____
7）to _____（if clearly inclusive, if clearly exclusive）	至_____ 至_____（含） 至_____（不含）
8）until _____	至_____（_____为止）
9）month	月
10）year	年
11）_____ or more	_____以上
12）_____ or less	_____以下
13）more than _____	超过_____
14）less than _____	低于_____

③ 将中方中文文本译成英文

中文	英文
1）_____后，_____以后	after _____
2）_____前	before _____
3）_____以前	on or before _____（by）
4）_____开始……_____终止	beginning _____ … ending _____
5）_____内	between _____

(续表)

中文	英文
6）自_____	starting _____
7）于_____，在_____	on _____
8）至_____（含）	through _____
9）至_____（不含）	to _____
10）至_____（为止）	until _____
11）月	month
12）年	year
13）_____以上	_____ or more（subject to context）
14）_____以下	_____ or less（subject to context）

本组词语里，2）可能会引起问题，"以前"也可译成"on or before"。

④ 起草中文文本并将其译成英文

中文	英文
1）_____后，_____以后	after _____
2）_____前	before _____
3）_____开始……_____终止	beginning _____ and ending _____
4）_____内	between _____
5）_____以前	on or before _____（by）
6）自_____（含）_____ 自_____（不含）_____	from _____（inclusive） from _____（exclusive）
7）于_____，在_____	on _____
8）至_____（含）_____	through _____
9）至_____（不含）_____	to _____（exclusive）
10）至_____（为止）	until _____
11）月	month
12）年	year
13）_____以上	_____ or more
14）_____以下	_____ or less

Chapter 4 How to Deal with *Number* and *Time* in Legal Documents ‖ 079

(5)"as of"用法及其翻译

Wilson Follett 在 *Modern American Usage* 一书中指出,"as of"是一个注明日期的行话。许多人认为这是注明日期的唯一方式,但是"as of"只能用来把一件事情定在一个时间,而在另一个时间承认这件事情,它常常用来赋予优惠溯及既往的效力。

> A letter dated Sept. 1 that promotes an employee as of the proceeding June 1.
> 一封日期注明为9月1日的信函要给一位雇员增加工资,从已过去的6月1日开始。

"The business outlook in the South as of mid-June"中的"as of"就用得不当,应该说"in/at mid-June"。"as of"可以用在2008年3月关于2007年会计年度的报告里,或用在对当前到以后某个日期的趋势做预测;如果所提时间是现在,用"as of"就没有意义。

中文参考书或词典对其释义存在偏差,如陆谷孙编《英汉大词典》中认为:1. as of = as from,自……起; 2. 直至;在……时。

> The new contract takes effect as of July 1.
> 新合同7月1日起生效。

这里用"起"一词是不对的。原文的意思是"在7月1日"(on July 1),虽说其法律效力与说如同"从7月1日"(as of it was from July)是一样的,但原文的意思并非"自7月1日起"(starting from July and then thereafter)。

> Notification letters had been delivered to 19 persons as of mid-July.
> 7月中旬以来,已向19人发出通知。

"as of mid-July"不是"7月中旬以来"的意思,而是"到(或截至)7月中旬"(by the middle of July)或"在7月中旬"(at the middle of July)。

> Termination of this Agreement shall cancel, as of the date the termination shall become effective, all orders that may not have been shipped.
> 本协议终止时,于终止生效之日起,停止一切尚未装运的订货。

把"as of"译成"于……之日起"是不对的,它的意思不是"从那个日子"(from the date)。"as of the date"的意思是"在终止之日"(on the date of termination),而不是"从终止之日"(from the date of termination)。

"from"与"on"之间可能有很大的区别,如有一份协议从英文译成中文,协议里提到"the amount of principal and interest outstanding as of January 1, 1999"。("在1999年1月1日未偿还的本金和利息数额"和"自1999年1月1日起至现在未偿还的本金和利息数额",显然这两者的差别会是巨大的。)英文"as of January 1, 1999"的含义是"在1999

年1月1日未偿还的……"。在正常情况下,如果一份英文合同说"[it is] 'effective as of a certain date'",我们应将其译成"[本合同]视为某年某月某日生效"。

(6) 用英文起草与时间有关的表述方式避免产生歧义的建议

不要写成	改写成
1. between ... and ... Seller may exercise its right between August 1, 2004 and August 29, 2004. (用了"between"是否包括"August 1"和"August 29",不清楚)	Depending on the meaning: (1) Seller may exercise its right <u>after</u> August 1, 2004 and <u>before</u> August 29, 2004. (2) Seller's right <u>begins on</u> August 1, 2004, and <u>ends on</u> August 29, 2004.
2. by Seller must exercise its right by August 29, 2004. (用了"by"是否包括"August 29",不清楚)	Depending on the meaning: (1) Seller must exercise its right <u>before</u> August 29, 2004. (2) Seller must exercise its right <u>on or before</u> August 29, 2004.
3. from From January 1 (用了"from"是否包括"January 1",不清楚)	Depending on the meaning: (1) on or after January 1 <u>commencing</u> (<u>with</u>) January 1 <u>beginning</u> (<u>with</u>) January 1 (2) <u>after</u> January 1
4. from ... to ... Seller may exercise its right from August 1, 2004 to August 29, 2004. ("August 1"和"August 29"是否包括在内,不清楚)	• Seller may exercise its right <u>after</u> August 1, 2004 and <u>before</u> August 29, 2004. • ... from August 2, 2004 to August 28, 2004, <u>both days included</u>. • ... <u>commencing</u> (<u>on</u>) August 2, 2004 and <u>ending</u> (<u>on</u>) August 28, 2004.
5. from [the time or event] 10 days from commencement of risk	Assuming period is to be measured in whole days: 10 days starting from <u>the date</u> of commencement of risk

6. to ...
... to August 15
(是否包括"August 15"? 不清楚)
	Depending on the meaning:
	(1) <u>ending with</u> August 15, <u>through</u> August 15
	    (包括"August 15")
	(2) <u>ending</u> (<u>with</u>) August 14, <u>through</u> August 14
	    (不包括"August 15")

(续表)

不要写成	改写成
7. until Seller's right is effective until August 29, 2004. (在"August 29"卖主能行使权利吗？不清楚)	• Seller must exercise its right <u>on or before</u> August 29, 2004. • Seller's right is effective <u>until and including</u> August 29, 2004. • … until, but <u>not including</u> August 30, 2004. • Seller's right <u>terminates (on)</u> August 29, 2004. • Seller's right <u>expires at 24:00 (on)</u> August 29, 2004.
8. month within one month (意思不清楚)	Depending on the meaning： (1) within one calendar month (2) within 30 days (3) within 28 days (4) within 30 working days

课后练习

将下列中文译成英文。

1. 付运：到6月底收到信用证后45天内／到5月底须已收到信用证2008年8月付运。

 付运：2008年8月，但到5月底须已收到信用证。

2. 第十一条　有效期间

 本合约须从上面首次写明的委托人（或供应商）和代理人（或经销商）签订本约的日期起生效并保持效力三年，并将按同样条件延长三年，否则与约任何一方至少须在原定时间期满前三十天给予另一方提前终止本合约的书面通知。

3. 成交日期：购买须按如下规定在12月31日或以前在某某律师行办公室完成，买款余额当时须完全付清，而卖主和其他所有不可或缺的各方（如果有的话）将签署正式财产转让书交付买主、其指定人等、凭本合约协议卖给买主的楼宇的转买人等，买方免受各种负担，只取决于下面出现的条件。

4. 楼宇、租期和月租：业主特此出租而租户租下苏州市十梓街××号四楼A座（下称"该楼宇"）连同租户、其应邀者、其所许可者和与他来往的其他人出入的权利并连带租户、其佣人和其他租户和住客使用通向和来自该楼宇的楼梯、通道和电梯（如果有的话）的权利。该楼宇租给租户，为期两年，从2008年1月1日起到2009年12月31日止，月租人民币5000元整，应在每月1日如数提前缴交，首次租金在2008年1月1日或以前支付。

5. 自乙方开工起,本工程合同工期为 50 天,另加 10 天场内清洁及保养期,工程总工期为 60 天。

6. 乙方清楚地知道工程逾期竣工或逾期交付工程时间超过 15 天,甲方作为一家已经订购生产设备及接获大量订单、准备投产的外商投资制造型企业,已制定的计划将无法实现,甲方每天的损失将超过合同价款的 10%,乙方逾期竣工或逾期交付工程的行为为恶意违约。逾期竣工或逾期交付工程的,乙方每迟延竣工或逾期交付工程一日,乙方支付甲方合同价款的 4‰作为违约金,逾期竣工或逾期交付工程时间超过 15 天的,每超过一天,乙方支付甲方合同价款的 6‰作为违约金,逾期竣工或逾期交付工程时间超过 20 天的,每超过一天,乙方支付甲方合同价款的 8‰作为违约金,甲方并有权解除合同,乙方须另行向甲方支付合同价款 30% 的违约金。

7. 案例阅读:本案是美国最高法院判决的法律文书中时间表达歧义方面的典型案例。US v. Locke. 471 U. S. 84 (1985).

Chapter 5　How to Read a Case

▶ 1. 为什么要阅读案例

习惯法由判决的累积而成。律师对于本案法院可能的判决做出预测,扮演着积极的角色。在进入正式诉讼以前,律师若对法律内容愈了解,则给予当事人的建议愈正确,对于解决案件的争议有极大裨益。欲找到与待决案件事实相类似的判决,找到后如何帮助待决案件问题的解决,犹如大海捞针、沙里淘金,故阅读案例是了解英美法的重要过程,帮助我们从判决先例的法律资料中归纳本案法律关系的连接因素,判断应该适用何种领域的法律规范,因此阅读案例的理由至少有:

(1) 增加理解法院系统及操作法律实务的能力

法院的功能是解决当事人的争议,重要的工作就是进行诉讼(litigation)。英美法实行"当事人主义",双方律师在进入诉讼前必须准备好诉讼材料,并且建议当事人采用何种方法最为有利。这些建议资讯的取得有赖于律师阅读案例的能力,使当事人得以充分的法律基础来进行诉讼。而律师受当事人委托,对于本案事实、法院可能的判决结论做出预测,建议当事人可主张的权利内容,分析对方可能提出的攻击防御方法、法院如何判决、对于相类似案件曾经有过何种判决先例,这些预测在找寻判决先例后以"案例分析"(Office Memo)方式找出适当的结论。阅读案例时必须全方位比较所有相关判决,比较事实部分是否相类似、法律适用是否恰当。当从各个角度比较判决先例是否相类似,难免产生模糊情形,一般称之为灰色地带(Grey Area)。律师为主张有利于自己当事人的结果,必须将先例产生的问题归纳整理出来,再找出对自己有利的部分,突破灰色地带的困难。

(2) 增加对各种法律内容的了解

判决书内容中以法律的解释(Construction)为重心,阅读案例可以帮助我们知悉法院对本案的见解。现就日常生活中可能发生的案例为例，分析其中可能涉及的法律规范：甲到家乐福超级市场买牛奶，15 分钟以前有一个客人不慎翻倒可乐，地板上湿滑，家乐福超级市场的工作人员没有及时清理，甲因而滑到并受伤，甲有哪些请求权可以主张呢？

本事实可能存在的请求权的法律渊源可分为三种：

- 第一种是立法规范（legislation），指经由立法机关依程序制订的法律规定。如有法律（law, statute）或法案（act）规定，超市负责人必须随时保持地板干净，保护顾客安全。若家乐福超级市场违反这种立法规定，甲依法可以请求赔偿。
- 第二种是行政法规（administrative regulation），行政主管机关经由立法授权自行制订法规（ordinance）。如卫生主管部门规定，如果超市未保持地板干净，可以撤销超市的执照。行政机关做出的决定称为"行政处分"（administrative decision）。
- 第三种是司法判决（judicial decision），依"遵循先例原则"，如果法院对类似上述事实作过判决，或对上述各种法规作过解释，则这些案例亦是本案的法律依据之一。

本案从上述归纳可能产生的诉讼是：

- 甲控告因家乐福超市负责人的过失行为致使损害，负责人应负侵权行为赔偿责任。
- 甲控告因家乐福超市负责人违反应保持地板干净的立法规定，请求损害赔偿。
- 甲控告家乐福超市负责人因违反应保持地板干净的行政法规，请求损害赔偿。
- 甲控告政府行政机关未履行定期检查家乐福超市的义务，请求行政机关负类似国家赔偿的责任。
- 国家行政机关可以因家乐福超市未注意地板干净，做出撤销家乐福超市执照的行政处分。
- 家乐福超市可以控告行政机关的不当行政处分，请求恢复原状，如有损害也可以请求国家赔偿。

以上这些可能发生的诉讼，唯有经过阅读相关案例，才可充分了解其可能的结果，做出预测，然后再选择出最有利的方式进行。

（3）案例分析可以帮助律师或法官搜寻法律资料

一个案件可以适用的法律资料很多，分析案例问题的所在，归纳出哪些法律可以解决这些问题，从案例书籍中，可提供线索与答案，这些问题曾经有哪些法院做出判决，有哪些相关资料可以作为判决的基础，找出有利的主张与判断依据。案例阅读愈多愈能培养分析事实及发现问题的能力。

（4）案例分析可以帮助律师制作法律文书

律师接受案件伊始，必须先搜寻法律资料，将取得的资料给予评估，写成报告，称为

"memorandum"。这种律师制作的法律文件大体上分为两种：一为"对内法律意见书"（internal memorandum or office memo），指律所内部的法律评估资料。律师处理案件先找寻所有与案件相关的法律规定及判决资料，研读后将有利本案与不利本案的法律观点、法院判决等详细内容撰写成法律评估报告书。另一种法律文件称为"对外法律意见书"（external memorandum），指诉讼时需要的法律文书，如答辩状、申请状、起诉状、预审听证会的举证资料等书面文件。"对外法律意见书"的目的是使法院相信律师的主张是正确的。要想完成内外法律意见书，需要阅读案例。

（5）提高律师调查事实和与客户谈话的能力

律师从与客户谈话中了解事实的经过，经由以前阅读案例的经验找出本案在法律上有关事实及法律上的解释，从客户的谈话中判断何谓本案的重要相关事实，这样才能建议对当事人有利的法律主张。

▶ 2. 案例汇编与案例结构

（1）判决书汇编

将法院判决结果以文字记载成为书面司法文书，这种书面司法文书称为"判决书或判例汇编（reports）"，判决后的案件一般称为"案例"（case）。判例汇编有两种：一为官方汇编（official report），法院将判决结果印成书面判决。二为非官方汇编（unofficial report），由民间出版商将判决整理后出版成册，除了判决内容外，书商请专家整理并加上与本案有关的注解、法律条文、相关法院判决等，参考价值大于官方判决汇编。

官方判例汇编有以下几种：美国联邦最高法院判例汇编（United States Reports，简称 U.S.）；各州最高法院也会出版判决汇编，如密歇根州最高法院判决汇编（Michigan Reports，简称 Mich.）；有些州第二审法院也出版判决汇编，如密歇根州二审法院判决汇编（Michigan Appeals Reports，简称 Mich. App.）。

美国现有 3 个比较大的法律图书出版商出版非官方判决汇编：西方出版公司（West Publishers）；律师出版公司（Lawyers Cooperative Publishing Company）；学徒殿堂图书公司（Prentice Hall Inc.）。实际上，一些国家已经不再继续出版他们的官方汇编了，而是交由私人公司负责出版。随着计算机和网络技术的发展，这两个公司逐步把美国联邦和各州的所有立法和司法判决都实行数据化和网络化。例如，西方出版公司整理出版《联邦最高法院判决汇编》（Supreme Court Reporter，简称 S.G.），律师出版公司出版《联邦最高法院判决汇编》（Unites States Reports, Lawyers Edition，简称 L. Ed.）。这两套书是联邦最高法院的判决累积一段时间后才出版的。有的判决汇编出版速度较快,一个星期整理出版一次(United States Law Weeks,简称 U. S. L. W);也有当天下午出版还未登录案号的当天判决(United States Supreme Court Bulletin,简称 S. Ct. Bull. C. C. H)。对于联邦高等法院/(巡回)上诉法院及地方法院的判决,西方出版公司出版有:《联邦上诉法院判例汇编》(Federal Reporter,简称为 F.)、《联邦上诉法院判例汇编·第二辑》(Federal Reporter, Second Series,简称为 F. 2d.);《联邦地区法院判例汇编》(Federal Supplement,简称为 F. Supp.)。为方便读者查询资料,西方出版公司将美国分为 7 个区域,将每一区域内的各州最高法院判决汇编为一套书,详见下表:

地区	判例汇编名称(中文)	判例汇编名称(英文)	简称
东北地区	《东北地区州法院判例汇编》	North Eastern Reporter	N. E.
	《东北地区州法院判例汇编·第二辑》	North Eastern Reporter, Second Series	N. E. 2d.
西北地区	《西北地区州法院判例汇编》	North Western Reporter	N. W.
	《西北地区州法院判例汇编·第二辑》	North Western Reporter, Second Series	N. W. 2d.
西南地区	《西南地区州法院判例汇编》	South Western Reporter	S. W.
	《西南地区州法院判例汇编·第二辑》	South Western Reporter, Second Series	S. W. 2d.
东南地区	《东南地区州法院判例汇编》	South Eastern Reporter	S. E.
	《东南地区州法院判例汇编·第二辑》	South Eastern Reporter, Second Series	S. E. 2d.
南部地区	《南部地区州法院判例汇编》	Southern Reporter	So.
	《南部地区州法院判例汇编·第二辑》	Southern Reporter, Second Series	So. 2d.
太平洋沿岸地区	《太平洋沿岸地区州法院判例汇编》	Pacific Reporter	P.
	《太平洋沿岸地区法院判例汇编·第二辑》	Pacific Reporter, Second Series	P. 2d.
大西洋沿岸地区	《大西洋沿岸地区州法院判例汇编》	Atlantic Reporter	A.
	《大西洋沿岸地区法院判例汇编·第二辑》	Atlantic Reporter, Second Series	A. 2d.

了解案例集或汇编之后,就有助于阅读案例的案号(citation:A reference to a legal precedent or authority, such as a case, statute, or treatise, that either substantiates or contradicts a given position, often shortened to cite),而案号常出现平行卷宗号(parallel citation:An additional reference to a case that has been reported in more than one reporter. For example, whereas a *Bluebook* citation reads "*Morgan v. United States*, 304 U. S. 1 (1938)", the same reference including parallel citations reads "*Morgan v. United States*, 304 U. S. 1, 58 S. Ct. 773, 82 L. Ed. 1129 (1938)", in which the main citation is to the *U. S. Reports* and the parallel citations are to the *Supreme Court Reporter* and to the *Lawyer's*

Edition)。有平行卷号的情形,一般是官方汇编在前,非官方居后,其结构一般为:

案件名称	+	官方判决书案号	+	非官方判决书案号	+	判决日期
Morgan v. United States		304 U. S. 1		58 S. Ct. 773; 82 L. Ed. 1129		1938

表示:摩根诉美国,收集在《美国最高法院判例汇编》第304卷第1页开始;同时收录在西方出版公司的《联邦最高法院判决汇编》第58卷,773页开始;律师出版公司的《联邦最高法院判决汇编》第82卷,1129页开始,1938年判决。又见下例:

Roe v. Wade	410 U. S. 113	93 S. Ct. 705	35 L. Ed. 2d. 147	1973
Case Name	Official Citation	Parallel Citation	Parallel Citation	Date of Opinion

案号可显示的内容有:

a. 案件双方当事人姓名(the names of the parties involved in the lawsuit);

b. 包含案件全文的汇编卷号(the volume number of the reporter containing the full text of the case);

c. 该案例汇编的缩写名称(the abbreviated name of that case reporter);

d. 案例开始的页码数(the page number on the case begins);

e. 案件判决年份(the year the case was decided)。

有时还包括案例判决法院(the name of the court deciding the case)。

(2) 案例的结构

为了解一般案例的结构,先来看下例:

Willie Louie CEREGHINO and Frances
Mary Cereghino, Appellants,

v.

Mary J. VERSHUM, Trustee, and
Janet Cooffyn, Respondents.

Supreme Court of Oregon,
In Banc.

Argued and Submitted July 10, 1975.
Decided Aug. 7, 1975.

① 判例的名称或抬头(Caption of Opinion)

从上诉人（Appellants）来看，这是一个上诉的案件。被上诉人（Respondents）中有一个是信托受托人（Trustee）。案件是由俄勒冈州的最高法院（Supreme Court of Oregon）的所有法官参加（In Banc）集体做出的。案件的上诉日期是1975年7月10日，审结日是同年8月7日。

从此例中可以看出，案例的名称或标题（name or title of the case）通常根据当事方的名字来进行设定。另外，从案例的题目中还可以获得其他有益的信息：

- 在"In re Payne"当中，"In re"是指在审判的过程中没有被告方（adversary parties）。在案例的名称前加上 In re 通常意味着只有一方当事人的案件，如：破产案件、遗嘱案件、监护人案件、藐视法庭案件、吊销律师资格或人身保护令等案件。

- 如果案例名称前有"ex parte"，如 ex parte payne 中，"ex parte"则表示可单方面进行的庭审程序，无须通知诉讼的另一方或无须让其出庭答辩。

- 如果案例名称中出现"et al."（Latin：and other persons），表明当事方一方或双方不止一人(一个单位)，如我们前面谈到的最高院的 UNITED STATES ET AL. v. LOCKE ET AL.。

- 如果案例名称中出现了州或联邦政府（State or Federal Government Agency）的字样，表明这是一起公诉或行政诉讼案件，如以国家或以州的名义提起的刑事诉讼（如 United States v. Stevens）。

- 最后，还可以对物提起诉讼，称为"actions based on in rem or quasi in rem jurisdiction"，如涉及查封或没收货物的案件就用被查封或没收的物的名称来表示（如 United States v. 45 Barrels of Whisky）。

② 判例总结(Syllabus)

判例总结是由出版者后来写进去的，法院的原始判决中并没有这个部分。这是出版者为读者提供的一种方便，其目的是为了让读者能尽快了解案情。当然作为法学院的学生应该阅读全部案例，而不应该图省事只读案件总结。

> In an action to reform a trust deed, plaintiff appealed from a decree of the Circuit Court, Multnomah County, William M. Dale, J., denying the relief requested. The Supreme Court held that reformation was correctly denied where there was no evidence to establish a mistake of the scrivener or mutual mistake, but where the evidence showed only unilateral mistake on the part of the plaintiffs unattended by fraud or other inequitable conduct on the part of defendants.
> Affirmed.

③ 关键主题词(Core/Key Terms)

在西方公司出版的案例汇编中，所有的案例都被分类并根据分类的结果在案例中加入关键主题词。这些关键主题词表明该案件涉及何种法律问题。例如，在所举上例中西方公司就在其提供的判例总结下加入关键主题词"reformation of instruments"，表明该案件是涉及契约修改方面的案件。如果我们想要找有关这方面的案件，只需要上网进入西方公司的法律数据库，输入关键主题词"reformation of instruments"，就可以检索到一系列关于契约修改方面的案件，其中就会有在此引以为例的"Cereghino v. Vershum"。

④ **关键数字**(Key Number)

在提供关键主题词的同时，为了进一步方便读者，西方公司又提供了一套关键数字(Key Number)，这些关键数字代表着不同法律问题的分类。你能够凭借这个关键数字去西方公司出版的法律或案例摘要(digest)中找到"Cereghino v. Vershum"案所涉及的法律问题和与之相关的其他案例。例如，该公司给这个案例提供的关键数字为45(8)。

⑤ **法律问题摘要**(Headnote)

该部分是法院基于案件中的特定事实所做的判决或适用的法律原则，由西方公司将其总结出来供读者迅速查阅。它是这些法律原则和相关事实的有机结合，是案例相关法律问题(a point of law)的概要。例如，在"Cereghino v. Vershum"这个案例中西方公司提供了如下法律问题摘要：

> Reformation of trust deed was correctly denied where there was no evidence to establish mistake of scrivener or mutual mistake, but where evidence showed only unilateral mistake on the part of plaintiffs unattended by fraud or other inequitable conduct on the part of defendants.

在"Cereghino v. Vershum"案例中只提供了一个法律问题摘要。但应注意由于许多案件会涉及很多法律问题，因此一个判例中含有若干个甚至几十个法律问题摘要都是极为常见的。有时候在官方的案例汇编中也会有案件总结(Syllabus)和法律问题摘要(Headnote)。它们通常是由法官助理(law clerk)而不是法官本人写的。但请注意，无论是官方或是非官方的案例汇编，案例的主体部分(即法院公布的判决)都是一样的。

⑥ **代理律师的姓名**(Names of the Attorneys Who Represented the Parties)

代理律师的名字一般会出现在案例中，如在"Cereghino v. Vershum"案的法庭意见书中有以下文字：

> Donald L. Alderton, Portland, argued the case and filed a brief for appellants.
> Francis F. Yunker, Portland, argued the case and filed a brief for respondents.
> PER CURIAM.

从以上可以看出，律师们都来自Portland这个城市。他们都向法院呈递了(filed)上诉法律意见书(brief)。案中的"per curiam"的基本意思是全体法院(a. & n. Latin: by the court as a whole）。通常情况下，书写判决的法官的名字要出现在判决的开头，但一旦判决书中出现"PER CURIAM"，指全体法官一致的判决结果，以法院的意见代替某个法官的姓名，其目的是为避免政治上或社会上的不良作用，由法官全体对审判负责。有时也用"Memorandum Opinion"来表示，通常由于案件的事实和法律非常清楚而法院认为无须对其判决做出详细论证或说明。这些名称以下出现的内容就是判决的内容。此类判决也可以被称为"Memorandum by the Court"或"Memorandum Decision"。应该注意的是，有些州的法院滥用"Memorandum Opinion"，对于一些案件只给判决（decision）而不给出原因（opinions or reasons），从而导致当事人依据宪法所享有的正当法律程序权受到侵害（right to due processes）。

⑦ 判决的开头(The Opinion Begins)

以"Cereghino v. Vershum"案为例，法庭判决书节选如下：

> This is a suit to reform a trust deed executed by plaintiffs on the ground that "by the mistake of the scrivener who drafted the trust deed * * * he included the home of plaintiffs" and that said trust deed, according to the agreement of plaintiffs and defendant Coffey and her agent who negotiated the loan, should have covered only property of plaintiffs in East Mount Tabor Addition, Multnomah County, Oregon. Plaintiffs appeal from decree denying the relief requested.
>
> There is no evidence to establish a "mistake of the scrivener". There is no evidence of mutual mistake. There is evidence of a unilateral mistake on the part of plaintiffs, but there is no evidence of attending fraud or inequitable conduct on the part of defendants. Webb v. Culver, 265 Or. 467, 509 P. 2d 1173 (1973). The record simply does not contain any evidence which would constitute grounds for reformation. Therefore the decree of the trial court is affirmed.
>
> Affirmed.

大多数已出版的法院案例都是上诉法院的案例。法院的"opinion"是对法院判决（decision）所做的解释，两者合起来就成为法院的"judgment"。案件在多数法官同意并判决后由其中的一名法官书写。其他同意该判决的法官如果有其他理由可以单独写成"concurring opinion"。不赞成法院判决的法官可以写出反对意见（dissenting opinion）。

(3) 具体案例分析

① Holding v. Dicta (案件的裁决与法官的附带意见)

> **Holding**——the rule of law or legal principle that comes from the decision or the judgment plus the material facts of the case; binding authority
>
> **Dicta**—Other statements in the decision that do not form part of the holding; persuasive authority

The precedent established by the case is the holding. In general, the holding of a case is binding authority, whereas the dicta are merely persuasive authority; arguments based on dicta are not binding. However, do not assume that dicta in a case are totally unimportant; sometimes the dicta become more important in later years than the actual holding. For example, the dicta in the famous Supreme Court ruling in *International Shoe Co. v. Washington* 326 U. S. 310, 66 S. Ct. 154, 90 L. Ed. 95 (1945) are still cited in many cases.

In *International Shoe Co.*, the US Supreme Court established the requirements for **personal jurisdiction** over a defendant in a civil action. Personal jurisdiction is important because it determines whether a court can force a defendant to appear before it in response to a civil lawsuit. The specific holding in this case relates to corporate agents in the state of Washington and the systematic conduct of business within the state. In its opinion, the court *discussed* but did not rule on traditional ideas of fairness. The dictum that arose from this discussion has become increasingly important in the jurisdictional decisions of other courts. The US Supreme Court stated:

It is evident that these operations [those of the corporation, Int'l Shoe] establish sufficient contacts or ties with the state of the forum to make it reasonable and just according to our traditional conception of **fair play and substantial justice** [emphasis added] to permit the state to enforce the obligations which appellant [Int'l Shoe] has incurred there.

Although the term *fair play and substantial justice* was part of the Court's opinion, courts to this day use the term when making decisions regarding personal jurisdiction.

Let's look at a hypothetical example of how we might try to separate holding from dicta. In a case of armed robbery, the plaintiff, a short college professor, was robbed while walking down a dark deserted street in downtown Memphis by an old Albanian man who waved a new Colt 45 pistol around and then shot into the air.

If the judge says that all of these facts (*armed robbery*, *short college professor*, *walking*, *dark deserted street*, *downtown Memphis*, *old Albanian man*, *waving a gun*, *new Colt 45 pistol*, *shoot one shot*, *into the air*) are essential in making the decision, the judge's decision will be binding only in cases in which all the same facts are present and that will never happen. In other words, the decision will be binding in no other cases except where the same facts are present. However, if the judge leaves out some of the nonessential facts and makes broader descriptions, the holding will be binding on more cases. For example, was it important that it was an *old* man? Probably not. Was it important that it was a *man* and not a *woman*? Again, probably not. But do we broaden the term to *person* or *adult*? Would we want our holding to apply to children or just to adults?

Eloyce DESHOTEL, Plaintiff and Appellant,

v.

The ATCHISON, TOPEKA & SANTA FE RAILWAY COMPANY (a Corporation), William M. Floyd, Defendants and Respondents.

(50 CAL.2d 664, 328 P.2d 449)

Supreme Court of California,

In Banc

July 31, 1958

Caption of Opinion (开头)
Citation (案号)
法院与审级
判决日期

Action by wife against railroad, taxicab company, train engineer, and cab driver, for loss of consortium allegedly resulting from negligence of such persons. The Superior Court, Alameda County, A. J. Woolsey, J., sustained the general demurrer by railroad and engineer without leave to amend, and the wife appealed. The Supreme Court, Gibson, C., J., held that wife, whose husband was injured in a train-taxicab collision as result of alleged negligence of railroad company, taxable company, train engineer and taxicab driver, could not maintain an action against them for loss of consortium.

Judgment affirmed.

DAMAGES k37

Syllabus (摘要)
判决
Key Topic (主旨查询索引)

115k37

Wife, whose husband was injured in a train-taxicab collision as a result of alleged negligence of railroad company, taxicab company, train engineer and taxicab driver, could not maintain an action against them for loss of consortium.

James A. Myers and D. W. Brobst, Oakland, for appellant. Robert W. Walker, Los Angeles, William J. Hayes; Hardin, Fletcher, Cook & Hayes, Oakland, and Cyril Viadro, San Francisco, for respondents.

GIBSON, Chief Justice.

Headnote (要旨)
(双方当事人律师之姓名)
主审法官姓名

Opinion of the Court(法院正式的判决书): Plaintiff's husband was severely injured when a taxicab in which he was a passenger collided with a train. He sued the railway company, the taxicab company, the train engineer, and the cab driver, obtaining a judgment in the amount of $290,000, which was affirmed on appeal (Deshotel v. Atchison, Topeka & Santa Fe Ry. Co., 144 Cal. App. 2d 224, 300 P. 2d 910). During the tendency of that action plaintiff brought this suit against the same defendants. She alleged that as a result of their negligence her husband was injured in such a manner that she has been denied his care, protection, consideration, companionship, aid, and society and that' by reason of the loss of the consortium of her husband she has been damaged in the sum of $100,000. A general demurrer by the railway company and the engineer was sustained without leave to amend, and plaintiff has appealed from the ensuing judgment.

Reading the Case

To the uninitiated, cases appearing in any of the reporters can at first seem very confusing. However, once a few basic organizational concepts are mastered, the researcher will appreciate that the cases are arranged in a way that provides the maximum amount of data in the minimum amount of time.

The order and nature of information given usually follow the same or a similar format based on a system used by West Publishers, the primary legal reporter publisher. Cases obtained from the Internet will not normally have headnotes but will go immediately into the opinion. Headnotes from West's simplify reading of the case because they attempt to summarize the important information. So, let's look at *United States v. White*, 552 F. 2d 268 (8th Cir. 1977), a criminal case, from a West Publication.

Headnote

The Parties

This section includes the names of the parties, identification of parties (plaintiff, defendant, etc.), an identification of the court in which the recorded case was heard, and the date of the opinion. In the following chart, we've printed an actual headnote as it would appear in its vertical format in the left column and explanations of each of the lines in the right.

UNITED STATES of America, Appellee v. David Lee WHITE, Appellant	prosecution versus defendant
No. 76—2047	docket number the court's system for finding the case in its files
United States Court of Appeals	the court hearing the case
Eighth Circuit	the federal circuit
Submitted March 24, 1977	date appeal filed
Decided April 6, 1997	date decision made

Procedural History

The procedural history is a brief recitation of what the courts have done with this case. This section also includes the basis for review and an abbreviated recitation of the previous court's holding. There is also a single line indicating the court's disposition of the case [what the court decided to do with the case]. We have added explanatory statements in bold to the various sections of the procedural history.

Defendant was convicted in the United States District Court for the District of Nebraska, Warren K. Urbom, Chief Judge, of interstate transportation of a stolen motor vehicle [previous court's holding—the District Court], and he appealed. The Court of Appeals held that the evidence was sufficient to support the trial court's finding that defendant knew the vehicle was stolen and that he caused it to be transported across state lines [basis for defendant's appeal implied-insufficient evidence to support power court's decision].

Affirmed [Court of Appeals' disposition of the case].

West Key Number System

Sections numbered according to a system of key words provide references to legal issues. General topics discussed in the case (e.g., Labor Relations, Sales, or Civil Rights) are in bold print followed by a key symbol and a number reference to sections in the reporters' indices that list similar case, that is, cases that rely on similar legal principles. When there is more than one key number in the headnote, these key numbers are numbered 1, 2, 3, and so forth. The opinion is then divided into sections by West: [1], [2], [3], and so on. The numbers indicate the sections in which a discussion of the particular legal discussion can be located within the text of the opinion. In our example, there is only one key note; however, a complicated case may contain references to many points of law.

[When an appellate court issues an opinion for publication, it makes the opinion available to a legal publisher. The publisher supplements the text written by the court by inserting various editorial material.

(The material added by the publisher is not "law" and cannot be offered as legal authority.) When a newly written opinion is reviewed by the publisher, the editorial staff notes the issues seemingly raised in the opinion. It inserts numbers in square brackets (e.g. "[4]"), in the text to note where the opinion discusses a particular issue. (Text contained within square brackets means that the material was not a part of the original text but instead was added by someone other than the author.) At the beginning of the case, the publisher inserts a summary. The summary is followed by the "headnotes", which consist of a list of numbers which correspond to each issue identified within square brackets in the opinion, together with a description of the point of law. The West Publishing Company, a major publisher of legal materials, has also developed what it calls its "Key Number System". Each headnote is assigned a key number, which refers to an extensive subject outline maintained by West. Just like statutes are organized by subject into Codes, Titles, Divisions, etc., the headnotes of cases are organized by subject and subdivisions. This subject index of headnotes is called the Key Number System. Various indexes permit an attorney to find headnotes, and thus cases, by locating the appropriate key number.]

Automobiles ⊙⟶ 355 (12) [Note: A section number would be before "Automobiles" if there were more than one key number in the opinion. Key and KeyCite West Group.]

Evidence in prosecution for interstate transportation of stolen motor vehicle was sufficient to support trial court's finding that defendants knew vehicle was stolen and caused it to be transported across state lines. 18 U.S.C.A. § 2312.

Legal Representatives

The names of the attorneys for both plaintiff and defendant, the attorneys' law firms, and the city within which the attorneys practice are listed.

Floyd A. Sterns, Lincoln, Neb., for appellant.

Daniel E. Wherry, U.S. Atty., and Robert F. Kokrda, Asst. U.S. Atty., Omaha, Neb., for appellee.

> **Opinion**
>
> The opinion includes the names of the judges who heard the case, the holding, and the rationale. This section is the official court decision and is what is used by attorneys when writing legal memoranda. The headnote, which we discussed earlier, while useful as a schema for understanding the case, is not the official opinion. In *U. S. v. White* the disposition of the case comes at the beginning of the opinion. In other cases, the disposition of the case is found after the recitation of the procedural history/facts and at the end of the opinion.

Judge or Judges Hearing the Case

Before HEANEY, ROSS. AND HENLEY, Circuit Judges.

PER CURIUM.

Procedural History

David Lee White was convicted by a jury of interstate transportation of a stole motor vehicle in violation of 18 U. S. C. A. § 2312. He appeals that conviction, contending that the evidence was insufficient to support the verdict.

We affirm.

Statutory or Common Law Basis for the Decision

After the specific procedural history, the court will often summarize the statutory or common law basis for its decision. Sometimes at the end of the summary, the court will give the disposition of the case.

To sustain a conviction under 18 U. S. C. A. § 2312, there must be some evidence before the jury which establishes that the defendant transported a motorvehicle in interstate commerce and that he knew that it was stolen. White concedes that the vehicle crossed state lines and was in interstate commerce. His principal contention is that the evidence did not establish either that he knew the vehicle was stolen or that he caused the vehicle to be transported.

When reviewing the sufficiency of the evidence to support a conviction, we must view evidence in the light most favorable to the government, *Glasser v. United States*, 315 U. S. 60, 80, 62 S. Ct. 457, 86 L. Ed. 680 (1942), and accept as established all reasonable inferences that tend to support the jury's verdict. *United States v. Overshon*, 494 F. 2d 894 (8th Cir. 1974), *cert. denied*, 419 U. S. 853, 95 S. Ct. 96, 42 L. Ed. 2d 85 (1974).

Facts/Background

A detailed recitation of the facts of the case is given. This includes identification of the parties, the series of events that precipitated the lawsuit, and often more detailed procedural history from the lower courts than the initial procedural information. In this case, *U. S. v. White*, the court is combining the facts with the legal conclusions to be drawn from the particular facts. This type of combining is not always done.

While in Connecticut, White and two acquaintances were in need of transportation. They located a station wagon which was unlocked with the ignition key inside. The three men got into the station wagon and drove away, traveled to Georgia, then Indiana, and finally abandoned the vehicle in Nebraska.

We conclude that a jury could infer from this evidence that White knew the vehicle was stolen. *United States v. Harris*, 528 F. 2d 1327 (8th Cir. 1975); *United States v. Wilson*, 523 F. 2d 828 (8th Cir. 1975).

White did not drive the vehicle during the journey. There was testimony by the other two men that White discovered some money in the station wagon which was used to pay for gas, that White read the road maps and instructed the driver as to the proper route, that he helped siphon gas from other vehicles, and that he was not coerced to remain in the vehicle. Based on these actions, the jury could find beyond a reasonable doubt that White had joint control over the vehicle and that he effectively transported it. *United States v. Williams*, 503 F. 2d 480 (8 th Cir. 1974); *United States v. Thomas*, 469 F. 2d 145 (8 th Cir. 1972), *cert. denied*, 410 U. S. 957, 93 S. Ct. 1429, 35 L. Ed. 2d 690 (1973).

Reasoning (Legal Discussion)

A discussion of the point of law important to a final disposition of the case and the rationale for the court's decision normally follow the facts/background section of the opinion. When more than one issue is involved, the court normally discusses the rationale for each issue separately.

Although this evidence was not all uncontroverted and a great deal of the evidence supporting the verdict was testimony of White's accomplices, it is the province of the jury to determine the weight and credibility of the evidence. Even the uncorroborated testimony of an accomplice may be sufficient to sustain a conviction. *United States v. Knight*, 547 F. 2d 75 (8th Cir. 1976); *United States v. Cady*, 495 F. 2d 742 (8th Cir. 1974).

Final Disposition of the Case

The last section of each opinion contains the conclusion of the court regarding the case. In some instances, the holding of the court is found in this section; at other times, however, you must make a determination of the holding by combining key elements from the rationale of the court. Here is the holding in this example case.

The jury had sufficient evidence before it to determine that White knew the car was stolen, and that he caused it to be transported across state lines. For this reason, we sustain the conviction.

Ex. 1 Reading for Details

* What is the first word that shows that this case is an appeal?
* Who lost in the original trial?
* Is this a federal or state case?
* Which word shows that the appeals court agreed or disagreed with the trial court?
* How many of the circuit judges agreed on the decision? How do you know?
* What kind of vehicle was stolen?
* How did they get the car to start?
* How did they get gas for the car?
* Was White being forced to travel with the two other men?
* What role did White play on the trip?
* What is interstate transportation?

Ex. 2 Reading and Analyzing

* What are the two elements necessary for conviction under 18 U. S. C. A. § 2312?
* Are they present in *U. S. v. White*?
* What's the difference between knowing and inferring that White knew the car was stolen?
* What allowed the jury to determine that White transported the car across state lines?
* Why is it important that the car be transported across state lines and not just driven around in one state?

Ex. 3 Statutory Interpretation and Paraphrasing

* Read and Translate 18 U. S. C. A. § 2312

§ 2312. Transportation of stolen vehicles

Whoever transports in interstate or foreign commerce a motor vehicle or aircraft, knowing the same to have been stolen, shall be fined under this title or imprisoned not more than 10 years, or both.

* Look back at the holding. What's the difference between "transported across state lines" and "caused to be transported across state lines"?
* Paraphrase the holding from this case to show that the elements of 18 U. S. C. A. § 2312 necessary for conviction have been met.

▶ 3. 案例典型结构

Notwithstanding the considerable variation in the structure of appellate opinions, they generally consist of four identifiable components:
- an introduction, which among other things, recognizes the Issues presented by the case;
- a discussion of the existing law and the recognition of an applicable Rule;
- the Application of the facts of the problem case to this rule, and
- the court's Conclusion as to how the issue, and therefore the case, is to be decided.

ISSUE—RULE—APPLICATION—CONCLUSION:

These four components should sound suspiciously familiar. For example, the following simple legal argument follows IRAC:

Is this will valid?	Issue
To be valid a will must be witnessed by two persons	Rule
This will was witnessed by only one person.	Application
This will is not valid.	Conclusion

Almost all legal argument roughly follows the IRAC structure: office memoranda, memoranda supporting motions, trial briefs, appellate briefs, the opinions of appellate courts, and even oral argument. While most opinions did not strictly follow the IRAC structure, they did roughly follow it. The classic structure of course is I-R-A-C. But an opinion might actually be structured I-R-A-R-A-C, or some other variation. Also, an appellate opinion usually deals with more than one issue, typically between two and four. That's because in prosecuting an appeal, a lawyer improves his chances of success by limiting the appeal to his best arguments; too many issues just distract the court's attention from his strongest arguments. Because there are usually several issues addressed in an appellate opinion, there is usually more than one IRAC structure in the opinion. The court usually addresses each issue in order, such as: first issue—IRAC, second issue—IRAC, and so on. The issues are often introduced like this: "Appellant first contends that …" That's the Issue; then the opinion sets out the rest of the R-A-C. Then the court may raise the second issue like this: "Next, appellant contends that ..." This second Issue is then followed by the R-A-C, or some variation of it.

Issue—The Introduction

Following the editorial material inserted by the publisher is the actual text of an appellate opinion. This normally begins with material which can be regarded as a type of "introduction". The introduction describes the procedural history of the case as to when and how the case proceeded through the trial and appellate courts. Also included is a description of the facts of the case. The introduction also usually states the issue or issues before the court. A case may contain one or many issues. Typically, a case will contain two to five issues. (Since there are typically several headnotes for each issue, the number of headnotes found at the beginning of the case is usually greater.) An issue is often introduced with words such as "Appellant first contends that ..." or "Petitioner complains that ..." Sometimes an opinion will list together all of issues raised in the case; more often, issues are identified separately and each is followed by the Rule, Application, and Conclusion sections applicable to that issue.

The Rule Discussion—The Raw Rule

Otto Von Bismarck is widely believed to have said: "If you like laws and sausages, you should never watch either one being made." You can think of an appellate decision as a sausage making machine. The raw material (that is an existing legal rule or doctrine, together with the facts of the problem case), go into the hopper and the sausage (a sort of "processed rule" created by that opinion), comes out the other end. The discussion of the raw rule usually follows the introduction. The court, with the assistance of its research attorneys and law clerks, researches and analyzes statutes and case law and derives from this material the raw rule applicable to the issue before it. This is the same process you would follow in analyzing a legal problem. And just as you may have difficulty finding all cases and synthesizing seemingly inconsistent opinions, the court may encounter similar problems. Naturally, the court and its staff bring great expertise and experience to the task and the analysis whose results is usually astute. In any event, even if others would disagree with the resulting analysis, the court's analysis carries the imprimatur of judicial authority. The raw rule is sometimes described in one short paragraph with citations to several leading case. Other times, the court may devote many pages to it, carefully discussing many cases and describing many steps in the analysis.

In substantive law classes students find the raw rule component of an opinion to be a very important tool. While of course in the opinion it is the raw material from which the "processed rule" of that case is fashioned, it may often be more important as a tool for understanding the area of law being considered. In other words, the raw rule discussion in an opinion is a bit like an encyclopedia or treatise article, in this instance written by the court, which helps you understand the existing law. However, if you confuse the raw rule component of the opinion as a description of the processed rule in that case, you may very well miss the point upon which that case is decided.

The Application Discussion

Following the analysis of the raw rule, the court usually applies the facts of the problem case to the rule and notes how they are similar and different from the facts of the cases from which the raw rule was derived. The court identifies the critical characteristics of these facts, often discussing the policies which make these characteristics important. This reasoning may rely upon assumptions as to legislative intent, deference to another branch of government based upon the separation of powers, concepts of fundamental fairness or desirable social policy, or practical considerations such as the workability of the resulting rule or burdens which would be imposed on individuals or governmental entities. Once again, this section of the opinion may be only one paragraph or it may be many pages long.

The Conclusion—The Processed Rule

The final component of the opinion is the Conclusion. The Conclusion may be one short sentence, or even one word (e. g. "Reversed"). However, implicit within this brevity is the "processed rule". In reaching its decision, the court applies the facts of the problem case to the raw rule, that is, the existing law. Through the recognition of critical characteristics and the reasoning applied, the court decides how these new facts will be treated, by refining, modifying, extending, limiting, or replacing existing law. Thus, the result sometimes leads to the articulation of an expanded, limited, or new rule, and thus the law changes. The court continues this process of shaping the law, when in future case, it begins its consideration with this earlier decision.

Understanding that an opinion is roughly structured according to IRAC is very useful. It's similar to getting a bird's-eye-view of a difficult text before actually trying to read it carefully and understand it. If you appreciate the structure or organization of a text in advance, it makes it much easier to understand, and your reading becomes much more efficient. It's like knowing that most textbooks have a table of contents at the beginning and an alphabetical index at the end. Knowing this allows you to quickly find and use these sections to extract the information you are after. If you didn't know about the index or how to use it, you would probably waste a lot of time searching through the text for particular information. Similarly, understanding the structure of an appellate opinion allows you to extract its meaning much more efficiently. Because of this benefit, we were taught to identify the structure of an opinion before getting down to carefully reading it.

While a section may consist of a single paragraph, usually it consists of a number of paragraphs.

Ex. 1 As you identify the following case in which section each paragraph belongs, please write the appropriate letter in the margin:

Included in the "I" section is the factual and procedural history of the case as well as any statement of the actual issue considered by the appeal;

The "R" section includes the court's review and discussion of the existing law;

The "A" section contain the application of the facts of the pending case to the existing rule of law;

And of course the "C" section is the decision of the court.

Dorothy Barker vs. Melody Dance Partners
(1993) 17 Cal. App. 4th 322

SPARKY, J.

Plaintiff Dorothy Barker sustained personal injuries when she slipped and fell while dancing. She filed a complaint for personal injury against Melody Dance Partners, the organization sponsoring the dance. The trial court granted summary judgment against plaintiff based upon her assumption of the risk.   [I]

The following facts, which were not in dispute, were submitted in support of defendant's motion for summary judgment. Before her accident, plaintiff attended at least six dances sponsored by the defendant in the past two years. When plaintiff first arrived at the dance on the night in question she observed a substance on the dance floor which she thought to be Avory Soap Flakes.

She had seen this substance used on the floor on at least three prior occasions and was aware that the substance made it easier for the dancer's foot to slide on the floor. At dances before her accident when she saw the substance on the floor, plaintiff would not dance until the floor was swept. On the evening of her accident, plaintiff waited until the substance had been swept before she danced. Plaintiff slipped and fell while dancing and fractured her hip. After her fall, plaintiff noticed the substance on her clothes. The trial court granted defendant's motion for summary judgment and this appeal followed.

Plaintiff contends that defendant's conduct increased the risk of harm inherent in recreational dancing, and therefore notwithstanding the application of assumption of risk, defendant owed her a duty of ordinary care such that defendant's motion for summary judgment should have been denied.

Our Supreme Court recently clarified the doctrine of assumption of the risk in *Nile v. Acme* (1992) 3 Cal. 4th 296. According to the *Nile* court, the principle of assumption of risk applies to two different situations: (1) those instances in which the assumption of risk doctrine embodies a legal conclusion that there is no duty on the part of the defendant to protect the plaintiff from a particular risk (so-called primary assumption of risk); (2) those instances in which the defendant does owe a duty of care to the plaintiff but the plaintiff knowingly encounters the risk (so-called secondary assumption of risk). (*Id.* at 308.) Further, primary assumption of risk bars a defendant's liability to the plaintiff for injury because the defendant has no legal duty to eliminate, or protect the plaintiff from, the risk; secondary assumption of risk permits an injured plaintiff to recover damages, but only to the extent of the defendant's proportionate share of fault.

The reasoning supporting this principle, the *Nile* court explained, is that persons have a general duty to use due care to avoid injury to others, and may be held liable if their careless conduct injures another person. (See Civ. Code § 1714.) Thus, for example, a property owner ordinarily is required to use due care to eliminate known dangers on his or her property. (See, e.g., *Reynard v. Janus* (1968) 69 Cal. 2d 108.) In a sports setting, however, conditions or conduct that otherwise might be viewed as dangerous often are an integral part of the sport itself. For example, moguls on a ski run pose a risk of harm to skiers that might not exist on a smoothly groomed slope. However, the challenge and risks posed by moguls are part of the sport of skiing, and thus a ski resort has no duty to eliminate them. Thus a skier who is injured on a particularly perilous mogul is barred from recovering damages from the resort, even if the mogul had been unreasonably constructed, because no duty of care is owed. In this respect, the nature of a sport is highly relevant in determining the existence of a duty care owed by a particular defendant. (*Id.* at 315.)

The plaintiff in *Nile* was injured in a touch football game when the defendant, another player, collided with her, knocked her over, and then stepped on her hand. Just before the play which resulted in the collision, the plaintiff had asked the defendant to be less aggressive. The *Nile* court held that this situation fell within the doctrine of primary assumption of risk because the risk of a collision and injury is inherent in the game. (*Id.* at 320.) While the conduct might very well have been negligent in a non-sport setting, it constituted conduct of a character inherent in the sport of football, and thus did not give rise to a duty of ordinary care. It is only if the conduct is "so reckless as to be totally outside the range of the ordinary activity involved in the sport" that a duty may be recognized.

The case now considered by this court involved recreational dancing, an activity which in some ways may be characterized as a contact sport. While it is an activity which is not normally associated with serious risk of harm; it does involve inherent risks, say by tripping on the feet of one's partner, by losing one's balance due to the nature of the steps required, or having one's toes tread upon.

Even assuming that falling is a risk inherent in dancing, dance hall operators still have a duty not to unreasonably increase the risk of injury to its patrons beyond the range of risks inherent in the sport. They very well may breach that duty by adding a substance to the floor which makes it too slippery and thus substantially increases the dancers' risk of harm by falling. After all, the nature of recreational dancing does not require the spreading of slippery material on the dance floor.

It is no answer to say that dancing is inherently dangerous because some dancers have been known to injure themselves by falling. The same could be said of driving a vehicle or virtually any human activity. Once a defendant has breached a duty of care, plaintiff is not precluded from recovery simply because she chose to encounter a known risk of harm. Although every driver of an automobile is aware that driving is a potentially hazardous activity and that inherent in the act another of driving is the risk that he or she will be injured by the negligent driving of another, a person who voluntarily chooses to drive does not thereby impliedly excused others from performing their duty to use due care for the driver's safety. Instead, the driver reasonably expects that if he or she is injured by another's negligence, i.e., by the breach of the other person's duty to use due care, the driver will be entitled to compensation for his or her injuries.

Consequently, we hold that defendant owed plaintiff a duty not to unreasonably increase the risk of injury from recreational dancing beyond those range of risks inherent in the sport. Whether defendant breached this duty to Ms. Barker by spreading Avory Soap Flakes on the dance floor is a question of fact to be determined by the jury. Whatever fault may be attached to plaintiff for dancing on the slippery floor, that fault does not operate as complete bar to recovery.

 We therefore hold that because defendant failed to establish as mater of law that plaintiff's asserted cause of action cannot prevail, it was not entitled to summary judgment. Accordingly, the judgment is reversed and the case remanded to the trial court with directions to enter a new and different order denying defendant's motion for summary judgment. Plaintiff shall recover her costs on appeal.

C

Chapter 6　Case Briefings

在传统法学的范畴里,美国法在相当程度上仍承袭着英国的普通法(Common Law)。所谓的"普通法",指由各个法院判决所形成的法规则累积而成的法律。因此,在学习传统法学时,不可避免地须大量阅读以往法院所做的判决。为了能准确地掌握且精简地陈述判决的内容,《法学研究与写作》(*Legal Research and Writing*)课程的老师一般在课程开始便会教如何去从事摘要判决的工作。判决摘要的学习通常有下述两大重点:首先须让法学院的新生能看懂法院判决书的格式;此外,使学习者熟悉一份完整的判决摘要通常应具备哪些项目,才能在日后复习此案例时达到事半功倍之效。

▶ 1. 如何做研究性案例摘要

学会做案例摘要是一个法律人所要具备的最基本的素质。对于中国的法学院学生而言,学会用英文做英文案例的摘要并形成习惯,实为提高法律英语能力的一个最佳途径。总结案例时,首先要明确为什么要这样做,是为了上课,还是为了研究或其他目的,然后依据这个特定目的来安排版式。无论设计何种版式,都要保证它是为你服务的,亦即判决摘要的格式须符合个人的需要。

一般来说,为研究所做的案例摘要需根据所要解决的问题来设计。当你设计自己的案例摘要格式时,可以参考下面格式:

(1) 编号索引(Citation)

一定要准确完整地写下该案例的全部编号索引,以后引用该案例时就会节省许多时间。

(2) 当事方(Parties)

这里包括本案的所有当事方和他们在诉讼中地位的变化。例如,某公司在一审中是以被告身份出现的,但在二审上诉中却可能成为上诉人,而且自始至终否认他们是侵权人。那么该公司的身份演变即为被告—上诉人—侵权人(defendant—appellant—tortfeasor),而另一方就应该被确认为原告—被上诉人—受害人(plaintiff—respondent—victim)。

(3) 诉讼历史(Prior Proceedings)

这里包括该案件以前所进行的诉讼程序和历史。例如,一审法院判决被告输(trial court found against the defendant)—被告上诉(defendant appealed)—上诉法院改判了一审法院的判决(court of appeals reversed the trial court's decision),改判判决后另一方不服再上诉到最高法院(and now this appeal is before the supreme court)。

(4) 当事人的诉由(Theories of the Parties)

这里包括原告或上诉人就本案所提出的法律理由,如非法拘押(false imprisonment)、合同违约(breach of contract),同时也包括被告可能提出的抗辩理由,如同意或出于自愿(consent)、缺乏对价(lack of consideration)。

(5) 寻求的法律救济(Objectives)

要求实际履行(getting specific performance),要求得到55000元的损害赔偿(getting damages in the amount of $55,000),要求被宣布无罪或释放,还清债务(getting acquitted)。

(6) 事实(Facts)

在这里写下对理解本案所必需的所有相关法律事实(legally significant facts)和背景资料(background facts)。

(7) 确定争点(Issues)

所谓争点,就是法院判决必须预先解决的关于事实和法律的争议。应根据自己的目的来设定和陈述争议的焦点。对争点的陈述一般应当具体清楚,避免太过含糊和笼统。例如,Did defendant Curtis falsely imprison plaintiff Butterworth when he drove around in the car for seven hours without stopping to let her out?(原告在被告驾驶的车中连续呆了7个小时不被允许下车,被告的这种行为是否构成对原告的非法拘禁?)

(8) 法院裁决(Holding)

法院裁决就是简要总结出法院就争点所做的答复及主要原因。例如,Yes; Curtis falsely imprisoned Butterworth because he used words or acts intended to confine Butterworth, he actually confined her in the car, and Butterworth was aware that she was confined.

(9) 法院推理过程(Rationale/Reasoning/Analysis)

这是案例摘要中最重要的部分。它应该包括相关法律原则(relevant rules)、这些原则的运用（the application of those rules）和法院的判决结果（the conclusion the court reached）。

如果可能的话，可以用三段论法（syllogism）来进行分析：相关法律原则是大前提（major premise）—原则运用是小前提（minor premise）—经过推理论证最后得出结论。例如，首先你可以陈述在某一管辖法院内（in the jurisdiction）关于非法拘禁（false imprisonment）的法则及其构成要件，然后你就要分析法院是如何对这一具体的案件适用该法则的。如此一步一步地推理下去，那么你在分析过程中所遇到的疑难问题就会逐渐变得清晰起来。最后再说明法院是如何做出判决的。

在法院推理的运用中，一般会牵涉到四种常用的分析方法，这是应该了解的，在此简述如下：① 归纳推理（inductive reasoning）；② 演绎推理（deductive reasoning）；③ 类比推理（analogical reasoning）；④ 规范推理（normative reasoning）。

（10）法官的附带意见（Dicta）

在有的判决中，有时法官会附带提出一些和该案无关的法律意见（obiter dictum）。它们是判决中的次要陈述，与该案的焦点没有直接关系，因此并不具有法律约束力。

（11）心得体会（Comments）

这部分内容是指在阅读并分析案例后所得出的心得体会（reaction）。无论你是要做学术研究还是要在课堂上陈述你对本案判决的意见，写出自己的心得体会都会显得尤为重要。当你用该案件与其他案件进行比较时，你会产生触电的感觉。另外，若你为课堂教学做案例摘要时，要问问自己："教科书的作者为什么要选择这个案例？它为什么会出现在这个位置？"与此同时你要写出这些问题的答案。诸如此类的内容就构成了你对此案的心得体会。

▶ 2. 课堂案例摘要

课堂案例摘要要根据教学的要求或根据所学课程的特点来做。一般来说，案例摘要应至少包括以下几部分：

（1）确定原被告双方当事人以及所有和他们相关的当事人，明确他们之间到底发生了什么事，并产生了怎样的法律关系。

（2）为了做好第一项工作，应该简要概括重要的相关事实（necessary and relevant facts）。所谓重要相关事实，是指法院判决所必须依据的事实或从诉讼双方当事人的角度来看与其诉求有直接关系的事实。在归纳总结重要事实的过程中要排除非相关事实

(irrelevant facts)。识别相关和非相关的事实是案例分析中必须具备的能力。

（3）明确原被告双方的诉求（claims）以及其用以支持各自诉求的事实和法理，还要搞清楚他们到底要求法院为其做出怎样的判决。

（4）在分析原被告双方的各项诉求过程中，一定要找出案件中的争点所在（issues），包括事实上争点（issues of facts）和法律上争点（issues of law）。对一个争点进行分析，然后确定原被告对此的观点以及法官对双方的观点进行分析后所做出的结论。最后，就某一个争点要搞清是原告赢了还是被告赢了？为什么赢？赢在什么地方？

（5）最后要总结并牢记该判决阐明了或创造了什么样的法律原则或理论。对法院的最后宣判（declaration），个别法官可以提出个别意见（concurring opinion）或反对意见（dissenting opinion），这些意见对于学习法律也很重要。

顾名思义，案例摘要的精髓在于根据摘要的目的和个人需要简要地摘取相关至为重要的内容。因此，不同教科书会有不同的格式，但总体上而言，一份完整的判决摘要至少应包含下列四个部分：

◆ 事实（facts）：须将复杂的案件事实加以精简，并仅摘要案例事实中基础且重要的部分。

◆ 争点（issues）与法院意见（holding）：争点与法院意见部分是成双成对的。法院意见部分乃是法院针对该案件当事人所提法律上争点的答复。当案件中的争点为复数时，相对应的法院意见亦为复数。此时，判决摘要的争点与法院意见栏皆须以复数来表示。

◆ 法院推理过程（rationale）：法院推理过程有时亦称为"判决理由"（reasoning）或"分析"（analysis）。在此部分中必须简要说明，法院就当事人所提的争点是如何推演出前述的"法院意见"。在分析法院的推理过程时，不应仅局限于该判决表面上的文义，应该尝试更深入地去推敲法院为何会得此心证的理由。

除了上述四个必要部分，有些教科书所提供的判决摘要格式可能包含其他项目，如诉讼程序（procedural posture）、判决（decision）、原告主张（plaintiff's arguments）、被告主张（defendant's arguments）等。一般来说，你不需要在你的判决摘要中纳入它们，但如果你认为它们对于你了解整个判决有帮助，也可将它们列入你的判决摘要中，或者你也可以选择将程序、判决、原被告主张等部分置于前述四个必要部分的适当项目之下。例如，若你认为该案件的程序部分有加以摘要的必要，且此程序的陈述与事实部分有密切的关联性，你可将其并入事实栏下一起讨论。

◇ Sample I

Swanson v. Martin

Facts: D landowner put spring-gun in his vineyard to prevent theft.

P was injured by the gun while trying to steal grapes.

Issue: May deadly force be used to protect property other than a dwelling?

Holding: No.

Rationale: Human life more valuable than property.

◇ Sample II

KIRKSEY v. KIRKSEY

Supreme Court of Alabama, 1845

8 Ala. 131.

Assumpsit [a common-law action for breach of a contract] by the defendant, against the <u>plaintiff in error</u> [plaintiff in error = appellant; defendant in error = appellee]. The question is presented in this Court, <u>upon a case agreed</u> [a formal written statement of the facts in a case, submitted to the court jointly by the parties so that a decision may be rendered without trial], which shows the following facts:

The plaintiff was the wife of defendant's brother, but had for some time been a widow, and had some children. In 1840, the plaintiff resided on public land, under a contract of lease, she had held over and was comfortably settled, and would have attempted to secure the land she lived on. The defendant resided in Talladega County, some sixty, or seventy miles off. On Oct. 10, 1840, he wrote to her the following letter:

"Dear Sister Antillico—Much to my mortification, I heard that Brother Henry was dead, and one of his children. I know that your situation is grief and difficult. You had a bad chance before, but a great deal worse now. I should like to come and see you, but cannot with convenience at present. * * * I do not know whether you have a preference on the place you live on or not. If you had, I would advise you to obtain your preference, sell the land and quit the county, as I understand it is very unhealthy, and I know society is very bad. If you will come down and see me, I will let you have a place to raise your family, and I have more open land than I can tend; and on the account of your situation and that of your family, I feel like I want you and the children to do well."

Within a month or two after receipt of this letter, the plaintiff abandoned her possessions, without disposing [the act of transferring sth. to another person's care or possession by deed or will; the relinquishing of property] of it, and removed with her family, to the residence of the defendant, who

> put her in comfortable houses, and gave her land to cultivate for two years, at the end of which time he notified her to remove, and put her in a house, not comfortable, in the woods, which he afterwards required her to leave.
>
> A verdict being found for the plaintiff, for two hundred dollars, the above facts were agreed, and if they will sustain the action, the judgment is to be affirmed, otherwise it is to be reversed.
>
> Ormon, J. — The inclination of my mind is that the loss and inconvenience, which the plaintiff sustained in breaking up, and moving to the defendant's, a distance of sixty miles, is a sufficient consideration to support the promise, to furnish her with a house and land to cultivate, until she could raise her family. However, my brothers think that the promise on the part of defendant was a mere gratuity, and that an action will not lie for its breach. The judgment of the Court below must therefore be reversed, pursuant to the agreement of the parties.

分析:课堂案例摘要(A Case Brief for Class)

(1) 当事人(parties)

① 一审原告(plaintiff)、上诉人(plaintiff in error):Mrs. Kirksey(the wife of defendant's brother)

② 一审被告(defendant)、被上诉人(defendant in error):Mr. Kirksey

(2) 重要的相关事实(necessary and relevant facts)

Defendant promised to let Plaintiff have a place to raise her family. In reliance, Plaintiff abandoned her possessions and came down to see Defendant, who put Plaintiff in comfortable houses and gave her land to cultivate. Two years later, however, Defendant forced Plaintiff to leave.

(3) 双方诉求及支持各自诉求的事实和法理

① 原告的诉求:Damages for breach of contract

② 被告的诉求:No contract because there was no consideration.

③ 支持原告诉求的事实和法理:The loss and inconvenience, which Plaintiff sustained in breaking up, and moving to the defendant's place, a distance of sixty miles, is a sufficient consideration to support Defendant's promise to furnish Plaintiff with a house and land to cultivate, until she could raise her family.

④ 支持被告诉求的事实和法理:The promise on the part of defendant was a mere gratuity, and that an action will not lie for its breach.

(4) 争点(issue)

Whether Plaintiff's loss and inconvenience constitute sufficient consideration to make Defendant's promise a binding contract?

(5) 该判决所阐明的法律原则或理论

Loss or inconvenience suffered in reliance on a promise made to the suffering party may render that promise a binding contract on the promisor.

◇ **Sample Ⅲ**

POTTS v. FIDELITY FRUIT & PRODUCE CO.

Court of Appeals of Georgia, 1983

165 Ga. App. 546, 301 S. E. 2d 903

BANKE, JUDGE

The appellant sued to recover for personal injuries which he allegedly sustained when he was bitten by a spider while unloading bananas from a truck. The incident occurred during the course of his employment with Colonial Stores. The defendants are the local distributor of the bananas, Fidelity Fruit and Produce Co., Inc., and the transporter Refrigerated Transport Co., Inc. Liability was originally predicated both on ordinary <u>negligence per se</u> [negligence established as a matter of law, so that breach of duty is not a jury question, usually arising from a statutory violation.] under the Georgia Food Act, former Code Ann. §§ 42-301 <u>et seq.</u> [and those (pages or sections) that follow] (OCGA ss 26—2—20 et seq.). However, the appellant has since conceded that the evidence would not sustain a finding of ordinary negligence. This appeal is from a grant of <u>summary judgment</u> [a procedural device allows the speedy disposition of a controversy without the need for trial.] in favor of Fidelity Fruit and Produce Co., as to the negligence per se claim, based on a determination that the appellant is not among the class of persons whom the Georgia Food Act was designed to protect. *Held*:

In determining whether the violation of a statute or ordinance is negligence per se as to a particular person, it is necessary to examine the purposes of the legislation and decide (1) whether the injured person falls within the class of persons it was intended to protect and (2) whether the harm complained of was the harm it was intended to guard against. Having examined the provisions of the Georgia Food Act, we agree fully with the following analysis made by the trial court: "Clearly, the Act is a consumer protection act, designed not to render the workplace a safe environment, but to prevent the sale and distribution of adulterated or misbranded food to consumers. While safety in the workplace, and compensation for injuries arising out of work activities, are indeed matters of contemporary concern, they

> are the subject of other legislative enactments on both the state and federal level." Because the appellant's alleged injuries did not arise incident to his consumption of the bananas, we hold that the trial court was correct in concluding that the Act affords him no basis for recovery.
>
> Judgment affirmed.

分析:课堂案例摘要(A Case Brief for Class)

(1) 当事人(parties)

① 原告、上诉人(plaintiff, appellant):Mr. Potts, a worker unloading bananas.

② 被告、被上诉人(defendants, apppellees):The bananas distributor—Fidelity Fruit and Produce Co., Inc. The transporter—Refrigerated Transport Co., Inc.

(2) 重要的相关事实(necessary and relevant facts)

While working for his employer, the appellant was bit by a spider hidden in the bananas that he was unloading from a truck. The defendants supplied and transported the bananas to the appellant's workplace.

(3) 双方诉求及支持各自诉求的事实和法理

① 上诉人的诉求:The appellant sued to recover for his injuries on the basis of negligence per se under Georgia Food Act.

② 被上诉人的诉求:A negligence per se claim is not sustainable because the appellant is not among the class of persons whom the Georgia Food Act was designed to protect.

③ 支持上诉人诉求的事实和法理:The appellant was injured on the job and a violation of the Georgia Food Act may constitute negligence per se.

④ 支持被上诉人诉求的事实和法理:The appellant is not among the class of persons whom the Georgia Food Act was designed to protect.

(4) 争点(issue)

As to the negligence per se claim, is the appellant among the class of persons whom the Georgia Food Act was designed to protect?

(5) 法院的结论(conclusion)

① 初审法院(trial court):The Georgia Food Act is a consumer protection act. It was designed to protect consumers, not workers like the appellant.

② 上诉法院(Court of Appeals of Georgia):The trial court was correct in concluding that the Food Act affords the appellant no basis for recovery, because the appellant's alleged injuries did not arise incident to his consumption of the bananas.

③ 哪一方获胜及其获胜原因：The defendants won, because the Georgia Food Act is a consumer protection act, and appellant's alleged injuries did not arise incident to his consumption of the bananas.

(6) 该判决所阐明的法律原则或理论

In determining whether the violation of a statute or ordinance is negligence per se as to a particular person, it is necessary to examine the purposes of the legislation and decide (a) whether the injured person falls within the class of persons it was intended to protect and (b) whether the harm complained of was the harm it was intended to guard against.

Courts must also determine whether a statute was intended to create tort liability at all.

Ex. 1　Use the above format and brief *U. S. v. White*

Brief：
U. S. v. White, 552 F. 2d 268 (8th Cir. 1977)
Facts：
Legal History：
Issue：
Holding：
Reasoning：
Rule of Law：

Ex. 2　Use the following format and brief *Dorothy Barker vs. Melody Dance Partners* (1993) 17 Cal. App. 4th 322

Dorothy Barker vs. Melody Dance Partners (1993) 17 *Cal. App.* 4th 322
Facts：
Issue：
Holding：
Rule：
Reasoning：

Chapter 7　Neutral Analysis—the Office Memo

▶ 1. "Legal Memo"简介

在美国的法学院,"memo"写作是一门非常重要的课程。"memo"写作不仅可以考察学生们的法律语言能力,同时能培养其法律分析和研究能力,并能够根据不同的写作要求写出适合不同阅读人员的"memo"。"memo"的写作也是考察法律人是否具备律师之严密思维和谨慎作风的试金石,故而为西方法学院所重视。随着中国经济的日益国际化,中国学生应当学会和掌握有关涉外法律写作中的基本知识,以便更好地参与法律业务国际化的进程。

当你找到第一份法律工作时,"office memo"大概会是你第一个被指派的工作,你的老板会要求你写一个"office memo"来回答与某位诉讼当事人相关的特定法律问题。当你向法院提交起诉书(compliant)或答辩状(answer)时,通常需要就法律和事实提交一份陈述状(memo)。在庭审(court proceeding)中,向法院提交一项动议(motion)时,也需要你提交一份支持该动议的法律陈述状(memo of points and authorities)。当你代理客户参加一起国际商事仲裁(arbitration)时,仲裁机构也往往要求当事方提交"memo",以阐明自己的观点。当你代表国家在国际法院(Int'l Court of Justice,简称"ICJ")参加诉讼时,国际法院也会要求当事国提交一份"memorial"(a written statement of facts presented to a legislature or executive as a petition),这也是一种"memo"。

根据提交的对象不同,"memo"可以分为两大类。第一类称为"internal or office memo"(简称"office memo")。"office memo"指在法律事务所内,助理律师根据合伙人或其他高级律师的要求,就特定案件中所涉及的法律和事实争议(issues)进行分析,提出相关意见,以供决策者参考。因其用于法律事务所内部参考,所以要求写作者以客观

(objective)、中立(neutral/detached)和全面(comprehensive)的角度分析当事人在案件中的利弊(positive and negative information)，最后根据法律和相关事实预测法院或仲裁机构对该案件可能做出的判决，并据此提出解决问题的最佳方案(recommendation)。如律师事务所在评估是否接一个胜诉才收酬金的案子(contingent-fee case)与一个以时薪计酬的案子(hourly-rate case)，其判断胜诉概率的措辞可能有所不同。

"office memo"的作者首先要分析案情，找出事实和法律焦点(issues of law and facts)。有时，客户或主任律师预先设定了焦点问题，作者只需在规定的时间内对焦点问题进行分析即可，"office memo"重在就利弊进行分析，其作用如下：

- to inform a senior attorney of the facts and law relevant to a client's problem；
- to assist a senior attorney in evaluating the merits of potential claims and defenses；
- to assist a senior attorney in planning litigation strategies and tactics, settlement options；
- to provide a foundation for drafting other documents, e.g. pleading documents, discovery requests and briefs；
- to assist in trial preparation；
- to document the factual and legal sources you rely on；
- to document your research for future cases.

另一类"memo"称为"external memo"，其提交对象主要是客户、法院、仲裁机构、政府等。其主要目的是说服对方接受你的观点或做出有利于自己的判决。"external memo"的最根本特点是必须具有说服力(persuasiveness)和感染力(effectiveness)，因此也被称为"advocacy memo"。"external memo"主要包括：

- memo of points and authorities：在向初审法院(trial court)提交动议(motion)时配合使用；
- trial memo：庭审法律意见书，又称"trial brief"；
- hearing memo：听证会使用的法律文书；
- appellate brief：向上诉法院提交的上诉法律意见书。

由此可见，"external memo"是一个泛称，其中第1和第4是最重要的两种。

▶ 2. "memo"写作一般注意事项

"memo"的写作宗旨是以读者为目标，根据读者的不同来设定语气和内容。一名合

Chapter 7　Neutral Analysis—the Office Memo　‖　117

　　格的律师必须学会将事实和法律有机地结合起来,善于通过演绎和归纳得出令人信服的结论。优秀的"memo"写作必须清楚、简洁、完整。每一句话中的每一个单词都应当认真斟酌;每个段落中的每一句话和每篇文章中的每个段落间须做到逻辑井然有序。

　　"memo"的写作是一个复杂的过程,通常要求作者在一定的时限内高效率地完成任务,还必须要求其遵循相应的写作程序和技巧。下面是"memo"写作的基本程序:

（1）Preparation
—Establish your objective
—Identify your reader
—Determine the scope of your coverage
—Develop a writing plan
（2）Research
—Develop and analyze facts
—Research statutes and cases
—Develop issues and short answers
（3）Organization
—Make an outline
—Select an appropriate format
（4）Writing the draft
—Develop and explain legal theories
—Apply the legal theories to facts
—Make conclusions
—Support your conclusions with further authorities if necessary
（5）Revision
—Check the accuracy of your citation and references
—Check for unity and coherence
—Check for completeness

撰写"memo"的建议:
—Don't be defensive about changing and improving your legal writing.
—Legal writing is not an exercise in creative writing, essay or composition. You must get to the point, be exact and follow the rules.
—The simpler, the better.

——You don't have to reinvent the wheel for every legal writing assignment. All memos demand only a slight variation in format.

——The courts care less about the reality; they only look into the facts and law as related to them by your memos and court hearing.

——Use consistent terms. After you have introduced an identifying term, stick with it until the end of your memo.

——Partners and professors will not necessarily give you clear directions for memo assignments. If you don't understand something, go back and ask them before you begin to work. Better now than later.

——A persuasive structure that works in memos will translate into a persuasive oral advocacy in the courtroom. Ask a respected trial attorney.

——It's the little things, like proofing and citation, which are easily fixed but too often overlooked. These kinds of errors will leave a poor impression of your work in the minds of court, partners and professors.

▶ 3. "Office Memo"的特点

如前所述,"office memo"应注意以下4个方面:

- Fully understand the <u>factual</u> and <u>legal</u> context of your assignment
- Assess the strengths and weaknesses of your position
- Assess the strengths and weaknesses of the opposing position
- Predict what the tribunal would decide as to each issue

这4个要求的核心就是"office memo"的客观性。所谓客观性,即要求在叙述事实时要如实客观,在寻找相关的法律依据时要实事求是;在根据事实和法律分析案情时要摒除主观偏见,在预测后果时要利弊兼顾。试比较以下两例:

> The majority of States consider surrogate motherhood unlawful; the United States and some European countries have not so considered.

> *Even though* a majority of states have considered surrogate motherhood unlawful, the United States and some European countries have *willfully ignored* its social ramification and *embraced it without qualification*.

▶ 4. "Office Memo"的结构

"office memo"的格式和结构没有一个特定的标准,许多律师事务所往往会根据自己的偏好制定一套格式和固定结构,甚至有些律所根本没有此类规定,任凭写作者自己决定。尽管如此,"office memo"一般包含下面几个部分:

- Heading　抬头
- Statement of Facts　事实陈述
- Statement of Issues　案件争点陈述
- Short Answer　简要回答
- Applicable Statutes or Cases　适用法律
- Discussion　案件分析讨论
- Conclusion and Recommendation　结论和建议

有些律师事务所要求在"office memo"的抬头部分后加上"statement of assignment"(对"memo"写作任务的说明)。

以下是"memo"的撰写格式

Format A	Format B	Format C
Ⅰ. Issue(s)	Ⅰ. Overview	Ⅰ. Facts
Ⅱ. Brief Answer(s)	Ⅱ. Facts	Ⅱ. Issue(s)
Ⅲ. Facts	Ⅲ. Issue(s)	Ⅲ. Conclusion
Ⅳ. Discussion	Ⅳ. Brief Answer(s)	Ⅳ. Discussion
Ⅴ. Conclusion	Ⅴ. Discussion	
	Ⅵ. Conclusion	

由此可见,"memo"的撰写格式不受任何规则或法则的拘束,只要所使用的格式能呈现你想表达的内容即可。比如,"memo"并不需要包含事实陈述部分,因为你的老板已经了解案件事实了,故当一份"memo"包含事实部分时,应该将其缩小集中在与你所分析的争点有关的部分,现将上面列明的每一部分进行逐一说明:

(1) 抬头(Heading)

"office memo"的抬头完整版一般包括:

- 标题(caption):要求居中放置,阐明"memo"的类型是"Office Memo of Law";
- "memo"的提交对象:一般为你的主管律师或教授;

- 作者姓名(writer's name and title);
- "memo"的分配日期和提交日期(assignment and submission dates);
- 案件名称或写作题目(如果知道当事人姓名,则应注明);
- 案件编号(case number,一般由律师事务所统一编号);
- 如果案件已经提起诉讼则应当列明法院案件编号(court docket number);
- 对"memo"主要内容的提示说明:一般要求在"RE"后面加上提示内容("re"表示"与……有关"),以表明该"memo"所涉及的法律内容,"memo"写作中将这一项的作用称为"subject matter description"。如下例所示:

	Office Memorandum of Law
TO:	Zhang San, Partner
FROM:	Li Si, Junior Associate
ASSIGNMENT DATE:	October 8, 2014
SUBMISSION DATE:	November 8, 2014
CASE:	China Veture Tech, Inc. v. Banco Pupula, N.A.
DOCKET NUMBER:	08-C00178NYS
OFFICE FILE NUMBER:	08-L016GY
RE:	Whether substitute service is allowed under the Civil Procedure Law of the PRC.

注意:"office memo"的"heading"以及在"memo"中若整段引述他人文章或者案例,应当采用单倍行距,其他情况则使用双倍行距。"RE"部分提示了接下来的"memo"正文中要处理的法律问题,如此既利于归档,又便于快速查档。

但下述简略版可能更为常见:

TO:	Susan Elias
FROM:	James Nelson
RE:	Enforceability of Julie Week's Promise to Act as Guarantor for Loan Obligation; File 06-127
DATE:	August 16, 2015

(2)工作任务说明(Statement of Assignment)

在主管律师或教授向你分配"office memo"写作任务后,你应当立即将其记录下来以明确工作范围,此部分有时候也被称为"background and purpose",见下例说明:

> **STATEMENT OF ASSIGNMENT**
> You have asked me to prepare a memo of law limited to the question whether our client, Mr. Defendant, has breached the contract between him and Ms. Plaintiff by directing his agents to withhold payment until SARS has been effectively controlled in China. Specifically, you asked me to discuss the applicability of the United Nations Convention on Contracts for the International Sale of Goods (CISG,联合国国际货物销售合同公约).

该部分内容若与"RE"部分相似,则可以和"RE"部分合并。

(3) 事实陈述(Statement of Facts)

事实陈述是整个"memo"中最为重要的部分,同时也是难度较大的一部分。一方面,作者必须找出相关的法律事实(legally relevant facts),即那些能够产生法定权利、引起法定义务或产生法律纠纷的事实,而此种法律事实又可分为重要的法律事实(legally significant facts)和背景事实(background facts);另一方面,事实陈述必须简洁(concise)、全面(comprehensive)、准确(accurate)并富有条理性(logical)。在事实陈述上的任何微小的疏漏都会造成决策者在预测法律后果或决定方案时出现偏颇。

要判断哪些是相关的法律事实,首先要通晓相关法律,以法律为准绳判定有关事实的法律地位;其次,还必须学会对比(contrast,即就类似案件的相关事实的不同点进行对比)与比较(compare,是就类似案件的相关事实的相似点进行比较),在复杂的事实中进行筛选。比如,国际法认为,战争中大规模的、有组织的强奸是一种战争罪(war crime),否则只能是一般的国内罪行。所谓的相关法律事实就可能包含以下几方面:

- 有没有人在战争中强奸妇女(rape against women);
- 规模如何(scale);
- 是否具有组织性(organized)。

上述任何一点事实都可能影响案件的审理结果。相关法律事实也可能涉及程序问题(procedure),如时效(statute of limitation),如果原告等了20年后才就某一合同提起违约之诉,则法院一般不会受理。

背景事实指那些可以帮助读者理解整个案件的事实。它对帮助理解重要法律事实是不可或缺的。但是,在叙述这一部分事实时应该尽可能简明扼要。

一篇好的事实陈述必须条理井然,使人一目了然。要组织好事实部分的写作,有两种途径:一是按照时间顺序(chronological order)来阐述,二是按照要点阐述。

按照时间顺序叙述事实,还可以分为列举式和陈述式。前者一般仅仅按照时间简单罗列事件,后者则按时间叙述事件。例如:

❏ 列举式：

STATEMENT OF FACTS

Year 2014

On December 7: Tianjin Co. (hereafter: CLAIMANT) emailed Shanghai Co. (hereafter: RESPONDENT), confirming the agreement reached through tele-conference earlier in the morning. CLAIMANT assured that RESPONDENT would always receive the "best price" and identified this price as 8% lower than the ordinary price quoted to CLAIMANT's other clients.

On December 15: REAPONDENT faxed CLAIMANT a purchase order, which was quickly acknowledged by CLAIMANT. No shipping and payment procedures were specified.

On December 27: CLAIMANT express-mailed RESPONDENT a standard contract in which an arbitration agreement designating a non-existing arbitration institution and a choice-of-law clause was incorporated. However, said contract did not contain the 8% discount as earlier agreed upon.

❏ 陈述式：

STATEMENT OF FACTS

On December 7, 2014, Tianjin Co., hereafter CLAIMANT, reached an agreement with Shanghai Co., hereafter RESPONDENT, through tele-conferencing. CLAIMANT assured that RESPONDENT would always receive the "best price" and identified this price as 8% lower than the ordinary price quoted to CLAIMANT's other clients. Immediately thereafter, RESPONDENT faxed CLAIMANT a confirmation letter.

Eight days later, RESPONDENT faxed CLAIMANT a bare purchase order containing no shipping or payment procedures, which order was quickly acknowledged by CLAIMANT. CLAIMANT, in addition, express-mailed RESPONDENT a standard contract in which an arbitration agreement designating a non-existing arbitration institution and a choice-of-law clause was incorporated. However, said contract did not contain the 8% discount as earlier agreed upon.

以上两种方法各有千秋，但陈述式更为普遍。

除了以上两种按照时间顺序叙述事实的方法以外，还可以按要点对事实进行组合。这一方法往往在按照要点展开比按照时间顺序叙述事实更为清晰、明了的情况下使用。无论如何，按照内容要点来进行说明的方法应当慎用，一般只有在按照时间顺序叙述不利于事实说明的情况下才使用。

Chapter 7   Neutral Analysis—the Office Memo

The Initial Agreement: On December 7, 2014, Tianjin Co., hereafter CLAIMANT, reached an agreement with Shanghai Co., hereafter RESPONDENT, through tele-conferencing. CLAIMANT assured that RESPONDENT would always receive the "best price" and identified this price as 8% lower than the ordinary price quoted to CLAIMANT's other clients. Immediately thereafter, RESPONDENT faxed CLAIMANT a confirmation letter.

The Subsequent Order: Eight days later, RESPONDENT faxed CLAIMANT a bare purchase order containing no shipping or payment procedures, which order was quickly acknowledged by CLAIMANT. CLAIMANT, in addition, express-mailed RESPONDENT a standard contract in which an arbitration agreement designating a non-existing arbitration institution and a choice-of-law clause was incorporated. However, said contract did not contain the 8% discount as earlier agreed upon.

在叙述复杂事实时,最好在段落开始部分使用一些具有提示性或概括性的用语,比如:

This case arises from an unlawful detention of Defendant by the police with arrest warrant …

Nanjing University and Soochow University both agreed to a merger plan in July 3000. Thereafter, however, a line of events has made this merger politically impossible …

由于事实陈述部分需要好好掌握,该部分写作要求注意事项:

—Do not simply quote from or paraphrase your source materials;

—Internalize the important facts, and then organize and articulate them to communicate the following:

- all legally significant facts
- all background facts necessary to understand the story and put it in context

—Legally significant facts are facts that tend to prove or disprove the existence of a legal element or factor;

—Background facts are those needed to tell a story and put the legally significant facts in context;

—State facts in the past tense;

—Do not use legal conclusions or cite legal authority in your statement of facts;

—Present facts accurately and objectively;

—Apply a consistent organizing principle;

—Chronology usually works best;

—If you have multiple issues or parties, you might organize the facts by separate topics;

—the facts should be described clearly and accurately and without argument;

—Be careful not to draw unwarranted conclusions from the facts;

—Avoid language which alters any of the facts.

(4) 争点陈述(Statement of Issues)

案件争点陈述在"memo"写作中又被称为"questions presented"。案件争点分为两种：一种叫事实争点(issues of facts)，另一种称为法律争点(issues of law)。事实争点是指对事实存在与否以及如何发生等所发生的争议；而法律争点指的是对法律规定以及应该如何适用所引发的争议。争点陈述要求使用非常简短的归纳性语言且必须使用疑问句形式。

① 争点陈述的格式

争点陈述要遵循一定的格式,必须包括以下三个要素：a. 在什么样法律规定下；b. 根据何种既成法律事实；c. 是否应该产生某一法律后果。

> Whether, under the practice of international judicial assistance [Rule], a U.S. citizen may apply to an English court for a worldwide Mareva Injunction [Facts] to restrict a Chinese joint venture operating solely within China? [Result]

"whether the injunction may restrict a Chinese joint venture operating solely within China"表明是否应该产生某一法律问题。只有以上三要素齐备,才能构成一个合格的案件争点陈述。

争点陈述的惯用表达法之一为"Under—does/do/is/are/can/should/etc.—when/if"的结构。如上例可改写为：

> Under the practice of international judicial assistance, can a Mareva Injunction be issued by English court restrict a Chinese joint venture operating solely within China, if it was a U.S. citizen who applied to the English court for such an injunction?

> Under California law that may hold a bartender liable for negligently selling alcohol to a driver, is Ms. Bartender Zhang liable for injuries caused by her customer in an automobile accident when she served the customer two drinks even though he was visibly intoxicated?

现在有为数不少的律师仍以"whether"开始一个"问题"（question），但以 whether 作为"问题"的起始是不好的构句方式，故请不要这样写："Whether lost profits can be recovered in a fraud action"（所失利润是否能在一个欺诈的诉讼中获得补偿），而要说 "Can lost profits be recovered in a fraud action?"（所失利润能否在一个诈欺的诉讼中获得补偿？）。

对一些复杂的法律关系，有时候争点繁多复杂，且难以用一个疑问句来单独陈述。因此，不要尝试以一句话来表达太复杂的问题，但是在写作上若无法避免以一句话来表达的情形时，可以选择用简短的句子来理清问题，以代替冗长的文句来陈述问题。在这种情况下可以通过一个小段落对案件争点加以说明，而无须使用上述的陈述方法，但一般情况下不宜采纳此法。

> **SUMMARY ISSUE**
>
> This memorandum discusses two doctrines related to transnational litigations: the doctrine of lis pendens [the jurisdiction, power, or control acquired by a court over property while a legal action is pending] and the doctrine of res judicata [an issue that has been definitively settled by judicial decision]. This memo focuses primarily upon scholarly treatment of these principles and how the courts have responded to the scholar opinions. The memo also analyzes how courts have applied the merger rule in analyzing and applying the two doctrines, particularly in the recognition and enforcement of foreign judgment.

② 如何设定案件争点

当事人把案件交由律师处理都是为了一定的目的。这些目的有些比较笼统，可能要求律师说明其打算从事的某一项商事交易（commercial transaction）是否合法，需要注意什么问题；有些目标则比较具体，比如说当事人想知道其刚赚取的咨询翻译服务费收入是否应该纳税、怎样纳税。律师所需要做的工作是将这些当事人的目的转化为法律问题，并考虑其在法律上的可行性。

要设定争点，第一步是分析当事人或律师认为应该进入的法律关系，再根据该法律关系确定应适用的法律。例如，一家美国公司打算在苏州全资收购（acquire）一家国有企业。这一问题涉及公司买卖的法律关系，而这种法律关系至少应当受《中华人民共和国公司法》以及相关配套法规的调整。找出适用的法律需要遵循一定的顺序。从纵向上看，可以法律渊源的层次高低来进行，以全国人大及其常委会制定的法律、与该法律相关的司法解释、国务院法规、部门规章、地方人大制定的法规和地方政府规章的顺序进行；从横向上看，可以按照该法律关系所涉及的不同部门法进行研究。如前述并购，可能涉及公司企业法、国有资产保护、外资企业准入、外汇交易、融资、劳动人事、环境保护等方面的法律法规。

明确了适用的法律并做了相关的研究之后,就可以结合当事人所要达到的目的,开始设定法律争点,一般其思考的路径如下:According to the potentially applicable rules of law, what specific things must the client establish in order to achieve its objective, and which of these specific things, if any, may present difficulties?

> 若当事人的案件涉及国际贸易中的合同纠纷,即当事人与对方订立的合同是否成立问题。纠纷起因于双方当事人之间对货物价格折扣条款约定不明确。我方当事人认为折扣优惠条款是价格条款的基本组成部分,因为折扣条款未协商一致,故合同因缺乏明确的价格条款而不能成立,但对于我方当事人的观点,对方不予认可。

经研究,以上纠纷涉及国际货物买卖合同关系。通过调查当事人所属国所缔结的国际条约,认定该法律关系受《1980年联合国国际货物销售合同公约》调整,依此可以将其法律争点设定为:Whether, under the United Nations Convention on Contracts for International Sales of Goods, the lack of an agreement on discount rate can preclude the conclusion of a sales contract?

③ 撰写问题陈述应注意的问题

- "问题"栏以成文法或判例法起头,并以案件事实结尾。

"问题"通常应包含法律(a reference to a legal rule)和事实(facts)两部分,把法律摆在"问题"栏的一开头能让读者了解并评估案件事实。下列"问题"中的判例法与援救(rescue)有关。

> Does a store owner have a duty to rescue an injured person in the store when the person is not a customer and was injured outside the store?

若"问题"栏中的法律系成文法(statute),那么请指明系何条文;若此成文法的名称广为人知,请在"问题"栏写明此成文法的名称。此成文法的引注(citation)在"问题"栏中可暂时略过不提,这部分留待"discussion","argument/advocacy"部分再提即可。

> Does a buyer have a claim under Minnesota's Lemon Law when the buyer's car was out of service for three months during the warranty period but was working perfectly by the time of trial?

若"问题"栏中的法律系判例法(case law),通常不需要交代此判例法的出处,然而当某一判例(case)对某"争点"(issue)有巨大影响时,也许会需要在"问题"中交代这个判例的简称(short-form name)。

> Is there personal jurisdiction over Sportco in California under International Shoe when Sportco has no retail stores in the state but makes an average of five sales a year to California customers by mail order?

即便你在"问题"中提到某个判例,但请记住不要因为引用这个判例而使"问题"显得杂乱无章。

上面最后一个例句中的"问题":"when"是法律(law)跟事实(facts)的一个大概的分界点,若你不了解怎么表示该"问题",你可以用以下的公式来呈现"问题":(a)"[law] when [facts]?"或(b)"[law] even though [facts]?"

若"问题"部分没有提到任何案件事实,会使读者无法在一开始就对整份"memo"有基本概念,也很难成为一份具有说服力的律师答辩状,如下例:

> Was a termination clause unconscionable under Section 2-302 of the Uniform Commercial Code?

在"问题"中提到的案件事实应该具体、明确,而不应该像下例包含太多写作者个人的意见:

> Was a termination clause unconscionable under Section 2-302 of the Uniform Commercial Code when it was used by a buyer to victimize a smaller seller?

下面点出了上例的重点,指出具体、特定的案件事实,且没有加入个人意见:

> Was a 30-day termination clause unconscionable under section 2-302 of the Uniform Commercial Code when the clause was contained in the buyer's form contract that the buyer refused to negotiate, and the buyer was five times the size of the seller?

除了"问题"栏以成文法或判例法起头并以案件事实结尾外,撰写问题陈述还应注意以下几方面:

- 决定使用诉讼当事人的姓名或称谓来指称当事人。
- "问题"栏切勿涵盖结论。
- "问题"栏只陈述主要争点。
- 谨慎选择及强调不具争议性的"案件事实",以使"问题"栏具有说服力。
- 在设定争点问题时,考虑一定要全面,要将所有的可能性都考虑进去。

在"memo"写作中,我们将这些可能存在的争点称为"contingency issue",其在法律实践中是大量存在的。例如,甲要求乙支付违约金,作为乙方代理人就应当提出两个争点问题:①是否存在违约? ②若法院认定乙违约,是否应该支付违约金? 第二个问题就是"contingency issue",因为法院很可能认定乙方没有违约而不再过问违约金问题。作为律师不应当因为违约金问题的不确定性而忽略对该问题的讨论。不管我们对前一争点问题有多大胜算,也不能忽略对"contingency issue"的讨论。在讨论"contingency issue"时我们可以用"on the assumption","even if","assume but not concede","if the court finds otherwise","in the alternative"等来连接。

- 在写作过程中,若发现已设定的案件争点问题有错误或偏差,此时就应当对其进行及时修改。一般情况下,随着写作进程的不断加深和对事实的不断认识,这种修改是完全正常的。

- 在语言方面应尽量使用主动语态,能用动词时就避免使用名词,语气尽量客观中立。

Writing the issues of the following cases:

Ex. 1

While driving his Dafa pickup truck(轻便小货车) home from work, Laozhang pulled over to the side of road, shifted the manual transmission lever into the "park" position, and left the cab to cover some tools in the open truck bed that had become exposed to the rain. He neither shut off the engine nor set the parking brake. As he jumped on the bumper to cover the tools, he suddenly realized the truck was moving in reverse. He leaped to the ground and ran to the truck's cab, but before he was able to re-enter the truck, he slipped on the pavement, fell, and the truck ran over both of his legs and one of his hands before a passenger sitting in the cab succeeded in stopping it. His subsequent action against Dafa was bottomed on allegations of defective design of the truck's shifting mechanism and on Dafa's failure to warn the propensity of the truck not to go completely into the "park" position. Dafa claimed that Laozhang negligently caused his own injury.

[Statement of Issue]

Ex. 2

Mrs. Wang purchased a *Chery* mini-car from defendant Suzhou Motors Resale Corporation and gave it to her son who was attending Soochow University. Ten days after delivery of the car, Mrs. Wang's son was injured in an accident that resulted when the steering failed suddenly and without warning. Up to this time the car had functioned properly. Mrs.

Wang's son sued both the reseller and car maker for breach of express and implied warranties and for negligence. Mrs. Wang joined in the action seeking compensation for her consequential losses. The sales contract signed by Mrs. Wang was a standard printed form. It contained the following language concerning the warranty: "It is expressly agreed that there are no warranties, express or implied, made by either the dealer or the manufacturer on the motor vehicle, chassis, of parts furnished hereunder." The defendants move the court to dismiss Mrs. Wang's son's action on the ground that he was not a party to the sales contract, and to dismiss Mrs. Wang's action on account of the warranty disclaimer clause.

[Statement of Issue]

(5) 对争点的简要回答(Brief Answer)

为了让"memo"的读者快速地知道法律研究的结果或律师的法律意见,"office memo"通常要求就法律争点问题提供"brief answer"。"brief answer"通常以"yes"或"no"开始,再附加一两句话说明其理由,其中最好不要引经据典,要直截了当、简洁明了。

> Statement of Issue: Under California law that may hold a bartender liable for negligently selling alcohol to a driver, is Ms. Bartender Zhang liable for injuries caused by her customer in an automobile accident after she served him two drinks even though he was visibly intoxicated already?
>
> Brief Answer: Yes. Ms. Bartender Zhang is liable for the victim's injuries because she negligently served two drinks to the driver customer who was already visibly intoxicated.

(6) 适用的法律(Applicable Law)

成文法国家的许多律师事务所要求在"office memo"中列明所适用的成文法规定,当然普通法国家自然还要列举所适用的普通法判例。同样,在解决国际经济纠纷中,也需要遵从很多条约(treaties)和公约(convention)的规定。但请记住,所列法律条文应加双引号,并使用单倍行距。

(7) 对案件的分析讨论(Discussion/Analysis)

此部分是整个"office memo"的核心内容。这一部分是以"issue"为单元展开的,一个"issue"构成一个单元。写作者要结合法律和事实对每一个"issue"进行全面而具体的分析。

在分析法律问题时,要求写作者能够结合事实引经据典。对于大陆法国家作者,必须准确引用成文法及相关司法解释,在必要时还需引用权威学者的观点或国家政策;对于普通法国家,这种分析既包括"statutory analysis",也包括"established common law"。在引用案例时应当注意比较和对比相似案件间的异同,这种被广泛重视的能力称为"the ability to distinguish cases"。援引案例时可以这样开始:"既然甲案可以如此判决,那么具有相似事实的乙案也不应当例外。"

案件分析讨论部分普遍采用 IRAC 法。根据此法:

首先:应当在每单元的开头就清楚地告诉读者本单元讨论的争点是什么;
随后:应当阐述相关的法律规则或案例;
接下来:是最为关键的法律适用部分,即要求将法律和事实结合并进行讨论,尤其是要比较法律和关键事实部分是否相匹配;
最后:应当对这个单元做出小结(mini-conclusion)。

这样,以问题开始,以结论收尾,整个结构严谨有序,有始有终。请看下面按照 IRAC 法写作的一个简单而又典型的例子:

[I] The issue here is whether the bankruptcy code exempted from discharging a judgment obtained against a doctor who had deliberately chosen a less effective course of treatment in order to save the client money. [R] 11U. S. C. §523(a)(6) makes non-dischargeable any debt "for willful or malicious injury by the debtor to another." [A] The plaintiff argued that the doctor's willful decision to use a cheaper method of treating plaintiff's injury qualified as deliberate under the statute. However, the court said that the section 523(a)(6) should be read as essentially identical to the category of intentional torts. In an intentional tort, the actor intends to cause the injury. Here, the doctor did an intentional act which injured the plaintiff, but the doctor did not intend to injure her. [C] Thus, the plaintiff's judgment against the doctor was dischargeable through bankruptcy proceeding.

若争点不止一个,有时可采用 CRAC 法来完成:

CRAC 是一个帮助写作者组织法律争点的讨论栏的工具,其与 IRAC 唯一的不同是:CRAC 以结论而非争点来起头。一开头就告诉读者结论,将有助于读者了解写作者所做的分析,就像推理小说一样,一开始就知道凶手是谁将有助于读者发现线索。如下列依 CRAC 格式所写的例子:

Chapter 7 Neutral Analysis—the Office Memo || 131

> Carol Sobel 在纽约北部拥有一处苗圃，里头种的是果树。从 1980 年开始，Sobel 大量贩卖所种的树给纽约的零售商。在 1985 年那年，她跟 Greenway 签了一份买卖果树的合约。Greenway 公司是一家比 Sobel 的苗圃规模大 5 倍的零售商。Greenway 公司坚持用它自己的制式合约，而且不接受 Sobel 的修改。Sobel 签约时的合约终止条款是：只要在 30 日前以书面通知对方，买受人或出卖人皆能任意终止这份合约。Greenway 公司与 Sobel 苗圃间的买卖关系维持了近 7 年，从没出过任何问题，然而在 1992 年 3 月 1 日，Sobel 接到 Greenway 公司的书面通知说这份合约将于 30 日内终止。对 Sobel 来说，这个通知的时间来得不巧，因为大部分的人都在春天种树，所以 4 月份是果树的销售旺季。合约此时终止，对 Sobel 而言影响很大。现在 Sobel 想要知道她是否能够从 Greenway 公司获得赔偿，故其向一位律师咨询，而这位律师要求其助手写一份关于这个案件的 memo，内容是这个终止条款根据纽约统一商法典（New York's version of the Uniform Commercial Code）是否合理。

针对 Sobel 的问题，下列采用了 CRAC 法写就的论题段落（thesis paragraph，通常在讨论部分的第一段应，简单介绍接下来要分析的部分）。

> Sobel is unlikely to recover damages under a theory that the termination clause was unconscionable. Such a clause will be held unconscionable under N. Y. U. C. C. Section 2-302 (McKinney 1964) when a seller can show (1) there was no meaningful choice but to deal with the buyer and accept the contract as offered and (2) the clause was unreasonable favorable to the buyer. <u>Worldwide Music v. CD City</u>, 578 N. E. 2d 80, 88 (N.Y. 1991). Because Sobel was not forced to deal with Greenway and because the clause gave both parties the same right to terminate the contract, the termination clause is likely to be held.

> Sobel's contract with Greenway is governed by Article 2 of New York's Uniform Commercial Code. Article 2 governs all transactions in "goods", which are defined in Section 2-107 to include "growing crops" or other things attached to reality capable of severance without material harm. Sobel grows her trees in the ground, but when she sells them she digs them up and transfers them. Because the trees are severed from the reality without harm, they are goods covered by Article 2.

上述最后一个例句中，第一个句子是结论，第二句是法律原则，第三句是将法律原则适用到事实，第四句则再次提到结论。该例刚好能适用一个完整的 CRAC，但通常情况下无法将 CRAC 作完整的运用，因为结论很短，而法律原则及将法律原则适用到事实部分通常比较长，因此有时你会需要数个段落来完整地解释一个法律原则，或将法律原则应用到事实中。

虽然 CRAC 法首尾皆为结论,但如用同样简短、一致的 CRAC 来表现开头跟结尾的结论部分,将使文章显得呆板。因此,通常第一个结论是简介,而第二个结论则是总结,而且第二个结论比第一个来得精确。

"适用要件"(application of element)通常是最令人混淆的部分。当把法律原则适用到案件事实中,首先你必须提到跟这个争点相关的案件事实,再将法律原则适用到那些事实中。在必要的范围内,你也必须依据相关的法律原则的适用来分析那些事实,因为 CRAC 中的 A 同时也代表 Analysis(分析),所以必须于必要时在 A 这个部分对案件事实作分析。

特别注意的是,如果法律规则比较复杂,就应当解析它们并将其分解为若干要件,然后再分别结合事实来分析,该方法的运用在以成文法为断案依据的大陆法国家中显得尤为重要。关于分解方法,参阅下例:

> The first issue to be discussed in this memo is the applicability of CISG Article 14 (1), which provides that "[a] proposal for concluding a contract addressed to one or more specific persons constitutes an offer if it is sufficiently definite and indicates the intention of the offer to be bound in case of acceptance. A proposal is sufficiently definite if it indicates the goods and expressly or implicitly fixed or makes provision for determining the quantity and the price." Here, four requirements must be established before a proposal can constitute an offer:
>
> ① The proposal must addressed to one or more specific persons;
> ② The proposal must indicate the intention of the offer to be bound in the case of acceptance;
> ③ The proposal must indicate the goods;
> ④ The proposal must expressly or implicitly fix or provide for determining the quantity and the price.
>
> I will discuss each of these requirements separately. Regarding the first requirement ...

通常你会有一个主要的 CRAC 争点,而其中会包含较小的 CRAC 次要争点。如若主要争点是关于是否有一个殴打事件,次要的争点就会是殴打的要件:(a)意图;(b)对另一个人;(c)造成伤害或攻击的接触。那此时的 CRAC 的运用形态示例如下:

```
CONSLUSION（是否构成殴打）
    RULE（殴打三要件）
    APPLICATION
        第一个要件：意图
            Conclusion
            Rule
            Application
            Conclusion
        第二个要件：另一个人
            Conclusion
            Rule
            Application
            Conclusion
        第三个要件：伤害或攻击的接触
            Conclusion
            Rule
            Application
            Conclusion
    Conclusion（是否构成殴打）
```

当然，当一个法律讨论部分复杂又包含纠缠不清且重复的法律争点时，也许不适用 CRAC。如遇这种情形，写作者必须放弃 CRAC 而该用某些处理特定问题的逻辑。CRAC/IRAC 是富有弹性的工具，帮助写作者建构一个法律的讨论部分，但又不强制写作者一定要依其完整版来写作。

分析过程应该注意语气的客观性，应当从正反两个方面对问题进行分析（analysis and counter-analysis），要时刻问自己：法官会同意我的分析吗？（Is it likely that the court will agree with what I have just written?）

此外，还应当注意"memo"的起承转合，重视过渡词汇（transitional words）的运用。如何将句子和句子以及段落和段落自然地连接起来是"memo"写作的基本要求。过渡突兀会阻碍读者的阅读和思考。法律英语中要掌握诸多语篇纽带的过渡词汇，如 therefore, consequently, in conclusion, on the other hand, conversely, arguably, in addition, finally, clearly, thereby, thus, shortly thereafter, contrast to, accordingly, notwithstanding, while, in any event 等一定要善加利用。

(8) 结论和建议(General Conclusion & Recommendation)

结论部分绝对不应成为"brief answer"的翻版或简单重复。二者的主要区别在于结论部分是对整个案件做出总体预测,包括对当事人的强项和弱项以及其胜诉可能性做全面的总结,并以此为依据给出相应的解决方案。该解决方案即为建议部分。而"brief answer"只是对每一个"issue"做简短的回答,它是零碎的、部分性的。

CONCLUSION

A motion to disqualify counsel under the advocate-witness rule is dependent on the facts, and thus Carter's probable testimony must be flushed out. Based on current information, it is likely that the court would find that Carter ought to testify. Our ability to successfully move to disqualify appears significantly greater under the prejudice test. If Carter ought to testify on behalf of his clients or might testify prejudicially to his clients, it might still be possible to move to limit his participation to pro se representation(自我代理). Moreover, it is possible that even his pro se representation could be barred, if not totally, then at least from trial advocacy.

建议部分要求给出解决问题的观点和思路,一般需要具体可行,还要说明如何扬长避短。建议应该是明确、直接和简明扼要的。比如说,可以直接提出这样的建议: To avoid litigation, Suzhou Co. should not discharge Mr. Workman.

一般来说,需要就下列问题给出建议:

- What do you recommend as a result of the analysis and conclusion you have presented?
- What do you think are the next steps?
- Should a suit be filed?
- Should further investigation be undertaken?
- Should further research be taken?

本部分介绍的是"office memo"一般的主体构成,有的"office memo"中可能因其具体需要会增加"table of contents"、"table of authorities"、"appendix"等。

Samples

Imagine that an attorney from the fictitious state of Calzona drafted the following office memorandum using only authority from the Calzona Supreme Court. Study the memorandum and consider the questions that follow it.

MEMORANDUM
TO: Susan Elias
FROM: James Nelson

RE: **Enforceability of Julie Week's Promise to Act as Guarantor for Loan Obligation; File 06-127**
DATE: August 16, 2013

I. ISSUE

By stating that he would refrain from demanding payment from Borrower on a loan obligation until he "needs the money", did Lender state a promise that provided consideration for Guarantor's promise to pay the obligation in the event that Borrower failed to pay on demand?

II. BRIEF ANSWER

Probably yes. Although the Lender's promise arguably is illusory, it probably satisfies the consideration requirement by committing the Lender to a performance, subject only to economic events not entirely within the Lender's control.

III. FACTS

One of our regular business clients, Julie Week (Guarantor), asserted the following facts in an interview.

On December 15, 2012, Guarantor's cousin, Don Caslin (Borrower), purchased a used Mercedes Benz sports coupe from a private owner, Thomas Beatty (Lender), for $20000. In a self-financing arrangement, Borrower paid $8000 on delivery and agreed in writing to pay the remainder of the purchase price in 12 monthly installments of $1000 each, beginning January 1, 2013.

From January to June 2013, Borrower paid Lender a total of $6000 in monthly installments. In late June, however, Borrower suffered unusual losses in his private business, and he failed to pay the installments due on July 1 and August 1. After Lender threatened to sue for the return of the automobile, Guarantor and Lender entered into a written agreement (the Guarantee Agreement) designed to give Borrower time to recover from his temporary financial difficulties. Dated August 5, 2013, the Guarantee Agreement refers to the agreement between Lender and Borrower as the "Credit/Sale Agreement," and it contains the following statement of mutual obligations:

1. Lender will refrain from asserting his claim against Borrower and from demanding payment on the Creit/Sale Agreement until Lender needs the money.
2. In the event that Borrower fails to pay all amounts due under the Creit/Sale Agreement upon demand by Lender, Guarantor will pay those amounts immediately and will pay further installments as they become due under the Credit/Sale Agreement.

On August 25, 2013, Lender demanded payment from Borrower, and Borrower explained that he could not yet pay. On September 2, 2013, Lender demanded immediate payment of $3000 from Guarantor; he also stated that he expects either Borrower or Guarantor to pay the remaining three installments as they become due on the first of each month.

We do not yet have any evidence that Lender engaged in fraud during formation of the Guarantee Agreement or that he did not in fact have a "need" for the money on August 25. You have asked me to analyze the question whether the Guarantee Agreement is unenforceable on its face for lack of consideration.

IV. DISCUSSION

Lender's promise to refrain from asserting his claim and demanding payment until he "needs the money" arguably is illusory. If so, Guarantor's promise is not supported by consideration and is unenforceable.

An enforceable contract requires a bargained—for exchange in which a promisor exchanges his own promise for a returned promise or performance. *Smith v. Newman*, 161 Calz. 443, 447, 667 P.2d 81,84 (1984). The requirement of an exchange is not satisfied if one party gives only an illusory promise, which does not commit the promisor to any future performance. *Atco Corp. v Johnson*, 155 Calz. 1211, 627 P.2d 781 (1980).

In *Atco Corp.*, the manager of an automobile repair shop purportedly promised to delay asserting a claim against the owner of an automobile for $900 in repairs. Specifically, he promised to forbear from asserting the claim "until I want the money". In exchange, a friend of the owner promised to act as guarantor of the owner's obligation. *See id.* at 1212, 627 P.2d at 782. The word "want" stated no legal commitment because it permitted the manager at his own discretion to refuse to perform any forbearance at all. Because the manager incurred no obligation, the guarantor's promise was gratuitous and unenforceable. *See id.* at 1213-14, 627 P.2d at 782-84.

On the other hand, even if a promisor leaves open the possibility that the promisor will escape obligation, the promise is valid if the promisor does not have complete control over the events on which the promisor's obligation is conditioned. *Bonnie v. DeLaney*, 158 Calz. 212, 645 P.2d 887 (1982). In *Bonnie*, an agreement for the sale of a house provided that the buyer could cancel the agreement if the buyer "cannot qualify for a 30-year mortgage loan for 90% of the sale price" with any of several banks listed in the agreement. Id. at 213, 645 P.2d at 888. In enforcing the agreement against the seller, the court distinguished *Atco Corp.* on the ground that the word "cannot" referred to the buyers' ability to obtain a loan rather than to his desire. Because his ability to obtain a loan was partly controlled by events and decisions outside his control, the promises in the sale agreement were non-illusory and binding. *See id.* at 214-15, 645 P.2d at 889-91.

Our client's case probably is more nearly analogous to *Bonnie* than it is to *Atco Corp.* Lender's promisor to forbear until he "needs" the money appears to condition the length of his forbearance on financial events that are at least partly outside his control. As long as his income and expenses create no need for the money, Lender has a commitment to forbear from demanding payment.

To convince a court to draw an analogy to *Atco Corp.* rather than to *Bonnie*, we should argue that the word "need" refers to a subjective perception of deprivation that is inseparable from one's desires. Lender arguably can control his financial needs through his personal spending decisions, subject only to his own discretion.

Unfortunately, the analogy to *Bonnie* is stronger because financial needs are almost certainly controlled partly by external factors. Lender's promise probably is not illusory.

V. CONCLUSION

The promises stated in the Guarantee Agreement appear to satisfy the consideration requirement, because Lender assumed a legal obligation by promising to refrain from asserting his claim and demanding payment until he "needs" the money. Unless we discover other serious defects in the Guarantee Agreement, Guarantor appears to be obligated to pay, and her defenses will not be worth litigating. We should urge Guarantor to settle Lender's claim, and we should try to persuade Borrower to indemnify Guarantor and to assume responsibility for further payments.

Questions:

a. Did the substantive labels assigned to the parties serve as helpful reminders of the respective roles of the parties, or would you have retained the parties' last names as less distracting references?

b. Does the statement of facts include any facts that you would omit or summarize further? Does it omit any important facts to which the author likely had access?

c. Identify the parts of the "Discussion" section that illuminate the issue, discuss the legal standards, analyze the facts, and state a conclusion.

d. Do you agree with the author's analysis? Does it adequately explore both sides of the dispute? Is it too pessimistic?

Chapter 8

Structuring Legal Writing: The CRuPAC Formula

▶ 1. Introduction

During your years in law school, you will learn an incredible amount of information. Torts, civil procedure, contract law and many other subjects will occupy you for years. Becoming an effective lawyer, however, requires more than just knowledge of the law; in order to succeed in both school and practice, you must learn to write like a lawyer. The ability to explain your legal analysis clearly and persuasively to clients, coworkers and judges is one of the most important skills you will develop as a young lawyer. Accordingly, here we want to help you develop the critical skills of legal advocacy.

In this chapter, we begin with the basic building block of legal writing: the paragraph. Each paragraph or section of your legal analysis should be designed to answer a specific question logically and effectively. Simply put, the goal is to apply the law to the facts of the case at hand and to arrive at a clear conclusion. The organizational method that we recommend here, called CRuPAC, is not only way to structure legal analysis, but it is useful and of particular value to those students who are new to legal writing.

Although we will discuss using CRuPAC to organize a paragraph of legal analysis, keep in mind that a single CRuPAC may take the form of one or several paragraphs, depending on the complexity of the legal issue at hand. After all, good legal writing should still observe the basic tenets of good writing generally, and a paragraph should not be so long that it becomes unwieldy.

▶ 2. Using CRuPAC

CRuPAC is an acronym designed to reflect the basic structure of a section of legal writing. It stands for Conclusion, Rule, Proof, Application and Conclusion, and it is meant to provide a framework for your analysis of a legal issue. When crafting a section of legal analysis, first state your conclusion. Second, state the legal rule upon which you based your conclusion. Third, prove the rule by providing appropriate citation to legal authority. Fourth, apply the rule to the specific fact pattern that you are analyzing. Typically, this application will require you to compare the facts of your case to the facts of the case or cases from which you derived the rule. Finally, you should close with a brief restatement of the legal conclusion that you articulated at the beginning of the paragraph.

(1) Leading with Your Conclusion

Most novice legal writers follow a similar pattern: first set out the legal and factual premises and then draw conclusions from them. The idea that a paragraph should begin with a conclusion may appear strange at first glance. However, busy attorneys, judges and clients are pressed for time and do not want to hunt for your conclusion under layers of legal analysis. Therefore, legal writers should articulate their conclusions at the beginning of each paragraph or section.

Leading with a conclusion also requires you to think through the entire paragraph before you write the first sentence. Your conclusion should be a succinct statement of the result of your legal analysis. In a predictive memorandum, a conclusion statement predicts the likely legal resolution of a specific issue or explains how the law applies to the case at hand. Examples of both these types of conclusion statements, taken from the Sample Memorandum in Appendix C, appear below:

> **Sample conclusion statements from a predictive memorandum:**
> "The court will probably find that Schmidt established minimum contacts with Illinois sufficient for the court to assert specific personal jurisdiction over her."
> "Schmidt's posting satisfies each prong of the Calder effects test."
> "Schmidt 'expressly aimed' the posting at Illinois."
> "Schmidt caused foreseeable harm to Baird in Illinois."
>
> (Sample Memorandum, Appendix C)

Note the different types of conclusions in the examples above. The first conclusion answers the broad question of whether Schmidt has established sufficient "minimum contacts" with Illinois so that the exercise of personal jurisdiction over her is proper. This conclusion is appropriate because it is directly reponsive to the question posed by the assigning attorney in this case. The next three conclusion statements answer narrower sub-questions about whether particular elements or tests for establishing personal jurisdiction are satisfied. When you write your own conclusion statements, be sure that they are properly tailored to answer the legal issue or issues in question, however broad or narrow they may be.

Finally, it is sometimes helpful to know how *not* to begin a paragraph of legal analysis. Below are some common mistakes that new law students should work to avoid:

Common mistakes to avoid in conclusion statements:
- Stating a general principle of law without applying it to your case:
"The First Amendment to the U. S. Constitution guarantees the right to freedom of speech."
- Describing the history of a legal principle:
"In Massachusetts, the exclusionary rule was first recognized in *Commonwealth v. Ford.*"
- Stating a central fact without rendering an opinion on its legal consequence:
"The accused did not intend to take the jacket from the store without paying for it."

Your conclusion sentence should connect the facts to the law. Each of the preceding three conclusions fails to do that, by omitting either the applicable law or the facts of the case at hand. A good leading sentence will make a conclusion about the connection between the two.

(2) Articulating the Rule

Next, state the rule upon which you relied immediately after your conclusion. Often, your rule will be derived from the cases that apply a relevant statute or that state an applicable common law principle. In the following example, the author of the Sample Memorandum concluded that "Schmidt caused forseeable harm to Baird in Illinois". To support this conclusion, the author provides a rule statement explaining how courts determine whether a defendant caused forseeable harm in a state:

> **Sample rule statement:**
> [Rule]: In Illinois, to satisfy the third prong of the effects test, a defendant must cause harm to the plaintiff in Illinois that the defendant knows is likely to be suffered in Illinois.
>
> (Sample Memorandum, Appendix C)

Note that the foreseeable harm rule here has two major requirements: (a) the defendant caused harm to the plaintiff in Illinois, and (b) the defendant knew that harm was likely to be suffered in Illinois.

(3) Providing Proof of the rule

At a minimum, you must provide proof of your rule by citing the authority from which you took the rule. When providing a rule derived from a statute or opinion, you must cite the statute or opinion you used. This citation serves two very important functions: (a) it tells the reader that your rule is supported by legal authority you cited when deciding whether or not to accept your conclusion. We will talk more about assessing the relative persuasiveness of authorities.

While citation of a legal authority is always necessary in many instances, it is not sufficient proof of a rule. Often, you should also provide a brief description of the relevant facts and disposition of the cited case or cases. Alternatively, you may need to include a detailed description of additional cases to explain sub-rules, exceptions or a judicial gloss on the primary rule. In that case, the rule-proof component of your CRuPAC alone could span two or more paragraphs.

Merely providing a case citation as your proof of rule, unless the rule is both clear on its face and well-established, is usually inadequate for two reasons. First, without the facts and disposition, a holding is just words. Courts may say one thing and do another—showing *how* courts apply a legal principle to a set of facts is what gives that principle practical meaning. Second, without the facts, it is difficult to determine how the precedent cited may be applied to the facts of your case. Remember, however, that the proof should include only the facts relevant to the issue you are analyzing. Do not attempt to summarize all the facts of the issue.

The Sample Memorandum in Appendix C provides many examples of detailed rule proofs. Building on the same sample CRuPAC analyzing foreseeable harm, note this time how the author provides extensive proof of the rule in the form of case citations and discussion of key facts and context:

> **Sample proof of Rule:**
>
> [Rule Proof]: *Euromarket Designs, Inc.* v. *Crate & Barrel Ltd.*, 96 F. Supp. 2d 824, 835 (N. D. Ill. 2000). The court in *Jackson* found that the brunt of the harm from the allegations of steroid use did not occur in Jackson's home state because he had a national reputation. *See* 406 F. Supp. 2d at 896. The *Jackson* court distinguished *Calder*, noting that "because the entertainment industry of which [Jones] was a part was centered in California, she experienced the most severe harm in California." *Id.* Other jurisdictions have found that the brunt of the damage done to a plantiff's personal (as opposed to professional) reputation occurs where she resides. *See*, *e.g.* *Zidon*, 344 F. Supp. 2d at 632.
>
> (Sample Memorandum, Appendix C)

Note here that the author, after providing us with the general rule and a case citation to support it, dives into the case law. She explains how the holding from different cases and jurisdictions fit together to provide us with a more detailed understanding of the scope of the rule.

While the example above uses textual explanations of the relevant holdings, at other places in the Sample Memorandum, you will notice that the author uses parenthetical expalanations of holding in her rule proofs. Explanatory parentheticals can be efficient and effective to briefly summarize a relevant holding, but they are best used when a detailed comparison of the facts of the case with the one at hand is unnecessary. If a case requires significant discussion or if it is central to your analysis, you typically should not use a parenthetical to describe the case.

(4) Application to Your Facts

Applying existing laws to a new set of facts is one of the practicing lawyers' most important skills. In a legal memorandum or brief, this part of the analysis explains why the conclusion that was stated at the beginning of the paragraph or section is the correct one. Returning again to the Sample Memorandum in Appendix C, note how the author follows the proof of rule section by applying the rule to the facts at hand:

> **Sample application section**:
> [Application]: Baird specifically alleges that Schmidt's actions have caused him in Illinois by damaging his reputation, causing emotional distress, and impairing his earning capacity, see Compl. ¶¶ 35–37, allegations that the court will accept as true. Though Baird is seeking jobs nationally, he has taken grants from foundations and the federal government, and has traveled frequently for business, Compl. ¶¶ 10–11, Schmidt Aff. ¶ 6, Schmidt will have difficulty convincing the court that Baird has a national reputation analogous to that of Jackson, who was a well-known professional athlete. However, even if the court accepts Schmidt's argument, Baird has nevertheless experienced "the most severe harm" in the forum where he lives and works. Baird's career and marriage are centered in Illinois. See Compl. ¶ 10. Because of the fallout from the posting, his wife forced him to move out of his Illinois home, Compl. ¶ 24, and his Illinois employer suspended him without pay, Compl. ¶ 27.
>
> (Sample Memorandum, Appendix C)

The application section of the paragraph requires significant thought. You must compare and contrast the cases you cited with your own case. Argument by analogy to precedent, also called analogical reasoning, is a key tool in the lawyer's arsenal for predicting the outcome of a new set of facts under the law. To master this tool, you will need to explain how the facts at hand could lead to a similar outcome or how certain facts may distinguish your client's case from past cases, leading to a different outcome.

It is very important that you make your analogies explicit; do not expect your reader to connect the dots by him or herself. Instead, tell your reader *exactly* how the cases you describe are similar to or different from the facts of your case. In the example above, note how the author directly contrasts Schmidt's experience with that of the plaintiff in the *Jackson* case. Below, you will find another example of the analogical reasoning from the Sample Memorandum, this time focusing on comparing the evidence in Schmidt's case with the evidence in prior cases where Illinois was the "focal point" of the relevant online posting:

> **Another example of reasoning by analogy**:
> Schmidt exhibited a similar intent to "particularly and directly target" Illinois with her posting on lovehimorleavehim.com. Like the posting in *Miraglia* and *Zidon*, Schmidt's profile page makes clear that Illinois was the "focal point" of her statements. Schmidt's entire profile page was exclusively concerned with the conduct and reputation of an Illinois resident. See Baird Ex. A. Moreover, Schmidt's profile page mentioned numerous Illinois persons and places in addition to Baird, including the University of Chicago (Baird's employer in Illinois), Baird's wife (a resident of Illinois), and the Latin school (Baird's wife's employer in Illinois). See Baird Ex. A. Schmidt also listed Illinois as one

> of the relevant locations for her posting, and users may search the profile pages on the website by their listed geographic locations, Compl. at ¶ 17.
>
> (Sample Memorandum, Appendix C)

When reasoning by analogy, do not forget the importance of policy arguments. Just as you can compare or contrast the facts in previous cases with the facts in your case, you can also compare the applicability of underlying policy argument. For example, imagine a court suggested in a prior opinion that its ruling on behalf of an injured employee was motivated in part by the desire to ensure swift and certain compensation for injured workers. If you represented an injured employee seeking workers' compensation, you would likely to want to argue that the court's policy rationale in the earlier decision is equally applicable in your case. This skill is particularly important in instances where your research has not turned up any cases with facts similar to yours. At that point, your ability to analyze the central policy concerns in factually dissimilar cases in the same area of law, and to apply those policy concerns to your case, can make all the difference.

(5) Reasserting Your Conclusion

The basic unit of legal analysis ends with a short restatement of your conclusion. This statement will usually be shorter than the sentence with which you began the CRuPAC and it can often be more conclusory, although some writers prefer to reverse that order by providing shorter initial conclusions and more comprehensive final conclusions. In either case, the purpose of this conclusion is essentially to remind your reader what conclusion is properly drawn from the preceding application of the rule to the facts, and to signify that you have dealt with that particular issue and will be moving on to another issue in the next section.

Returning once more to the Sample Memorandum in Appendix C, we can now see the completed CRuPAC in its entirety.

Putting the CRuPAC together:

[Conclusion]: Baird felt the brunt of the harm caused by Schmidt's posting in Illinois. [Rule]: In Illinois, to satisfy the third prong of the effects test, a defendant must cause harm to the plaintiff in Illinois that the defendant knows is likely to be suffered in Illinois. [Rule Proof]: *Euromarket Designs, Inc. v. Crate & Barrel Ltd.*, 96F. Supp. 2d 824, 835 (N. D. Ill. 2000). The court in *Jackson* found that the brunt of the harm from the allegations of steroid use did not occur in Jackson's home state because he had a national reputation. *See* 406 F. Supp. 2d at 896. The *Jackson* court distinguished *Calder*, noting that "because the entertainment industry of which [Jones] was a part was centered in California, she experienced the most severe harm in California." *Id.* Other jurisdictions have found that the brunt of the damage done to a plaintiff's personal (as opposed to professional) reputation occurs where she resides. *See, e.g., Zidon*, 344F. Supp. 2d at 632.

[Application]: Baird specifically alleges that Schmidt's actions have caused him harm in Illinois by damaging his reputation, causing emotional distress, and impairing his earning capacity, see Compl. ¶¶ 35–37, allegations that the court will accept as true. Though Baird is seeking jobs nationally, he has taken grants from foundations and the federal government, and has traveled frequently for business, Compl. ¶¶ 10–11, Schmidt Aff. ¶ 6, Schmidt will have difficulty convincing the court that Baird has a national reputation analogous to that of Jackson, who was a well-known professional athlete. However, even if the court accepts Schmidt's argument, Baird has nevertheless experienced "the most severe harm" in the forum where he lives and works. Baird's career and marriage are centered in Illinois. *See* Compl. ¶ 10. Because of the fallout from the posting, his wife forced him to move of his Illinois home, Compl. ¶ 24, and his Illinois employer suspended him without pay, Compl. ¶ 27. [Conclusion]: The Court will thus likely find that the primary effects of Schmidt's posting were felt in Illinois even if Schmidt's statements did harm Baird's job prospects across the country.

(Sample Memorandum, Appendix C)

▶ 3. A Final Note on The CRuPAC Formula

Although we refer to CRuPAC as a formula in this chapter, we do not mean to suggest that the elements of CRuPAC are inflexible. When looking at the Sample Memorandum in Appendix C, you may have noticed that some of the CRuPACs are significantly longer than others or are structured a little differently from one another. In a perfect world, legal issues would all be simple enough to fit each part of the CRuPAC in a single paragraph in order.

However, the law is rarely so simple, so do not be alarmed if your CRuPACs span multiple paragraphs in a section.

Always bear in mind that the purpose of legal writing is to communicate clearly to the reader your conclusions and analysis. We recommend CRuPAC as the best way to accomplish this goal, and your legal writing will benefit from its application. Although in time you may wish to deviate from the CRuPAC system, you must know the rules before you can break them. Mastering CRuPAC is well worth the effort.

Chapter 9   Identifying and Synthesizing Rules

▶ 1. Introducion

Rules are a common feature in our lives. The rules of the road tell us how to drive our cars. Rules of a game or sport define the limits of acceptable actions. Even mathematical and scientific formulas are rules that help us solve complex problems. In the legal world, a rule is a statement of the law on a given topic that, when applied to a set of facts determines the legal result. In a way, legal rules are similar to mathematic formulas; they tell us what outcome a particular set of facts or variables should produce in the context of that rule or formula. If the facts satisfy the rule, then the legal outcome should be X. If the facts fail to satisfy the rule, then the legal outcome should be Y.

When a lawyer approaches a new set of facts, he must determine which legal rules are applicable to those facts before he can predict the likely outcome of the case or advocate effectively for his client. Through his research, he endeavors to find the relevant rule or set of rules within his jurisdiction that will control his case. The ability to take a case or series of cases and to derive a rule that you can apply to the facts at hand is one of the most important skills you will develop as a lawyer. Mastering the skill of rule synthesis also will pay dividends throughout your legal career.

This chapter will give you the tools you need to pinpoint and define the rule from a case or set of cases. We first outline the different types of rules that you are likely to come across in your research. Next, we discuss the hierarchy of authority; that is, the relative persuasive value of different sources of rules. We then focus on finding the rule in a particular case.

And finally, we walk through the process of synthesizing a rule statement from a collection of related case laws.

▶ 2. Types of Rules

In US judicial system, rules come from a variety of sources and take many forms. Federal and state constitutions, statutes and regulations contain countless rules that courts must interpret. In addition, many rules in common law system are judge-made and derive from prior judicial opinions.

A regulation prohibiting smoking within fifteen feet of a building is easy to understand and apply. Other more complex rules may have multiple elements, one or all of which must be satisfied in order for the rule to apply. For example, a theft statute might criminalize the taking of another's property *without* permission and *with* the intent of converting the property to the taker's use. In other words, you would need to establish both the absence of permission *and* the presence of intent to convert property to satisfy the statute. A vandalism statute, on the other hand, might criminalize defacing, damaging, *or* destroying someone else's property. A vandal could violate that statute in any one of the three ways and still face prosecution.

Some of the most complex rules take the form of multi-factor test and balancing tests. For example, a state court trying to determine whether a worker acted as an employee or an independent contractor at the time of her injury may apply a multi-factor test, considering such factors as the amount of skill required for the job, the length of time involved, the supplier of tools, the method of payment, and the beliefs of the parties. With multi-factor tests, typically no one factor is controlling and the court will look to the weight of the factors considered in context. Similarly, balancing tests ask the court to weigh one factor (or set of factors) another to determine the correct legal outcome. In the due process context, for example, courts may need to weigh a defendant's interest in additional process against the burden that additional process might impose on the government.

No matter what the type of rule you are dealing with, be alert to possibility of exceptions. In a statute or regulation, watch out for critical words like "unless" or "except". Exceptions to common law rules may be less obvious, but a thorough search of the relevant jurisdiction's case law should reveal whether or not judges have developed any exceptions to the rule in question.

▶ 3. Hierarchy of Authority

(1) Binding Versus Persuasive Authorities

In order to determine which rules will govern your case, you must pay careful attention to the source of the rule. "Binding" or "mandatory" authorities are those that all lower courts and administrative bodies in a jurisdiction must follow. For example, the United States Supreme Court's decisions on federal law are binding on all courts. "Persuasive" authorities may carry a great deal of weight because of the authoritativeness of the author, but a court need not follow them. For example, a judge sitting on the U.S. Court of Appeals for the First Circuit might find an opinion written by Judge Posner from the Seventh Circuit to be very persuasive, but the judge is not bound by an opinion from another circuit.

In the Sample Memorandum provided in Appendix C, the writer analyzes a personal jurisdiction issue for a case in the United States District Court for the Northern District of Illinois. Accordingly, she cites binding decisions from the U.S. Supreme Court and the Seventh Circuit Court of Appeals. In addition to these binding authorities, the writer also draw upon persuasive, factually similar cases from other jurisdictions, including the Fifth Circuit Court of Appeals and the United States District Court for the Northern District of Texas. Though persuasive, these cases do not bind the Northern District of Illinois, no matter how similar the fact patterns are.

The following paragraphs briefly outline which sources of case law are binding on the various levels of state and federal courts. Keep in mind that individual state rules may differ, so you should always double-check the rules of your jurisdiction before tackling your research.

State Courts: On matters of state law, lower state courts are bound by the decisions of the intermediate appellate court for their area (or all state intermediate courts, depending on the rules of the state) and the highest court of the state. Intermediate state courts are bound by the highest court of the state, but they are normally not bound by the decisions of other intermediate courts. The highest court of the state is bound only by its own precedent on questions of state law. This is known as the principle of *stare decisis*, which is a presumption against disturbing legal matters that have already been decided by the court. Of course, courts sometimes decline to follow *stare decisis* and instead choose to overrule outdated or poorly reasoned precedent. Finally, on issues of federal law, all state courts are bound by the decisions of the United States Supreme Court.

Federal Courts: On questions of federal law, federal district courts are bound by decisions of the court of appeals for the circuit in which they are found and by Supreme Court decisions. Federal courts of appeals are bound by the decisions of the United States Supreme Court and by their own past precedent under the principle of *stare decisis*. Federal district courts and courts of appeal may look to the decisions of other districts or circuits, but these are not binding. The Supreme Court is bound only by its own precedent under the principle of *stare decisis*. And when a federal court interprets state law—for example, in a civil suit with diversity jurisdiction—it is bound by the decisions of the highest court of the state in question.

(2) Evaluating Persuasive Authorities

Even when an opinion with a favorable rule statement is not binding on your court, it may be useful as a persuasive authority. However, not all persuasive authorities are created equal. When deciding whether to bring a non-binding opinion to your reader's attention, you must keep in mind the hierarchy of authority, or the relative persuasiveness of a given source of law. Highly persuasive case law in a factually similar case may push a judge to accept your rule statement, while indiscriminate use of unpersuasive authorities may cause the court to question the strength of your research and analysis. Accordingly, learning how to evaluate the relative weight of the authorities you encounter is a critical part of learning how to find and compose well-supported rule statements.

Binding case law is of course the gold standard at the top of the hierarchy while unpersuasive authority is at the bottom. In order to determine the relative persuasiveness of non-binding authorities, considering the following factors:

The Identity of the Issuing Court: Even if the particular decision is not binding on your court, it is likely to carry more persuasive weight if it came from a higher source. For example, decisions of the Federal Courts of Appeal can be very persuasive, even where they are not binding.

The Date of the Decision: Recent decisions are more persuasive than older decisions.

The Power of the Court's Reasoning: Not all opinions are models of legal reasoning and writing. Well-thought out and well-argued decisions are likely to be more persuasive than cursory and poorly supported opinions.

The Centrality of the Language to the Holding: Legal reasoning that is used to determine the outcome of the case is more persuasive than a legal proposition mentioned only in passing or in a hypothetical. Words that are part of an opinion but not a necessary part of the court's holding are called *dicta* and have less persuasive value.

The Number of Judges: Unanimous opinions are more persuasive than divided opinions. When dealing with opinions with pluralities or with judges concurring or dissenting in part, be very careful that you understand the precedential value of the portion of the opinion you are using.

The Subsequent Treatment of the Opinion: Some opinions are often cited in other decisions or in secondary sources. Opinions that are often cited may have strong persuasive value, even where they are not binding.

The Reputation of the Authoring Judge: Some judges are highly respected and opinions written by these judges may carry weight even if they are not binding.

▶ 4. Finding the Rule

Once you've familiarized yourself with the different types of rules and the relative persuasiveness of their sources, the next step is to distill an explicit rule statement from those authorities that you can use in your analysis. Be sure not to confuse the rule, which is a generalizable principle that can be applied to other fact patterns, with the holding, which is specific to the facts of the case. If you are lucky, the opinions you use will state a rule explicitly and apply that rule in a straightforward manner. However, in many instances, you will be required to derive an implicit rule from the court's analysis. This section will focus on how to identify both explicit and implicit rules.

Explicit rules will often contain language signaling that the court is stating a rule. For example, the court will refer to the principle as a rule or a test, or will number the parts of the rule to clarify the definition. Explicit rules are, as expected, relatively easy to identify.

Just be sure to read the opinion carefully so as not to be fooled by a statement that sounds like a rule statement but is not actually the rule the court is applying. If they are concisely written, explicit rules are also easy to quote for quick use in your CRuPAC rule statement.

Implicit rules, on the other hand, must be derived from an often extensive discussion. As you read the case, you will have to pay close attention to the facts, the discussion and the holding to determine the rule that the court is applying. Because you cannot excerpt the court's entire discussion in your CRuPAC, you will have to articulate your own version of the rule.

Example of an explicit rule:

"A three-pronged test has emerged for determining whether the exercise of specific personal jurisdiction over a non-resident defendant is appropriate: (a) the defendant must have sufficient 'minimum contacts' with the forum state, (b) the claim asserted against the defendant must arise out of those contacts, and (c) the exercise of jurisdiction must be reasonable."

—*Zippo Mfg. Co. v. Zippo Dot Com, Inc.*, 952 F. Supp. 1119, 1122-23 (W. D. Pa. 1997).

Example of an implicit rule:

"The allegedly libelous story concerned the California activities of a California resident. It impugned the professionalism of an entertainer whose television career was centered in California. The article was drawn from California sources, and the brunt of the harm, in terms both of respondent's emotional distress and the injury to her professional reputation, was suffered in California. In sum, California is the focal point both of the story and of the harm suffered. Jurisdiction over petitioners is therefore proper in California based on the 'effects' of their Florida conduct in California."

—*Calder v. Jones*, 465 U. S. 783, 788-89 (1984) (citations omitted).

Possible articulation of the implicit rule:

A state can properly exercise personal jurisdiction over a defendant where the defendant's allegedly tortious conduct was focused on that state and resulted in harmful effects in that state.

▶ 5. Synthesizing Rules

Try as you might, it is not always possible to find a single case that clearly lays out the current state of the law on your issue. As a result, you may need to draw on multiple cases to get a full picture of the applicable law in your jurisdiction. Synthesizing a rule from multiple cases will require you to pay careful attention to the interplay between opinions. Is a later case refining the meaning of a rule in an earlier case or resolving a tension in the case law? Is it simplifying a rule or articulating a new one? In order to understand the legal landscape, you must know if an opinion is explicitly or implicitly overruling past case law or building on and refining a prior rule. Accordingly, you should pay careful attention to the dates the opinions were issued and the way in which they discuss prior case law.

Often, you will come across rules that each provides incomplete articulations of the law in your jurisdiction. In this situation, you must first determine if each rule is still a good law by using a citator as the Shepardized function on Lexis or the Key Cite function on Westlaw. If you find that each of the complementary rules is still a good law, your rule statement should reflect a complete statement of the law based on a combination of the rules. For example, imagine that Case A establishes a two-factor test, and Case B emphasizes two additional, different factors. In this situation, you will want to tell your reader first that different cases have emphasized a number of different factors, and then list those factors provided in the two cases. Note that a complete rule statement may require using more than one sentence and more than one citation.

In other instances, one case may provide an important judicial gloss on the rule of prior cases, perhaps expanding or narrowing an earlier rule. You will then need to synthesize a comprehensive rule statement using two or more cases. Imagine that Case A says that in order to prove constructive eviction, a tenant must show that the landlord's actions had a permanent character. Case B held that two days was insufficient to prove permanence, and Case C held that two months was more than sufficient. A complete rule statement should identify the permanence requirement and explain that while the court has not specified the precise amount of time required, it is between two days and two months.

Sometimes, multiple cases that are binding on your client's case will have rules that seem to be in conflict. To make sense of the conflict, you need to know whether the tension signals that an earlier case was overruled or whether the outcome of the cases can be harmonized. Are the two different rules simply alternate ways of stating a similar proposition? Are the two cases distinguishable based on differences in the facts? Or was a policy concern that motivated the court's decision in the first case not applicable to the second?

The Sample Memorandum in Appendix C provides a good example of an instance where the conflicting case law must be harmonized in creating a complete rule. In the Memorandum, the author used her research skills to locate several Seventh Circuit cases interpreting the Supreme Court's *Calder* "Effects Test". However, the three main cases dealing with this issue include rule-like statements that are apparently in tension with one another. See if you can identify the potential tension(s) in the case law excerpted below.

> **Case excerpts seemingly in tension:**
>
> ***Wallace***: The Supreme Court in *Calder* did not make the type of dramatic change in the due-process analysis of *in personam* jurisdiction advocated by the plaintiff. Rather, the so-called "effect" test is merely another way of assessing the defendant's relevant contacts with the forum State. The defendant must still "purposefully avail [himself] of the privilege of conducting activities within the forum State, thus invoking the benefits and protections of its laws". The forum State cannot hale the defendant into court "solely as a result of 'random', 'fortuitous', or 'attenuated' contacts". Jurisdiction is proper "where the contacts proximately result from actions by the defendant *himself* that create a 'substantial connection' with the forum State".
>
> ***Indianapolis Colts***: In *Calder* as in all the other cases that have come to our attention in which jurisdiction over a suit involving intellectual property (when broadly defined to include reputation, so that it includes *Calder* itself) was upheld, the defendant had done more than brought about an injury to an interest located in a particular state. The defendant had also "entered" the state in some fashion, as by the sale (in *Calder*) of the magazine containing the defamatory material. Well, we have that here too, because of the broadcasts, so we needn't decide whether the addition is indispensable.
>
> ***Janmark***: [T]here can be no serious doubt after *Calder* that the state in which the victim of a tort suffers the injury may entertain a suit against the accused tortfeasor. [*Indianapolis Colts*] applies this understanding to a case with many features in common with Janmark's ... Applying the principle that there is no tort without an injury, we held that the tort (if there was one) occurred in Indiana rather than Maryland. If operating a football team in Maryland can be a tort in Indiana, inducing the customers of an Illinois firm to drop their orders can be a tort in Illinois—and given 735 ILCS 5/2-209(c), whether or not it is a tort in Illinois, it is *actionable* in Illinois.

How would you describe the tensions among these three cases? *Wallace* seems to require something more than the basic Effects Test, in the form of a "substantial connection". *Indianapolis Colts* also states that some form of "entry" into the state may be a requirement for personal jurisdiction to be exercised. *Janmark*, on the other hand, suggests that the tortious effects of the defendant's act are enough to satisfy the requirements for personal jurisdiction. The following excerpt from the Sample Memorandum demonstrates one possibility for resolving this tension.

> **Synthesizing a rule from cases in tension:**
>
> On its face, the "entry" requirement of *Indianapolis Colts* appears to conflict with *Janmark's* unqualified assertion that anyone who intentionally causes a tortious injury in Illinois is amenable to suit there. *See Caterpillar, Inc. v. Miskin Scraper Works, Inc.*, 256 F. Supp. 2d 849, 851-52 (C. D. Ill. 2003) (describing the tension between *Janmark* and *Indianapolis Colts*). However, since *Janmark*, district courts in the Seventh Circuit have resolved this linguistic discrepancy by equating the "entry" requirement of *Indianapolis Colts* with "express aiming". *See, e.g., id.* at 852; *Richter v. INSTAR Enters. Int'l*, 594 F. Supp. 2d 1000, 1010 (N. D. Ill. 2009); *Nerds on Call, Inc. v. Nerds on Call, Inc.*, 598 F. Supp. 2d 913, 917, 919 (S. D. Ind. 2008).
>
> In other words, regardless of whether it is characterized as "entry" into the forum State or as "intentional and purposeful tortious conduct ... calculated to cause injury in the forum State", *Caterpillar*, 256 F. Supp. 2d at 851, there must be some "express aiming" at the forum State in order for a court to assert personal jurisdiction over a non-resident tortfeasor. *See id.* Thus, despite the varying language used, courts in the Northern District of Illinois have all adopted some version of the traditional three-factor "effects test".
>
> (Sample Memorandum, Appendix C)

In this example, the author was able to explain the relationship between seemingly contradictory case law in the first paragraph and to synthesize an appropriate rule statement in the second paragraph. She draws from useful persuasive authorities to highlight a trend in the case law and now, armed with her synthesized rule, she is ready to begin crafting a strong legal memorandum that will apply the relevant rule to the facts of her case.

Chapter 10: Approaching a Case and Developing a Core Theory

At their core, lawyers are advocates for their clients. When a lawyer takes on a client's case, she must persuade a neutral third party that the client is in the right. Thus, the ability to write persuasively is one of the most important skills that a lawyer can develop. Before you can begin writing an effective and persuasive brief, however, you must learn how to approach a case and develop a core theory.

A core theory, or theory of the case, is central to the persuasiveness of a brief. A core theory is a concise theme or story that weaves together the favorable legal, factual and policy elements at play in the case. A strong core theory will motivate the court to find for your side.

Core theory can be a difficult concept to grasp, because law students and young lawyers often want to make arguments based solely on the legal standards they found during their research. However, your experiences in other first-year classes should illustrate the importance of core theory. First-year law students quickly discover that very similar facts applied to the same legal standard can, at times, lead to radically different outcomes. It is often the core theory of a case—the policy considerations, factual distinctions, and sometimes simple common sense—that derives judges' decisions. Therefore, development of a core theory that is compelling, logical and appealing is one of the most important parts of legal advocacy.

▶ 1. Facts in Context

Facts can lend themselves to more than one interpretation. It is your job to examine the facts critically to discover which ones are important to your case. A strong presentation of the facts, with effective organization and the appropriate tone, will help persuade the court to view the case from your perspective.

For example, consider the fairy tale of *Goldilocks and the Three Bears*. From the bears' perspective, the important facts are that they came home to find their house a wreck, their food eaten, and a potentially dangerous intruder passed out in their bedroom—an open and shut case for breaking and entering, robbery and trespass. From Goldilocks's perspective, she was lost, starving, and could barely make it to the door of the bear's home. To avoid starvation, she entered the house, ate some porridge and passed out in a bed only to be terrified by the arrival of angry bears. She had no malicious intentions and only did what she needed to survive. Creating a cohesive story is central to developing a strong core theory. For the bears, the story was of a grievous violation to the sanctity of their home by a shameless stranger. For Goldilocks, the story was one of fear, desperation and necessity.

As you review your case, try to view the facts from different perspectives. In order to make a compelling argument, you need to develop an appropriate and credible narrative that will inform your core theory. In *Bell-wesley v. O'Toole* ①, Rebecca Bell-wesley gave birth to a healthy baby boy, Frank. Dr. O'Toole viewed the birth as a benefit to the Bell-wesleys, who had tried unsuccessfully to conceive a healthy child over a period of years. For the Bell-Wesleys, however, the conception and birth of their son violated a conscious choice they had made to forego having children and irrevocably changed their lives. These alternate views of Frank's birth will influence the way each side addressess the legal issues.

Finally, remember that this process is dynamic. Your understanding of the facts will

---

① It is a fictional appellate case used in a law school moot court program, *Bell-Wesley v. O'Toole*, the techniques apply across a range of situations. In *Bell-Wesley v. O'Toole*, Rebecca and Scott Bell-Wesley sued Dr. Stephen O'Toole for damages arising from his negligent performance of a vasectomy and sperm count. These injuries included damages suffered by the Bell-Wesley during Rebecca Bell-Wesley's subsequent pregnancy and childbirth, as well as future damages associated with the cost of raising their healthy son to majority. Although the trial court found that Dr. O'Toole had been negligent, the court limited the Bell-Wesleys' recovery to out-of-pocket costs, pain and suffering, emotional trauma, lost earnings, and loss of consortium for a total damage award of $ 100,000. The Bell-Wesley appealed the decision on the grounds that the trial court improperly failed to recognize child-rearing costs as an element of damages in a wrongful pregnancy action. The Court of Appeals for the state of Ames affirmed the trial court's decisions of law. You are brought into the problem after the Ames Supreme Court has granted certiorari. Damages in a wrongful pregnancy action are an issue of first impression in the State of Ames. Thus, whether you represent Dr. O'Toole or the Bell-Wesleys, you must solve the legal problem using the facts, policy, case law, and creativity. You should use *Bell-Wesley v. O'Toole* to understand the principles we will suggest in the following chapters.

often change, sometimes radically, over the course of the research and writing process. A clear understanding of the facts is always essential, but the context and importance of many of the facts will be influenced by your research and by reflection on your core theory. In other words, the relevance of otherwise-favorable facts will largely depend on the core theory that you present. Be prepared to re-evaluate your interpretation of the facts in order to make the strongest arguments for your client.

▶ 2. Developing a Core Theory

Work on the core theory begins upon an initial review of the facts and continues throughout the process of legal research and writing. Consider first the non-legal reasons that justify a decision in your favor, such as policy implications or factual distinctions. Many times, other cases discussing your issue will address such considerations. Then, as you research, incorporate the law into your core theory. The legal aspect of your core theory is important for two reasons: it contains the policy and other arguments that you can make, and it becomes in itself a part of the story that you tell.

Developing a core theory takes time and thought. As you review the record and your research, try to structure your ideas around a theory that captures the essence of your case. Next, try articulating your core theory into a narrative of several words or sentences. It is a challenging step, but the process of distilling your ideas into a few sentences ultimately voill prodllce the strand that connects your ideas into a cohesive whole. Note that in many cases, you may not want to write your theory verbatim into your brief; rather than use your theory explicitly, it is often more effective to incorporate it implicitly, using it as an internal guidepost to orient you as you weave together the facts, law and policy into a compelling narrative.

When you first receive an assignment to write a brief, you may wonder where to begin and how to approach your case and develop a core theory. The following list of tasks, explained in more details below, will help direct and focus your work:

A. Read the entire record.

B. Creat a chronology or diagram of what happened.

C. Identify the issues on appeal and begin developing a core theory.

Chapter 10   Approaching a Case and Developing a Core Theory   ‖   159

    D. Determine and consider the standard of review.
    E. Connect the facts to the legal issues.
    F. Formulate arguments.
    G. Refine your core theory.
    H. Reread the record, consider opposing arguments and core theories, and adjust your core theory as needed.

(1) Read the Entire Record

An initial review of the entire record will help you understand what is happening both legally and factually. Your job on appeal is to examine the lower court's decision closely to dertermine the precise legal grounds for the opinion, the potential issues of reversible error, and the available arguments for your position. Because the record is your only source of factual information, a mastery of the record is a prerequisite to an effective appeal.

As you read the record, be aware of the varying importance different courts will attach to different types of facts. Typically, the appellate court will give the greatest weight to the lower court's findings of fact. Remember also that the extent to which the appellate court defers to the lower court's findings of fact depends on the standard of review.

A comprehensive understanding of the record will also facilitate the initial stages of your research and help you plot a logical course of action. By rushing to research without carefully considering the intricacies and nuances that inevitably exist in the record, you may find yourself exploring many unproductive or irrelevant paths. Your research will be more efficient and effective from the outset if you begin with a solid understanding of the case.

(2) Create a Chronology or Diagram of What Happened

The items in a record are not necessarily arranged in the order in which events actually happened. By preparing a chronology of events, you will have a comprehensive understanding of the factual setting. This is important because many cases depend equally on what happened and when it happened.

For example, in *Bell-Wesley v. O'Toole*, one of the important issues is whether Frank's birth harmed Rebecca Bell-Wesley's career goals. You need to examine the trial record of Rebecca's testimony to learn about her potential lost career opportunities. A reading of the record shows that Rebecca became pregnant after she accepted a new position at the attorney general's office. This is very important, because if Rebecca had become pregnant before she accepted the new position, she would be less likely to succeed in her claim for damages.

In any court record, some facts will be missing or ambiguous. Once you notice which relevant facts are missing, look more closely at the record to see if these facts are hidden or if they can be resonably inferred from available facts. Facts inferred from the record should become a part of your argument. If you choose to include them in the Statement of Facts, however, be sure to preface them in a way that signals to the court that you are making an inference. The misuse of facts or the use of inference as undisputed facts will reduce your credibility with the court.

(3) Identity the Issues on Appeal and Begin Developing a Core Theory

On appeal, the legal issues are narrower and more defined than at the trial court level. At the trial level, both parties raise all the legal issues they think are at stake, but at the appellate level, the court certifies only particular questions of law for appeal. It is very important that both parties brief only those issues within the scope of the appeal. For example, the court certified a question on the last page of the *Bell-Wesley v. O'Toole* record telling the parties to focus on the issue of whether the cost of raising a child should be included in the damages calculation for a wrongful pregnancy action. (See Appendix D, pg. 285 – 286.) This tells the parties that they need not and should not raise the possible negligence arguments concerning the vasectomy, as that issue is beyond the scope of the appeal.

The best places to discover the relevant legal and factual issues on appeal are in the lower court opinion and in the certified questions. They discuss the reasons for the court's ruling and frame the issues for appeal. In *Bell-Wesley v. O'Toole*, the judge's fifth and sixth conclusions of law point you to the two vital issues on appeal: can the court award damages for a wrongful pregnancy, and what items should enter into the calculation of these damages? See Record, Appendix D, pg. 282.

In other cases, the opinion and record will not frame the issues so clearly, but a careful reading of the relevant documents should provide you with the important legal issues for the appeal. In non-moot-court contexts, the narrowing of the issues may be considerably more difficult and may itself require a significant amount of legal research. In that case, be sure that you are selective when choosing the issues for appeal. If you think you have nine different grounds for appeal, you are often served best by selecting and focusing only on your

Chapter 10   Approaching a Case and Developing a Core Theory || 161

strongest handful of arguments so as not to dilute the strength of your appeal.

In narrowing the issue, you will also be presented with policy implications that should prompt refinement of your core theory. *Bell-Wesley v. O'Toole* presents several policy issues:

- Should society allow parents who keep a child to force the doctor who negligently performed a vasectomy to pay for all of the costs incurred in raising a child?
- What impact would such payment have on a child?
- What impact would such payment have on the medical profession?
- What impact would such payment have on other potential plaintiffs and defendants in a similar situation?
- Would a decision against the doctor make it more difficult for patients to find other doctors willing to perform a sterilization procedure?
- Should the court be concerned about the possible expressive function of an order treating a child's healthy birth and life as a cause for damages?

You need not, and probably cannot, determine all of the legal and policy issues presented by the case before beginning your research. Indeed, in the course of your research, you should continuously refine issues and consider new ways of looking at the case. Legal research is a dynamic process of defining issues, developing arguments and finding support for those arguments.

(4) Determine the Standard of Review

When a higher court reviews a lower court's ruling, the standard of review defines the extent of the actions that the appellate court can take with respect to the issues before it, as well as the deference it must give the lower court's decisions. In some instances, the standard of review will be mentioned in the record. When the standard of review is not stipulated, you should research it as you would any other legal issue.

Potential standards of review range from "do novo" review to "abuse of discretion" or "clearly erroneous" review. An appellate court nearly always reviews conclusions of law de novo, which means that it shows no deference to the lower court's decision and reviews the legal issues as if they were being considered for the first time. Findings of fact are often reviewed for clear error, which means that the appellate court does not disturb the lower court's decision unless it strongly believes the lower court clearly made a mistake. Thus, it is important to distinguish the lower court's legal findings from its factual findings.

The standard of review will have implications for both your written and oral advocacy. For example, if you are arguing that there was an abuse of discretion at the trial court level, you likely will want to focus your arguments on the facts. On the other hand, if the court is reviewing a question of law de novo, you may wish to spend more time arguing the relevant law.

(5) Connect the Facts to the Legal Issues

By this point, you will have a solid grasp of what actually happened and of the legal considerations. You should begin to synthesize the two sets of information. The key to an effective argument is your ability to relate the legal arguments to the specific factual situation. This synthesis requires you to look critically at the information in the record to determine which facts matter the most to your arguments. In the *Bell-Wesley* case, not every fact concerning Dr. O'Toole's performance of the vasectomy is relevant. The important facts for the appellants are those that demonstrate how the wrongful pregnancy of a child can be a real injury to the parents. For example, evidence of the economic and emotional costs to Rebecca and Scott Bell-Wesley can be used for this purpose.

Highlight these important facts when making your legal argument. The best arguments not only state the relevant law persuasively and accurately, but also show how the facts of the present case fit the law. The stronger your connection of the facts to the law, the more persuasive your brief will be.

The process of relating the facts to the law helps you continually redefine the factual and legal issues. There is a symbiosis between the facts and the legal issues. The important facts are determined by the legal issues, and the legal issues are determined by the facts of the case. Neither can be evaluated in a vacuum and both must be considered and reconsidered in light of the core theory.

(6) Formulate Arguments

The arguments you make in your written and oral presentation to court answer the questions raised in your case and stated in the "Questions Presented" section of your brief, which we will discuss in more detail in the next chapter. These arguments are the reasons the court should find in your favor. Formulating arguments is a process, involving analysis of precedent and analogical reasoning. You should prepare arguments in conjuction with your

Chapter 10   Approaching a Case and Developing a Core Theory   ‖   163

development of a core theory, as a strong core theory will link all parts of your legal argument together into a cohesive and compelling whole.

Do not be afraid to rely on your intuition. If you had to explain to a parent or friend why you think your client should win, what would you say? Begin thinking about how you can best frame the arguments for (and against) the position you wish to support. Consider also the following list of types of arguments to help you generate ideas:

- Arguments based on common-sense notions of justice and equity;
- Arguments based on authorities and case law that you have already studied;
- Arguments by analogy or comparison to other cases and situations with which you are familiar;
- Arguments typically associated with the subject matter of the case;
- Arguments based on the potential consequences of the court's decision; and
- Arguments drawing upon public policy.

This list is a starting point. During the course of your research, you will discover new arguments to add to the list and reject some as frivolous. As you can see, many of the argument considerations are also those that drive the core theoryies.

(7) Refine Your Core Theory

After identifying the legal, factual and policy issues and generating a series of useful arguments, try to unite them into a core theory. Any case can give rise to a number of alternative core theories. Here are some examples of what a core theory could look like for the appellant and appellee in *Bell-Wesley v. O'Toole*:

Sample Core Theories:

Appellant: The Bell-Wesleys's wrongful pregnancy claim is indistinguishable from any other medical malpractice claim. They must be compensated for all of the injuries flowing from Dr. O'Toole's repeated negligence, and that includes the substantial cost of raising a child to adulthood.

Appellee: The Bell-Wesleys wanted a healthy child and they got one. Rather than being injured by their son's birth, the Bell-Wesleys benefited from it, as would any parents fortunate enough to have a healthy child in our society.

---

(8) Reread the Record, Consider Opposing Arguments and Core Theories, and Adjust Your Core Theory as Needed

Anticipating the opposing side's arguments gives you a window into your opponent's mind and an opportunity to identify weaknesses in your own arguments and core theory. How you use your opponent's arguments in your brief is part strategy and part personal preference. At this stage, however, you should strive to brainstorm all of the other side's best theories and arguments.

Next, consider whether you want to make changes to your core theory in response to your opponent's likely arguments. Imagine you are a defense attorney and that you are defending a teacher who you believe was wrongly accused of assaulting a child. You might be tempted to build your defense around the theory that the crime is incompatible with your client's nature; he is a respected teacher who has dedicated years of his life to educating children and would never harm them. However, if the record includes previous, similar allegations against your client, you could anticipate that the prosecutors will respond by arguing that the defendant is a predator who continues to use his position as a teacher to prey upon children. As a result, you will want to think of an alternative theory of the case that will be less susceptible to reversal and thus less damaging to your client.

Another advantage in preparing for all of your opponent's viable arguments is that even if not all of them are raised in the briefs, the judge or judges might raise them during oral argument. By anticipating counterarguments and preparing a response, you will be in better shape to respond persuasively to the judges' questions. Your repeated reading of the record will also position you well for both writing a brief and an oral argument. You may discover inconsistencies and omissions in the record as you become more familiar with it. The better you understand these problems, the better your ability to confront them. This step is probably the most tedious in the process, but it is important nonetheless.

* * *

A core theory brings together the law, facts and policy into a concise statement of why your client should win. A strong core theory appeals to the judge's intellect and common sense in a way that makes him or her want to side with your client. The best briefs combine comprehensive legal research, persuasive highlighting of the most favorable facts, and an intuitive statement of why that side should win. The approach laid out in this chapter will help you formulate a strong core theory and, ultimately, a compelling brief.

Chapter 11
How to Write an External Memo—a Brief

▶ **1. Introduction**

(1) The Purpose of a Brief

An advocate almost always submits her case to a court in written form. In appellate courts, these documents are called "briefs". A brief is a persuasive legal document designed to convince a court to rule in a party's favor. In trial courts, these documents are sometimes called "memoranda of law". Despite the similarity in title, memoranda of law differ substantially from the objective legal research memoranda. To avoid confusion, this chapter uses the term "brief" to refer to a persuasive legal document, regardless of the context in which it is submitted to a court. The sample briefs in *Bell-Wesley v. O'Toole* are written for submission to the Supreme Court of the State of Ames, an imaginary state supreme court. The same general principals of brief writing apply, however, to documents submitted to lower courts. A successful brief in either setting will draw upon the skills discussed in the preceding chapters, including performing legal research, synthesizing rules, developing a core theory, and structuring paragraphs of legal analysis.

A brief presents the advocate's view of her case's strongest arguments, authority and background material in a clear and assertive manner. A strong brief is well-organized, interesting, complete and reliable. An effective brief compels the court to rule in favor of the writer's party. The brief also serves as an aid to the court, frequently providing the foundation for a judge's decision and the resource for writing an opinion.

(2) Rules of the Court

Before beginning to draft your brief, be sure to review the rules of your particular court, be it moot or otherwise. Doing so prior to drafting will help avoid unnecessary shocks down the line. The rules will supply information about deadlines, page limits, format, and the sources you may consult. Follow them carefully. While these guidelines are usually included with moot court documents, you should be aware that "real-world" rules are set out both in national compilations, such as the Federal Rules of Appellate Procedure, and in local or circuit court rules.

(3) Outlining

After you have thoroughly researched the legal issues relevant to your case and reviewed the rules of the court, the next step is to outline your brief. It can be tempting to dive straight into the writing process, but time spent outlining pays dividends when it comes to writing a well-organized, persuasive brief. At a minimum, outline your argument section. This can help you think critically about how the parts of your argument fit together, recognize areas that require more research, and structure your brief in the most persuasive manner. You will also find that the writing process goes much faster if you take the time to outline first.

(4) Style

Good brief writing builds on the skills of good writing. The challenges of phrasing and structure still apply. Nonetheless, a brief is a persuasive piece of writing, and each element of your brief should work to convince the court to decide in your favor. In accomplishing this goal, a brief writer has discretion in selecting a particular writing style. Reasonable minds differ over what tone is the most persuasive. Some advocates are dispassionate, while others are more aggressive and adversarial.

No matter what tone you adopt, you should keep in mind these four basic principles:

1) Strategically select every word by analyzing its tactical value. For example, even choosing the names of the parties in the case can be significant. The overuse of "appellant" and "appellee" in a brief can be confusing to a reader who does not share your intimate understanding of the record. Instead, you should characterize the parties in a manner that will influence the reader's perception of them. For instance, you might try to evoke the reader's sympathy for a client by using a personal title while using a more formal title for an adversary. Regardless of the route you choose, you should be consistent throughout the brief.

2) Use the active voice. A forceful argument uses action verbs rather than passive forms of the verb "to be". However, keep in mind that you can downplay damaging facts and arguments by selectively and purposefully using the passive voice to minimize their impact.

3) Avoid needlessly complex language, including "legalese".

4) Avoid extended quotations. An impatient reader will skip lengthy quotations. Short quotations can be used to add variety or emphasis, but if there is no concise quotation, a paraphrase with a citation may be a better choice. Be sure to explain the relevance of the quotation; do not expect the court to figure out how it applies to your case.

(5) Editing

Some writers say that there is no good writing, only good rewriting. In any case, careful editing is an essential component of a good brief, and you must budget sufficient time to edit your brief before submission. True editing, however, is more than mere proofreading. Resist the temptation to become overly attached to your writing, and think critically about how the organization of your brief could be improved. Did you follow the CRuPAC structure? Is your analysis easy to follow? At the sentence level, look out for certain word patterns that can invariably be eliminated without any loss of meaning. The following are examples of such "throat-clearing" terms: "It can be argued", "It seems that", "Cases have clearly held", "It is beyond argument that", and "One might think that". Without such phrases, prose is much clearer, stronger and more direct. To bolster your credibility, also eliminate superfluous adverbs and adjectives where nouns and verbs will convey the same points. Be particularly careful to avoid typographical errors; careless mistakes compromise your credibility. Good form and attention to detail inspire the court's confidence in your research and analysis.

(6) Convention

There is no set formula for drafting a successful brief, but there are recognized conventions. This is not surprising, since writers of briefs have similar training and the common goal of persuasion. Creativity is important, particularly in crafting arguments, but it is best employed within the confines set by common practice and by the rules of your court. Accordingly, this chapter will introduce you to common brief-writing practices and the traditional components of a comprehensive appellate brief.

▶ 2. Parts of a Brief

A brief consists of several parts, each designed to convey a specific type of information. While brief writers sometimes add or omit parts depending on the particular case or court, most appellate briefs contain the following sections:

A. Title Page;

B. Table of Contents;

C. Table of Authorities;

D. Preliminary Statement;

E. Questions Presented;

F. Statement of Facts;

G. Summary of the Argument;

H. Argument;

I. Conclusion; and

J. Signature Block.

(1) Title Page

The title page of a brief sets forth the caption, which includes the name of the court, the docket number, the names of the parties and their procedural designations (e.g., "Plaintiff-Appellant"). In most state jurisdictions and lower federal courts, the original order of the parties is maintained in the case on appeal. The Supreme Court of the United States names the appealing party first. You should also include counsel's names, formal titles (e.g., "Attorney for the Appellee"), and the date and place of the oral argument in the lower right hand corner of the page.

(2) Table of Contents

The Table of Contents should list the components of the brief, including the Table of Authorities, Preliminary Statement, Questions Presented, Statement of Facts, Summary of Argument, Argument (including complete headings and subheadings), and the Conclusion, along with the page number on which each can be found.

(3) Table of Authorities

Here, the writer lists all of the authorities used and notes the pages where each authority is cited in the brief. The Table of Authorities demands great technical care. Citations must be accurate and complete, and must include all of the information required by *The Bluebook* and/or the local rules of the court. All page numbers, volume numbers, underlining, parentheses, brackets and spacing should be checked carefully before submitting a brief.

The list of citations is divided into at least three sections: "Cases", "Statutes", and "Other Sources". Arrange cases alphabetically. Sources under the "Statutes" and "Other Sources" categories should be subdivided by source type before being listed alphabetically. Under the "Statutes" section, the writer should include any constitutional provisions, court rules or administrative regulations that are cited in the brief, expanding the section heading as needed to reflect the additional types of sources cited. Any secondary sources should be placed under the "Other Sources" category, which can be further subdivided based on the types of sources used into "Restatements", "Treatises" and "Law Review Articles".

Note that the pages of the Table of Authorities, like the Table of Contents, are traditionally numbered separately from the body of the brief, and are paginated using lowercase roman numerals. As a result, Page "1" of a brief begins with the Preliminary Statement.

(4) Preliminary Statement

The Preliminary Statement, sometimes called "the Statement of the Case", introduces the court to the procedural posture of a case on appeal. It identifies the parties to the dispute and briefly describes the relevant procedural events leading up to the present case, including a short description of the decision and reasoning of the lower court. The preliminary statement presents the first opportunity for persuasion, so be sure to frame your statement in a compelling and succinct manner.

(5) Questions Presented

The function of the Questions Presented in a brief is similar to their function in a legal research memorandum. Unlike those in a memorandum, however, the Questions Presented in a brief aim to persuade the reader to adopt a particular conclusion with a careful balance of advocacy and accuracy. A judge's initial reaction to the merit of a motion or appeal is often based upon this formulation of what the counsel considers to be vital to her case. Like the brief as a whole, the questions must be simple, interesting, complete and reliable.

Sketching out the Questions Presented at the start of the writing process is useful because it forces the writer to frame and clarify the key issues. Some brief writers, however, prefer to save this task for last, after they have articulated their argument in detail. If you do elect to write your Questions Presented before your argument, be sure to review them afterwards to ensure you remain satisfied with them. Regardless of whether you write them first or last, you should take great care in crafting your brief's questions because the Questions Presented provide another important opportunity to present your version of the case.

a. Structure

The Questions Presented are placed at the beginning of the text in the order in which the corresponding arguments appear in the brief. Each question should be independent and require no reference to any point contained in a previous question. Although an argument may be complex, the questions should be clear and easy-to-read. Questions with many sub-clauses tend to be convoluted and should be avoided, as should wordy or overly long questions. A good rule of thumb is to keep each Question Presented under seventy-five words. However, you should not be afraid to use multiple sentences in a single Question Presented; a sentence or two of relevant factual background followed by a brief statement of the relevant law and then the question can make for a more effective and persuasive question.

b. Substance

The questions should suggest the answers the writer wants the court to reach. Put in another way, a reader should always be able to tell which side wrote a brief simply by reading the Question Presented. An effective Question Presented gently suggests that the court can reasonably rule in only one way—in the writer's favor. Be careful, however, not to irritate the court with overly biased questions that suggest by their stridency the inevitable counter-argument. To achieve this balance, questions should mesh important facts with the law that the writer wants the court to apply. It may be tempting to craft lofty, abstract questions of law, but you should resist the temptation and remember that fact-filled questions will help you impart some of the flavor of your argument to the reader from the very start.

Be careful in your questions not to assume the issue in dispute. For example, the question "Does an unreasonable search violate the Fourth Amendment?" assumes that the search in question was unreasonable. This question is poorly crafted, because the real issue is whether the particular search in the case was an unreasonable search. There is no question that if the search were unreasonable, it would violate the Fourth Amendment.

Finally, the Questions Presented should be answerable by either a "yes" or a "no". For purpose of symmetry, try to frame all of the questions in a brief so that they are answered the same way—either all "yes" or all "no"—in support of your position.

c. Sample Questions

Different advocates arguing *Bell-Wesley v. O'Toole* might draft the following Questions Presented:

(a) Is a doctor who negligently performs a vasectomy liable for the costs of raising a child when the husband subsequently impregnates his wife and they have an unplanned baby?

(b) Where a couple, after having several congenitally deformed children who died soon after birth, has a child conceived after an unsuccessfully performed vasectomy, and refused to abort, or give the child up for adoption, should the doctor who performed the vasectomy be held liable for all the costs of raising that child when the couple could well afford to have the child, and benefited from the doctor's negligence by receiving the healthy child that they had always wanted?

(c) O'Toole negligently performed a vasectomy and follow-up testing on Scott Bell-Wesley. As a result of O'Toole negligence, the Bell-Wesleys unexpectedly conceived and gave birth to a son, incurring the costs of his delivery and upbringing. Under fundamental tort law principles, individuals are liable for all injuries flowing naturally and foreseeably from their negligence. Should O'Toole be held liable for the full results of his negligence, including the extensive costs associated with raising a child?

The most effective question is the third one. It clearly suggests the answer the litigant wants the court to reach: "yes". It incorporates key facts of the case, such as the negligent sterilization, and uses phrases like "full results of his negligence" and "extensive costs" to set the tone for the subsequent argument. It also clearly identifies the core legal issues.

By contrast, the first question is not persuasive enough. The reader cannot tell which side the author represents. The use of "negligently" suggests she represents the couple, but the phrase "unplanned baby" is not favorable to the couple and the author does not lead the reader to any answer. Additionally, few facts are incorporated into the question. While a brief writer should strive for concise Questions Presented, this question is incomplete.

Complicated and difficult to follow, Question 2 errs in the other direction. Although it is clear the writer represents the doctor, the author uses too many clauses and is likely to lose rather than persuade her reader. While certain slanted phrases, like "the healthy child that they had always wanted" show promise, they are lost in the complexity of an unwieldy question.

A good brief should avoid overly simplistic questions, like Question 1, and confusing questions, like Question 2. Instead, seek a middle ground, as in Question 3.

(6) Statement of Facts

The Statement of Facts presents your view of what happened in the "real world" to bring this case into court. For example, each side in *Bell-Wesley v. O'Toole* informs the court about the couple's decision that Scott would have a vasectomy:

Sample Statement of Facts Excerpts:

The attorney for the Bell-Wesley writes:

The Bell-Wesleys made a conscious decision to forego having children. R. at 1. They made this difficult decision after they previously had given birth to three children, all of whom tragically died within six months of birth due to a genetic congenital disorder. Id. Their doctor, Defendant-Appellee Stephen O'Toole, advised the Bell-Wesleys that there was a seventy-five percent chance that any future child they conceived would suffer from the same lethal congenital disorder. Id. Based on O'Toole's advice and their fear of bringing another ill child into the world, the Bell-Wesleys chose to remain childless. R. at 1, 11. They did not adopt. See id. Instead, they devoted their lives to each other and to their careers. See R. at 3, 9.

(See Appendix E, pg. 289 – 290)

In contrast, the attorney for Dr. O'Toole writes:

On three occasions before the January 2011 birth of their son, the Bell-Wesleys attempted to start a family. R. at 1. Each time, however, Ms. Bell-Wesley gave birth to a sick infant that died within six months due to a fatal congenital abnormality. R. at 1. Dr. O'Toole accurately informed the Bell-Wesleys that there was a seventy-five percent chance that any child they conceived would suffer from the same abnormality. R. at 1. For the sole purpose of avoiding the conception of another sick child, the Bell-Wesleys decided to have Mr. Bell-Wesley sterilized. R. at 7.

(See Appendix E, pg. 298)

Note that both sides describe the same essential facts but use very different language. The Bell-Wesleys stress the "conscious decision to forego having children", while Dr. O'Toole emphasizes that the "sole purpose" of the decision was to avoid the "conception of another sick child". The authors cite the Record in the case throughout.

The Statement of Facts in a brief, unlike the Statement of Facts in a legal memorandum, should be persuasive rather than objective. Note that persuasive does not mean false or distorted. While the Statement of Facts in each sample brief tells the story from a different perspective, neither writer crosses the line into drawing unsupported conclusions, exaggerating, or misleading the court.

Both sides must present a complete and reliable, yet easy-to-understand and interesting, version of the facts of the case. To some judges, a fair yet persuasive Statement of Facts can be more dispositive than a carefully crafted Argument. After reading your Statement of Facts, the judge should want to interpret the law in your favor.

a. Choosing the Facts

Separate the relevant facts from the irrelevant ones in the record. Be careful, however, not to omit the most relevant facts supporting your opponent's position. A failure to disclose important, albeit unfavorable, facts is likely to impair your credibility with the court. Still, a good Statement of the Facts will do more than just summarize the record; it will shape the relevant facts into a narrative that interests the reader and favors the author's position.

Also make sure that your Statement of Facts includes every fact mentioned in your Argument; there should be no factual surprises buried in your Argument. To this end, make sure to reread your Statement of Facts after you have finished writing your Argument section to be sure that all necessary facts are included. While a seemingly obvious point, it is easy to recognize the importance of a particular fact while crafting your Argument but then forget to include it in the Statement of Facts once the Argument is finished.

b. Using the Record

Use only the facts found in the record or facts of general knowledge, which are subject to "judicial notice". You can use admissions by the other side as positive proof of a fact considered material. Regardless of the source, be sure to support your factual assertions with proper citations.

The creativity you demonstrate in presenting a persuasive fact must not extend to fabricating or exaggerating information. A judge will not let a fabricated "fact" slide by as a clever inference. All assumptions of fact must be firmly grounded in the record. Certain undeniable assertions, however, such as the fact that apples do not fall up, can be used without appearing in the record. Other information, like the conclusions of relevant sociological studies, can be used even though they are not part of the record as long as proper authority is cited.

Holes in the record can also prove useful in a brief. You can successfully use "negative facts" to buttress your position. Negative facts are facts that the other side can neither establish nor disprove, because they do not exist in the record. For example, the *Bell-Wesley v. O'Toole* record is silent on the issue of whether Scott and Rebecca ever considered adopting a child after learning that there was a high likelihood that any child they conceived would suffer a congenital birth defect. Nonetheless, in the appellants' brief, the author uses this negative fact to support a favorable inference:

Based on O'Toole's advice and their fear of bringing another ill child into the world, the Bell-Wesleys chose to remain childless. R. at 1, 11. They did not adopt. See id. Instead, they devoted their lives to each other and to their careers. See R. at 3, 9. (See Appendix E, pg. 289)

Do not be afraid to make effective use of holes in the record that can help shape a favorable presentation of the facts of the case.

c. Organizing the Facts

The organization of the facts is critical because how the judge views the facts will undoubtedly influence how she views the case. Every word in the Statement of Facts should be geared toward making the brief a better instrument of persuasion and a more complete and reliable resource. A chronological, carefully constructed narrative is often the most persuasive structure for telling the story of your case. Alternatively, you can try starting with the conflict or injury and later describing what preceded it. With either approach, remember these points:

- Use labels that appropriately characterize the parties.
- Use words with effective connotations for your argument.
- Never assume the reader has any prior knowledge of the case. Introduce the parties and avoid abbreviations with which the court may not be familiar.

d. Handling Adverse Facts

Glaring omissions of adverse facts central to the other side's case will decrease your credibility with the court and lessen the persuasive power of your brief. More strategically, omitting adverse facts also costs you the opportunity to mitigate the damage those facts can cause. Carefully disclosing adverse facts in the Statement of Facts thus serves the dual purpose of preserving your credibility with the court and allowing you to present otherwise damaging facts in the best possible light.

Downplay unfavorable facts by being strategic about how you present them. Consider using the passive voice to help dilute their force. You can also place damaging material in subordinate clauses of longer sentences or in the middle of a paragraph to minimize its impact. Once a harmful fact is mentioned, there is no need to emphasize it. For example, while an appellant needs to disclose that there was an adverse judgment below, she need not disclose that the district judge rejected each and every contention. Rest assured that the appellee will mention that. For another example, in Bell-Wesley v. O'Toole, the doctor's attorney minimized his client's negligence by saying Dr. O'Toole "performed a vasectomy" and "mistakenly informed" Mr. Bell-Wesley that he was sterile. On the other hand, the Bell-Wesleys' attorney used language like "botched the procedure" and "then compounded his surgical error" to characterize the same acts in a light favorable to his clients.

e. Separating Fact from Argument

Paint a persuasive factual picture, but guard against the temptation to cross the boundary into argument. The facts are used to support conclusions, but they must not be expressed as conclusions. For example, a Statement of Facts should not contain conclusions of laws such as "the defendant acted knowingly and recklessly". Instead, explain what the defendant did, allowing the court to reach its own conclusion that the defendant acted in that manner. The court should be left to draw the appropriate legal conclusion once you have provided the factual foundation. One exception to this rule—as demonstrated in the sample briefs—is that you may report the conclusions of law of the lower court(s) in a Statement of Facts for an appellate brief.

(7) Summary of the Argument

A one- or two- paragraph road map outlining the party's essential arguments is incredibly useful, particularly in complex cases. A good Summary of the Argument is clear and concise and contains few citations. You should also use the section to acquaint the reader with your core theory of the case. For example, the attorney for the Bell-Wesleys used her Summary of the Argument to stress her view that Dr. O'Toole's negligence should not be excused simply because one of the products of his negligence was a child. Rules governing the location of the Summary of the Argument vary by jurisdiction, so be sure to check your court's rules.

(8) Argument

The argument section comprises the majority of the brief. After considering legal precedent, policy, and the facts of the case, choose the strongest arguments to include in your brief. Discard weaker or less clear arguments because including them will dilute the force of your main points. Buttress your arguments with authority, and strive to anticipate, preempt, or rebut your opponent's core arguments and to distinguish opposing cases.

a. Argument Headings

Each argument begins with a complete sentence called an "argument heading". The heading should be a concise summary of the argument. The heading identifies the specific portion of the argument to be advanced in that section of the brief, and it is particularly important given the heavy caseloads many judges face. To create an effective heading, imagine that a judge only has a few minutes to scan through your brief and that she focuses on your heading alone. She should be able to understand and follow the general progress of your argument if your headings are crafted properly.

The argument headings should state affirmatively the resolution of the issues raised in the Questions Presented. An effective argument heading will identify the applicable law, the way in which the law applies to the facts of the case at hand, and the conclusion that follows from that application. A good rule of thumb is that if you could copy your heading into another brief and it would still fit, you have not sufficiently tailored your heading to the facts of your case. Of course, not every relevant legal or factual issue can fit in a heading, and headings should not be so long as to be difficult to read and understand. Argument headings are conventionally identified by roman numerals and comprised of bolded, single spaced, capital letters.

b. Subheadings

Subheadings may be used effectively to partition arguments, especially complex ones. When an argument is relatively simple, however, subheadings may interrupt the flow of the argument. Subheadings are identified by capital letters, while the text of the subheading itself typically uses lower case letters and is bolded.

> **Example of an Argument Heading and Subheadings:**
> I. THIS COURT SHOULD NOT AWARD THE APPELLANTS DAMAGES FOR THE COSTS OF RAISING THEIR NORMAL, HEALTHY SON TO MAJORITY
>   A. Frank's Birth Did Not Injure the Appellants Because Giving Birth to a Healthy Child Cannot Be an "Injury" B. Even if the Birth of Appellants' Son Constitutes an "Injury", Frank's Birth Did Not Cause a Compensable Economic Injury to the Bell-Wesleys Because They Sought Sterilization for Purely Non-Economic Reasons.

(See Appendix F, pg. 297)

The sample argument heading above identifies the legal issue of damages and the author's position. The subheadings describe how the law relates to the specific facts of the case: *because* the Bell-Wesleys sought sterilization for non-economic reasons, they suffered no legally cognizable injury. Furthermore, the subheadings neatly break the main argument down into its legal and policy components. Finally, the argument heading and subheadings are not bolstered by unnecessary adverbs or adjectives.

Depending on the complexity of a case's legal arguments, a brief may also incorporate additional layers of subheadings, typically marked by Arabic numerals. You should be careful not to make a brief's outline overly complex, but another layer of subheadings is useful if a particular subheading can be cleanly divided into substantial, independent sections. A judge should be able to read through the headings and subheadings of a brief and have a complete picture of the arguments.

   c. Standard of Review

An appellate brief should set forth the appropriate standard of review explicitly in the Argument section of the brief. The standard of review dictates how an appeals court must treat the findings of a lower court and guides the court's analysis. You should provide the Standard of Review for each Question Presented. Generally, an appeals court must defer to a trial court's findings of fact, disturbing them only if they are "clearly erroneous". However, an appeals court typically may make its own determinations on the law regardless of the trial court's decision. This is called "de novo" review.

This distinction between issues of fact and law is not always readily apparent, so consider your case carefully and be sure to research the standard of review for the particular cause of action involved. A case from the appropriate jurisdiction will usually clarify the standard of review. For example, in some contract cases, an appellate judge may make new findings on the interpretation of a contract term, but she should defer to the trial judge's assessment of oral testimony.

If the parties disagree about the appropriate standard of review, then the "correct" standard of review should be argued rather than merely asserted. Logistically, the standard of review may be included in the first paragraph of the first argument. Alternatively, it may be placed in a separate section between the Statement of Facts and the Argument. In some instances, you will want to present the standard of review in an argument subheading. The prominence of the standard of review in a brief will depend on how favorable it is to your side and whether it is a point of contention.

If the standard of review is favorable, you should use it to frame your arguments throughout the brief. For example, you may frame the Questions Presented or Argument headings in light of the standard of review. Similarly, an attorney for the appellee who won in the trial court will often stress the "clearly erroneous" standard. The appellant, however, will emphasize that no deference should be given to the trial court's interpretation of the law.

> Discussing the Standard of Review:
> The Bell-Wesleys' brief:
> Whether the Bell-Wesley family can recover the full cost of raising a healthy child as an element of damages in a wrongful pregnancy action is a question of law and thus reviewed *de novo*. See Lovelace Med. Ctr. v. Mendez, 805 P. 2d 603, 614 (N. M. 1991).
>
> (See Appendix E, pg. 291)

In the example above, the attorney for the appellants, the Bell-Wesleys, stressed that the appellate court need not follow the trial court's refusal to recognize a cause of action for wrongful birth. In contrast, the attorney for Dr. O'Toole downplays the standard of review for legal findings by keeping the discussion succinct.

d. Form of the Argument

The argument should follow the CRuPAC method. You should choose what legal issues to discuss so that they proceed in a logical order and mirror the structure that you have laid out elsewhere in your brief in your Questions Presented and Summary of the Argument.

e. Substance of the Argument

The argument musters facts and law to persuade the court to rule in your side's favor.

Do not devote long sections of the brief, for example, to the historical evolution of a current legal standard. This style is simply not persuasive to a court which must apply principles of law to the particular facts of the case. A skillful brief writer will attempt to incorporate direct reference to the relevant facts of the case into every paragraph of the argument.

Because unsupported assertions are not persuasive, you must provide citations to the cases and other authorities that give the court the tools to reach a particular decision. When properly used, authorities aid in convincing the reader to adopt the propositions asserted. The authorities with the greatest relevance (those most "on point") and the greatest weight should be cited. Cases with similar facts and issues are usually the most relevant, and decisions that bind your court have the greatest weight. Citing a variety of jurisdictions, however, may be useful to show that courts widely accept a proposition. Uncontested propositions of law, such as the definition of negligence, rarely require more than one authority in a citation.

While major cases should be discussed at appropriate length, others can be effectively summarized by using parentheticals. In some instances, the best way to use a case is to paraphrase the principle it stands for and follow that with a citation. However, an unelaborated or "bare" citation, giving only the case name and the reporter, will not often help the court. Parentheticals, abstracting the holding of the case or quoting critical language, aid the reader by explaining the relevance, similarity or difference of the cited case to the case at hand.

> **Example of an Explanatory Parenthetical**:
> The general rule in tort cases is that "a person has an obligation to exercise reasonable care so as to not cause foreseeable harm to another". Marciniak v. Lundborg, 450 N. W. 2d 243, 245 (Wis. 1989) (citation omitted) (holding that costs of raising child to majority may be recovered by parents as damages for negligently performed sterilization procedure).
>
> (See Appendix E, pg. 291)

While parentheticals can be useful, do not overuse them. Your most important cases will often need more extensive treatment than a parenthetical provides. An advocate might include a paragraph explaining how the legal principle in an opinion governs the issue before the court, or why it must be distinguished. In either situation, the relevant facts from the case before the court should be emphasized for their similarities or difference to the facts of the opinion cited.

For the sake of reliability and completeness, you should also cite important cases standing *against* the propositions advanced in your brief. The ethical rules of most jurisdictions require citation of controlling contrary authority. However, you can lessen the effect of contrary authority in two ways: (a) by distinguishing your case based on the facts or the rationale, or (b) by undermining the rationale of the contrary authority. The first method allows you to argue that the contrary authority should not be controlling in your case because the facts are too dissimilar or because the rationale that motivated the court's decision in that instance does not apply to your case.

The second method, undermining rather than distinguishing a contrary authority, requires a more direct attack on the contrary court's reasoning and should be used with care. When cited as adverse to the proposition raised, a contrary authority should be signaled with "*but see*". Citation of contrary authority shows thoroughness, enhancing your credibility with the court. It also negates the damage done by the adverse cases because it gives you the opportunity to shape the way the court interprets the contrary authority.

Once you have discussed the legal precedent that supports your position and dealt with any binding, contrary authorities, be sure to survey the case law for any relevant policy arguments. Roughly speaking, any argument that the outcome benefits the public interest falls into this category. Some brief writers place public policy arguments under separate headings. Often, however, they appear in a separate paragraph under a particular argument heading. For example, the attorney for Dr. O'Toole makes a public policy argument about the effect of awarding full damages. According to the writer, deciding in Dr. O'Toole's favor furthers the public policy against unreasonable liability for physicians. When analyzing and interpreting precedents, try to determine what policy rationales underlie them and the implications of those rationales for your case.

Finally, an advocate who urges a change or modification of the law as it has developed in cases should include reference to scholars or other authorities that have also argued for such a change. This may make the court more "comfortable" with departing from precedent or navigating uncharted territory. (For examples of using law review articles, see the sample briefs in Appendix E, pg. 293 and Appendix F, pg. 300.)

f. Preemption and Rebuttal of Arguments

A good appellant brief should anticipate the appellee's best counterarguments and respond to them, explaining why those arguments ultimately fail. Similarly, effective appellee briefs must address the appellant's best arguments. Avoiding or concealing the difficult points in your argument may leave their resolution to the court without the benefit of your guidance. Instead, try to show the logical deficiencies of your opponent's argument, demonstrate how the facts fail to support their legal conclusion, or point out the unfortunate consequences that would flow from a decision for the other side.

Regardless, the tone of each brief must remain affirmative and not convey a defensive posture. Blanket statements characterizing the other side as wrong are useless and may detract from your credibility. When responding to counterarguments, however, be careful not to simply summarize the other side's arguments. This wastes space and puts the writer in a purely defensive position. You should counter the arguments effectively and succinctly, and watch that you do not cross the line into making your opponent's arguments for him.

A respondent or appellee should use any opportunity to review the brief of the moving party, or appellant, before she files her own brief. Because the time between filings is usually short, the respondent must not wait until she has received the appellant's brief before she begins researching and preparing her arguments. Once she has the appellant's brief, however, the respondent should use it to highlight the weaknesses of the moving party's arguments. Still, a point-by-point refutation is rarely the ideal format for a respondent's brief. Independent arguments are stronger and more persuasive.

g. Arguing in the Alternative

For some legal arguments there are "fall-back" positions. If the court fails to agree with one side's main position, the court can turn to the advocate's alternative argument. For example, the Bell-Wesleys' attorney argues that based on the law and facts, the Bell-Wesleys should receive full child-rearing damages. In the alternative, she argues that if the court does not award full child-rearing damages, the court should award full recovery offset by the value of the emotional benefits the Bell-Wesleys receive from Frank. (See Appendix E, pg. 294)

Arguing in the alternative should never force you to compromise your core theory. If an alternative argument contradicts your core theory, you might choose to omit it from the brief and reserve it for oral argument. If the judges are not receptive to your main argument, then you may raise the alternative one.

(9) Conclusion

The brief ends with a section entitled "Conclusion", which clearly states the remedy or relief sought. A summary is usually *unhelpful* here. Because it is difficult to determine which components of an argument a court will find persuasive, emphasizing one or the other in summary may undermine the persuasive effect of the winning argument. Also, page limits may require you to leave out details.

What you should always do in a Conclusion is tell the court what you want it to do—to reverse or affirm the lower court's judgment in an appeals case, or to hold a certain way in a district court case. Always remember that your job as an advocate is to achieve a certain outcome for your client. Make sure that you clearly articulate at the end of your brief what you want that outcome to be.

(10) Signature Block

Different courts have different requirements for the Signature Block, but typically you can expect to include a closing line (e.g., "Respectfully submitted"), the typed names of the brief's authors, their addresses, their signatures, and the date of submission.

▶ 3. Sample Briefs: *Bell-Wesley v. O'Toole*

Sample briefs for the appellants and appellee in the case of *Bell-Wesley v. O'Toole* appear in Appendix E and appendix F, respectively.

As you know from reading the sample Record in Appendix D, this case involves a wrongful pregnancy action. On appeal, the legal issue is whether or not the Bell-Wesleys should receive damages for the costs of raising their son Frank, who was born after Dr. O'Toole negligently performed a vasectomy and sperm count.

The brief for Dr. O'Toole argues that the Bell-Wesleys should not receive any child-rearing costs. It cites supportive legal authority, stressing that the reason the Bell-Wesleys obtained sterilization, to avoid the birth of another sick baby, means they cannot recover for any costs beyond the prenatal period. It also reviews public policy reasons for this position.

The attorney for Dr. O'Toole recognizes that the Bell-Wesleys will argue that they should receive full costs, but that the court could still apply the equitable "benefit rule" to offset damages by the amount of the benefit the Bell-Wesleys receive from having their son

Frank. Therefore, the brief for Dr. O'Toole contests that the "benefit rule" is inapplicable when the intangible benefits of a child are involved. Nonetheless, the writer maintains that even if the court adopts the "benefit rule", it should still find that the benefits to the Bell-Wesleys outweigh the costs.

The brief for the Bell-Wesleys argues that they should receive all damages flowing naturally from the negligence of Dr. O'Toole. Their side has far less legal authority upon which to rely, but they have many convincing policy arguments. The Bell-Wesleys also argue in the alternative that if the judge refuses to award full damages because of the benefit bestowed on them through the birth of a healthy child, the judge should apply the offset rule (providing them with full recovery less the amount of the benefit they derive from the child).

Take a moment now to read through both briefs to get a better idea of what the tips and tools presented in this chapter look like in practice.

Chapter 12

Introduction to Oral Argument

The oral argument is the culmination of your efforts as an advocate. Although only used sparingly in trial courts (e.g. summary judgment motions), oral argument plays an important role in appellate advocacy and has become a historic part of American advocacy. In the early years of the Supreme Court, arguments lasted for hours, if not days. Although increased caseloads have caused modern courts to reduce the availability and length of arguments, oral argument still presents a valuable opportunity to convince the court of the merits of your case and to dispel any doubts particular judges may have after reading the briefs.

Presenting an effective oral argument is different from brief writing in a number of ways. First, it is an interactive effort requiring spontaneous responses to the judges' questions. Second, it takes place under strict time limits, so you must prioritize arguments even more radically than in the brief. Finally, the effectiveness of oral argument depends in large part on the attorney's physical presence and speaking style. Despite these differences, the oral argument is a logical extension of the brief, building on its foundations. If you are prepared to defend your core theory and are familiar with the supporting case law and the record, you will be able to answer the judges' question confidently. As in brief writing, diverse styles and approaches may be equally successful. There is no right way to frame an oral argument. There are, however, some basics to master and tips to help you succeed. Accordingly, in this chapter you will find information on how to respond to questions, and how to present yourself effectively.

In appellate litigation, our model for this chapter, the structure of an oral argument is simple and direct. The appellant (or "petitioner") rises first to introduce the case and to explain why the court should reverse the lower tribunal's decision. The appellee (or "respondent") then argues her side of the case, defending the lower court's decision. Finally, the appellant may choose to rebut her opponent's assertions. Throughout the argument, the judges are likely to interrupt counsels' presentations with questions. Attention to the judges' concerns and creative responses to any hypothetical situations they may pose are often the most important features of a good oral argument.

▶ 1. Preparing for Oral Argument

In preparing for oral argument you should focus on both substance and style. Carefully study the record, relevant authorities, and arguments that will enable you to defend your brief and to answer the judges' questions. Practice delivering your argument so that you become comfortable with public speaking and the phrasing of your case. This practice will also help ensure that you are not distracted or trapped by questions, that you can transition effectively between different parts of your argument, and that you emphasize your key points. At the same time, you should avoid rote memorization and canned, mechanical responses. A good oralist is both prepared and flexible, inventing appropriate responses on the spot when necessary and being sensitive to the personalities and concerns of the judges.

Now that you know some of the qualities of an excellent oralist, you may wonder where to begin your own preparation. The following is a step-by-step outline of basic techniques to help you prepare your oral argument.

(1) Study the Record and Authorities

Success in oral argument requires detailed knowledge of the record. It is important to understand, and have an identifiable point of view on the events giving rise to the cause of action and the facts and issues discussed in the lower court's opinion. The court is more likely to trust other aspects of your argument if you have a solid command of the record, whereas an incomplete knowledge of the record will only hurt your credibility in the eyes of the judges.

Likewise, studying the cases included in both sides' briefs is a vital step in your argument preparation. Judges often use the oral arguments to determine which cases should guide their decision and whether the parties' arguments based on precedent are consistent.

You should prepare to analogize your case to helpful precedents and distinguish it from harmful ones. Writing short case abstracts and indexing the record is both a helpful study process and can enable easy referencing during the argument. However, these notes should not become a crutch. An advocate who can discuss the cases and facts without frequently referring to notes will have a more natural dialogue with the judge, and thus, may be more successful.

In addition to considering the authorities cited in both briefs, you may also want to consider authorities that were not raised previously. Depending on the rules of the court (some courts restrict the use of cases not cited in the briefs), new authorities that were not presented in your brief sometimes may be raised orally before the court. You may use this opportunity to correct what the judges perceive as ambiguities or flaws in the original brief.

(2) Analyze the Arguments

Not every aspect of your brief can make it into your oral argument. You will need to make strategic choices as to which arguments are most important and amenable to oral presentation. Choosing effective arguments for oral presentation often means separating the wheat from the chaff of an argument. Before you do so, try to break down the arguments presented in both parties' briefs. A fresh look at the arguments will give you a complete background against which to make strategic and tactical choices concerning both substance and style. Although there may be many reasons to find for your client, your job is to emphasize what you see as the most important reasons, the most compelling reasons, or those reasons that may have the most influence on the court. The following guidelines can aid you in selecting and refining arguments.

a. Use Your Core Theory

The demands of oral argument illustrate the importance of having a pithy, convincing core theory—a one or two sentence explanation of the essence of a party's position. Both a good brief and a good oral argument will stress a central theme, approaching that theme from different angles based on the relevant facts, law and policy. Yet in oral argument, you should be prepared to express your core theory even more simply and memorably than in your brief. Accordingly, when organizing your argument, keep in mind the relationship between each assertion and your core theory. Try to weave your points together with your core theory to craft a cohesive argument that the judges will remember. With your core theory as your guide, you should be able to place your answers to the judges' questions in context and to rebut your opponent's arguments. In the end, know that you are not shackled to your brief during oral argument and that you are free to focus on the points you choose. Thus, while you may have spent a relatively small portion of your brief addressing public policy concerns, you are free to emphasize those concerns in your argument if you feel it will persuade the judges and fit with your theory of the case.

b. Review and Prioritize Specfic Arguments

Working from the briefs, you should outline and review the specific arguments made by both parties. This may require some new thought about which arguments are the most convincing or the most controversial. The limited time frame of oral argument means that not all of a party's arguments will be developed fully. Keeping in mind the desired results of the litigation, rank arguments in terms of their importance in achieving those results. There is no single method for prioritizing. Some factors to weigh include: (a) whether a written argument is simple enough to make orally; (b) what policy considerations may move a judge to rule favorably; (c) what argument the judges are likely to want clarified; (d) what argument is most closely related to the facts; and (e) whether an argument follows or goes against current trends in the law.

Arguing for a change in the law may be a strong choice in some situations, but often it meets with greater resistance from the court and will require more justification than an argument for the status quo. Thus, you should typically avoid characterizing your legal position as something novel or unique. Rather, you should emphasize how—under your theory of the case—precedent and reason dictate a verdict in favor of your client. To do so, you must know exactly what the lower court did what you seek to have affirmed or reversed.

Finally, when prioritizing your arguments, be sure to consider what opposing counsel will likely focus on during oral arguments. This will help you identify the key issues on which the case might turn, allowing you to anticipate lines of questioning from the judges. It will also help you to identify potential weaknesses in your own arguments that you will need to explain under tight time constraints. While you want to use the majority of your argument time to present your own case affirmatively, you may also choose to use a few moments to explain why a particular counterargument is incorrect or otherwise not persuasive.

(3) Strategy and Style

The oral argument should be a conversation with the judges in which you discuss your view of how the case should be resolved and address any doubts the judges have about your interpretation of the facts and the law. While you absolutely should conduct yourself as a zealous advocate for your client, a conversational demeanor in oral arguments will serve you well. In other words, yelling, podium-pounding and sarcastic responses make for great television but terrible oral arguments. Instead, you will want to let the strength of your position shine through your arguments to the court and your answers to the judges' questions. By providing believable answers that eliminate their doubts, you will persuade them to decide in favor of your client. The judges' questions may not be predictable, but in the overwhelming majority of cases, they are not designed to trick you. If you are well-prepared and a good listener, you will have no trouble answering any questions they may raise.

A good oral argument is neither an overly rehearsed monologue, nor is it an oral recitation of the brief. The argument should be lively, vivid and occasionally improvised. If need be, use a clever illustration to make a point clear. Pick up on the judges' metaphors and hypothetical situations, and suggest your own. Often, nothing is more persuasive than using an example that the judges can picture vividly in their minds, because that image is likely to be remembered long after your presentation.

Another key preparation strategy is to think about the institutional factors that might influence a judge's attitudes. What arguments are likely to appeal to a particular judge based on ideological preferences? Will the bench be "hot", where the judges ask many questions, or "cold", where the judges rarely intervene? Are the judges likely to have read your brief before your argument? Any predictions as to these factors will be just that—predictions—but often, devoting some thought to these factors will better prepare you for the nature of your conversation with the panel.

Similarly, you should know the different advantages of representing the appellant or the appellee. The appellant speaks first and has the opportunity to raise particular issues and to set the tone of the argument. The appellee, on the other hand, can tailor her argument to concerns of the court as demonstrated in questions to the appellant. The opportunity for rebuttal gives the appellant the coveted last word, but in another sense, the appellee has the upper hand since the appellant seeks to overturn a lower court judgment already entered against her. Both parties should also be aware of the applicable standard of review and, at the very least, be ready to advise the court about that standard. At best, you can use the standard of review advantageously in making an argument either to respect or to reverse the district court's judgment.

(4) Practice, Practice, Practice

To best prepare yourself for oral arguments, you should rehearse in the most realistic way possible. Practice your delivery out loud and experiment with different emphases and timing. If you have the opportunity, try recording your performance—reviewing a recorded performance will expose weaknesses in your delivery like awkward phrases, hesitations, wordiness, distracting movements, or mumbling. You should also recruit at least one practice questioner to act as a judge and force you to practice responding to questions on the spot. In addition to making your delivery stronger, these practice techniques also lead to substantive improvements because flaws in your argument become clearer when stated out loud and questioned. Finally rehearsing this new skill will build your confidence, which will in turn make you a more effective oralist.

▶ 2. Organizing the Oral Argument

(1) The Basic Structure of Oral Argument

There are many ways to build an effective argument, and an appellee's argument in particular may differ from the traditional model we describe below as a matter of strategy. However, most oral presentations do conform, at least roughly, to this framework. What would a judge like to know first about the case? What manner of presentation would immediately inform the judge of the central issue? What is an interesting, logical, respectful and positive approach? The oral argument model we discuss here is a common-sense way of answering these questions.

a. The Opening Statement

The opening statement introduces you as counsel and describes the nature of the case. You should introduce yourself in a formal and simple way by giving your name and the names of your clients. For example:

> May it please the court, my name is Jane Harvey. I represent the appellants, Rebecca and Scott Bell-Wesley.

In moot court exercises with teams of speakers, the first speaker should introduce both herself and her teammate. The second speaker will repeat her own name before launching into her half of the argument.

In addition, the first speaker should outline for the court the issues that each of the advocates will develop. A proper introduction of the issues should combine essential facts and legal analysis to describe the case in a nutshell, and it should enable the judges to focus on specific issues presented. The introduction should highlight the core theory and give the court enough information to follow the arguments. Consider the following sample introduction, given on behalf of the Bell-Wesleys:

> This case is here on appeal from the Court of Appeals for the State of Ames. The Bell-Wesleys urge this Court to overturn the lower court's ruling that child-rearing costs are not recoverable in a wrongful pregnancy action.
>
> I will argue that the fundamental principles of tort law dictate that child-rearing damages are recoverable to the same extent as any other reasonably foreseeable consequence of standard medical malpractice. My co-counsel, Yvonne Smith, will argue that even if this Court will not award full damages, it should compensate the Bell-Wesleys for the extensive costs of raising a child, offset by the benefit of having the child.

From this statement, the court knows at the outset what the questions are and will be able to listen to the facts and arguments with some appreciation of their relevance.

By comparison, an opening that launches into a contorted description of procedural history or immediately begins reciting facts will not give the court adequate background. Confusing openings like these should be avoided:

> **Introductions to Avoid:**
>
> *The overly procedural introduction:* This case comes here on appeal of a judgment entered by the Superior Court for the State of Ames. The Superior Court rejected Plaintiff's claim for damages, and the Court of Appeals also declined to award the requested damages. The Plaintiffs then petitioned this Court, which granted certiorari to determine whether the Bell-Wesleys can recover the costs of raising their son.
>
> *The overly factual introduction:* The Plaintiffs here seek damages in the form of full child-rearing costs because Dr. O'Toole performed a negligent vasectomy on Mr. Bell-Wesley on October 16, 2011, when he failed to sever the tubes of Mr. Bell-Wesley's vas deferens properly, leaving him capable of fathering another child. Dr. O'Toole then negligently conducted a sperm count, incorrectly informing Mr. Bell-Wesley that he was sterile. As a result of Dr. Toole's negligence, the Bell-Wesleys gave birth to a son, Frank, on January 4, 2014.

As these contrasting examples demonstrate, a clear presentation is crucial. You should not plunge into facts or procedural history without a true introduction.

b. Roadmap of Legal Argumfents

After introducing yourself and the case, you should give the court a concise outline of the legal arguments you will develop to support your position. The appellant in *Bell-Wesley v. O'Toole*, speaking on the first issue (recovering full damages), might present her outline in the following manner:

> There are two bases for the Bell-Wesleys' claim for child rearing damages. First, Dr. O'Toole's behavior contains all the elements necessary to prove medical malpractice such that fundamental tort law principles require full and fair compensation for the Bell-Wesleys. Second, awarding compensation to the Bell-Wesleys would support public policies favoring family planning, self-determination, and trust between doctor and patient.

This summary outline gives the judges a pattern in which to fit later arguments, indicates the order in which matters will be discussed, and enables the court to defer its questions until the appropriate time. Moreover, announcing the arguments at the beginning of a presentation—albeit in abbreviated form—will at least communicate that these particular arguments are important, even if lengthy questioning on an early point precludes discussing all of the topics prepared for discussion.

c. Statement of Facts

The parties' briefs provide the relevant facts of the case. Accordingly, the oral statement of the facts should be relatively concise. Absent a particular strategic rationale, i. e. the facts are extremely important or particularly strong, any lengthy exposition of the facts wastes valuable time and raises the risk of getting bogged down in factual minutiae. Therefore, rather than providing an exhaustive chronology, the most important function of the oral statement of facts is drawing attention to key facts that will become important in subsequent arguments. The statement should be as short as possible to achieve the desired goal. In moot court situation, only the first speaker should state the facts, including facts important to the arguments of both teammates.

When representing the appellee, you must make a judgment call about how many facts to state. Undisputed facts stated by the appellant usually should not be repeated. However, the appellee can use a statement of facts to tell her own story, dispelling the vision of the case created by the appellant. Furthermore, if the appellee truly believes that the appellant has omitted or mischaracterized important facts, she can draw attention to these misrepresentations.

d. The Argument

You should present your strongest points early in the argument, using an "inverted pyramid" structure: begin with the most important and weighty arguments and end with the least. This order both attracts the court's attention and ensures that the most important points are not omitted if time runs out. As in the brief, you should always state conclusions first and then support them with facts and law. The opposite approach (setting out a series of premises that only later lead to conclusions) is often too complicated to be effective because judges will interrupt with questions before you have reached your point.

e. Conclusion

Whenever possible, try to save yourself enough time for a proper conclusion that will allow you to summarize your most important arguments. The conclusion should be a brief explanation of the relationship among all of the arguments presented, integrating them into your core theory. When there is nothing left to say and no further questions, thank the court and end the presentation, even if time is left. The attempt to fill the remaining time with a makeshift argument could distract the court or dilute the strength of your primary arguments.

(2) Additional Considerations Specific to Each Party

Given the format employed for oral argument, each party faces particular challenges.

Depending on which party you represent, consider the following:

a. Appellee's Argument

As the traditional appellee's argument is structurally similar to the appellant's, the guidelines listed above will be helpful. Appellee's counsel, just as much as appellant's, should develop an independent core theory, and should not limit herself entirely to a reactive role. However, the need to answer the appellant's arguments does create unique issues for the appellee. When the two sides explicitly disagree, the appellee may challenge the appellant's assertions directly. This affirmative method brings to sharp attention the distinctions between the two parties' cases. Counsel should listen closely to the appellant's oral presentation and the questions the judges ask, taking notes as the argument proceeds. Although the appellee's counsel should have an outline prepared before the argument, she should also be ready to respond to any significant misrepresentations made by opposing counsel or to any issues that obviously concerned the judges when they questioned the other party.

b. Appellant's Rebuttal

At the beginning of the argument, the appellant may wish to reserve time for rebuttal. Rebuttal time should be used to clarify any prior arguments or respond to the appellee's presentation. Because it is the court's last impression of the case, rebuttal can be very important.

The time reserved for rebuttal should not be extensive, as reserving too much time may detract from the effectiveness of the main argument. In many circumstances, it may even be effective to decline the use of rebuttal time, indicating to the court that the case as first presented was solid and remains so even after the other side has presented its argument. An ill-prepared or rambling rebuttals can undermine even the best points made in the first argument. Rebuttals can also give the judges an opportunity to ask more difficult questions about the initial argument. Generally, rebuttal time should be used only to contest directly a point made by the appellee.

▶ 3. Questions by the Court

(1) The Value of Questions

Questions from the court reveal the judges' perceptions of the case, as well as their biases and policy concerns. Listening carefully to the judges' questions and noticing their nonverbal cues make it easier to frame persuasive answers and to budget time. If it is apparent from the nods of the judges or from their questions that they already agree with your position on an issue, it may be a good idea to finish discussing that issue relatively soon and move on to a new issue. If the questions indicate that the court disagrees with certain contentions, you should take time to present arguments that might convince the court of the position's validity.

Not every question asked is meant to attack the position presented, so you should not assume that interruption for questions is a hostile act. Some questions are designed to support your view and some simply seek to clarify points about which the judge is confused and has no preconceived opinion. Furthermore, some "softball" questions are asked to allow the attorney to argue a point more fully. For example, a judge could ask the Bell-Wesleys counsel:

> What policy goals would be served by allowing the Bell-Wesleys to recover child-rearing costs?

You should seize this chance to elucidate your position and impress a judge who is already an "ally". Do not miss the opportunity presented by a judge who offers you an open question, restates your argument in a new way, or supports your position with a new argument. Remember that a judge who agrees with you may be attempting to persuade the other panel members, so treat questions as an opportunity to shore up support for your client.

(2) Effective Answering

a. Be Responsive

To respond to questions adequately, you must understand what the judge has asked. Always stop speaking when the judge interrupts you. If the question's wording is unclear, ask the judge to repeat or rephrase it. If the substantive implications of a question are unclear, repeat what the judge appears to be asking and inquire whether that is what the judge means. It is often wise to pause and reflect briefly on the question before beginning to speak. Taking a few seconds to collect your thoughts usually results in a more focused response. A prompt but disorganized answer may confuse the judge further, leading either to more questions or to a weak showing on the issue.

A judge's questions may spring from confusion, misunderstanding, concern about the consequences of broadening a legal rule, hostility born of a personal conviction that a position is wrong, or a genuine desire to help the speaker regain footing after a tough interrogation from a less-than-friendly colleague. Answers should be framed to address the judge's concerns, as evasive answers usually provoke judges to repeat questions and badger the speakers. In some cases, if a judge finds a party to be unduly evasive, she may grow exasperated and simply rule against that party. A judge also likes to think that her question is unique and will probably resent what sounds like a "pat" answer.

If the judge tries to elicit a "yes" or "no" response that seems to corner the speaker into a contrived position, the speaker should provide the one-word response but follow up quickly explaining why the question is not so clear-cut and unwillingness to answer at all signals disrespect.

b. Advocate

You should use questions to advance your argument, even if the questions require bringing up a point before its planned place. Questions can also be used to put a positive spin on the client's position. You could make a concession, but show that it is not inconsistent with your client's case or that it is minor in comparison with the main point. You could also show that the judge's concern is even more reason to find for your client. Once the court seems satisfied with an answer, make a smooth transition from that response to another related topic and continue through your planned argument. Maintaining continuity and minimzing awkward silences is important, although a brief pause between arguments can be used advantageously.

Using a question as a vehicle to advance a line of argument is not an easy skill to master. The following is an example of how an attorney for the appellant in *Bell-Wesley v. O'Toole* might proceed.

> **Sample Question and Answer:**
>
> *Judge:* If the Bell-Wesleys didn't want to pay child-rearing costs, why did they conceive children on three prior occasions?
>
> *Appellants' attorney:* Your Honor, it may seem logical that if the Bell-Wesleys were prepared to assume the financial burden of raising children in the past, there is no reason they should not be similarly now. Before experiencing the tremendous emotional anguish accompanying the births and deaths of three deformed children, the Bell-Wesleys had indeed decided to take on the financial burden of raising children. However, after suffering immeasurably when each of their children died in infancy, they made a conscious choice to forego having children. Once they made that decision, they no longer accounted for children in their financial decisions and long-term planning. The issue is not whether, since they previously conceived and gave birth to children, they should now be presumed to be in the same financial position to raise Frank Michael. Rather, the issue is whether Dr. O'Toole's negligence caused the Bell-Wesleys a financial loss. Dr. O'Toole gave the Bell-Wesleys reason to believe that they would not have children and could plan their life accordingly. Dr. O'Toole must be held liable for all the foreseeable consequences of his negligence, including the costs of raising a healthy child to majority.

The first sentence of this sample answer restates the question. By restating the question counsel has shown that she fully understands the question asked. (Indeed, the judge could have interrupted and corrected any misperception of the question.) Then, counsel uses the question as a platform to advance her argument that damages ought to be awarded, to remind the judge of the Bell-Wesleys' personal suffering, and to reframe the question from "why did the parents attempt to have children before?" to "what responsibility does Dr. O'Toole have for his negligence now?"

Good preparation is the key to answering questions. Although it is natural to feel unprepared and apprehensive going into oral argument, an advocate who has reviewed the record, authorities, and briefs will often be pleasantly surprised and find that the court's questions are manageable. Finally, if there seems to be no good answer to a question, be very honest with the court. Being evasive is more detrimental than simply saying, "I don't know."

c. Be Sensitive to the Types of Questions Asked

When responding to questions from the judges, try to concentrate on the central thrust of their inquiry. Generally, questions focus on one of the following concerns: the facts, the policy considerations, the cited authorities, or the legal arguments. Each category of questions calls for a different type of response.

Generally, when a judge asks about the facts of the case, he is looking to move from abstract legal principles to a concrete application of the law to the current case. In this situation, you should provide explicit facts and citations to the record in a framework conductive to your side of the case.

In contrast, questions about policy concerns are generally looking for arguments arising from information outside the facts of the current case. Here, a judge is likely seeking a better understanding of the potential consequences of her decision.

Questions about cited authorities typically call for more than simple facts and holding of a case. Instead, the judge wants to know how the authority relates to the case being argued. Is it binding in this jurisdiction? Does it show an existing framework of law into which the desired result must fit? Can a valid and consistent exception to the precedent be made without detracting from the force of the precedent as a whole? In response, you should focus on telling the judge why a particular precedent is controlling, persuasive and based in sound policy.

Finally, questions about the legal arguments often focus on hypothetical situations to test the limits and illustrate the implications of the legal principle argued. Be sure that you are completely comfortable with your arguments and their limits if you want to avoid being tricked into supporting a legal argument that has absurd outcomes. If you find yourself being drawn into far-reaching hypotheticals and slippery slope arguments, remember that the case being argued involves specific parties in a single fact situation. Weaving the facts neatly into your answers can help prevent you from getting trapped into defending a broad general principle against all possible attacks.

(3) Questioning in Team Situations

Although judges should refrain from questions one member of the team about issues for which the other member is primarily responsible, each co-counsel should understand her partner's basic arguments. If questioning becomes too specific, ask the court either to permit co-counsel to return to the lectern or, in the case of the first oralist, to await your teammate's later appearance. If properly prepared, the second speaker may also take the opportunity to cover crucial points that her co-counsel inadvertently omitted and to develop further any answers that may have been inadequate.

▶ 4. Presenting the Oral Argument

(1) Be Yourself

If there is one general rule of presenting an oral argument, it is "be yourself". An ordinarily even-tempered and moderate person usually should not affect a flashy, fist-pounding display of rhetoric. Trying too hard to create a different, "effective" personality for the argument diverts your energy and attention away from the issues in the case, and it can be hard to maintain. There is no single right way to argue a case, and the more comfortable you are, the more effective the argument is likely to be. You should assess your personality and speaking style ahead of time and think of ways to use your unique strengths in the argument and to polish your own delivery.

(2) Effective Delivery

A clear presentation that is easy to follow is crucial in oral arguments. The general rules of effective public speaking apply equally well to oral arguments; speak loudly enough to be heard, and slowly enough to be understood. You should not read from notes unless absolutely necessary, because a paper barrier between the court and counsel inhibits effective presentation. The best advocates have a thorough knowledge of relevant materials. This does not mean memorizing case citations. Rather, it means dealing quickly and surely with the issues and calling forth relevant arguments without fumbling through a mound of written materials for a case or fact. Eye contact with the judges is extremely helpful, both in terms of keeping the judges focused on you and convincing them that the argument is defensible. With good eye contact, you are most likely to involve the judges in an active process.

Quoting cases to support arguments is sometimes useful, but quotes should be short and used sparingly if at all. In general, paraphrasing the language of cases cited in the brief is a more effective way of communicating their essence to the judges and a more efficient use of time.

The most effective oral arguments have the tone of a conversation rather than a speech. In this way, oral argument is quite different from a presentation to a jury. It need not be as heightened or dramatized as a statement before a jury, partially because the judges know the applicable law thoroughly, and partially because judges may interrupt you. Still, within this conversation, you should remember that your goal is to persuade and to get across a point of view. Toward that end, you should speak clearly and convey your brief in what you are arguing.

You should avoid legalese and other jargon when there is a simpler way to make your point. Overly complex sentence structure may make your argument hard to follow. Remember that a person's attention span when listening to a speaker is significantly less than when reading a brief. Therefore, it is useful preparation to take an especially complicated sentence from the brief and figure out how to express it orally by colloquializing it, simplifying it, and imbuing it with feeling without becoming too informal.

To some extent the conversational character of a presentation will depend on how many questions the judges ask. But regardless of the behavior of the judges, remember that oral argument is still an exercise in public speaking and should be treated as such. Speak clearly, projecting your voice towards the judges. Speak a little more slowly than you would in everyday conversation to make sure you do not mumble or sallow the ends of your sentence. Keep your delivery interesting by varying your tone and cadence to emphasize key words and concepts. Pausing for emphasis, if used sparingly, can also be powerful. Finally, be aware of your body language. Maintain eye contact with the judges and try to minimize distracting movements like pen-clicking or nervous hand motions. When kept to a minimum, gestures can become more effective as a means to emphasize the key sections of your argument.

It is unrealistic to expect to be allowed to deliver a complete prepared speech. In fact, the procedural rules for the federal appellate courts prohibit the reading of briefs at argument. Some speakers feel most comfortable after writing out at least the first minute (about a page) of their argument. Although reading this introduction may make the opening moments easier, counsel usually should resist the temptation to read. Use notes as a back-up, but focus on talking to the judges and maintaining eye contact.

(3) Attitude Toward the Court

Your attitude toward the court should be one of respectful equality: you should not be servile to the court, but you should accord judges due deference. Even in the heat of hard questioning, you should be receptive and cooperative. If a particular judge or question annoys you, do not show it. Giving definite answers to the court's questions, speaking with an animated and positive tone, and being confident in the strength of your argument is more likely to promote listening than adopting an aggressive interpersonal manner. Hostile behavior can be perceived as "defensive" and may suggest that you are unable to support your own argument.

You should attempt to be helpful to the court and to make sure everything is clear. You should not treat anything as obvious or as a waste of time, but rather you should act as a true "counselor" and respond empathetically to judges' concerns. Of course, once you have answered a question, you can indicate politely but firmly that you will now move on to the next point.

A few customs of formal conduct should be observed in oral argument. The customs do not vary much from courtroom to courtroom. When beginning the argument, speakers should rise and say, "May it please the court", or "If the court please", before introducing themselves. In answering questions, address the judge as "Your Honor". In referring to members of the court, "Judge Smith" or "The Chief Justice" is appropriate. Opposing counsel should be referred to as such, or as "Mr. Neuville" or "counsel for the defendant" but never as "my opponent". Associate counsel is called "my colleague", "my associate", "co-counsel", or "Ms. Harvey".

(4) Handling Miscitations and Misreprensentations by Opposing Counsel

Bring any miscitations and misrepresentations of opposing counsel to the court's attention when they are important to the case. If a misrepresentation influences an essential argument, if the court will be unable to find the correct citation, or if the judges' questions reveal that they do not realize that a fact or doctrine has been misrepresented, you should call attention to the misrepresentation. When appropriate, corrections can help your credibility. However, you should not appear to be attacking opposing counsel personally. For instance, an advocate in the *Bell-Wesley* case might say:

> It appears that opposing counsel is claiming that Dr. O'Toole guaranteed the 100% effectiveness of the vasectomy. If the Court would please refer to Exhibit 4 in the record, the Court will see that the Bell-Wesleys signed an acknowledgment that Dr. O'Toole had informed them of the chance that any given vasectomy would not be successful.

▶ 5. How to End Gracefully and Persuasively

Oral argument is not a natural exercise for most first-year law students. It is full of procedural requirements and formality that you may not have been exposed to before law school. But this does not mean that the task must be a daunting one. With adequate preparation and a bit of practice, oral argument can become an opportunity to showcase the hard work you have put into refining your argument and to demonstrate how well you know your case.

The best oral advocates will often be those who have mastered their party's position so well that they can speak about it naturally and compellingly. While a feeling of nervousness is almost inevitable, knowledge of your facts, cases and arguments will reduce the opportunities for you to be caught off guard. The better prepared you are, the more oral arguments can start to resemble a conversation. After all the time you have spent researching your case and writing your brief, it can be very gratifying—and even fun—to engage with respected judges on a subject you know so well.

Once you have completed your argument, remind the court what action you would like it to take (e. g. "we therefore ask that you affirm the Superior Court's judgment"), thank the court, and take your seat. And, when you leave the courtroom and have a moment, congratulate yourself on your achievement. You learned how to organize legal writing, how to synthesize rules, how to conduct legal research, how to draft predictive and persuasive legal writing, how to approach a case and develop a core theory, and how to present an oral argument. These are all tremendous accomplishments, and though you will spend your career honing these skills, you are well on your way to becoming a skilled legal advocate.

Appendix A History of Soochow University Law School

TRAINING CHINA'S EARLY MODERN LAWYERS: SOOCHOW UNIVERSITY LAW SCHOOL *

▶ 1. INTRODUCTION

    Late imperial China produced neither a private, independent legal profession① nor a formal program for training legal specialists. ② The introduction of legal and educational reforms in the closing years of the Qing

---

    * This article was selected from *Journal of Chinese Law* (8 J. Chinese L. 1) written by Alison W. Conner—Lecturer in Law, University of Hong Kong. This article is part of a larger project on the history of Soochow Law School and the role its graduates have played in the development of the modern Chinese legal profession. Earlier versions were presented as papers at the American Society for Legal History 1989 Annual Meeting, the Association for Asian Studies 1990 Annual Meeting and the 1992 Symposium on Civil Society in East Asian Countries, and have appeared in Alison W. Conner, Legal Education during the Republican Period, 19 Republican China 84 (1993) and Alison E. W. Conner, Soochow Law School and the Shanghai Bar, 23 H. K. L. J. 395 (1993). The research for this article was conducted with the assistance of research grants from the Language and Research Program (jointly sponsored by the Committee on Scientific and Scholarly Cooperation with the U.S., the Academia Sinica, the Inter-University Program and the Luce Foundation) and from the Committee on Scholarly Communication with China; their support is gratefully acknowledged. I would also like to thank Wejen Chang, Jiang Xiaowei, Zhao Yuesheng, Tian Jigeng, the staff of Shanghai Higher Education History Materials Center, the Soochow Alumni Association of Shanghai, and the teachers and graduates of both Comparative Law School of China and the Soochow University College of Law for the information they kindly provided me. I am also grateful to Jerome A. Cohen, R. Randle Edwards, William C. Jones, Richard S. Kay and Stephen B. Nathanson for comments and suggestions on an earlier draft of this article, and to Albert Lam Kwok Ming for the research assistance noted below.

    ① Most scholars agree on this point. See, e.g., Sybille van der Sprenkel, Legal Institutions in Manchu China: A Sociological Analysis 1 (1962); Derk Bodde and Clarence Morris, Law in Imperial China: Exemplified by 190 Qing Dynasty Cases 4, 113, 180 (1973). This view is apparently held on both sides of Taiwan Straits. Zhan Hengju, Zhongguo Jindai Fazhishi [Modern Chinese Legal History] 292 – 293 (1973); Chen Haisheng, Jiu Zhongguo de Lushi he Lushi Zhidu [Lawyers and the Lawyer System of Old China], in Fazhi Ribao [*Legal System Daily*], Mar. 2, 1989, at 3.

    ② For a discussion of traditional legal education, see Wejen Chang, Qingdai de Faxue Jiaoyu [Legal Education in the Qing Dynasty], 18 Faxue Luncong [*Collected Law Essays*]: 1 (1988).

Dynasty (1644 – 1911), however, led to the establishment of schools offering courses in "law and government", not only in the capital but also throughout the provinces. Their main purpose was to train officials for judicial and tax positions while providing an alternative to the traditional examination system. ③ Such law and government schools soon outnumbered other new schools and attracted most students because they offered several fields of study, the government permitted them to be established privately, and legal talent was seen as necessary for the proposed constitutional government. Consequently, according to one source, they became the core of higher education at that time. ④

But the real development of modern legal education—and of the legal profession itself—came during the Republican Period (1912 – 1949) with the founding of more professionally oriented schools and the enactment of legislation officially recognizing private lawyers. ⑤ The years from 1912 through 1927 in particular represented an era of relative freedom for many schools. The increase in the number of educational institutions was arguably facilitated by the weakness of the central government, which also made it possible for a more autonomous and diverse system to develop. ⑥ Many more law colleges were founded during this period; there were already forty-nine by 1915 – 1916, and many students continued to enroll because it seemed an easy route to becoming officials in the new government. ⑦

---

③ Ministry of Education Yearbook Compilation Committee, Diyici Zhongguo Jiaoyu Nianjian [First China Education Yearbook] 465 – 468 (Zhuanji Chubanshe 1971) (1934) [hereinafter Education Yearbook]; 2 Xuebu Guanbao [Official Reports of the Department of Education] 20 – 21 (1907); Chuzo Ichiko, Political and Institutional Reform, 1901 – 1911, in 11 The Cambridge History of China 375, 376 – 383 (John K. Fairbank and Kwang-Ching Liu eds., 1978). But the Qing authorities were "extremely cautious" about anything new and concerned that the wrong lessons (e.g., "people's rights or freedom") not be learned, even if it was necessary to study foreign law and government. Id. at 381.

④ Education Yearbook, supra note 3, at 465 – 468. See also Joseph K. Cheng, Chinese Law in Transition: The Late Ch'ing Law Reform 1901 – 1911, at 143 – 154 (1976) (unpublished Ph. D. dissertation, Brown University). Thousands of Chinese students were also sent abroad during this period, particularly to Japan, where a large number of them studied law. Marius Jansen, Japan and the Chinese Revolution of 1911, in 11 The Cambridge History of China, supra note 3, at 339, 348 – 352.

⑤ Cheng, supra note 4, at 153 – 154. Many texts state that the "lawyer system" was adopted around 1901, and some provisions of the Qing 1910 drafts of criminal and civil procedure refer to lawyers or legal representatives. Zhan, supra note 1, at 293; Wu Lei, Zhongguo Sifa Zhidu [The Chinese Judicial System] 354 (1988). But the first general regulations on lawyers were not enacted until September 16, 1912. Lushi Zhanxing Zhangcheng [Provisional Regulations on Lawyers], 5(1) Zhengfu Gongbao [Government Gazette] 108 (1912); Liao Yuren, Zhonghua Minguo Xianxing Sifa Zhidu [The Current Judicial System of the Republic of China] 248 – 257, 949 ff. (1982).

⑥ E-Tu Zen Sun, The Growth of the Academic Community 1912 – 1949, in 13 the Cambridge History of China, supra note 3, at 361, 367 (John K. Fairbank and Albert Feuerwerker eds.). The government's attitude was not encouraging, however. An educational convention in 1922 even recommended that the government law colleges be abolished because they produced "disorderly graduates" or "case-multiplying lawyers". W. W. Blume, Legal Education in China, 1 China L. Rev. 305, 308 (1923).

⑦ Statistics vary, depending on the source. Another compilation shows a total of forty-two "law and government" schools in 1915, down from a high of sixty-four in 1912. Education Yearbook, supra note 3, at 469 – 470. The latter's charts also show real fluctuations from year to year, but a large number of these schools certainly operated during this period.

One of the most influential of these new institutions was Soochow University Law School, whose graduates still stress its special character as well as the high quality of its training. Soochow University Law School was the only law school sponsored by the American Christian missionary movement (whose separate professional schools were otherwise founded to teach medicine or theology). ⑧ Though not the only school to teach foreign law⑨, Soochow University Law School alone specialized in "comparative law" and maintained an important place in its curriculum for such study long after the promulgation of the basic Chinese codes. It was, moreover, the only law school to offer a formal program in "Anglo-American law" (*yingmei fa*), to use the case method of teaching and to maintain close ties with American lawyers, teachers and law schools.

In part because of its unique character, the school contributed to the emergence of a modern legal profession in China during the Republican Period. Though many institutions taught law in Shanghai⑩, Soochow University Law School held a pre-eminent position: It was the best and most famous law school in South China. Its graduates played prominent roles in the legal profession and in civic life during the 1920s and 1930s, and almost anyone of importance in Shanghai's legal world was affiliated with the school at one time or another. In contrast with many other law schools, Soochow University Law School produced lawyers rather than legal officials, and its emphasis on ethics and standards as well as professional competence prepared them to take an active part in both political and commercial life.

Now that legal education has been re-established in a major way and over 60,000 lawyers are engaged in practice in the People's Republic of China (the "PRC")⑪, the approach and experience of Soochow

---

⑧ Earl H. Cressy, Christian Higher Education in China: A Study for the Year 1925 – 1926, at 6 – 9 (1928). For a time Yenching University also had a law department (not a separate law school), but it was established for the purpose of meeting the government's requirement of three colleges to constitute a university. Jessie G. Lutz, China and the Christian Colleges 1850 – 1950, at 313 (1971). Although Shanghai's St. John's University (Shengyuehan Daxue) also considered establishing a law school, Soochow University founded its school first and the St. John's administration did not think there was room in Shanghai for another such institution. In the 1920s, the St. John's authorities recommended cooperation with Soochow University in the management of a law school in Shanghai, but the plan was never implemented and Soochow University continued to run the Law School by itself. Mary Lamberton, St. John's University, Shanghai 1879 – 1951, at 63, 74, 111 (1955).

⑨ Shanghai's Aurora University (Zhendan Daxue), whose law faculty opened a few years before Soochow's in 1911, taught French as well as Chinese law. Université L'Aurore, Université L'Aurore, Shanghai 63 – 88 (1935).

⑩ At least eight institutions, both public and private, taught law in Shanghai during the thirties, including Fudan University, Aurora University, the Shanghai College of Law and Political Science and the Shanghai College of Law. Shanghai Shi Tongzhi Guan [Shanghai Municipal Encyclopedia Office], Shanghai Shi Nianjian [Greater Shanghai Annual], at N17 – 19 (1935) [hereinafter Greater Shanghai Annual]. For more on the two Shanghai law colleges, which were both independent schools of law, see Shanghai Gaodeng Xuexiao Yange [History of Shanghai Schools of Higher Education] 192 – 193, 201 – 207 (Xin Fuliang and Zhao Andong eds., 1992) [hereinafter History of Shanghai Schools].

⑪ Timothy A. Gelatt and Frederick E. Snyder, Legal Education in China: Training for a New Era, 1 China L. Rep. 41 (1980); Timothy A. Gelatt, Lawyers in China: The Past Decade and Beyond, 23 N. Y. U. J. Int'l L. & Pol. 751 (1991); Chang Hong, Capital Gets First Private Law Office, *China Daily*, Apr. 18, 1994, at 3; Liu Weiling, Lawyers, Lifted by Boom, Find Success and Status, *China Daily* (Bus. Wkly.), May 29-June 4, 1994, at 1.

University Law School may once again be worthy of emulation. The purpose of this article, therefore, is to analyze the reasons for the early prominence of Soochow University Law School and its general significance in the development of Chinese legal education. The article will examine the school's history, educational program and goals, faculty and students, and its most important contributions. In particular, it will focus on the school's students and their backgrounds: Why were they attracted to Soochow University Law School and the new legal profession? What was most valuable about their training?

▶ 2. THE LAW SCHOOL, 1915 – 1952

Soochow University (Dongwu Daxue, the "University") was established in 1900 in the city of Suzhou (i.e., Soochow) [12] by American missionaries from the Methodist Episcopal Church South. [13] The University's law school was founded in 1915 by Charles Rankin, a lawyer then teaching political science at the University. When he was sent in 1914 to head the University's second middle school in nearby Shanghai, he was given the freedom to explore other educational possibilities, provided he did not involve the University in any "unauthorized expenditure". What he found was a "God-given opportunity to render an outstanding service to the young Republic"[14] and in Shanghai (China's most important commercial and industrial center) all the resources with which to provide it. Rankin's idea was to establish a law department for Shanghai students by using the facilities of the University's middle school at night and by recruiting lawyers and judges

---

[12] The University continues to use the older romanization of the city in its English name, not the official *pinyin* version now used in the PRC.

[13] For a general history of the University, see W. B. Nance, Soochow University (1956); Chen Tingrui (D. S. Chen), Sili Dongwu Daxue [Soochow University], in Zhonghua Minguo Daxue Zhi [*University Annals of the Republic of China*] 153 – 155 (Zhang Qiyun ed., 1953). The University was one of the thirteen Protestant colleges in China under the general direction of the Associated Boards for Christian Colleges in China (later known as the United Board for Christian Colleges in China). See Lutz, supra note 8, for a comprehensive history of those colleges, including the University.

[14] Nance, supra note 13, at 71.

from Shanghai's foreign concessions (particularly the International Settlement) as teachers. ⑮

As a result of Rankin's efforts, Soochow University Law School, also known as the "Comparative Law School of China" (the "CLS" or the "Law School")⑯, opened in fall 1915 with its first class of seven students and more than ten instructors. ⑰ The scheme was a truly inspiring one, as the school's later history was to show. Rankin's religious fundamentalism led to early difficulties for the CLS, however; according to some of its supporters, his "narrow attitude continued to cause trouble". But the arrival of W. W. Blume from Michigan, who served as the Law School's second dean from 1921 until 1927, "saved the day" and the CLS then began a "steady approach toward the ideals and standards of the best American Law Schools"⑱.

During the late 1920s and 1930s, the Law School entered a period of rapid growth in terms of its students, faculty and prestige. In 1924, the school was able to move into its own Kunshan (Quinsan) Road classrooms, offices and dormitories⑲, and it began serious efforts to build up its library, which by 1935 had

---

⑮ Under the terms of the nineteenth-century "unequal treaties" between China and the Western powers, foreigners had been granted extraterritorial privileges (the right to be tried in consular courts under their own laws rather than by the Chinese legal system) and territorial "concessions" (i.e., large areas of land leased in perpetuity at low rates) in the treaty ports along the coast of China. John K. Fairbank et al., East Asia: The Modern Transformation 144 – 145, 340 – 342 (1973). Shanghai was effectively divided into three sections, consisting of the Chinese-administered city, the French Concession and the International Settlement. The latter, by far the larger of the two foreign concessions, had been formed from the merger of the British and American areas in 1863. Id. at 340. British and American lawyers based in Shanghai practiced before (or served as judges in) the foreign consular courts in Shanghai, and until its replacement in 1927, the Shanghai Mixed Court as well. The United States Court for China, for example, was created in 1906 to replace consular staff with professional legal experts; it ordinarily sat in Shanghai and in practice held the same position as a United States District Court, with appeals to the Circuit Court of Appeals for the Ninth Circuit in San Francisco. Its jurisdiction covered probate matters, matters relating to marriage and divorce of Americans, and the activities of U. S. corporations in China. G. W. Keeton, 2 The Development of Extraterritoriality in China 78 – 80, 126 – 131 (1928); William C. Johnstone, Jr., The Shanghai Problem 159 (1937). Great Britain exercised jurisdiction over its nationals in all civil and criminal matters through its provincial courts and the Supreme Court, which normally sat in Shanghai. Keeton, supra, at 77 – 78. In addition to the foreign courts, the International Settlement was also served by the Shanghai Mixed Court, established in 1864. A Chinese magistrate presided but a foreign consular "assessor" sat with him as a co-judge, sharing the judicial function. The Mixed Court used Western judicial procedure and handled cases between Chinese and cases in which Chinese were defendants. Fairbank, supra, at 341. For a detailed treatment of the Mixed Court, see A. M. Kotenev, Shanghai: Its Mixed Court and Council (1925).

⑯ The Law School was originally known as the *Dongwu Daxue Fake* (Law Department of Soochow University). In 1927 the school changed its name to *Dongwu Daxue Falü Xueyuan* (Soochow Law School), and in 1935 to *Dongwu Daxue Faxueyuan* (Soochow Law School). History of Shanghai Schools, supra note 10, at 149 – 152. Charles Lobingier, whom Rankin had consulted about his idea for a law school, suggested the "Comparative Law School" as part of its English name, and this title was used throughout the school's life on the mainland. Charles S. Lobingier, Legal Education in Twentieth Century China, Law. Guild Rev., July – Aug. 1944, at 1, 2.

⑰ Nance, supra note 13, at 72.

⑱ Lobingier, supra note 16, at 2 – 3. Lobingier, a Roman and comparative law specialist, was appointed Judge of the U. S. Court for China in 1914 and later organized the Far Eastern American Bar Association. He was instrumental in organizing support for the new school and helped to plan its courses and draft its early rules and regulations. W. W. Blume, Judge Lobingier (An Appreciation), 1 China L. Rev. 264, 265 (1923).

⑲ Nance, supra note 13, at 78.

Appendix A History of Soochow University Law School

grown to "more than 20,000 volumes purely in law subjects" and was proudly described as "one of the best in the Far East"[20]. In 1926, the CLS became one of the few law schools in China to establish a graduate program, offering students (mostly its own graduates) the opportunity to earn an LL.M. without overseas study. The Law School's classes proved increasingly popular, and in 1934 it graduated eighty-four students, the largest class to that date.[21] When the Nationalist government established by Chiang Kaishek attempted to restrict the number of students in "non-essential" courses like law[22], the CLS opened an accounting section and thereby kept overall student numbers to a "reasonable" level[23].

During these growth years, the Law School became increasingly independent of its parent university in Suzhou, financially and otherwise, and at one point its students outnumbered those of the University.[24] But the school's further expansion was curtailed by the difficulties of the central government in Nanjing and the widening Japanese encroachment in China during the 1930s. After the outbreak of the Sino-Japanese War in 1937, the Law School took refuge south of the Suzhou Creek in Shanghai's International Settlement, and law classes were conducted in a series of temporary venues, including the Moore Memorial Church. At the beginning of the Pacific War, however, the Japanese occupied the International Settlement, and by early 1942 the Chinese government had suspended the operation of registered universities like Soochow University in the Japanese-occupied areas.[25] Nevertheless, loyal members of the Law School managed to operate the school informally in Shanghai under a new name, *Zhongguo Bijiaofa Xuexiao* (the "Comparative Law

---

[20] 8 China L. Rev. inside cover (1935). According to Dean Sheng, the library was better than anything to be found in Manila or Tokyo. During the war with Japan, CLS students and teachers managed to preserve the library's books by taking them away and hiding them, and it was a "great pity" when the library was broken up in 1952. Interview in Shanghai (July 30, 1990). The Law School's files support his claims for the library, particularly documents relating to the school's closure, Shanghai Municipal Archives, Q245 – 231 to Q245 – 234. For an American comparison, the Association of American Law Schools (the AALS) resolved in 1932 that all member schools should have at least 10,000 volumes in their libraries and spend at least $2,000 per year to maintain them. Robert Stevens, Law School: Legal Education in America from the 1850s to the 1980s, at 176 (1983).

[21] According to a list [hereinafter 1946 List] of CLS graduates from 1918 – 1947 contained in the 1946 student yearbook. Soochow University School of Law, The Woolsack [no pagination] (1946) [hereinafter 1946 Yearbook].

[22] A 1932 regulation prohibited universities from enrolling more students in arts and social sciences than in science and engineering, subjects the government considered more useful to national development. Within a few years there was a marked drop in the number of law students, from 11,500 in 1929 to a low of around 7,000 in 1938. The number of students admitted to law departments, which had formerly ranked first in terms of enrollment, fell to fourth place—a "satisfactory result" in the government's view. Education Yearbook, supra note 3, at 425 – 427; Cressy, supra note 8, at 24 – 27.

[23] Nance, supra note 13, at 83.

[24] In 1925, for example, the Law School had almost as many students as the University (146 and 195 respectively), and in 1930 the Law School enrolled 594 students whereas the University had only 450. Cressy, supra note 8, at 9; Lutz, supra note 8, at 184.

[25] Nance, supra note 13, at 108, 113; 1946 Yearbook, supra note 21, at sections "1937 Fall – 1941 Winter", "1942 Spring – 1946 Spring".

School of China"). ㉖ At the same time, some Soochow University Law School students and faculty had retreated inland to the wartime capital of Chongqing, and they revived the CLS there as well, at the government's request and in association with the Shanghai Baptist College (*Hujiang Daxue*) and Hangchow Christian College (*Zhijiang Daxue*). ㉗ In 1945, at the end of World War II, the Law School officially reopened in Shanghai in 1945 and, despite heavy damage sustained by its facilities during many years of disruption, returned to its Kunshan Road campus the next year; graduates of both wartime branches were recognized and received their diplomas at the school's 1946 commencement. ㉘

After the war, both the Law School administration in Shanghai and its mission board officers in the United States assumed that the CLS would resume normal operations, perhaps as a reorganized and independent law school. ㉙ A new judicial section to train judges was approved by the government, the graduate division was restored, and student enrollment exceeded its highest pre-war levels. ㉚ Although the CLS continued to operate for a few more years, the school was closed during the PRC's 1952 – 1953 reorganization of higher education; its library was broken up and the books redistributed, and its students and teachers were reassigned. ㉛ Although the school was transpanted to (and has flourished in) China's Taiwan, the class of 1952 proved to be the last ever to graduate from Shanghai's Comparative Law School of China.

㉖ This translation of its English name had previously never been used in Chinese but easily identified the school to anyone familiar with the institution.

㉗ Nance, supra note 13, at 114 – 115. It was known as the "Associated College of Law and Commerce of Soochow University and Shanghai Baptist College" (*Dongwu, Hujiang Lianhe Fashang Xueyuan*). Shanghai Baptist College and Hangchow Christian College were also among the thirteen Protestant colleges. 1946 Yearbook, supra note 21, at section "1942 Spring – 1946 Spring". For a description of the migration of Chinese universities from the coastal provinces to the interior, see Chinese Ministry of Information, China Handbook 1937 – 1944, at 240 (Ch'eng Wen Publishing Company 1971) (1944).

㉘ Nance, supra note 13, at 130; Minutes of Board of Trustees meeting (Jan. 26, 1946), Shanghai Municipal Archives, Q245 – 55.

㉙ According to Soochow University files, United Board for Christian Higher Education in Asia Archives, Day Missions Library, Yale University, No. 271/4315 [hereinafter United Board Archives]. The proposal was for the merger of St. John's, Hangchow Christian College and Soochow University into a "China Christian University", with Soochow University to keep the Law School and its name. 1946 Yearbook, supra note 21, at section "Fall 1946"; news reports, 1940s scrapbook, Shanghai Municipal Archives, Q245 – 268.

㉚ History of Shanghai Schools, supra note 10, at 151.

㉛ China Handbook Editorial Committee, Education and Science 16 (1983). Lutz, supra note 8, at 445 – 461, 477, 481, describes the reorganization process and the resulting closure of the mission colleges, including Soochow University. Most of the Law School's library books went to the newly established East China Institute of Politics and Law (*Huadong Zhengfa Xueyuan*); law students and many teachers were also assigned there, while accounting students were sent to Shanghai Institute of Finance and Economics (*Shanghai Caizheng Jingji Xueyuan*). Documents relating to the school's closure, Shanghai Municipal Archives, Q245 – 231 to Q245 – 234. The main classroom and office building at 146 Kunshan Road is still standing and until recently was still being used as classrooms and offices by a division of Shanghai University of Finance and Economics.

▶ 3. THE LAW SCHOOL'S EDUCATIONAL MISSION

A. Comparative Law

The most fundamental task for the CLS (as for other law schools of the time) was the definition of the appropriate goals or purposes of legal education in China. When the Law School was founded in 1915, China had neither promulgated its basic codes nor fully established its new legal system. ㉜ Writing a few years later, in 1923, Dean Blume saw three main problems facing law schools in China: the extremely low academic standards, the lack of legal ethics and the difficulty of providing a suitable education for law students. ㉝ These problems continued to be of concern to the CLS throughout the twenties and thirties, and the solutions it adopted contributed to the influence of both the school and its graduates in the profession.

The first and most basic problem was simply to provide students with a "legal education suited to the needs of the country" ㉞. The Law School's answer was to teach comparative law, an approach it continued throughout its life on the mainland. ㉟ The aim of the CLS, according to an early course bulletin, was "to give the students a thorough mastery of the fundamental principles of the world's chief legal systems, an important object being to turn out students who can contribute to the making of a new and better jurisprudence for China" ㊱. Consequently the program of study included a broad range of courses from three different legal

---

㉜ Serious efforts at law drafting began in 1904, and as a result a criminal code (including civil as well as criminal matters) was promulgated and a new court system established by two organic laws at the end of the Qing Dynasty. Both were adopted by the Republican Government and continued with some modifications after 1912. Other legislation was enacted during the 1910s and early 1920s, but the most important laws, including the Civil Code and a new Criminal Code, did not appear until 1929 – 1936. Some of the main enactments, based on civil law models, were: the Criminal Code (1935), the Code of Civil Procedure (1935), the Code of Criminal Procedure (1935), the Civil Code (1929), the Law of Insurance (1929), Company Law (1929), Maritime Law (1929), Bankruptcy Law (1935), Negotiable Instruments Law (1929) and Trademark Law (1936). Jyh-pin Fa, Early 20th-Century Law Reform in China (Hungdah Chiu ed.), in Contemporary Republic of China: The Taiwan Experience 1950 – 1980, at 287 – 290 (James C. Hsiung ed., 2d ed. 1983); Wang Chung-Hui, Law Reform in China 9 – 13 (1919). Early efforts to establish a legal education system therefore preceded the appearance of much of China's modern legislation.

㉝ Blume, supra note 6, at 310 – 311.

㉞ Id. at 311.

㉟ Id. The comparative law approach was initially adopted by other schools besides the CLS, at least during this early period. When Cai Yuanpei, President of National Peking University, for example, was organizing its law department, he decided to use comparative law as a starting point, in order to make the best use of existing resources at a time when the legal system was still undergoing development and revision. Sun, supra note 6, at 372. The Law School of National Beiyang University, founded at the end of the nineteenth century in Tianjin, had also begun by teaching Anglo-American law, but it was merged into Peking University in 1918. Yuen-li Liang, The Harvard Law School, Some of its Chinese Alumni and Some Chinese Law Schools in Relation to It, 2 Soochow L. Rev. 82, 83 (1978). The CLS was unusual, however, in that it continued to teach comparative law and to stress its importance long after the twenties.

㊱ Soochow University, Courses and Announcements, 1919 – 1920, at 31 [hereinafter 1919 Announcement].

systems, with a strong emphasis on Anglo-American law. Students took courses in continental, Anglo-American and Chinese law, the idea being that by studying basic areas of law in the three systems simultaneously they would be able to make their own comparisons. ㊲

In its first few years, the CLS in fact taught very little Chinese law; only in 1923 – 1924 were general Chinese law courses introduced into the curriculum. By 1926, students were taking at least basic courses in China's family, criminal, procedural, civil and commercial law, but the bulk of their studies remained common law and comparative law. ㊳ The enactment of the major Chinese law codes during the late 1920s, however, transformed teaching methods and course content; thereafter, the study of these fundamental laws necessarily constituted the core curriculum for most law schools, including the CLS. At the same time, greater government regulation after 1928 also meant closer supervision of law school coursework. Thus, minimum requirements for all recognized law programs were set, and increasingly enforced, by the central government. By 1930, therefore, CLS course announcements all listed standard Chinese law courses taught in Chinese, as well as courses on continental law (on which the new Chinese system was based) and Anglo-American law. ㊴

Nevertheless, the comparative approach was strongly supported by the school's faculty, like Dean Blume's student Shelley Sun (Sun Xiaolou, class of 1927), who taught at the Law School from 1932 to 1939 and also served as associate dean. In his sensible and persuasive *Legal Education*, published in 1935, Sun argued that comparative law study was necessary in an increasingly interconnected world; the development in China of new law based on legal principles (*fali*) might also require a review of foreign developments. ㊵ For Sun the ultimate purpose of such study was the improvement of Chinese law and not simply the study of foreign law for its own sake. He thought comparative law was especially important in China, where foreigners had long justified their refusal to abandon extraterritorial privilege by arguing that Chinese law was unsuited to the modern world. If Chinese lawyers studied the law of other countries, Sun argued, they could improve Chinese law and thereby overcome those foreign rationalizations. ㊶

The Law School therefore maintained its distinctive character even after the promulgation of the Chinese codes and the increased government involvement in legal education. Although other law schools of the day also taught some comparative law courses, few could match the depth or range of the CLS, where such

---

㊲ Nance, supra note 13, at 75.

㊳ According to transcripts contained in student files for 1918 – 1927 graduates, Shanghai Municipal Archives, Q245 – 273.

㊴ From the early 1920s, the government required that Mandarin be taught in elementary schools, but that policy was difficult to implement in Shanghai area, where many teachers could not speak it well enough to teach in it. Nance, supra note 13, at 154 n. 1.

㊵ Sun Xiaolou, Falu Jiaoyu [Legal Education] 74 – 78 (1935).

㊶ Id. at 71 – 78.

Appendix A   History of Soochow University Law School   ‖ 211

courses still constituted one-third of the curriculum during the thirties.[42] In 1934, for example, the CLS program was advertised to include courses in (1) Chinese law, (2) modern continental law (French, German, Japanese and Soviet Russian civil law), (3) Anglo-American law, (4) Roman law and (5) both public and private international law.[43] Students were required to take not only Roman law and legal Latin but also continental civil law (German or French); comparative electives included world legal history and comparative criminal law.[44] Since those courses covered past as well as contemporary law, the school's comparative approach was described by one thirties graduate as being both "vertical" and "horizontal"[45]. The CLS graduate program also stressed the study and research of comparative law.[46]

The Law School's policy of presenting the broadest curriculum possible led to some dubious offerings: A January 1933 notice announced the introduction of a course on "Italian Fascist Corporative Law", which was described as the "fundamental organic law of the Fascist system and a most original and expressive political conception"[47]. But Dean Sheng maintained that the school should be free to teach all kinds of law (including Soviet or fascist law); one did not have to agree with everything taught—"just see what it is and then criticize it if you want to"[48].

When in 1937 the school's program was finally shortened from four to five years, comparative work was still required, and later students continued to be attracted by the school's emphasis on foreign languages and foreign relations.[49] Even after 1949, the CLS faculty retained their belief in the school's mission to teach comparative law, because it had "always been the specialty of the school". In the first few faculty meetings held after the Communist victory, CLS teachers resolved to continue teaching such courses (though now emphasizing civil rather than common law) and, if possible, to increase their foreign law courses in order to

---

[42] Sheng Zhenwei (Robert C. W. Sheng), Shijiu Nianlai zhi Dongwu Falu Jiaoyu [Nineteen Years of Legal Education at Soochow], 7 Faxue Zazhi [The Law Journal] 241, 246 (1934).

[43] 7 China L. Rev. inside cover (1934).

[44] Sun, supra note 40, at 189, 194, 196.

[45] Interview in Shanghai (Nov. 24, 1992). During the last few years, I have interviewed or had discussions with more than fifty CLS graduates and teachers or others knowledgeable about the school and its graduates. This article cites interviews with twenty-eight graduates and teachers, whom I interviewed in the following places and dates: Taipei, 1987: Sherman J. K. Chang, Wilson Faung, John Y. Kuei, William C. S. Ma, Ruchin Tsar and Yao Chi-Ching; Taipei, 1989: Andrew Lee; Shanghai, 1990: Sheng Zhenwei; Shanghai, 1992–1993: Allegiant C. Chen, Fu Jizhong, Hong Shi, Hu Wenzhi, Gu Hao, Lu Shengzu, Pu Zengyuan, Qiu Riqing, Qiu Shaoheng, Sun Miaoxin, Xu Daquan, Xu Junmin, Xu Kaishu, Xu Zhisen, Yu Zhenlong, T. F. Wu and Wu Yaole; Hong Kong, 1993: Huang Yulin, Herbert H. P. Ma and Zhang Mengbai.

[46] News clipping, 1940s scrapbook, Shanghai Municipal Archives, Q245–268.

[47] Italian Law in China, in Current Events, 6 China L. Rev. 1, 4 (1933).

[48] Interview in Shanghai (July 30, 1990).

[49] Interview in Shanghai (Nov. 18, 1992).

enhance the school's tradition of comparative study.[50] As late as 1950, the administration still hoped to strengthen the international law program, using the school's past excellence in foreign languages and comparative law as a base. The founding of the new government, they argued, made it even more important to provide international law training for diplomatic and government officials so that they could better fulfill their duties.[51]

Despite many curriculum revisions, Anglo-American law (like comparative law generally) also retained its special position at the CLS until 1949.[52] The Law School continued to attach great importance to the required torts and contracts courses, and a wide range of Anglo-American law electives, including agency, company law, trusts, partnership, remedies and equity, was offered each year.[53] In one sense, of course, these common law courses were not really taught as comparative law. Classes were still conducted in English, even after Chinese became the main language of instruction at the Law School.[54] More importantly, the Anglo-American faculty had all completed at least some study in the United States or England[55] and they employed the American case method of teaching rather than lecturing: Casebooks were used and students were expected to state the case in class with the book firmly closed.[56] Their "comparative" common law study therefore proved of great practical use to CLS graduates, enabling them to dominate foreign work in the International Settlement because of their good English and their insider's understanding of common

---

[50] Minutes of CLS faculty meetings (Aug. 10, 1949 and Aug. 12, 1949), Shanghai Municipal Archives, Q245 - 123.

[51] Undated discussion of the proposed curriculum, prepared for submission to the East China educational authorities, Shanghai Municipal Archives, Q245 - 153.

[52] The school has always used the term "Anglo-American law" (yingmei fa) rather than "common law" (*putong fa*) to refer to its special courses, a usage partly reflecting the participation of both American- and English-trained lecturers in the school's early days. But this usage also reflects the era in which the school was founded: its formative years coincided with the high point of closeness or common views on legal issues on the two sides of the Atlantic. See Richard A. Cosgrove, Our Lady of the Common Law: An Anglo-American Legal Community, 1870 - 1930 (1987).

[53] The Comparative Law School of China, Annual Announcement 1930 - 1931, at 7 [hereinafter 1930 Announcement]; course lists in student files, Shanghai Municipal Archives, Q245 - 273 ff.; Sun, supra note 40, at 189 - 191.

[54] Nance, supra note 13, at 76. Even the classes of 1927 and 1928 had almost all their classes and examinations in English, according to graduates of those years. Interview in Taipei (July 29, 1987).

[55] As late as 1946, the Anglo-American faculty numbered sixteen, including not only Chinese teachers trained in the United States but also two Americans (Judge Milton Helmick and Blaine Hollimon). 1946 Yearbook, supra note 21.

[56] According to Dean Blume, the case method replaced the textbook method in 1922 or 1923. Nance, supra note 13, at 76. It was George Sellett who introduced casebooks and the case method to the CLS. Interview in Hong Kong (Nov. 10, 1993). Students were required to brief all the cases, stating the facts, issues, judgment and reasons, and they found it very difficult. Interview in Taipei (July 29, 1987); Interview in Shanghai (Sept. 19, 1992). The CLS approach stood in marked contrast to that of other law schools, which might occasionally offer common law courses but taught in Chinese and employed civil law teaching methods to do so.

law systems. (57)

B. Academic Standards

In his 1923 essay, Dean Blume stressed the widespread lack of standards then prevailing in many Chinese law schools. Poor teaching, inadequate textbooks and the admission (even graduation) of unqualified students were all said to be common problems, not only during Blume's tenure as dean but even after tighter supervision by the Nationalist government over course requirements, standards of instruction and educational facilities brought some improvement. (58) Blume thought the solution was to raise entrance requirements to completion of at least two years of college, which the CLS did. Although a few students were admitted on the basis of an entrance examination, the two-year requirement was rarely waived(59), and the school later introduced its own preparatory program (*yuke*) to ensure a higher standard of pre-law college training. (60)

During the mid-1930s, the preparatory program required courses in modern history, sociology, political science, economics, psychology and logic. (61) The "idea was that a lawyer should know something about everything", so students had to study a broad range of courses before they embarked on their professional training. (62) Shelley Sun argued that such subjects formed the basis of law study and were therefore necessary for a true understanding of law itself. He thought that economics was the most important supplementary course for law students because the economy formed the basis for the legal system and the law had concrete links with land, inheritance and labor problems. He saw philosophy and logic as the necessary foundation for legal reasoning. (63)

At the same time, Sun proposed raising entrance requirements even further, believing it to be the

(57) Interview in Taipei (July 30, 1987).

(58) The Joint Office of the Educational and Cultural Organizations of China, Higher Education in China 2 - 4, 12 - 13 (n. d.).

(59) Blume, supra note 6, at 310; student files, 1918 - 1927 graduates, Shanghai Municipal Archives, Q245 - 273. The files show that CLS administrators did indeed check applications to see that all entrance requirements were met.

(60) The University's pre-legal course consisted of either two or three years of social science and other courses; if the full three years of study were completed, the student could obtain both a B. A. and an LL. B. After two years of the pre-legal course, the student could also transfer to the first year of the Law School but would obtain an LL. B. only. Soochow Law School, Sili Dongwu Daxue Falü Xueyuan Yuanzhang [Regulations of the Soochow Law School] 14 (1930 - 1931) [hereinafter CLS Regulations].

(61) Sun, supra note 40, at 188.

(62) Interview in Shanghai (Nov. 24, 1992).

(63) Sun, supra note 40, at 13 - 18.

inevitable trend at American law schools.⑭ Other CLS faculty members agreed, but at that time the school was still requiring five years of study (two years of college plus three years of law school) instead of the four years prescribed for government-supported institutions⑮, and the proposal proved impossible to implement.⑯ The CLS and University administration did, however, for years resist all suggestions to reduce the length of their program, which in their view would have meant a lowering of standards.⑰ It was not until the end of the 1930s that the school was compelled by government decree to introduce the standard four-year course of study.⑱ Moreover, although the numbers fluctuated from year to year, many students during the late twenties and early thirties had already obtained a first degree before entering the Law School.⑲

Equally important to the Law School and the University was the maintenance of standards once students had been admitted. According to Sun, law schools often admitted large numbers of students for budgetary reasons but rarely enforced attendance requirements. If 100 students registered, said Sun, probably only fifty or sixty—not necessarily the same ones—attended any given class from day to day, but all would be permitted to graduate.⑳ But the CLS was no diploma mill; students were indeed required to attend class most of the time and to maintain satisfactory standing in their courses or they could be asked to leave.㉑ Sun cited

---

　　⑭ Sun, supra note 40, at 92–95. He was right. The 1922–1945 period in the U. S. was marked by an ever-rising commitment to higher standards in legal education by the AALS and the American Bar Association (ABA). Stevens, supra note 20, at 172–174. By 1937, for example, the ABA had adopted the requirements of two years of college study and three years of full-time or four years of part-time study at a law school that had a library of at least 7,500 volumes, a minimum of three full-time professors and a student-faculty ratio of no more than one hundred to one. Id. at 179. But the CLS was still able, before war-time conditions, to meet most of those requirements.

　　⑮ During this period, law was taught in departments or colleges (or "schools") of universities (*daxue*), or at independent colleges/institutes (*xueyuan*). Law study ordinarily constituted a four-year program at the undergraduate level, with introductory and general courses given in the first year. Most law colleges had several departments, including political science, economics or accounting as well as law, and they granted the LL.B. degree for completion of studies in any of their departments. Hugh Chan [Chen Sheau], Modern Legal Education in China, 9 China L. Rev. 142, 143–146 (1936).

　　⑯ Following the American model would have meant a total of seven years of study, which was simply too long a program for most students.

　　⑰ President's Report to the Board of Trustees of Soochow University (1936), United Board Archives, No. 271/4312.

　　⑱ 1937 Ministry of Education order dated October 19, 1937, requiring the CLS to institute a four-year day program commencing with the first and second-year students then enrolled at the school, Shanghai Municipal Archives, Q245–230.

　　⑲ See infra pp. 28–29. Adopting the four-year program meant that most students were admitted directly from middle school to an undergraduate course of study, which necessarily resulted in some lowering of standards. The students were younger, they had less work experience and, although there were exceptions, in general their English was not as good as that of the earlier students. A late-1940s student recalled how he struggled through the cases in his Anglo-American law courses; at first he could hardly understand them at all. Interview in Hong Kong (Apr. 7, 1993). Moreover, with only four years to cover the required curriculum, the program could offer—or at least require—less in the way of comparative and foreign law courses for the students. Most commentators would therefore agree that general student standards were lower during the forties than during the twenties and thirties; that was certainly the view of one thirties graduate who returned to teach at the CLS in the forties. Interview in Shanghai (Nov. 25, 1992).

　　⑳ Sun, supra note 40, at 97.

　　㉑ CLS Regulations, supra note 60, at 17 ff.

the example of his own class: Although eighty-four students began the program, in the end—owing to the strict coursework—only twenty-eight graduated. ⑫ Yearbooks and class lists lend some support to his assertion, consistently showing more students enrolled than ever finished the course; CLS files are also full of student petitions for supplementary examinations or reinstatement after their suspension for poor marks. ⑬

Another issue relating to standards was the timing of classes. CLS classes were held in the late afternoon and early evening (ordinarily from 4:30 to 7:30, until 1937), which allowed ambitious Shanghai students to work and to attend school at the same time. But this practice had required special permission from the Ministry of Education after 1928 and continued to be a matter of concern to the University, which believed that teaching at night was "not the most desirable arrangement"⑭. The University administration wished to switch to day classes, and in 1933 – 1934 the CLS initiated a separate day section. This approach had to be abandoned, however, when government regulations restricted enrollment in law study and there were too few students to support both sections; it was not until the 1940s that the CLS was consistently able to maintain both day and evening sections. ⑮

As a CLS graduate himself, Shelley Sun did not believe evening classes posed any real obstacle to providing quality education, and his fellow students were quick to assert that the Law School was "not just a night school"⑯. He conceded the disadvantages of holding night classes but still argued that evening sessions were appropriate to China's social needs: The country was poor, universities could not expand their enrollments sufficiently, and the Depression had forced many students to abandon full-time education. Moreover, law students were often working in courts or legal offices already, so their practical experience meant they had less need for special extracurricular activities. If the degree program was lengthened or students had already completed some university training (as at the CLS), Sun believed high standards could

---

⑫ Sun, supra note 40, at 99. This seems an unusually small percentage to finish, however.

⑬ The 1930 Announcement, supra note 53, for example, lists ninety-six students in the class of 1931, but seventy-eight graduated; the class of 1932 graduated seventy-six students but ninety-two are listed in that announcement. Of course, some students could not finish for financial reasons, and others graduated but fell behind their original class. It was only during the war years of the 1940s that very large numbers—hundreds and hundreds—of students dropped out. Student files, Shanghai Municipal Archives, Q245 – 402 to Q245 – 410, Q245 – 417 to Q245 – 421.

⑭ Soochow University, President's Report for the Year 1933 – 1934, at 11, United Board Archives, No. 271/4312 [hereinafter President's Report]. The Ministry of Education opposed the operation of night schools and had pressured Shanghai night schools to close on a number of grounds, including their failure to offer extracurricular activities, to carry out military exercises and to fully supervise students (because they did not usually live on campus). Sun, supra note 40, at 103.

⑮ As reflected in student files, Shanghai Municipal Archives, Q245 – 286 ff.

⑯ The evening schedule was only a "convenience of scheduling for the teachers". Interview in Taipei (July 29, 1987). Others viewed it as a night school, however. Interview in Taipei (July 26, 1987); Interview in Taipei (July 31, 1987). The CLS did in some respects resemble proprietary law schools in the U.S., although the school's model was always the better national law schools so many of the faculty had attended. The Law School's standards were higher than at many of the proprietary schools, even if it filled some of the same social roles. Stevens, supra note 20, at 75 – 76.

still be maintained. Indeed, based on his own experience, CLS graduates who had worked and studied at the same time were more successful in their careers than the graduates of most day schools. ⑦

Finally, as part of its efforts to raise legal standards, the Law School introduced a graduate program in the late 1920s. Its Research Institute (*yanjiusuo*), one of the few in China, offered a two-year program of courses and research leading to the LL. M. degree. ⑱ Shelley Sun was a strong advocate of graduate training in China because he thought it would make it possible to train specialized legal talent, to foster law teaching and to stimulate interest in legal research and learning generally. While he acknowledged the accomplishments of those who studied abroad (and had done so himself), he also noted that China could not afford to send everyone overseas for further training. In any event, he thought studying in China would make students more familiar with the situation in their own country. Although not many students planned to teach or to engage in research, those who wished to do so needed opportunities in China; otherwise, even students returning from abroad had nowhere to pursue their research interests. ⑲

C. Ethical Standards

The third problem facing law schools, according to Dean Blume, was related to the moral character of judges and lawyers, a critical issue in a society lacking a long tradition of an independent legal profession bound by ethical rules. In Blume's view, this situation had been exacerbated by the low standards of professional behavior tolerated during the 1910s. ⑳ The national lawyers regulations and local bar association regulations did contain some rules of professional conduct, and, considered together, these rules no doubt provided simple guidance for lawyers. ㉑ But some Chinese lawyers as well as educators believed that the system was inadequate and therefore advocated the enactment of a more general "legal ethics law" to raise moral standards of the legal profession.

The Shanghai lawyer Liu Zhen, for example, argued in his 1934 book on legal ethics that such a law was essential if China wished to "improve its judiciary, receive the true benefits of the 'lawyer system' and increase the trust of society in lawyers". The reasons for his concern were clearly stated throughout the

---

⑦ Sun, supra note 40, at 103 – 107.

⑱ Nance, supra note 13, at 82. At times, it was the only law school to do so. Chan, supra note 65, at 146. During the 1930s and 1940s, only four to five law schools were authorized by the government to offer graduate law programs. Education Yearbook, supra note 3, at 574 – 576.

⑲ Sun, supra note 40, at 80 – 82. Few students pursued that option, however. Overall, the CLS awarded only thirty-one master's degrees in law: fourteen in the decade 1928 through 1937, one in 1944, and the remaining sixteen in the postwar years, 1947 – 1951. Eighty-four percent (twenty-six students) were CLS graduates. Student files, Shanghai Municipal Archives, Q245 – 319.

⑳ Blume, supra note 6, at 310 – 311.

㉑ See, e.g., Provisional Regulations on Lawyers, supra note 5; Shanghai Lushi Gonghui Zhanxing Huize [Provisional Regulations of the Shanghai Bar Association], in Liu Zhen, Lushi Daode Lunli [Lawyers' Ethics] app. at 21 – 32 (1934).

book: He wished to distinguish China's modern lawyers from its traditional pettifoggers and the bad practices for which they were notorious. Despite the potentially vital role lawyers could play in the judicial system, Liu feared that the layman would find it difficult to make that distinction. Only the enforcement of ethical standards would make that possible—hence the necessity for an ethics law and its propagation in law schools. [82]

Blume thought the solution to the low moral standards was the teaching of ethics and the stressing of moral values along with the teaching of law. [83] Certainly, the school's religious character was prominent during its early years, when many of the students and faculty were Christian and ties with the University were particularly close. Throughout Dean Blume's tenure, courses in both "Christian Ethics" and "Legal Ethics" were required of all students. After 1928, however, the government discouraged the teaching of Christianity, and religious instruction could no longer be made compulsory at government-registered schools. [84] The CLS therefore took on an increasingly secular character, and as classes expanded fewer students were Christian or products of the mission schools.

Nevertheless, the Law School's influential teachers continued to emphasize the ideals and ethics of the profession, and the CLS continued to offer ethics courses when few other schools did so. [85] Echoing Dean Blume's concerns about the moral standards of the profession, Shelley Sun argued that legal ethics should be a required first-year course; he thought that students should be introduced to the topic at the beginning of their studies, regardless of whether they ever intended to practice. Although Sun recognized that teaching legal ethics could not guarantee the production of ethical lawyers, he thought that law students should at least be given some idea of their true mission and their responsibilities to society. [86]

Charles Rankin, the school's founder, also emphasized this aspect of legal education when in 1949 Dean Sheng asked him to restate the reasons for the Law School's founding. "Lawyers," he replied, "are naturally and rightly leaders of the people ... They should lead in opposing corruption and upholding virtue. With skill and judicial wisdom they should be quick to discern the approach of public danger, and instant and courageous in opposing it. And as counsel of the people and advocates before the court, their course should be such that on whatever side they may be, their sole purpose is to render all possible assistance to the litigant and the court in arriving at a just and righteous decision." [87]

---

[82] Liu, supra note 81, at 3–5.
[83] Blume, supra note 6, at 310–311.
[84] Interview in Shanghai (July 30, 1990). The CLS offered a course on "Hebrew Law" from time to time as a substitute (and a way of evading the government restrictions). Id.
[85] Ethics and Legal Ethics were offered as second-year electives during the 1930s. Sun, supra note 40, at 191.
[86] Id. at 33–34. He noted with approval the strict standards of bar associations in the U.S., and the possibility that lawyers could be disbarred for violations of legal ethics.
[87] Letter from Charles Rankin to Dean Sheng (Mar. 12, 1949), Shanghai Municipal Archives, Q245–399.

How could the lawyer achieve those goals? "[H]e should not only seek skill and learning, but he should be a man of unspotted character, of unquestioned integrity." "Our purpose," Rankin concluded, "was, with God's help, to try to help in making Christian men and women, Christian lawyers."⑧⑧ Long after the CLS had ceased to teach or emphasize Christianity, it still honored Rankin's general intention through its emphasis on legal ethics and a principled profession.

D. Student Activities

A similar concern for professional competence, comparative study and social responsibility was reflected in the wide variety of student activities organized and encouraged at the CLS. All students, for example, were required to participate in the moot court, introduced in 1921 and described in the student yearbook as one of the "new and unique features" of schoolwork that year. The sessions, which were held every two weeks, followed the procedure of the regular Chinese courts, the Shanghai Mixed Court, the U. S. Court for China or even the American judge and jury system. Students played the roles of the attorneys, witnesses and jurors, and lawyers, judges and faculty members served as the judges for the sessions. ⑧⑨ Holding such formal sessions was unusual for the time, according to Shelley Sun, since most schools paid little attention to practical exercises. ⑨⓪ Sun also advocated the establishment of legal aid societies to be run by students, in order to give them actual experience in legal work, and during the 1940s the Law School did introduce a legal aid society (*falü qiuzhu she*) for its students. ⑨①

A more enduring activity was the publication of the CLS law journal, which was edited by the students under the supervision of a faculty editorial board. Their quarterly journal was actually composed of two publications, one in English (*The China Law Review*) and the other in Chinese (*faxue zazhi*). Most contributors were CLS students, faculty and graduates, but practicing lawyers and judges from the Chinese and foreign bars in Shanghai also submitted articles. ⑨② The journal's policy, declared in the inaugural issue, was both ambitious and consistent with the CLS approach to law study: Its first purpose was to "introduce the principles of foreign laws to China, and to acquaint foreign countries with the principles of Chinese law". The English articles would therefore be concerned with Chinese law and the Chinese articles with

---

⑧⑧ Id.

⑧⑨ Soochow University, The New Atlantis, at 144d (1922).

⑨⓪ Sun, supra note 40, at 111. At the CLS, however, students participated in moot court for three years and were graded on their performance. Student files, 1918 – 1927 graduates, Shanghai Municipal Archives, Q245 – 273.

⑨① Sun, supra note 40, at 113 – 114; clipping from *Xinwen Bao* (Feb. 4, 1947), Shanghai Municipal Archives, Q245 – 268. A doctor without experience might kill someone, but if a lawyer lacked experience, Sun said, the consequences might be much worse, since the resulting mistakes would affect society as a whole. Sun, supra.

⑨② As a review of the journals' tables of contents shows. *The China Law Review* was republished by Oceana Publications in 1975 and is therefore available in many American law school libraries.

foreign law.⁹³

The second purpose of the journal was to "facilitate a comparative study of these principles of law", so the comparative method of the investigation of law was to be emphasized; the editors argued that this approach would constitute the best way for China to establish its own laws. The third purpose was to "extend widely in China knowledge of these principles as a preparation for legal reform", since it was claimed that no journals devoted solely to legal matters were then published in China. In general, the editorial policy was "not merely to restate the present law, but also to show what the law ought to be"⁹⁴.

The English-language journal consequently published a variety of articles on such diverse legal topics as "The Nature and Origin of Law," The "History of Judicial Reform in China" and "The Registration of Corporations". Editorials, book reviews, texts of recent speeches and notes on current events appeared as regular features, and the journal often carried translations of Chinese court cases as well as cases decided by the Mixed Court and the U. S. Court for China. It published English translations of major new laws then being promulgated, together with comments and analyses of the legislation. The Chinese journal carried a similar range of articles and also produced a series of issues devoted to topics of particular importance, such as legal education and comparative constitutional law.⁹⁵

In addition to the journal and moot court, student yearbooks show CLS students engaged in a variety of other activities, both inside and outside the Law School. In the early twenties, students participated actively in Shanghai-wide groups as well as in their own student government. Students were regularly sent as representatives to the Shanghai Student Union, and Pao-li Tsiang (Jiang Baoli, class of 1922) served as the union's president in 1921.⁹⁶ Many of Shanghai's outstanding practitioners began their activities as students at the CLS. Eugene Y. B. Kiang (Jiang Yiping, class of 1923), for example, served as editor-in-chief of the law journal, class president, student body president, general manager of the yearbook, and chairman of the legislative body of Shanghai Student Union. The yearbook praised his "skill as a public speaker" and described him as a "born lawyer"—so it is perhaps not surprising that he later became a leader of Shanghai Bar Association.⁹⁷

---

⁹³ Editorial, 1 China L. Rev. 33 (1922).

⁹⁴ Id. at 33 – 34.

⁹⁵ The January and March 1934 issues of *Faxue Zazhi*, for example, published thirty-six articles on different aspects of Chinese and comparative legal education.

⁹⁶ The Student Body of the Comparative Law School of China, The Woolsack [no pagination] (1923) [hereinafter Woolsack]; 1924 Woolsack [no pagination], supra; student files, 1918 – 1927 graduates, Shanghai Municipal Archives, Q245 – 273.

⁹⁷ 1923 Woolsack, supra note 96.

▶ 4. THE LAW SCHOOL FACULTY

Rankin's original plan was to use lawyers and judges from the foreign concessions and Chinese returned students to lecture part-time, essentially creating a volunteer faculty. The early instructors were therefore drawn from the ranks of the Shanghai international bar and included many Americans. Besides Judge Lobingier and Dean Blume, some of the more notable teachers including H. C. Mei, George Sellet, Stirling Fessenden, T. R. Jernigan and Norwood F. Allman, all members of the American bar in Shanghai. The distinguished Dr. Wang Chunghui (Wang Chonghui), a deputy judge of the permanent Court of International Justice and translator of the German Civil Code into English, and Tung Kang (Dong Kang), who served as chief justice of the Supreme Court and later as Minister of Justice, also taught at the CLS during the early years.

Although most of the original Law School teachers were foreign, the faculty was increasingly "localized" as more Chinese instructors joined the faculty during the 1920s. When, as part of a "long-cherished policy", the Law School moved in the late twenties towards the employment of full-time instructors and administrators, it particularly sought out its own graduates. Anticipating the Nanjing government's regulations requiring that Chinese rather than foreigners serve as administrative heads even in private colleges, the University in 1927 named Robert C. W. Sheng (Sheng Zhenwei, from Shanghai) as the first Chinese dean (*jiaowuzhang*) and John C. H. Wu (Wu Jingxiung, from Ningbo) as the school's first "principal" (*yuanzhang*), a newly created position. Most other new faculty members, including those who had been educated in north China, also came from Jiangsu or Zhejiang, and from then on the school's administration was dominated by this group, particularly those from Shanghai and Suzhou.

Both Sheng and Wu were CLS graduates who had completed their studies at American law schools (Northwestern University and the University of Michigan, respectively) and both took an active role in the

---

⑨⑧ Instructors were later paid for their services.

⑨⑨ Born and educated in the U.S., Mei taught at the CLS from its opening in 1915 until 1925. He also served as chief defense counsel in the May Thirtieth case of 1925. 1936 Who's Who in China 187 – 188 (*China Weekly Review* 5th ed.). Jernigan was the former U. S. Consul General in Shanghai and author of China in Law and Commerce (1905). Fessenden served as secretary general of the Shanghai Municipal Council (the governing body of the International Settlement); Sellett was district attorney for the U. S. Court for China; Allman was the author of *Shanghai Lawyer* (1943). Sellett was the longest-serving of all non-Chinese teachers at the Law School. The CLS had foreign teachers for much of its life; even in the late 1940s there were still two Americans teaching part-time on the faculty. 1946 Yearbook, supra note 21.

⑩⓪ 3 *Biographical Dictionary of Republican China* 340 – 341, 376 – 378 (Howard L. Boorman and Richard C. Howard eds., 1979) [hereinafter Biographical Dictionary]. Both Wang and Tung received LL. D. degrees from the Law School in 1924 (Lobingier had received one the previous year). 1946 List, supra note 21.

⑩① Nance, supra note 13, at 80 – 81. Wu served in that office from 1927 until 1938; Sheng served as dean from 1927 to 1940 and as principal from 1942 to 1950. Dean Sheng's handwritten notes (on file with author).

legal developments of the Nationalist government in Nanjing. Dean Sheng (class of 1924), who later served as principal himself, was associated with the law school until its closure; the son of a Methodist clergyman in Shanghai, he received his B. A. degree from Soochow University in 1921 before entering the CLS. Dr. Wu (class of 1920) was a research fellow at the Universities of Paris and Berlin as well as at Harvard Law School. No doubt the Law School's most famous graduate, he later served as a judge of the Shanghai Provisional Court but is better known as a drafter of the 1946 Chinese Constitution. [102]

The Law School was able to attract (and retain) other talented and prominent graduates, most of whom had also studied abroad. D. S. Chen (Chen Tingrui, class of 1920), a leading member of the Shanghai bar, taught at the Law School on his return from graduate study at Michigan. Although he entered law practice shortly thereafter, he continued to teach part-time at the CLS, co-founded its alumni association and served on its board of trustees, remaining closely connected with the school during most of his career in Shanghai. Shelley Sun returned to Shanghai after receiving his doctorate from Northwestern; a prominent legal educator during the 1930s, he often wrote on education issues and served as an editor of the school's legal journal. [103]

Although few women taught on the regular law faculty (and none before World War II), in the late forties the Law School also began employing its own women graduates. In 1947, the faculty included five women, four of whom were CLS graduates (three in law and one in accounting). Of the five, however, only two taught law[104]: Cecilia Sieu-ling Zung (Cheng Xiuling, class of 1934) and Grace M. T. Tan (Tan Mingde, class of 1937). Both joined the faculty in 1946 after obtaining their J. S. D. degrees from New York University Law School, Tan in 1939 and Zung in 1942. Tan, the daughter of a lawyer and a legal practitioner herself, taught criminology at the University and English literature at Shanghai's St. John's University before becoming an instructor at the CLS. [105] Zung received her B. A. and M. A. degrees from Columbia University (in 1938 and 1939) and, according to her classmates, was probably the best-known woman graduate of the Law School, partly because of the numerous degrees she had obtained and the breadth of her interests. (Besides practicing law in Shanghai, she had taught mathematics at the city's elite McTyeire Girls School and later taught Chinese opera at colleges in the U. S.). [106]

---

[102] Interview in Shanghai (July 30, 1990); Who's Who in China, supra note 99, at 40; *Biographical Dictionary*, supra note 100, at 421.

[103] They were joined by Henry H. P. Chiu (Qiu Hanping, class of 1927), Arthur Yao (Yao Qiyin), Ao Sen (E Sen) and Henry K. F. Ai (Ai Guofan), all class of 1928; Fei Ching (Fei Qing, class of 1929); Joffre Lu (Lu Jun, class of 1930); Hugh Chen (Chen Sheau, i.e., Chen Xiao), who received his LL.M. from the CLS in 1937.

[104] Two of the others taught English and the third taught accounting.

[105] Based on forms completed by CLS teachers in 1946 – 1949, Shanghai Municipal Archives, Q245 – 283, Q245 – 284.

[106] Id.; Interview in Shanghai (Nov. 24, 1992); Who's Who in China (1940 Supp.), supra note 99, at 11.

The goal of employing a predominantly full-time faculty proved harder for the Law School to realize, however, as even most CLS graduates taught only part-time.[107] In his 1933 – 1934 annual report, the University president noted the appointment of the former judge Tsao Chieh (Cao Jie) as the first full-time CLS professor, as well as two more full-time resident officers (a proctor and an associate dean) in addition to the dean.[108] But other records indicate that most instructors at the CLS continued to be practicing lawyers or judges[109] and some were lecturing at several schools each year. In the administration's view, having such a high proportion of the faculty teaching on a part-time basis created obvious disadvantages; few teachers, it was feared, could devote their full attention to the school.[110]

Despite the administration's concerns, however, many part-time instructors taught at the CLS for lengthy periods and actively involved themselves in its affairs. Many were also excellent teachers and, when the Law School introduced regular day sessions, students often preferred to attend the evening sessions because the instructors were practicing lawyers and judges.[111] Popular part-time teachers included Francis Liu (Liu Shifang) and C. H. Chang (Zhang Zhengxue), both of whom joined the faculty in the late 1920s and taught there for over twenty years. After receiving his LL. B. from Yale, Liu pursued advanced study in France and Germany for three years. A prominent lawyer in Shanghai, he taught German civil law as well as Anglo-American law.[112] C. H. Chang, a graduate of Beiyang University, had served as both a judge and procurator in Shanghai before going into law practice there. He too specialized in civil law.[113]

In any event, according to its graduates, the Law School's "standard of teaching was high and the teachers strict" and in general its "teachers were very good"[114]. In interviews, former students have expressed their appreciation for both the common and civil law faculty, and for their foreign as well as Chinese teachers ("many foreign teachers devoted their whole lives to the school").[115] Blume, for example,

---

[107] The heavy reliance on part-time teachers posed a difficult problem for many schools, not just for the CLS. Shelley Sun depicted a very commercialized teaching profession during the 1930s. Because salaries were so low, teachers had to take on multiple posts; some taught as much as five or six hours a day and twenty to thirty hours per week. Many teachers saw no need to specialize, lecturing in any subject required. Sun, supra note 40, at 63 – 67.

[108] President's Report, supra note 74, at 10 – 11.

[109] In 1941, for example, there were five full-time and thirty part-time professors; in 1943 in Chongqing, there was one full-time professor (the dean) and twenty-five part-time teachers. Those admittedly were unusual circumstances, but it seems that the CLS was still far from having a full-time faculty. Soochow University files, United Board Archives, No. 269/4294.

[110] President's Report, supra note 74, at 11.

[111] Interview in Hong Kong (Apr. 7, 1993).

[112] Who's Who in China, supra note 99, at 169; 1946 Yearbook, supra note 21.

[113] CLS teacher files, Shanghai Municipal Archives, Q245 – 187.

[114] Interview in Taipei (July 29, 1987); Interview in Shanghai (Oct. 12, 1992); Interview in Shanghai (Nov. 24, 1992).

[115] W. B. Nance, the former president of Soochow University, and George Sellett, for example. Interview in Shanghai (Nov. 24, 1992).

was "honest, sincere, kind and energetic"; Sellett very "eloquent and clear-minded"; and the American-trained common law teachers "could really talk"[116]. Tsao Chieh, the author of important books on Chinese property and domestic relations law, was "very popular" and his views "progressive"[117].

One 1940 graduate praised his CLS teachers for avoiding the "stuff the duck" method of teaching (just cramming the students' heads with facts) that he thought was often employed in Chinese schools today. He also admired the "independent" approach of the civil lawyers, who distributed fewer materials than the common lawyers, thereby placing greater responsibility for class preparation on the students themselves.[118] One thirties graduate particularly admired Judge Helmick, who taught him contracts. The judge used a casebook and worked through it very slowly, but "what he got out of the cases, the principles and policies, made it very interesting". If you studied with him, moreover, "you really learned how to read the cases yourself—that was the important thing"[119].

▶ 5. THE LAW SCHOOL'S STUDENTS

A. Native Place and Shanghai Ties

The Law School was in many respects a national institution, with a national reputation and a student body drawn from throughout China, as Dean Sheng and other alumni all attest.[120] Its 1918 – 1949 graduates came from sixteen provinces and a large number of cities and towns, with the later and larger classes increasingly diverse. The Law School was also well-known outside China's borders; during the twenties and early thirties in particular, it attracted a number of overseas Chinese from Hong Kong and Southeast Asia.

Nevertheless, in other respects the CLS remained a regional institution, with its greatest appeal to students from the prosperous, densely populated and commercially-oriented South and East China. Few CLS students were from North China and indeed the vast majority of 1918 – 1949 graduates cited native places (*jiguan*) in Jiangsu (44%), Zhejiang (28%) and Guangdong (13%) provinces, with 93% of the students drawn from just five provinces. CLS students also tended to come from certain cities, with Shanghai,

---

[116] Interview in Taipei (July 29, 1987); Interview in Shanghai (Nov. 24, 1992).
[117] Interview in Shanghai (Nov. 25, 1992).
[118] Interview in Shanghai (Sept. 29, 1992).
[119] Interview in Shanghai (Oct. 12, 1992); Interview in Shanghai (Nov. 24, 1992).
[120] Interview in Shanghai (July 30, 1990).

Suzhou, Ningbo, Wuxi and Hangzhou the most frequently listed on their application forms. ⑫

Moreover, whatever their native place, many CLS students had attended middle school or college in Shanghai; of the first ten graduating classes (1918 – 1927), for example, 30% had studied at a local college before entering the Law School⑫, and by the 1940s a high percentage of Jiangsu and Zhejiang students (ranging from 65% – 94%) had actually grown up in Shanghai. After graduation, these students also tended to make their careers locally; thus, the Law School's 1936 survey found the majority of its graduates still in Shanghai, whether teaching, working in banks or other companies, or engaged in law practice. ⑫

B. Previous Education

Many students from the first ten graduating classes (1918 – 1927) at the CLS had ties with mission schools: One-third had attended Soochow University for at least one year, and 20% had studied at other Christian colleges, such as Shanghai Baptist College, Hangchow Christian College or St. John's University. ⑭ During the next ten years (1928 – 1937), when classes were larger, CLS graduates came from a broad range of institutions of every description, from the very best to the highly questionable. ⑮ The seventy-six members of the class of 1932, for example, had studied at a total of twenty-six colleges or institutes, and many of them had attended two or three colleges before enrolling at the CLS. ⑯ Nevertheless,

---

⑫ The statistics cited herein are based on information contained in the files for the approximately 1250 students graduating from the CLS from 1918 through 1949, Shanghai Municipal Archives, Q245 – 273 to Q245 – 299. The materials, including student application forms, are more complete for some years than for others, and the information required (or supplied) also varied over time. Complete files are available for graduates only, not for all students who attended the CLS, but I believe most of my conclusions would apply equally to CLS students in general and not to graduates alone. The percentages from Jiangsu and Zhejiang hardly vary from class to class.

⑫ Student files, 1918 – 1927 graduates, Shanghai Municipal Archives, Q245 – 273. In 1931 and 1932, nearly 40% of the students entered the CLS directly from the Soochow pre-law program, and another 20% were studying in Shanghai schools. CLS Regulations, supra note 60, at 50 – 60. These figures include all members of the class at that time, not just those who went on to graduate.

⑫ Sili Dongwu Daxue Faxueyuan Tongxue Lu [Student Register of Soochow Law School] (1936), Shanghai Municipal Library [hereinafter 1936 List].

⑭ During the school's first few years, almost half its graduates came from the Nanyang Institute or Beiyang University, which in some respects resembled the CLS. Shanghai's Nanyang Institute (later Communications University), for example, maintained high standards of training for the new technical professions and "offered the sons of the less well-to-do an opportunity to move up". Wen-hsin Yeh, The Alienated Academy: Culture and Politics in Republican China, 1919 – 1937, at 96 (1990). The statistics in this paragraph are based on information contained in the 1936 List, supra note 123, as supplemented by student files, 1918 – 1927 graduates, Shanghai Municipal Archives, Q245 – 273.

⑮ For an excellent analysis of the different cultural styles, social composition and standards of Republican tertiary institutions, see Yeh, supra note 124, at 59 – 116.

⑯ This not only resulted from the admission of larger and more diverse classes but also reflected the growing number of colleges and universities in Shanghai and environs during the twenties and thirties, which apparently allowed students to "forum-shop" around the city. Judging from these records, it seems to have been a common phenomenon. See Yeh, supra note 124, for a discussion of Shanghai colleges and universities.

during this period a core of students still entered the CLS directly from the University or had attended the Law School's preparatory program, and their numbers increased during the 1930s as the CLS tried to standardize college preparation with the introduction of its own program. [127]

The percentage of college graduates also fluctuated over time, partly as a result of changing admission requirements. Few students in the first ten classes were college graduates when they entered the CLS, but during the late twenties and early thirties (1927 – 1933) from 20% to 50% of the school's students had already obtained a first degree. [128] By the late thirties, very few CLS students were already graduates—though they still met the school's entrance requirement of two years of college study. The class of 1941 (entering in 1937), however, was for the first time admitted directly from secondary schools to the new four-year program mandated by the educational authorities. Thereafter, the occasional student had a college degree or a few years of college, but the majority came directly from middle school. [129]

C. Soochow Connections

Students often had closer or more personal connections to the Law School than attendance at the University or its middle schools. Three graduates of the 1930s and 1940s, for example, were CLS employees when they enrolled, including Charles Y. S. Yu (Yu Youxin), who served as the school's librarian from 1931 until 1952 and received his LL. B. in 1946. [130] Teachers at the CLS received free tuition for their children, and a number of faculty members, such as John Wu, D. S. Chen, T. F. Wu and C. H. Chang, sent their sons or daughters to study there. CLS alumni also sent their children (e.g., the son of a 1931 graduate in 1937, the daughter of a 1926 graduate in 1940) or, more commonly, were followed by nephews, cousins or other "relatives" (*qinqi*). At least ten groups of siblings or cousins studied together, graduating in the same class or only a few years apart, including brothers (1921, 1926), sisters (class of 1943, 1940 and 1945), uncle and nephew (1941) and cousins (1927, 1930 and 1934)—and they

---

[127] For example, 45% of the 1933 graduates had studied at Soochow University, after the preparatory program was moved there in 1929.

[128] Based on information contained in student files, Shanghai Municipal Archives, Q245 – 273 to Q245 – 279.

[129] Beginning with the class of 1931, student application forms began to ask for the student's middle or preparatory school, although the data are not complete until later in the thirties. As with universities, a very broad range of middle schools was represented. Each year contained a core of students from one of the three Soochow middle schools or another mission school, and others were graduates of elite private schools like St. John's and McTyeire. Nevertheless, many students were products of cheaper (and in many cases less prestigious) provincial middle schools.

[130] Student files, 1946 graduates, Shanghai Municipal Archives, Q245 – 292. The other two were members of staff (*zhiyuan*); they obtained their degrees in 1931 and 1936. Id. at Q245 – 277, Q245 – 282.

sometimes went on to practice together after graduation. ⑬

D. Religion

Despite its origins in the Christian missionary movement, the Law School never required that its students be Christian, and even in its earliest days the CLS probably had a lower percentage of Christians than most other mission schools. ⑬ Not surprisingly, however, many of the earlier students were Christian (virtually all Protestant though by no means all Methodist): At least 30% of the students graduating between 1918 and 1929 identified themselves as Christian on their application forms. Though most of these had converted while attending missionary primary or middle schools, as indicated in their "history of conversion", a sizeable percentage reported that they were "born in a Christian family" or were "Christian for several generations", or that "grandfather was a pastor". In later years, however, the numbers of such students fell considerably, as the school expanded and students came from a broader range of middle schools; thus only 12% of the students graduating from 1932 – 1945 listed themselves as Christians. ⑬

E. Women Students

The earliest classes were all male (the University's English motto, also used by the Law School, was "Unto a fullgrown man"). In 1928, however, the University formally became co-educational, and the first

---

⑬ Based on information contained in student files for those years, Shanghai Municipal Archives, Q245 – 273, – 276, – 280, – 287, – 289, – 291. The true number of CLS relatives and other connections was probably much higher than these files reveal, however, as applicants were not asked to list relatives who attended the CLS on their application forms and full student files are available only for graduates, not all students who ever attended. Interviews also suggest that it was common. Actually, many students maintained a long, even life-long connection to the University, its middle schools and the Law School. The CLS teacher T. F. Wu, for example, graduated from the University (class of 1921) and one of its middle schools; all three of his sons also graduated from the University (his daughter attended the CLS). He himself taught at the University's middle school in Suzhou, at the University and at the CLS, serving as dean of the arts college in the late forties. Interview in Shanghai (July 28, 1993). Zhang Mengbai's career followed a similar pattern: A 1926 graduate of the University, he had also attended its primary and middle schools. He taught world history at the University and the Law School for many years and continues his affiliation with the PRC's Suzhou University (which occupies the old Soochow University campus). Interview in Hong Kong (Dec. 9, 1993). It is no wonder that CLS teachers and graduates felt such loyalty to their school—though such close ties could also be a disadvantage. See Jessie Lutz, Materials on the China Christian Colleges at Harvard University, paper presented at the International Symposium on Historical Archives of pre-1949 Christian Higher Education in China (Dec. 9 – 11, 1993) (on file with author).

⑬ One 1920s student thought it was "preferable" for a student to be a Christian (and he became one), but he stressed that it was not necessary to do so. According to graduates of the 1930s and 1940s, most CLS students were not Christian and no pressure was placed on them to convert—religion simply was not an issue. Interview in Taipei (July 29, 1987); Interview in Shanghai (Sept. 15, 1992); Interview in Shanghai (Nov. 24, 1992). By comparison, 88% of the students at Beijing's Yenching University were Christian in 1924, and in 1935 the number was still 31%. Philip West, Yenching University and Sino-Western Relations, 1916 – 1952, at 126 (1976).

⑬ Student files, Shanghai Municipal Archives, Q245 – 273 to Q245 – 295. For several years (1930 – 1931) the student application forms failed to ask the applicant's religion, so those years cannot be included in the calculations here.

woman graduated from the CLS three years later.[134] Overall, women comprised only 12% of the CLS graduates from 1931 to 1949 and only 10% of the 1918–1949 total. But their numbers grew in the Law School's later years, from almost 9% of law graduates during the thirties (1931–1940) to 18% during the forties (1941–1949), an increase vividly reflected in yearbook photos and other less formal student records, as well as the employment of the first women on the regular law faculty.[135]

The Law School's smaller and newer accounting section, however, attracted a far higher proportion of women from its inception; about the same number of women graduated in accounting during 1941–1949 as in law, but they represented 38% of the total accounting graduates during those years. According to some sources, this was because accounting was considered a more appropriate course of study for women—with the result that accounting ended up with "too many girls"[136]. The admission of more women to both the law and accounting sections in the forties and fifties led to many Law School marriages, but even during the thirties some classmates met and married as a result of their study together ("Soochow people liked to marry Soochow people").[137]

F. Family Background

The great majority of CLS students, both male and female, came from commercial or professional families, the group most likely to appreciate the value of professional training and qualifications.[138] Throughout the thirties and forties, almost half (45%) of the school's graduates identified their family head's occupation as "business" or "commerce" (*shang*), 7% identified it as government (including customs and the post office) and more than 20% identified it as professional (including law, medicine, engineering and education). Within these categories, a wide variety of other occupations was represented, including editors, journalists, YMCA employees and pastors, and even a few workers, farmers, policemen and railway employees. "Business" also encompassed a diverse set of commercial occupations, ranging from tea merchants, silk traders, bank directors and managers of foreign hongs to small businessmen or company

---

[134] Helen Clark, Co-education at Soochow University, 3 *Tung Wu Magazine of Soochow University* 86 (1935); 1936 List, supra note 123.

[135] Student files, 1918–1949 graduates, Shanghai Municipal Archives, Q245–273 to Q245–299.

[136] Soochow University Law School Accounting Department, SUDECAC 1939–1947 [no pagination] (1947) [hereinafter Sudecac]. Professor C. H. Chang sent two daughters through the CLS; the first graduated in law (class of 1940) and the second, who attended after the accounting section had been established, in accounting (class of 1945). Student files, 1940 and 1945 graduates, Shanghai Municipal Archives, Q245–286, Q245–291.

[137] Interview in Shanghai (Aug. 14, 1993). A 1950 graduate was able to point out some five sets of classmates in his graduating class alone who married each other. Interview in Hong Kong (Apr. 7, 1993). Hugh Chen, a CLS teacher for many years, married a graduate of the accounting department. Sudecac, supra note 136.

[138] Application forms for the classes of 1930 and thereafter (that is, those entering the school from 1927) asked for the occupation as well as the name of the applicant's family head (*jiazhang*). The information on family heads is much less complete during the 1940s, however.

clerks.

The legal profession itself was well represented during the 1930s and 1940s. In every graduating class but one from 1930 through 1949 at least one student identified his family head's occupation as "lawyer". Overall, more than 10% of the graduates during those years had a legal professional of some kind for a family head, half of them lawyers; many other students named lawyers, usually a relative or close connection, as their guarantors. Women CLS graduates had a slightly stronger connection to the legal profession, with almost 10% listing a lawyer as family head and another 8% naming a lawyer-relative as their guarantor. [139] Remarkably, by the late thirties—only twenty-five years after the formal recognition of the private legal profession—some 20% to 30% in each class of CLS graduates had lawyers for family heads or guarantors. [140]

Some CLS students clearly came from wealthy families, a fact reflected in the photographs they submitted with their applications (e.g., young women in silk gowns holding fur coats or other well-dressed students posed in front of large residences) and in accounts of students driven to school in chauffered limousines. A few thirties graduates listed no occupations for themselves in the school's 1936 directory—they were "too rich" to work, according to their classmates, and had studied law as a form of "self-protection" for their property, not because they had to earn a living. [141]

Most students, however, were not the products of such moneyed backgrounds, and professional status was no guarantee of wealth, as some professionals (particularly educators) were notoriously ill-paid. But it was not necessary to be rich to attend the Law School, despite its relatively high tuition and the miscellaneous fees and charges it also levied. [142] The school offered scholarships on the basis of merit and need, as shown by the many approvals of student petitions noted in their files, and the school's administrators in general tried to help in cases of financial hardship because, in the words of one graduate, "it was a missionary school" [143].

---

[139] Some women had even closer connections to the profession. One 1940 graduate, for example, listed both her father and her aunt as lawyers. Student files, 1940 graduates, Shanghai Municipal Archives, Q245 - 286.

[140] Particularly for the graduating classes beginning in 1937, as reflected in student files for those years, Shanghai Municipal Archives, Q245 - 283 ff.

[141] 1936 List, supra note 123; Interview in Shanghai (Nov. 24, 1992).

[142] Tuition was much higher at private schools, which relied very heavily on tuition for financing, than at publicly-supported institutions. Lutz, supra note 8, at 167 - 168; Yeh, supra note 124, at 196 - 197. Tuition at the Law School was $80 per year in 1919 - 1920, and $100 per year in 1926 - 1927. By the early 1930s, tuition had risen to $60 per term and was further supplemented by library, student organization, lecture materials, journal and miscellaneous fees totaling $15.50. Sili Dongwu Daxue Faxueyuan Yilan [A Guide to Soochow University Law School] 1932 - 1933, at 20 - 21 (1932). One 1927 graduate accurately remembered his tuition in an interview forty years later because it was so "expensive": $100 (he was earning $30 per month at the Commercial Press, where he worked during the day). Interview in Taipei (July 26, 1987). Textbooks were also expensive in the earlier years, because they were imported from the United States or England. Interview in Taipei (July 29, 1987).

[143] Interview in Shanghai (Nov. 24, 1992); student files, Shanghai Municipal Archives, Q245 - 273 ff.

The work records of students are incomplete, but they do at least suggest that for many the CLS offered real social mobility, allowing them to move on to better, different or higher-paying positions after graduation.[144]

The Law School's convenient location in Shanghai and in particular its late afternoon and early evening schedule also meant that students could support their studies through part-time or even full-time work, and many did so. Some found jobs after their admission to the CLS, such as the 1934 graduate who began his long career with the Jiaotong Bank as a law student, or the 1940s student who taught English at the University's middle school (though he found it a "heavy load").[145] Others with jobs already were drawn to the Law School because they could attend classes after regular office hours. A few of the latter applicants had advanced degrees and established careers, usually in higher education: One 1931 graduate taught chemistry at two Shanghai universities and enrolled in the CLS under a pseudonym and two Fudan University professors (husband and wife) went through the CLS together in the thirties (class of 1933).[146]

More typical Law School applicants during the twenties and thirties were junior clerks in banks or insurance companies, primary school teachers and post office employees, or even law clerks or legal interpreters, who yearned to further their education or to improve their prospects.[147] One such young man (class of 1931) wrote a touching series of letters in support of his application for admission despite his failure to meet some school requirements:

"[M]any students whose families prove incapable to support their children to pursue collegiate education on monetary or other questions have suspended their further career. This always makes me heartbroken when pondering one of Chinese proverbs, saying, Those who like to study, cannot study; those who can study, do not like to study ... In struggling for a better living and to accomplish obligations of being a citizen, I though bound to work, still deem a higher education is necessary for me.

Day by day I have been looking for the school which most meets my requirements and has nothing affecting my working hours in C. P. O. [China Post Office]. Although correspondence schools are to some

---

[144] Application forms for the classes graduating from 1930 through 1947 asked for the applicant's occupation. The data are incomplete, but comparisons with positions they later held (as given in the 1936 List, supra note 123) show that in a number of cases, the graduates clearly moved into better positions. A few are dramatic: for example, a 1933 graduate who worked at the CLS and listed his father as a worker went on to become a part-time lawyer and insurance company employee. Primary and middle school teachers often became lawyers (classes of 1931, 1932, 1934, 1935, for example), or court clerks became lawyers (class of 1932). Student files, Shanghai Municipal Archives, Q245 – 277, – 278, – 280, – 281. See also Lutz, supra note 8, at 302 – 303.

[145] Interview in Taipei (Aug. 3, 1987).

[146] Student files, Shanghai Municipal Archives, Q245 – 279.

[147] In some classes a large percentage (as high as 23% in 1931) gave some current occupation (other than the usual "student"). Twelve students during those years listed occupations relating to law: legal interpreters (2), court clerks (3), the Shanghai Municipal Council legal department (2), and clerks or typists in law offices (5). Student files, Shanghai Municipal Archives, Q245 – 276 to Q245 – 293.

degree helpful, I find difficulties in discussion of hard problems. Your university, Soochow Comparative Law School, I have verily appreciated it since a copy of your catalogue has been perused."[148]

An obvious result of the reliance on outside jobs was that CLS students worked very hard, and most apparently expected to do so. In the twenties at least, they were "serious and ambitious students, they didn't gamble or fool around"[149]. One 1936 graduate, in petitioning the Law School for extra scholarship help, apologized that he could only work part-time to support his study because he had to spend mornings with his readers (he was blind).[150] Those without outside jobs often engaged in other study during the day, like the 1928 graduate who attended Fudan University at the same time as the CLS and commuted between the two schools on the motorcycle his father bought him for that purpose. Nevertheless, some students still found time for extracurricular activities despite their jobs and other study. Eugene Y. B. Kiang, for example, was able to combine all three during the twenties: He worked part-time, attended Fudan University classes to complete his B. A. degree—and still managed to chair most Law School activities for his class.[151]

G. Reasons for Law Study

The social composition of Law School graduates outlined above suggests the reasons they wished to study law and, more particularly, to enroll at the CLS. It is true that many early students came from mission schools, were Christian or had special ties with Soochow University, and these factors continued to be relevant to some degree. More important factors, however, were family background and native place, which remained remarkably consistent from the school's founding through the end of the forties. That the CLS held special appeal for the Jiangnan commercial and professional sector is also borne out by the testimony of Law School graduates themselves.

Thus, many students were directed towards law by their families, who wished them to have a solid profession. According to one 1928 graduate, his family stressed education and getting a skill; law was a "way to make a living". A thirties student, the son of a doctor, was advised by his father that only three professions were "for people" (the rest were only "for money"): clergymen, doctors and lawyers, in that order (lawyers placed last because they "told lies"). Since the son seemed ill-suited to the first two professions, he chose law by default. A late forties student wanted to become a singer, but his parents disapproved and refused to permit it, on the grounds that "such people led immoral lives". In the end the

---

[148] Student files, Shanghai Municipal Archives, Q245 - 277. Dean Sheng admitted him on examination, and his records show that he subsequently did well at the CLS.

[149] Interview in Taipei (July 29, 1987).

[150] Student files, Shanghai Municipal Archives, Q245 - 282.

[151] Interview in Taipei (July 31, 1987); student files, Shanghai Municipal Archives, Q245 - 273. Some parents insisted that their children concentrate on their studies (at the CLS only) and would not allow them to work. Interview in Hong Kong (Apr. 7, 1993).

son studied law like his father, and his brothers also followed practical professions in banking and accounting.[152]

Others chose law themselves, like the 1927 graduate who studied law because his father "was a jurist" and he shared an interest in the subject, or the thirties student who thought law might play an important role in Chinese society. A 1947 graduate was "very argumentative", always getting into disputes with his classmates, so he thought law practice might be a good career for him.[153] Other students were less focused, like the thirties graduate who was "going to do science but got tired of memorizing scientific rules"—until someone suggested that he try law instead (and his older brother was already a lawyer). Or the late forties student who did not do well enough on his mathematics examinations to pursue a career in science; if he chose literature he was afraid he would only be able to teach, so he "thought he would try law and then he could always become a judge"[154].

Why did they attend the CLS and not one of the many other law programs in the Shanghai area? For essentially three reasons (besides its evening hours): its good reputation, the professional nature of its training and its specialty in comparative and Anglo-American law. According to its graduates, the CLS had "high standards", it was "the best school in Shanghai", much better than the two law colleges and even Fudan University's law department, not to mention various "wild chicken" schools in the city. The Law School, moreover, was "very famous", "famous and prestigious", it had "very high status and its graduates were well-known lawyers and judges"—one thirties graduate said he came all the way from Guangzhou just to study there.[155]

Equally important was the kind of training the CLS offered. During the 1920s and 1930s, the CLS was the "only truly professional law school", known for its "practice orientation", whereas the others were "just undergraduate colleges"[156]. So one 1943 graduate enrolled because he wanted to practice law and the CLS "was the place for that"[157]. (Fudan University "really only trained you to become a judge", while the CLS trained its students for broader careers.[158])

The CLS, moreover, provided its students with the best preparation for Shanghai's international

---

[152] Interview in Taipei (July 29, 1987); Interview in Taipei (Nov. 9, 1989); Interview in Shanghai (Nov. 18, 1992).

[153] Interview in Taipei (July 27, 1987); Interview in Shanghai (Sept. 29, 1992); Interview in Shanghai (Nov. 25, 1992).

[154] Interview in Shanghai (Oct. 12, 1992); Interview in Hong Kong (Apr. 7, 1993).

[155] Interview in Taipei (July 29, 1987); Interview in Shanghai (Sept. 19, 1992); Interview in Shanghai (Nov. 25, 1992); Interview in Shanghai (July 30, 1990).

[156] Interview in Shanghai (Nov. 20, 1992); Interview in Shanghai (Nov. 24, 1992).

[157] Interview in Taipei (July 30, 1987).

[158] Interview in Shanghai (Nov. 20, 1992).

commercial environment. It was the only school that taught Anglo-American law, enabling students to practice in the International Settlement after graduation and, by all accounts, to dominate that practice. Lawyers in Shanghai "had to have that background and the language to deal with the Shanghai Municipal Council higher-ups". Many students, moreover, were "already working for insurance, banking and other companies where English was very important, so they thought Soochow University's course would be useful to them"[159]. Even later students were attracted by the school's specialty, including its emphasis on foreign languages and foreign relations.[160]

H. Study Abroad

Besides offering its own graduate program, the Law School also encouraged students to go abroad for further study. In the early days, students "all wanted" to study overseas: it was their "warm hope", though financially out of the question for most of them.[160] A foreign J. S. D. degree meant not only a prestigious title but a higher status and greater recognition upon their return to China (automatic promotion to associate professor during the 1930s, for example).[162] As a result, at least 15% of CLS graduates from 1918 through 1936 (a total of ninety-three students) obtained advanced law degrees from overseas institutions or were engaged in study abroad at the time of the school's 1936 survey.[163] In the late 1940s, Dean Sheng estimated that, despite all the difficulties of going abroad during the war years, 10% of the Law School's graduates overall had studied in the United States or Europe.[164]

Not surprisingly, given the school's close ties with American schools and teachers, most CLS graduates pursued their advanced study in the United States, although a handful also went to England, France or Germany. Students graduating between 1918 and 1936 attended more than fifteen institutions, including Harvard, Yale, Indiana and the University of Washington, but the most popular were New York University

---

[159] Interview in Taipei (July 30, 1987); Interview in Taipei (Aug. 3, 1987); Interview in Taipei (Nov. 9, 1989); Interview in Shanghai (Sept. 15, 1992). Some students attended the CLS through accidents of geography. One forties student, for example, was also admitted to Fudan University, which as a public institution would have been cheaper than the CLS. But Fudan University was a long way from his home and the CLS only fifteen minutes away by bus, so his father paid the extra tuition and sent him to the Law School. Another lawyer did *not* attend the CLS for similar reasons—it was too far away from his home and his father thought the area was unsafe during the war. Interview in Hong Kong (Apr. 7, 1993); Interview in Hong Kong (Feb. 8, 1993).

[160] Interview in Shanghai (Nov. 18, 1992).

[161] Interview in Taipei (July 29, 1987).

[162] Interview in Shanghai (Nov. 23, 1992). That situation has its parallels in the PRC today, with a foreign law degree often more highly valued than a Chinese one and returned students placed on an accelerated promotion track.

[163] 1936 List, supra note 123. My thanks to Albert Lam Kwok Ming for his help in organizing these statistics. By contrast, as noted above, only fourteen students obtained LL. M. degrees at the CLS during the 1928 – 1937 years.

[164] Interview with Dean Sheng in *Xinwen Bao* (Feb. 4, 1947), Shanghai Municipal Archives, Q245 – 268.

(twenty-one students, the largest number at any school), the University of Michigan and Northwestern University.⑯ For many students, CLS connections played a major role in determining their destination: Michigan was Dean Blume's school as well as Dr. Sellett's alma mater, and many students were given recommendations for NYU.⑯ Religion was at least partly the reason for some early choices; thus, Dean Sheng, a devout Methodist, chose Northwestern because of its Methodist origins as well as his desire to study evidence with Wigmore.⑯ Cost was also an important factor. Indiana, for example, "was a good school and relatively inexpensive" ($800 for all of a student's expenses in the mid-thirties)⑯, and one 1943 graduate attended Yale rather than Harvard because the latter refused to recognize all his CLS credits and would have required extra coursework (and therefore greater expense).⑯

I. CLS Careers

The Law School's graduates pursued a wide range of careers in government, business, teaching, the judiciary, and even church work, news reporting and translation.⑰ But by far the largest group of CLS graduates became lawyers. Unlike Beijing's Chaoyang Law School⑰, with which it was often compared, the CLS was known for training legal practitioners rather than legal officials ("Chaoyang produced judges, but Soochow produced lawyers")⑰, and the school's statistics bear this out. According to the 1936 directory of the Law School's first eighteen graduating classes (1918 – 1935), 41% were engaged in full-time and another 8% in part-time practice⑰, and even in later years the percentage of graduates in private practice

---

⑯ 1936 List, supra note 123. My thanks to Albert Lam Kwok Ming for these calculations.
⑯ Interview in Taipei (July 29, 1987).
⑯ Interview in Shanghai (July 30, 1990).
⑯ Interview in Shanghai (Nov. 23, 1992).
⑯ Interview in Taipei (July 30, 1987).
⑰ 1936 List, supra note 123; 1930 Announcement, supra note 53.
⑰ According to a popular saying, "In the north there is Chaoyang, in the south there is Soochow" (*Bei*, *Chaoyang*, *nan*, *Dongwu*). For more on Chaoyang, see Yu Fengxiang, Sili Chaoyang Xueyuan [Chaoyang College], in Zhang Qiyun, Zhonghua Minguo Daxue Zhi [University Annals of the Republic of China] 179 – 181 (1953). It was also said that "without Chaoyang Law School the judiciary could not be staffed." Except for a minority who went into teaching and research, almost all its graduates entered the judicial service. Id. at 181.
⑰ Interview in Shanghai (July 30, 1990); Interview in Shanghai (Oct. 12, 1992). According to Dean Sheng, only 10% of the Law School's graduates became judges; the other 90% went into practice, where they could make more money. Interview in Shanghai (July 30, 1990).
⑰ Many part-time practitioners were law teachers but others worked for banks or insurance or other companies. Companies often allowed their employees to engage in outside practice, and many teachers needed to do so in order to supplement their salaries. It was also sometimes difficult for outsiders (e.g., Cantonese without connections in the city) to break into full-time practice or to set up on their own in Shanghai. Interview in Shanghai (Nov. 23, 1992); Interview in Shanghai (Nov. 24, 1992).

remained high.⁽¹⁷⁴⁾ CLS graduates specialized in both civil and criminal law, and (according to a 1930s student) if you wanted someone to represent you, "you would never look for a Chaoyang University graduate, but only for someone from Soochow University".⁽¹⁷⁵⁾

Although they practiced law in some eighteen cities, most CLS practitioners remained in Shanghai: a total of 84% in 1936.⁽¹⁷⁶⁾ In that year, therefore, the school's graduates comprised more than 18% of Shanghai Bar Association's membership, even though the CLS was only one of the city's many law schools.⁽¹⁷⁷⁾ CLS graduates, moreover, were among the most active and distinguished members of the association; D. S. Chen, Loh Ting-kuei (Lo Dingkui, class of 1920) and Eugene Y. B. Kiang, in particular, served on its governing committees for many years.⁽¹⁷⁸⁾ Other famous Shanghai lawyers during the twenties and thirties—all qualifying as "important lawyers" (*da lüshi*), at least according to their advertisements—including Chang Nieh-yun (Zhang Nieyun), class of 1918; Herbert Chung-tao Lee (Li Zhongdao), Afman S. C. Hsi (Hsi Yafu) and Ruchin Tsar (Cai Liucheng), class of 1924; and Tsai Ju Tung (Cai Rudong), class of 1925.⁽¹⁷⁹⁾

▶ **6. CLS CONTRIBUTIONS**

The Comparative Law School of China was very much the product of its particular place and time: Shanghai and the foreign concessions between the two world wars, during a critical period in the

---

⁽¹⁷⁴⁾ These percentages are based on the careers of the 587 then living graduates for whom there is career information in the 1936 List, supra note 123. The list almost certainly underreports CLS graduates who ever practiced law, as legal professionals tended to change jobs frequently and to enter practice after engaging in further study or other legal work. Thus, the percentage of practicing lawyers in the earlier classes is somewhat higher: 55% of the first ten classes (1918 – 1927) were in full- or part-time practice in 1936. Moreover, these figures do not include the eight CLS graduates working as lawyers for the Shanghai Municipal Council in 1936. By contrast, 4% of CLS graduates were law teachers, 3% were judges, almost 16% held other government positions and 11% held jobs in banking, business or industry. Id. My thanks to Albert Lam Kwok Ming for help with these statistics. Despite all the changes the school's program underwent in later years, 39% of the school's graduates were still engaged in full-time practice in 1948. Soochow University School of Law, Gexiang Tongji Tubiao [Miscellaneous Statistical Charts] 63 (n.d.), Shanghai Municipal Archives, Q245 – 260.
⁽¹⁷⁵⁾ Interview in Taipei (Nov. 9, 1989).
⁽¹⁷⁶⁾ 1936 List, supra note 123.
⁽¹⁷⁷⁾ Shanghai bar membership is based on the statistics contained in 1936 Greater Shanghai Annual, supra note 10, at G237.
⁽¹⁷⁸⁾ 1935 Greater Shanghai Annual, supra note 10, at G121; 1936 Greater Shanghai Annual, supra, at G236; 1937 Greater Shanghai Annual, supra, at G169.
⁽¹⁷⁹⁾ These graduates all had entries in the major who's who directories of the day. Chen, Chang, Lee, Hsi and Tsai appeared in successive editions of Who's Who in China; and Jiang, Lo and Lee appeared in Men of Shanghai and North China. Who's Who in China, supra note 99, at 13, 35, 84, 138 and 231; George F. Nellist, Men of Shanghai and North China 195, 206, 246 (1933). For examples of their advertisements, see The Students of Soochow University, The Soochow Annual (1929).

establishment of a new legal system. It flourished during the "Nanking Decade", when China was most oriented to the West, and it succeeded because it offered practical and creative opportunities ideally suited to its era. But it offered something more and its influence has therefore survived beyond the circumstances that formed it.

A. Initial Contributions

Largely because of its emphasis on standards, ethics and the comparative approach, Soochow Law School made significant contributions to China's emerging legal system during the Republican period. First and most obviously, the CLS trained many lawyers, judges and law teachers, producing more than 1,200 graduates by 1949.[180] According to Hugh Chen, in the Law School's first twenty years alone, seventy-two graduates were teaching in colleges and universities, four were presidents of law schools, thirty-one were serving as judges, forty-one were working in the government, and seven were members of the Nationalist government's Codification Commission.[181] Some alumni have emphasized the role of CLS graduates as law teachers and drafters[182], while others name the distinguished judges associated with the school.[183] But CLS graduates tended to be versatile, serving in a number of capacities during their careers, and many occupied prominent positions in the legal world, as who's who directories of the day all attest.

Of course, numbers alone cannot tell the whole story. Other law schools could claim more graduates: Chaoyang Law School, for example, graduated almost 10,000 students over a twenty-one year period, and other Shanghai law colleges had much higher enrollments than the CLS.[184] As noted above, however, the CLS trained lawyers rather than legal officials, and many students enrolled there because they hoped to enter law practice. From the school's founding through the 1940s, a very high proportion of its graduates actually did so, and they played an important role in the private legal profession, particularly in Shanghai.

Equally important is the contribution made to legal scholarship by the CLS style of research and teaching; its law journal, for example, published articles of a high standard, and it remains a valuable resource for the study of that period. Whatever its limitations, moreover, the case method of teaching

---

[180] 1946 List, supra note 21; student files, Shanghai Municipal Archives, Q245 – 273 to Q245 – 299.

[181] Chan, supra note 65, at 148.

[182] Stressing the role of graduates like John Wu, Robert Sheng, Shelley Sun, Henry H. P. Chiu, Ho Shih Chen, etc. Interview in Taipei (July 29, 1987).

[183] According to Dean Sheng, for example, all China's judges who have served on the World Court were CLS graduates or teachers. Interview in Shanghai (July 30, 1990); Dean Sheng's handwritten list of CLS graduates and teachers (on file with author). Well-known CLS judges include Lloyd L. C. Char, Sherman J. K. Chang and Ni Zhengyu. The chief justice in Hong Kong, Sir Ti Liang Yang, attended the CLS for three years (1946 – 1949), although he completed his legal education in England. Lindy Course, Top judge gets term extended, S. China Morning Post, Sept. 14, 1993, at 1.

[184] Yu, supra note 171, at 181. See, for example, statistics contained in the 1935 Greater Shanghai Annual, supra note 10, at N18 – 19.

employed in many courses was more creative than the recitation of lectures and rote learning that often prevailed in law schools of the day. Certainly, CLS graduates still speak highly of the school's teaching fifty and even sixty years later. Moreover, beyond the active participation by many CLS teachers in drafting legislation, their general encouragment of scholarship and discussion of important national issues played a useful role during the 1920s and 1930s.

While the Nationalist government undoubtedly wished to raise educational standards, it also sought to control legal education (and ultimately lawyers), as Qing officials had earlier attempted to eliminate pettifoggers entirely. The authorities clearly viewed law as less important than science and technology—and even as dangerous and necessary to curb. By contrast, the CLS presented a different and broader view of legal education and the legal profession, one whose constraints were ethical and professional, and its teachers tried to demonstrate through their teaching and example the honorable nature of their calling. In so doing the Law School helped to introduce and to develop in China the idea of a modern legal profession, private and independent, with high standards of competence, ethical behavior and social responsibility. The CLS, moreover, imparted to its students a modern, outward-looking world view; it was above all that outlook and not simply the practical training they received that distinguished them from the quasi-professional of the past.

B. The Post-1949 Legacy

But has the Law School left any more lasting legacy? After 1949, the CLS was suspect from the beginning, too foreign in origin and too closely linked to the bourgeoisie throughout its history (it "was very hard to find a Communist" at the CLS). [185] The Chinese laws it had taught were all abolished, and within a few years of the Communist victory the school itself was closed. CLS connections also proved a liability for many graduates and teachers. Some, like Dean Sheng, had early problems: He was not only removed from his position but also declared a counterrevolutionary and sentenced to ten years of reform through labor in Gansu. [186] Hugh Chen, who was accused of being an American agent, also had a "very hard time" after 1949. Once a tall man who held himself erect, by the end of the Cultural Revolution he was bent over like an old man ("you could hardly recognize him as the same person"). [187]

Many other alumni were mistreated during the 1957 Anti-Rightist movement or the 1966 – 1976 Cultural

---

[185] Interview in Shanghai (Nov. 20, 1992). Foreign connections proved totally unacceptable and indeed were interpreted as control over Chinese education by Americans and other foreigners. "During more than 20 years under the Kuomintang rule, the United States strengthened its influence and control over Chinese education." China Handbook Editorial Committee, supra note 31, at 7.

[186] He was released after six years, on the intercession of Song Qingling, however. Interview in Shanghai (July 30, 1990).

[187] Interview in Shanghai (Nov. 25, 1992); Interview in Shanghai (July 14, 1993).

Revolution years. One thirties graduate, for example, was branded a rightist and forced to "wear a cap" simply because he wrote an article arguing that guilt should be proved beyond a reasonable doubt.[188] A 1946 graduate who had studied in the United States was subjected to protracted "examination in isolation" and finally demoted to a street market to sell pork.[189] Some CLS graduates died early because they "suffered a lot during the Cultural Revolution"; others "could not stand it and killed themselves"[190]. By the early 1970s, therefore, the Law School had seemingly disappeared without a trace, its graduates punished and their training wasted.

Yet any assessment of the CLS must take account of its continued influence outside the mainland, particularly in China's Hong Kong and Taiwan, where the Law School's graduates have by contrast prospered. Although the treaty port system was swept away forever in 1949, the internationalization of law and business has grown rapidly. In both territories the good English and solid legal foundation of CLS graduates, their practice orientation and genuine understanding of other systems have all proved advantages and enabled them to work in an increasingly international framework.[191] In China's Taiwan, moreover, the Law School—along with much of what it represented—has survived, if in a somewhat different form. Although the majority of its graduates remained on the mainland after 1949, many others, particularly those most closely connected with the Nationalists, fled to China's Hong Kong or Taiwan. In 1951, members of the Soochow Alumni Association in China's Taiwan began the process of re-establishing the University, beginning with its preparatory school, and three years later CLS graduates succeeded in reviving their school as the Soochow University Law College. Since its restoration in China's Taiwan, the law college has continued to emphasize Anglo-American law; it still offers its students the choice of enrolling in either the civil law or the comparative law section, in which many of the courses are classified as Anglo-American law and are still taught in English.[192] Its comparative approach has influenced other schools in China's Taiwan[193], and the school's faculty have taken an active role in international legal issues, including China's Taiwan's

---

[188] Interview in Shanghai (Nov. 20, 1992).

[189] Shop assistant returns to law school podium, *China Daily*, Mar. 8, 1983, at 3. He was later re-assigned to Nanjing University's newly-established law department, where I taught with him in 1983 – 1984.

[190] Interview in Shanghai (Nov. 20, 1992); Interview in Shanghai (July 14, 1993).

[191] Interview in Taipei (July 30, 1987); Interview in Taipei (Aug. 3, 1987).

[192] Course materials provided by the College of Law in China's Taiwan (on file with author); Soochow University Anniversary Catalogue (1982). CLS graduates were very actively involved in its refounding; D. S. Chen, Henry H. P. Chiu, Lloyd L. C. Char, J. K. Twanmoh all served on the early Board of Trustees. Arthur Yao and J. K. Twanmoh also taught at the School of Law. Bulletin of Soochow University (Taiwan School), 1952 – 1953, United Board Archives, No. 269/4289.

[193] CLS graduates and former teachers have taught at other law schools in Taiwan, where they were instrumental in introducing and teaching courses on the Anglo-American legal system. Interview in Shanghai (Nov. 24, 1992); Interview in Shanghai (July 28, 1993).

relations with the mainland. ⑭

Even on the mainland, many of the Law School's graduates and teachers have now made a comeback from exile or retirement, and consequently the school's name and influence have also been revived in the PRC. Since the implementation of economic reforms and the open policy in 1979, CLS graduates have resurfaced at courts, law offices, universities and other institutions. Despite the passage of thirty or forty years, their legal training has stood them in good stead, enabling them to participate in the re-establishment of China's legal system. ⑮ The Law School's graduates have also returned to teach another generation; many younger lawyers trained during the eighties, particularly in Shanghai, have had CLS teachers. ⑯ This suggests that the school has made a continuing contribution to legal education on the mainland as well as outside it—and that there may be greater continuity with the Republican period than scholars have previously thought.

▶ 7. CONCLUSION

CLS files and yearbooks as well as interviews with its graduates all demonstrate that students and faculty alike thought their school unique and were very proud of it. Their strong attachment is not unusual, since many graduates of other missionary schools (and government institutions) have expressed similar loyalty to their own "mother schools" (*muxiao*). ⑰ In the Law School's case, however, at least part of that feeling derives from its distinctive identity, including its emphasis on Anglo-American and, more broadly, comparative law.

Though it was based on a foreign model and taught foreign law, the Law School was not in the end simply a foreign institution. Like most other mission schools, the CLS had moved to Chinese administration,

---

⑭ Chiang son for seminar, S. *China Morning Post*, Feb. 10, 1993, at 8; Angel Lau, Chiang's grandson gets warm welcome, The Standard, Aug. 23, 1993, at 10; Agnes Cheung, Plan to boost Taipei as hub for mainland laws, The Standard, Feb. 11, 1993, at 10.

⑮ Interview in Shanghai (Nov. 20, 1992); Interview in Shanghai (Nov. 24, 1992). Some qualified to practice law and began practice for the first time after 1979. Interview in Shanghai (Nov. 24, 1992); Interview in Shanghai (Aug. 2, 1993).

⑯ CLS graduates may still be found at Peking University, Chinese University of Politics and Law and the Chinese Academy of Social Sciences in Beijing; and at the East China Institute of Politics and Law, the Shanghai Academy of Social Sciences and the Shanghai Institute of Foreign Trade in Shanghai. Dongwu Daxue Beijing Xiaoyou Hui Tongxun Lu [Address List of the Soochow University Alumni Association of Beijing] (1985); Dongwu Bijiaofa Jinxiu Xueyuan Zhaosheng Jianzhang [General Regulations on Enrollment of the Soochow Comparative Law Advanced Studies Institute] (1989) [hereinafter General Regulations]. CLS alumni still have high standards: When I asked a Chinese friend why he (unlike so many) made good use of footnotes, he replied that his strictest teacher, a 1940 CLS graduate, had always insisted on it.

⑰ St John's University, for example. Marlowe Hood, College's old boy network leads way to world, *Sunday Morning Post*, Dec. 18, 1988, at 17.

language and courses[198], and it was always firmly rooted in Shanghai, where it provided avenues of social mobility for many ambitious and eager young people, just as its founder had foreseen. Admission to the Law School did not require a classical education, family connections or a great deal of money, but it opened the door to many opportunities in Shanghai's commercial world. The Law School was above all a *Shanghai* institution, which in large part explains its success. Shanghai may have been the "other China"[199], but it was still China, and lawyers with special training had an important role to play there.

CLS graduates have now sought to revive their school in Shanghai, which is re-emerging as China's commercial and financial center. In 1989 the Soochow Comparative Law Advanced Studies Institute (*Dongwu Bijiaofa Jinxiu Xueyuan*) obtained official approval to begin offering courses to specialized cadres engaged in foreign economic work or legal duties.[200] That institution is currently a limited one, but the CLS model—high standards, a comparative approach and a broad understanding of other systems, all taught in China—may still have something valuable to offer as the PRC seeks to rebuild its legal system and to expand trade and investment with the outside world. Could the Law School, which in the words of former students was founded on a "whim" and refounded by a "fluke"[201], now be reborn in Shanghai?

---

[198] Unlike the more Westernized St. John's University, Soochow University did register with both the Nationalist government and its predecessor, and it attempted to comply with official regulations applicable to universities and colleges. Lutz, supra note 8, at 264-265, 267-270.

[199] See Marie-Claire Bergere, The Other China, in Shanghai 1-34 (Christopher Howe ed., 1981).

[200] More than a third of the originally listed faculty were graduates of the old CLS, and the Soochow Alumni Association has been active in running the Institute. General Regulations, supra note 196; Interview in Shanghai (July 14, 1993).

[201] The "whim" was Charles Rankin's. The Law School's refounding was something of a "fluke" and was due in part to the intervention of Wang Chung-hui, the recipient of a CLS honorary degree who continued to serve on its board of trustees in China's Taiwan. Interview in Taipei (July 26, 1987); Interview in Taipei (Nov. 9, 1989). Other influential graduates of the University or its middle schools also pressed for its re-establishment in Taipei. Interview in Shanghai (Nov. 24, 1992); Interview in Shanghai (July 28, 1993).

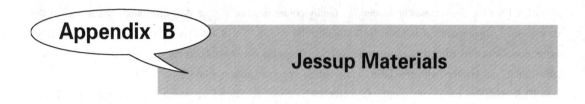

Appendix B: Jessup Materials

Writing Jessup Memorials

▶ 1. Introduction

The Jessup Compromis (also called the "Jessup Problem") is released by the International Law Students Association (ILSA) in September of each year. During the first four months of the Jessup Competition, teams analyze the Compromis and write their Applicant and Respondent memorials. These can be very challenging tasks, especially for first-time competitors. Like any other legal research and writing assignment, there is a great deal of work which must be done in a short period of time in order to produce quality memorials. It is important that you devote sufficient time to writing the memorials. Teams which leave the drafting to the last few weeks before the deadline will almost never produce a high-quality memorial. More importantly, you will not get the full benefit of what the Jessup Competition has to offer.

This part provides advice on how to write well-structured memorials that contain clear and coherent arguments. This advice is not intended to be prescriptive or exhaustive; there are different approaches to writing a Jessup memorial. The suggestions below, however, are based on many years of judging Jessup memorials and provide advice that will assist your team throughout the memorial writing process.

▶ 2. Purpose and Function of Memorials

Official Jessup Rule 6.0 governs the writing and submission of memorials. You need to review and follow the rules carefully: failure to adhere to the strict limitations set out in the rules can result in penalties.

Remember the ultimate purpose of memorials is to convince the Court that your side should prevail on the facts and on the law. Jessup memorials are expected to contain *written advocacy*; a Jessup memorial is not a neutral or carefully balanced research paper. You must make strong arguments and strive to persuade the reader that your case should win.

A. What Are Memorials?

Each Jessup team is required to draft and submit one Applicant memorial and one Respondent memorial. These documents contain submissions intended to persuade the International Court of Justice ("ICJ" or "Court") to rule in favor of the respective party. The use of memorials in the Jessup Competition attempts to mirror some aspects of the use of memorials in real cases before the ICJ.

Although the rules governing the memorials in the Jessup Competition are substantially different than the ICJ procedural rules, the essential purpose remains the same: the memorials are intended to allow each party to advocate its position by making legal submissions on the basis of its view of the facts. The major difference is that the Jessup Compromis sets out all the "agreed" facts, and the parties have limited scope with respect to manipulation of those facts.

Article 49 of the International Court of Justice's Rules of Court (1978) includes the following provisions:

- A Memorial shall contain a statement of the relevant facts, a statement of law, and the submissions.
- A Counter-Memorial shall contain: an admission or denial of the facts stated in the memorial; any additional facts, if necessary; observations concerning the statement of law in the memorial; a statement of law in answer thereto and the submissions.

Jessup memorials contain the same basic elements: facts, law and arguments.

B. Role of Memorials

a. Setting Out Your Case

Each memorial should set out the case for the relevant party and contain as much research as possible. However, most Jessup teams find that they will enhance or refine their arguments even after the memorials have been submitted. Further research, practice and competition after the memorial submission deadline often lead Jessup teams in directions not fully appreciated while writing memorials. You should therefore see the memorials as the first, albeit critical, attempt at setting out your case.

b. Foundation for Oral Argument

Official Jessup Rule 7.3.2 states that each team's oral arguments are not limited to the scope of its memorial. Accordingly, you are permitted to enhance or add to your memorial arguments or choose not to raise those arguments during the oral rounds. Although contradicting or retracting arguments in a memorial is permissible under the Official Jessup Rules, this may be noticed by the judges and your opponents, and may damage your team's credibility. For those reasons, it is important that your written arguments are chosen and drafted carefully.

Many teams rely on their memorials when developing their oral arguments, using them as a form of script. Doing so makes it all the more important that the arguments in your memorial are easy to follow, and presented as clearly and logically as possible. If a Jessup memorial judge finds it difficult to understand your arguments, you will find the same when it comes time for oral pleadings.

c. Memorial Scores

Each memorial will be graded and given a score. That score will go towards determining your team's:
- Win/loss record
- Relative position to other teams if a tie-break is required
- Ranking for memorial awards

The memorial score contributes up one third of the points for your team, with oral pleading making up the remaining two thirds. Accordingly, your memorial scores can be decisive in determining how well your team performs in the Jessup. For the Jessup teams that compete in the advanced stage of the International Rounds, the memorials are graded differently, but can still be the decisive factor in determining which team is eliminated.

▶ 3. How Memorials Are Graded

A. Memorial Scoresheet

Prior to grading memorials, Jessup judges are provided with a number of documents to assist in the grading process. These include the Bench Memorandum (a confidential document for judges only that addresses each issue in the Jessup Compromis, with citations to legal authority and scholarly works), a guide to judging memorials (a brief description of the role of the memorial judge and what parts of the memorial should be taken into account to determine a memorial score), and the memorial scoresheet. A sample memorial scoresheet can be found on the "ILSA" website (www.ilsa.org/jessup/admin.php).

The memorial scoresheet is detailed, and provides a good degree of guidance as to how to assess the memorials. For each category, memorial judges are expected to determine what factors to consider, and what weight to give to those factors, in deciding the score for the particular category.

B. Subjectivity of Judging

The categories in the scoresheet represent concepts that will be familiar and understood by each memorial judge and Jessup competitor. It is important to remember, however, that memorial judges (just like oral round judges) come from many different backgrounds and legal traditions, and may have different preferences for writing styles. For example, there is a difference between the common law advocacy style and the civil law advocacy style, and, even within each system, there are differences in memorial drafting style (for example, British and American lawyers may differ with respect to their preferred tone in a memorial). As another example, in assessing the citation of authority, different judges will have different expectations about how much authority they want to see for propositions of law.

Therefore, there is a degree of subjectivity in grading memorials which is unavoidable. It is possible that the same memorial will receive both very high and very low scores. To reduce the impact of such potential differences and subjectivity, each memorial is graded by three judges. You should keep in mind that, in the real world lawyers often are required to appear before, and submit written pleadings to, judges who come from very different backgrounds, with different preferences and expectations, so the Jessup memorial judging process mirrors the same subjectivity inherent in real international legal practice.

The advice in this part of the Jessup Guide is intended to reflect what, in our experience, most Jessup judges look for when grading memorials. If you follow this advice, your memorials will probably be well-regarded by most, if not all, memorial judges.

C. English Language Skills

Since teams from all over the world participate in the Jessup, varying degrees of proficiency in the English language are represented. Memorial judges are aware that English is not the native language of most Jessup teams and take this into account when grading the memorials. While judges are not told the identities of the teams (hence the use of team numbers rather than school names), they are generally able to distinguish memorials submitted by native English speakers from teams competing in a foreign tongue. Most judges, therefore, will allow for certain grammatical and syntactical differences which arise from non-native English speaking teams, and focus on the substantive quality of the arguments.

Nonetheless, the quality of the English in your memorials is important. The Official Jessup Rules state that English is the primary language of the International Rounds, and memorials are required to be in English for the International Rounds. The memorials written in a language other than English, within the rules of their National Rounds, must be translated into English if the team advances to the International Rounds.

In general, most memorial judges are primarily concerned with the quality and organization of the legal arguments. Memorials which provide good legal arguments arranged in a logical flow will generally score higher than memorials which, while grammatically correct, do not contain solid legal arguments. Teams should never sacrifice the strength of a legal argument in favor of better language skills, but should strive for excellence in both.

D. Memorial Word Count

The word count limit is an important consideration when preparing your memorials. Teams should not ignore the specific limitations in the Official Jessup Rules, as word count violations can result in substantial penalties to your memorial scores.

Please note that the *word count rule applies to footnotes*. Many Jessup teams receive substantial penalties because they did not take into account the number of words contained in their footnotes, which can alter the word count of the document by hundreds of words. Do not make this easily avoidable mistake.

> Official Jessup Rule 6.4 States:
> The word count shall be conducted using the standard "Word Count" feature in Microsoft Word 2003 or Microsoft Word 2007.
> (a) The total length of the Pleading, including the Conclusion/Prayer for Relief and any associated footnotes, must be no longer than 9,000 words.
> (b) The Summary of Pleadings must be no longer than 700 words.
> (c) The Statement of Facts must be no longer than 1,200 words.

> Official Jessup Rule 11.1 States:
> The penalty for excessive length of pleadings is the following:
> 1 – 100 words over = 3 points
> 101 – 200 words over = 6 points
> 201 – 300 words over = 9 points
> 301 – 400 words over = 12 points
> 400 + words over = 15 points
> The penalty for excessive length of the Summary of Pleadings is 2 points (one-time penalty).
> The penalty for excessive length of the Statement of Facts is 2 points (one-time penalty).

▶ 4. Preliminary Sections of Memorials

A. Required Parts of a Memorial

This section addresses the required preliminary parts of the memorial which come before the Pleadings: cover page, table of contents, index of authorities, statement of jurisdiction, questions presented, statement of facts and the summary of the pleadings. Section 5 provides advice on drafting the Pleadings themselves (including the Conclusion and Prayers for Relief).

Most of the drafting of the preliminary parts will have to wait until your team has almost finished the memorials (for example, the table of contents and the table of authorities cannot be finalized until the entire memorial is finalized). However, you should start your preparations early and bear the preliminary parts in mind as you draft the Pleadings, since the content of some of the preliminary sections will depend on the content of your Pleadings. Do not wait until the last minute to draft these sections—writing a statement of facts, for example, will take more time than you might think.

Apart from being mandatory under Jessup rules, the preliminary parts are important because, when drafted effectively, these sections can enhance the judges' perception of your team's substantive arguments and result in a better memorial score.

There is no official template for each preliminary part. If you review the award-winning Jessup memorials from previous years, it is possible to identify what should be included in each of the preliminary parts. Official Jessup Rules 6.3.2–6.3.5 also provide some explanation about the content of these parts. The best applicant and respondent memorials from 2006 through 2009 can be found on the "ILSA" website (www.ilsa.org/jessup/archives.php).

Despite the lack of an official template, the rules regarding the preliminary parts of a memorial have remained largely unchanged for many years, so the approach taken by successful Jessup teams in the past allows for the identification of some good practices.

B. Cover Page

A Cover Page should contain all the mandatory elements specified in Official Jessup Rule 6.3.2. Many teams use ornate Cover Pages, which incorporate the logo of the ICJ, different fonts, various borders or other formatting. As long as there are no careless mistakes on the Cover Page and it is in an easy-to-read font, its visual attractiveness makes no difference to a judge when grading a memorial. It is sufficient to have a plain Cover Page, with plain fonts and no borders, provided it is well-presented and contains the required elements.

C. Table of Contents

a. Purpose

A good Table of Contents will assist a reader in finding key sections of the memorial. Apart from this basic function, a good Table of Contents should also allow a reader to see, at a glance, that you have organized the memorial appropriately and logically.

The Table of Contents should include a list of headings contained in the Pleadings (see Appendix 1 for an example of a list of headings). This will allow a memorial judge to quickly review the structure and substance of your arguments, and assess whether your Pleadings include the key arguments required by the Jessup Problem. Many judges use the Table of Contents as a basic introduction to the detailed arguments. If you can create a good first impression with the list of headings, this can assist the judge when grading and improve the judge's overall perception of your memorial.

> Official Jessup Rule 6.3.1 States:
>
> The memorial must contain only the following parts:
>
> (a) Cover Page
>
> (b) Table of Contents
>
> (c) Index of Authorities
>
> (d) Statement of Jurisdiction
>
> (e) Questions Presented
>
> (f) Statement of Facts
>
> (g) Summary of Pleadings
>
> (h) Pleadings (including Conclusion/Prayer for Relief)

> Official Jessup Rule 6.3.2 States:
>
> The front cover of each memorial must have the following information:
>
> (a) The Team number in the upper right-hand corner followed by "A" if an Applicant Memorial or "R" if a Respondent Memorial (e.g., Team Number 123 would put "123A" in the top right-hand corner of the front cover of its Applicant memorial)
>
> (b) The name of the court (i.e., "International Court of Justice")
>
> (c) The year of the Competition
>
> (d) The name of the case
>
> (e) The title of the document (i.e., "Memorial for Respondent" or "Memorial for Applicant")

> Official Jessup Rule 6.3.3 States:
>
> The Index of Authorities must list all legal authorities cited in any part of the memorial and must indicate the page number(s) of the memorial on which each authority is cited.

b. Creating the Table of Contents Using Automated Features

When creating the Table of Contents, it is advisable to use the automated features in the word processing software. Creating the Table of Contents manually may result in formatting problems, cause page number errors and lead to unnecessary work and stress.

c. What Should Be Included in the Table of Contents?

The Official Rules do not prescribe format or content for the Table of Contents. However, over many years, the elements of a good Table of Contents have evolved to include the aspects found in Appendix 1 (this example was taken from a memorial used in a previous year, with its formatting adjusted for illustrative purposes). While there is no requirement to do so, most teams list the preliminary parts in the order in which they are found in the Official Rules. Alternatively, some teams believe that the "Questions Presented" should follow the "Statement of Facts", and precede the "Summary of Pleadings". With this order, the

"Summary of Pleadings" can be seen as answers to the "Questions Presented". Either method is acceptable.

The following formatting is suggested:

- Try to use only three (maximum four) levels of headings in the Table of Contents, per below:

I. Level 1
    A. Level 2
        1. Level 3

Using only two heading levels is not usually very helpful, while four heading levels can sometimes be unwieldy. See Appendix 1 as an example, as well as Jessup memorials from previous years on the "ILSA" website.

- The formatting of the headings should mirror the actual headings used in the Pleadings (that is, the Table of Contents should contain the same headings as those that appear in the Pleadings).

- No matter how many heading levels you include, you should make sure that each level is clearly distinguished from the others, using indenting and text formatting. You should be able to manipulate the formatting using the automated Table of Contents features in your word processing software.

D. Index of Authorities

a. Purpose

The Index of Authorities provides the location(s) in your memorial where a particular case, treaty or other authority is cited. Memorial judges use the Index of Authorities to obtain a quick impression of whether you have cited all the key treaties, cases and other sources of law which are relevant to the Jessup Compromis. They will also use the Index of Authorities to get an idea of the depth and breadth of your research—for instance, if you have cited too many domestic cases, or too many obscure journal articles, or done too little research because you cite only a few international cases. Judges can be immediately influenced—positively or negatively—by a quick perusal of the Index of Authorities.

b. What Should Be Included in the Index of Authorities?

Over many years, most Jessup teams have adopted a common approach to the Index of Authorities: sources of law are divided into major groupings, and within the groupings the sources of law are listed in alphabetical order (see Appendix 2 for a sample Index of Authorities). Beyond this, teams differ in how they group their sources of law, and the order in which they are listed.

The following groupings are suggested:

(i) Treaties and Conventions

(ii) United Nations Resolutions and Other Documents

(iii) International Cases and Arbitral Decisions

(iv) Municipal Cases and Laws

(v) Treatises and Other Books

(vi) Journal Articles

This is the recommended order because it roughly mirrors the hierarchy of the sources of law to which the ICJ is permitted to have access to when deciding cases, pursuant to Article 38(1) of the Statute of the ICJ.

Jessup teams often use their own labels for these sources of law. Sometimes they use a slightly different order and sometimes break down these groupings into further sublevels (for instance, international cases and arbitral decisions may be subdivided into Permanent Court of International Justice cases, ICJ cases, other international cases and arbitral cases). This can become unwieldy and may make it more difficult to quickly locate a particular authority. Whatever labels you choose for these groupings must be accurate.

E. Statement of Jurisdiction

a. The Usual Position Regarding Jurisdiction

In most years of the Jessup Competition, the jurisdiction of the ICJ is not disputed by the parties in the Jessup Problem. In such cases, the Statement of Jurisdiction is a standard statement that refers to the special agreement procedures derived from Articles 36(1) and 40(1) of the Statute of the ICJ.

There are various ways in which you can draft the Statement of Jurisdiction when there is no dispute as to the Court's jurisdiction. Some examples include:

- "The Republic of Appollonia and the Kingdom of Raglan submit the present dispute to this Court by Special Agreement, dated May 15, 2004, pursuant to Article 40(1) of the Court's Statute. The parties have agreed to the contents of the Compromis submitted as part of the Special Agreement. In accordance with Article 36(1) of the Court's Statute, each party shall accept the judgment of this Court as final and binding and shall execute it in good faith in its entirety."

- "The Republic of Appollonia (Applicant) and the Kingdom of Raglan (Respondent) have agreed *ad hoc* to submit the present dispute concerning the 'Vessel the *Mairi Maru*' to the International Court of Justice, pursuant to Article 40, Paragraph 1 of the Statute of this Court and by virtue of a Special Agreement (*Compromis*) signed in Washington, DC on May 15, 2004, and jointly notified to the Court on June 1 of the same year. Both parties have expressly agreed that no other State is a necessary party for the resolution of any of the issues that are the subject of the *Compromis*."

b. When the Court's Jurisdiction is Disputed

In some years, one of the parties in the Jessup Problem disputes the jurisdiction of the Court to hear the case or to hear one of the issues raised by the Jessup Problem.

In these situations, the Statement of Jurisdiction needs to be altered; the standard references to Articles 36(1) and 40(1) are not appropriate in circumstances where one party disputes jurisdiction notwithstanding its agreement to the case proceeding to the Court for consideration. The Statement of Jurisdiction for the party disputing jurisdiction must refer to the fact that the party does not accept that the Court has the relevant jurisdiction to consider the matter (with substantive argument on this point being left to the Pleadings). Similarly, the party asserting that the Court has jurisdiction must make this explicit in the Statement of Jurisdiction (with substantive argument being left to the Pleadings).

There is no particular formula for a Statement of Jurisdiction in such cases. It will depend on the nature of the dispute as to jurisdiction. However, to illustrate the concept, we have extracted two samples from Jessup memorials submitted in previous years:

- *Sample for party asserting that jurisdiction exists (Kuraca)*: "The governments of Kuraca and Senhava have agreed to submit by Special Agreement the present dispute for final resolution by the International Court of Justice, subject to Senhava's reservation of its objection to the jurisdiction of the Court. Although both Kuraca and Senhava have declared their acceptance of the Court's compulsory jurisdiction pursuant to Article 36(2), Senhava is seeking to invoke Kuraca's reservations, maintaining that the Court is without jurisdiction over the subject matter of this case because: (a) the dispute exclusively concerns matters which are essentially within the domestic jurisdiction of Senhava as determined by Senhava, and (b) the dispute arises under a multilateral treaty and some affected states are not parties to this case."

- *Sample for party disputing jurisdiction (Senhava)*: "The Governments of the State of Kuraca and the Republic of Senhava have recognised as compulsory ipso facto in relation to any other State accepting the same obligation, the jurisdiction of the International Court of Justice in accordance with Article 36, Paragraph 2. Senhava objects to this Court's jurisdiction on several grounds. It observes that Kuraca's declaration restricts this Court's jurisdiction by placing two reservations. Senhava, under the principle of reciprocity, relies on those reservations. Alternatively, Senhava contests the validity of Kuraca's declaration. Accordingly, Senhava requests that the Court decline jurisdiction."

ICJ Statute Article 36(1) —

The jurisdiction of the Court comprises all cases which the parties refer to it and all matters specially provided for in the Charter of the United Nations or in treaties and conventions in force.

ICJ Statute Article 40(1) —

Cases are brought before the Court, as the case may be, either by the notification of the special agreement or by a written application addressed to the Registrar. In either case the subject of the dispute and the parties shall be indicated.

F. Questions Presented

Teams generally take one of three approaches when drafting the Questions Presented:

- Repeating the relief claimed by the relevant party in the Compromis, but rewording the relief into questions

- Identifying the one or two key issues arising from each item of relief sought by the relevant party
- Breaking down the relief sought by each relevant party into a large number of questions which reflect the many issues and sub-issues raised by the Jessup Problem

There are usually four Prayers for Relief sought by each party. Your team should consider carefully whether it is sufficient to include only four questions which mirror the items of relief, or whether there are more issues involved. There will generally be more than four key issues raised by the Jessup Problem, even though most Jessup Problems are divided into four main topics.

On the other hand, the Questions Presented usually should not include more than eight questions. Each item of relief will generally raise one or two key issues. There is seldom justification for including more questions, and including more than eight questions may indicate that you have not thought carefully about the key issues and how they are interrelated.

G. Statement of Facts

Remember that the Statement of Facts is part of your memorial and, therefore, should aim to *persuade* the Court of your case.

It is very tempting for Jessup teams when preparing the Statement of Facts to do little more than copy and paste most or all of the facts from the Compromis, only slightly restructuring those facts. Resist this temptation: a well-drafted Statement of Facts usually distinguishes the very best teams from the average teams.

There is an art to drafting the Statement of Facts to comply with the restrictions in the Official Jessup Rules, while still presenting the facts in an advantageous way to support the particular party's position. A good Statement of Facts will demonstrate that the team has thought about which facts are relevant and how to present those facts to maximum advantage in light of the issues raised by the Jessup Problem, even in spite of the deliberate gaps and ambiguities included in the Compromis (you should have considered these matters in the process of analyzing the Compromis). Unfavorable facts must not be ignored, but they should be presented in such a way as to draw the readers' attention to more favorable facts. This takes practice and cannot be effectively accomplished at the last minute.

Some teams will find it easier to draft the Statement of Facts once significant progress has been made in drafting the Pleadings. Once you have considered the stated facts, the necessary inferences and how these should be used in the Pleadings, you will be in a much better position to draft the Statement of Facts without merely copying and pasting from the Compromis.

H. Summary of Pleadings

The Summary of Pleadings is crucial and is often the first section read by memorial and oral round judges (i.e., where the judges form their first impressions). The Summary of Pleadings must be more than a mere reproduction of the section headings contained in the Pleadings. The goal of the Summary of Pleadings is to distill the essence of the arguments in relation to each major pleading. This requires careful consideration and drafting.

As an example, consider the headings used for Pleading I in the sample Table of Contents included in Appendix 1. The major pleading has been broken down into three sub-headings, and two of those sub-headings are broken down into two further sub-subheadings. However, that detail needs to be turned into an effective summary of the major pleading:

"Raglan is responsible for the attack on and the wreck of *The Mairi Maru*. Customary international law dictates that states have an obligation to prevent piracy within their waters. Raglan failed to discharge this obligation by not addressing the piracy plaguing its waters for years. Even when Raglan instituted an anti-piracy program, it negligently administered it providing an opportunity for Thomas Good to commandeer *The Mairi Maru*. Moreover, as required by principles of state responsibility, Good's actions are attributable to Raglan. Thomas Good was an agent of Raglan hired and trained by the Raglanian Navy. Good's actions remain attributable to Raglan even if they are ultra vires because he was acting under the pretence of his status as a Raglanian naval officer."

The essence of the pleading has been concisely and effectively explained by this summary.

> Official Jessup Rule 6.3.4 States:
> Teams are advised that judges will take the following into account in evaluating the Statement of Facts. A well-formed Statement of Facts should be limited to the stipulated facts and necessary inferences from the Competition Problem. The Statement of Facts should not include unsupported facts, distortions of stated facts, argumentative statements, or legal conclusions. The Competition Problem typically omits certain facts which might be relevant or dispositive to the outcome of the case. Participants will be judged on their ability to conform the facts to their arguments without creating new facts or drawing unreasonable inferences from the Competition Problem.

> Official Jessup Rule 6.3.5 States:
> A well-formed Summary of the Pleadings should consist of a substantive summary of the Pleadings of the memorial, rather than a simple reproduction of the headings contained in the Pleadings.

▶ 5. Writing the Pleadings

The Pleadings section of the memorial demonstrates the quality of your analysis of the Compromis, the depth and breadth of your research, and, ultimately, your skills with respect to written legal argument. This is the most important part of a memorial, and requires significant attention during the first few months of the Jessup Competition.

A. Substance of Arguments

a. Avoid Unnecessary Arguments

The Jessup Competition is not only a test of a competitor's legal reasoning skills, but his or her ability to focus an argument on the important issues, while avoiding unnecessary arguments. This is especially important in the Jessup, as the Compromis is often drafted to purposely include false paths intended to lead the competitor to make such unnecessary arguments. As oral arguments are limited by time, and as memorials are limited by word count, the elimination of unnecessary arguments will give your team more time in oral rounds and space in the memorial, for the relevant issues raised in the Compromis.

When drafting a Jessup memorial, always keep in mind the main goal of the document: to persuade the Court to rule in favor of one of the parties to the dispute. A Jessup memorial is not a legal treatise on all topics which might be relevant to the subject matter of the Competition. Thus, a successful Jessup competitor will always keep in mind the Prayers for Relief when drafting the memorial, and ensure that the legal arguments do not stray from the relief requested.

In determining whether you should include an argument in a memorial, consider two interrelated questions:

- "Does this argument convince the Court to grant the relief requested?"
- "Do I *have* to make this argument?"

This requires:

—A careful assessment of what matters you *must* establish to succeed in your case

—Good judgment about what matters will be raised by your opponent which you can be expected to address on a preemptive basis (see Section 5(A)(d))

Jessup memorial judges devote significant amounts of time to reviewing numerous memorials, so they will find it frustrating to read through legal arguments that turn out to be meaningless or unhelpful to the team's ultimate goals. This frustration will be reflected in memorial scores, so make sure each argument that appears in your memorial is necessary to your case.

b. Avoid the Repetition of Facts in the Pleadings Section

Just as omitting unnecessary arguments frees up space for necessary arguments, avoiding a repetition of facts in the Pleadings sections will ensure that much-needed room for legal arguments is preserved. The memorial already contains the Statement of Facts, so repeating the facts in any detail in the Pleadings section wastes space.

Judges may react negatively to Pleadings which contain large quotes, paraphrasings, or other lengthy references to the facts of the case which are not integrated with legal argument. Keep such isolated statements of facts to a minimum. Instead, consider ways of referring to important facts in concise statements (properly footnoted), in connection with the larger legal position the memorial is advocating. For example, compare the two following quotes taken from Jessup memorials and note how the first example conveys the same meaning in a much more concise manner:

- " Thomas Good was clearly acting as an agent of Raglan when he boarded *The Mairi Maru*, since he had been selected by the Raglanian Royal Navy to pilot the ship and boarded the ship under the ostensible authority of the navy. He was still acting as an agent of Raglan when he took over *The Mairi Maru*".

- "Thomas Good was one of 100 Raglanian citizens selected and trained as pilots as part of an antipiracy program run by the Raglanian government. He was selected by the Raglanian Royal Navy to pilot *The Mairi Maru* through Raglan's archipelagic waters. In that capacity, he boarded the ship and once aboard, he took control of the ship. Thomas Good was therefore acting as an agent of Raglan."

c. Address Weaknesses in the Legal Argument

Many Jessup competitors fail to address weaknesses in their own side's case. If there is a well-known ICJ or other international court case that directly opposes one of your arguments, but you neglect to mention it, distinguish it, or otherwise attempt to persuade the Court to rule in a different manner, judges may assume you have not discovered it in your research or you have no effective response to the opposing case law. This can negatively impact your memorial scores, and you may also be called to account by the judges during the oral rounds.

Jessup memorial judges are well-versed in international law and will be aware of relevant case law and academic authority on the issues addressed in the Jessup Problem. Accordingly, it will become apparent to a memorial judge when a team is advocating a position without sufficient support or is ignoring contradictory authority. Thus, the memorial should show the judges that your team realizes and effectively deals with the key weaknesses in its arguments, while highlighting the positive authority which favors the team's arguments.

There are several ways to address weaknesses in a Jessup argument without undermining your own case, as explained below using examples from actual memorials submitted by successful teams in the past.

(a) Mention and Distinguish Negative Authority

If, as noted above, there is a case which holds against the legal argument advocated, a competitor may distinguish it factually. For example:

"Furthermore, Raglan has not breached its obligation to exercise due diligence in light of the decision in the *Corfu Channel* case, which obligates a state to notify other states of any danger to navigation within its jurisdiction. This is because such obligation only applies to risks that are unknown to other states. In our case, the fact of the piratical problems in Raglanian waters is a well-known fact due to the International

Maritime Bureau's Annual Piracy Report." (Footnotes omitted).

The case may be from a domestic or regional court that does not necessarily reflect the state of the law in the international community as a whole. For example:

"Although the granting of immunity to foreign States in cases involving human rights violations is frequently recognized by municipal courts, this position results in the denial of redress for the victims of human rights violations by third States. For this reason, scholars increasingly sustain that States do not have immunity or, that they implicitly waived it, when they breach their international human rights obligations." (Footnotes omitted).

The case may be old, predating significant developments or alterations in modern international law, or may be new, reflecting progressions in the law that have not yet gained the status of international custom. For example:

"Maritime violence and terrorism are relatively new concepts under international law that are still developing. There is not even a comprehensive or generally accepted definition on terrorism. As such there is [not] yet any consistent state practice in relation to maritime violence and terrorism, to constitute an obligation under customary international law. The United Nations itself has yet to produce a convention defining and prohibiting maritime terrorism, even though a report and recommendation has been issued in 1979. This shows that although steps have been taken, it fails to be finalized since the international community is not yet ready to create a strict legal obligation upon itself, mainly due to political difficulties in the current international arena." (Footnotes omitted).

The particular legal theory for which the case is cited might be mere obiter dictum or precatory language that does not create legal obligations. For example:

"A duty of notification to coastal states for shipments of nuclear materials has been proposed in treaty negotiations, but has never been accepted. Of those States who have requested prior notification, few have characterized the request for notification as a legal entitlement (opinio juris). Furthermore, of those States whose vessels have shipped nuclear materials few have accepted the existence of a legal obligation to notify coastal States." (Footnotes omitted).

The particular legal theory may be one arising from a convention obligation that does not actually bind one of the parties. For example:

"*The Convention on the Prevention of Marine Pollution by Dumping of Wastes and Other Matter* 1972 ("London Convention"), prohibits the dumping of radioactive waste except where the conditions set out in Article V of the treaty are established. Appollonia is not a party to this treaty. Pursuant to the *pacta tertiis* principle, the rights of Appollonia cannot be altered by this treaty without its consent. Raglan cannot rely on the treaty to defend its interference with an Appollonian flagged vessel on the High Seas." (Footnotes omitted).

As you can see from the above examples, a Jessup competitor need not always avoid the mention of negative authority. An advocate is expected to *assist* the Court with difficult legal issues, and to be candid about authority which may seem contrary to the advocate's case, because the Court must consider both sides of the case before reaching its decision. In both the Jessup Competition and the real world, failure to bring the Court's attention to such negative authority may cause the Court to form a negative opinion of the advocate.

(b) If the Law Is Not on Your Side, Make an Appeal to Equity

Occasionally, a Jessup Compromis will include a certain issue for which the great weight of the authority is in favor of only one side. In such instances, the judge reviewing a memorial arguing the minority side of that argument will look for the drafter to mention such great weight of authority, but perhaps focus more attention on the equitable arguments which may be supportive of the minority view. For example:

"The granting of an immunity can constitute a denial of justice. In the circumstances of the present case, the granting of an immunity to the Raglanian Royal Navy has denied effective remedies to Appollonian nationals and constitutes a denial of justice." (Footnotes omitted).

While an appeal to equity is certainly an important consideration when the ICJ—or a Jessup panel of judges—reaches a decision, judges would generally prefer an argument based on law and facts, as opposed to an overly emotional argument. An appeal to equity should generally be an argument of last resort, or an additional point to arguments supported by more persuasive authority. But if no such authority exists, an equitable argument based on public policy or real world effects may be the competitor's best and only option. Further, a good argument that appeals to the judges' sense of justice can raise your profile and credibility in the face of the Court, even if you "lose" on the law.

(c) Make Strategic Concessions

Jessup teams sometimes have to make a strategic decision as to whether and when to make concessions. At times, if the great weight of authority is against a particular argument, and the equitable considerations are likewise unfavorable, then a judge might be more impressed by a team that concedes that particular point of law, rather than wasting time arguing something that is sure to fail. A team that concedes that a particular legal theory supports the other side's position and concentrates the argument on a different legal avenue that might lead to the relief requested might be more successful with the judges than a team that argues against overwhelming odds.

Be careful when conceding a point. Concessions should be made only when there is no legitimate reason to argue about a particular legal point (for example, when the issue is very minor compared to others in the Compromis). Although you may have to concede a legal point, you will never have to concede an entire Prayer for Relief. Also, be aware of how a conceded point may affect the other arguments in the memorial.

(d) Alert the Judges When a Legal Rule Applies Differently in Different Situations

Most Jessup Problems require a team to make a contradictory argument in the same memorial, using the same rule of law to justify one position but refute another. For example, when addressing the issue of state responsibility, an Applicant team may have to argue that a person referred to in the Compromis is *not* an agent of the Applicant state for the purposes of attributing responsibility to the Applicant state for that person's conduct. On the other hand, that same team may find itself having to argue that a different person referred to in the Compromis, with a similar position of authority and in similar circumstances, *is* an agent of the Respondent state, and that such person's conduct is directly attributable to the Respondent state. Thus, a team will have to use the same rule of state responsibility to justify one position but refute another. This is a difficult balancing act and a team *must* let the judges know that this is happening and justify the distinction as to why the same rule of law applies to the two situations differently.

Most of these apparent inconsistencies can be addressed by carefully examining the facts in the Compromis, which usually provide some basis for a principled factual distinction. This must be made clear to the judges. Failure to address such inconsistencies could lead a memorial judge to believe that the contradictory arguments were written by different team members, without the team's reconciliation of the sections into a comprehensive, internally consistent brief (see Section 5(B)).

d. Predict and Address the Arguments of the Other Side

All Jessup teams are required to argue both sides of the Compromis, so both sides of a team should be able to anticipate most of the arguments that their opponents will raise. All teams, therefore, should have the ability to preemptively rebut the other side's arguments before ever encountering another team. Successful memorial drafters not only advocate their side's position, but respond to the anticipated arguments of their opponents.

When reviewing memorials, Jessup judges expect the teams to outline the law and how the law applies to the teams' arguments—a team that does so will receive decent or slightly-above-average scores. Judges are more impressed, however, when teams go even further, by stating how the law *does not* favor their opponents. Thus, judges often look for phrases such as "Applicant will likely argue …" (in a memorial for the Respondent) and "Respondent's only legal authority is …" (in a memorial for the Applicant) as a sign that a team is not only able to advocate a position, but can also anticipate the main points of the other side and address them. The following are examples of teams addressing their opponents' argument:

"Appollonia may argue that there were intervening factors that broke the causal link between the damage and the unlawful shipment. However, a closer examination of the facts revealed that the damage to the Norton Shallows resulted from Appollonian illegal act and is not severable from it." (Footnotes omitted).

"Notwithstanding, Rubria may argue that the few objections made bar Acastus' claim, equating this case to that of Yugoslavia. However, in such case, rejection of the continuity was expressed by the vast majority of States and rested primarily on political grounds given the ongoing atrocities in the region.

Conversely, Acastus' continuity claim was generally accepted and there are no major political reasons for rejecting its claim. " (Footnotes omitted).

A word of caution: your team must exercise careful judgment about how much preemptive rebuttal to use and which arguments to preemptively rebut. Remember that your primary responsibility is to establish your own case and you should not sacrifice too much space in favor of dealing with anticipated opposing arguments. Reserve preemptive rebuttal for only the most important opposing arguments which are obvious and could undermine your own case if you do not comment on them.

e. Respect the Hierarchy of Authority in ICJ Statute Article 38(1)

Article 38(1) of the Statute of the ICJ sets out the hierarchy of legal authority that Jessup competitors and judges must refer to when considering the relative strength of particular arguments: (a) treaties, (b) customary international law, (c) "general principles of law recognized by civilized nations" and (d) "judicial decisions and the teachings of the most highly qualified publicists". While some scholars and international lawyers might disagree, the prevailing view is that this list outlines a hierarchy of importance; that is, treaties will generally be thought of as more important than customary international law, while customary international law will be more important than "general principles of law", and so forth.

Jessup judges are well-versed in the hierarchy set out in Article 38(1), and will recognize when an argument relies on legal authority that falls further down on that hierarchy than an opponent's authorities. If a team's legal authority consists mostly of subsidiary works like law review articles, domestic judicial decisions, or studies by international organizations, a judge will likely give that team a lower score than a team whose authority consists of more persuasive sources such as treaties or custom. Whenever possible, teams should base the vast majority of their legal arguments on Article 38(1)(a) and (b) authorities, while using Article 38(1)(c) and (d) authorities as additional support.

There are ways to use subsidiary authorities with greater credibility than its relative position in the legal hierarchy would suggest. For instance, it can often be difficult to find and refer to evidence of relevant state practice and opinio juris to prove a rule of customary international law. However, teams can use subsidiary authority (such as scholarly works and judicial decisions) to support the argument that the stated rule is a rule of customary international law, thereby converting subsidiary sources into a primary argument. For example:

"Actual practices of states show that the international community requires shipping states to inform them and seek their consent of transboundary movement of nuclear materials through their territorial waters. This includes Canada, Djibouti, Libya, Malta, Pakistan, Portugal and the United Arab Emirates, Egypt, Guinea, Iran, Malaysia and Turkey and Mediterranean nations. Meanwhile, other states completely prohibit passage by ships carrying nuclear or other inherently dangerous or noxious substances.

In the absence of consent from coastal states, ships carrying nuclear materials had avoided passing through their territorial sea and exclusive economic zone as evidently shown in the incident involving the *Akatsuki Maru* and the *Pacific Pintail*. This shows that the duty to seek prior consent as obligatory under customary international law, thus proving opinio juris. Thus, the duty to notify coastal states of nuclear shipments is a rule of customary international law as it satisfies both the requirements of widespread state practice and opinio juris."

(Footnotes omitted, which cited scholarly works—i.e., Article 38(1)(d) subsidiary sources and national statistical reports to justify the statement that the theory is customary international law).

In short, unlike citing treaty provisions, it is not enough simply citing journal articles or other materials without explaining *how* these materials assist in establishing a rule of customary international law. Similarly, your team needs to consider carefully how and why you are citing cases, in light of the subsidiary status of judicial authority under Article 38(1). Teams that realize and demonstrate that they know treaties and custom rank higher than "general principles" and subsidiary authorities will impress judges more than those who ignore the Article 38(1) hierarchy.

B. Organization of Arguments

The organization of a Jessup memorial is an important consideration for judges when determining scores. Jessup Problems always involve a large number of legal issues, and presenting the arguments in a logical, flowing manner that the judges can understand and easily follow can be almost as important as the legal arguments themselves. Even the most brilliant legal arguments can be undermined if presented in an illogical manner.

The following advice includes several ways to improve the organization of a memorial.

a. The Order of the Four Main Submissions

Many Jessup teams use the Prayers for Relief in the Compromis (there are usually four paragraphs in the Prayers for Relief) as the basis for the order of main submissions in the Pleadings section of the memorial. It is common to organize the presentation of the main submissions/pleadings in the order in which the four paragraphs appear in the Prayers for Relief in the Compromis.

There is much to be said for this method. The first submission as listed in the Prayers for Relief often involves a threshold question of the ICJ's jurisdiction or competence to hear the case, which is a question which must be addressed before the Court can consider the merits of the case. Using the order of the submissions in the Compromis also provides consistency among the memorials submitted by the teams—and for judges who grade a large number of memorials each year, consistency is certainly helpful. Finally, the order of the submissions in the Compromis is also often split into the claims brought by the parties; that is, the first two submissions are generally regarding relief sought by the Applicant, while the second two submissions are generally relief sought by the Respondent.

On the other hand, there are times when a Jessup team might want to depart from the order set out in the Prayers for Relief and present arguments in a different sequence. As noted in Section 5(A)(c)((d)), Jessup Problems often require competitors to argue different interpretations of the same legal doctrine in different submissions. For instance, if the second submission and the fourth submission (in the order used in the Prayers for Relief) present the need for a team to argue divergent interpretations of a certain legal point, it might be more logical for a team to address those two divergent interpretations consecutively, rather than in sections separated by a completely different topic. This decision will also depend on how the submissions are divided among the oralists, so keep this in mind when determining which oralist will address which arguments.

Whether to rearrange the order of the submissions or not is a decision for each team to make. The most important consideration, though, is whether the flow of the Pleadings section is improved by such rearrangement. Judges are more likely to give high scores to teams whose memorials are organized in a logical flow, rather than in a haphazard assembly of legal arguments.

b. Separate the Submissions into Logical Sub-Points

Because a Jessup Problem involves so many legal topics, and because each topic usually involves the analysis of a number of different factors, it is important for Jessup memorial drafters to provide a logical breakdown of those topics and sub-topics to the judges. Rather than including a single heading for a large, general topic like "jurisdiction", a well-organized memorial will split the larger jurisdiction topic into logical subparts (for instance, "the text of the Statute of the ICJ", "decisions of the ICJ interpreting the text", "application of the law to the facts in the Compromis", etc.). The authorities collected during the research phase almost always provide logical partitions, which will help Jessup competitors structure their arguments, and will help the judges by providing a logical organization for them to follow.

c. Maintain a "Flow" Throughout the Memorial

The best writing, legal or otherwise, is that which brings the reader from start to finish without confusion. The easiest way to confuse a reader is to jump suddenly, without warning, from one topic to another with little or no transition to ease the reader into a new line of thought. As noted above, many Jessup judges read large numbers of memorials each year. When a judge encounters a memorial that does not flow easily from one topic to the next, he or she must re-read certain sections in an attempt to discover the intent of the drafters. Needless to say, such duplication of effort is not appreciated, and often causes judges to deduct points from that team's score.

Thus, it is important for a memorial drafter to ensure that the large numbers of legal issues addressed fit seamlessly together in a logically organized fashion, using clear headings and subheadings, and concise transitional phrases which link one section or subsection to another.

d. Using the Headings to Summarize Your Argument

As outlined in Section 4(C), the Table of Contents in a memorial is often used by judges to obtain an overview of the Pleadings. Accordingly, you should draft your headings so that they convey exactly what your argument is, not just the general topic of the relevant section.

For example, the following headings (contained in the sample Table of Contents in Appendix 1), are drafted so that they make submissions at each heading level:

> I. Raglan Is Responsible Under International Law for the Attack and the Wreck of *The Mairi Maru*
>
>   A. Raglan has breached its obligations under international law to suppress and prevent piracy.
>
>   1. *Thomas Good's acts of violence fall within the definition of piracy.*

Breaking down your Pleadings in this way will provide a good test of whether your legal arguments make sense, whether they are well-organized, and whether you have created a "flow". Summarizing your arguments by drafting the headings in this way will also assist the reader in following each step in your argument throughout the Pleadings.

C. Citation of Sources

Citation of sources is an absolute necessity, and the Jessup Competition maintains strict citation rules, the violation of which may lead to penalties assessed by the competition administrators.

Citation of sources is also helpful for the judges who score the memorials. Proper footnotes and source references allow the judges to verify how fully the competitors understand the facts and the law of the Jessup Problem.

Citation rules and methods are outlined in the Official Jessup Rules 6.5 and 6.6. However, *when* to cite sources can sometimes be a point of confusion for Jessup teams. There is a relatively simple rule to follow: citations should be offered for every statement of fact, quotation of another's words, definition or assertion of legal theory. This means that most sentences in the Pleading section will require footnoting with the exception of statements that are truly original thoughts from the drafters of the memorial. Plagiarism is a serious violation of the Jessup Rules and will be penalized accordingly.

Certain authorities are used many times in a memorial, and it would be very cumbersome for the drafter to include a full citation every time such a source is referenced. Citation signifiers *such as infra* (appearing later in the document), *supra* (appearing earlier in the document), *id.* or *ibid.* (appearing in the footnote immediately preceding) are useful. You should also include abbreviations of longer titles in the index of authorities and use these abbreviations whenever possible instead of signifiers like *supra*, *infra* and *ibid*. (for example, use *Barcelona Traction* rather than *Case Concerning the Barcelona Traction, Light and Power*

Company Limited (Belgium vs. Spain)).

Although insufficient citation is a problem, excessive citation is equally a problem. Some teams cite 10 to 15 authorities, or more, in support of some propositions of law. This is often referred to as "string citing", and is a problem which memorial judges note quickly. There are very few occasions where citing that many authorities is justifiable—perhaps the only justification is where the team is attempting to show widespread and uniform state practice. Whenever citing authority to support a point, you should cite only the authorities that are necessary in support of the point.

D. Writing Style

a. Consistency of Language

Jessup is a team competition, and therefore the research and written memorials are usually done collectively by more than one team member. While this team effort makes the research phase much easier for competitors by separating the duties and avoiding repetition of efforts, each memorial submitted to the judges should not appear as though multiple individuals wrote it.

To avoid this problem, teams should ensure that all of the research and drafting of memorial sections is completed much earlier than the submission deadline, leaving sufficient time for one team member to review and revise the *entire* memorial. This will help ensure that grammar, syntax and "voice" will remain consistent throughout the entire document. Rules allow a fifth member of the team to act as co-agent; it may be a good idea for this fifth member to act as the central memorial editor to ensure the level of English proficiency. Some teams prefer to conduct the final review and revision of memorials together as a team, so that all members are expected to agree on each line of drafting in the Pleadings. This approach can work, as long as your team leaves enough time for a group review.

b. Use Spell-Check and Grammar-Check

Most, if not all, word processing software includes both automatic spell-check and automatic grammar correction, and most of them will include both British and American English resources even if the standard language used by that team is not English. Memorials should not contain spelling or grammar mistakes since a quick and easy means of avoiding these problems involves simply pressing a button. However, teams should carefully read the memorials prior to submission and not rely *completely* on such automatic corrections.

E. The Conclusion/Prayer for Relief

This is a required element of the Pleadings, but there is no prescribed format or content for this section. Many Jessup teams simply copy and paste the paragraphs from the Prayer for Relief in the Compromis for the relevant party and use this as the Prayer for Relief in the memorial. This may be preceded by brief concluding remarks. Teams often include this final section on the last page of the Pleadings. Please refer to

Appendix 3 for examples of Prayers for Relief.

▶ 6. Getting the Most Out of Writing Jessup Memorials

The objective of this part of the Guide is to help you write high-quality memorials for the Jessup Competition. However, the advice herein is not obligatory, prescriptive or exhaustive. Each team needs to find its own way of approaching the task of writing the memorials. If you keep in mind the main tasks involved in writing memorials, the main problems which teams encounter throughout the writing process and our suggestions for overcoming those problems, you will have a solid foundation upon which to write your memorials. Remember: your task is to persuade.

Appendix 1—Sample Table of Contents

Table of Contents

Index of Authorities ·· iv

Statement of Jurisdiction ·· xiii

Questions Presented ·· xiv

Statement of Facts ··· xv

Summary of Pleadings ··· xviii

Pleadings ··· 1

   I. **Raglan Is Responsible Under International Law for the Attack and the Wreck of the Mairi Maru**
··· 1

     A. **Raglan has breached its obligations under international law to suppress and prevent piracy**
··· 1

        1. Thomas Good's acts of violence fall within the definition of piracy ············ 3

        2. Raglan failed to fulfill its obligations under international law because it failed to suppress piracy in its archipelagic waters and failed to properly respond to the attack on the Mairi Maru ······ 4

     B. **Raglan is responsible for the attack and the wreck of the Mairi Maru because Raglan failed to respond appropriately to the pirate attacks in violation of its obligations under international law** ·· 5

     C. **Raglan is responsible for the attack and the wreck of the Mairi Maru because Thomas Good's acts are attributable to Raglan** ·· 6

        1. Thomas Good was an agent of the Raglanian government ·························· 6

        2. Thomas Good's actions are attributable to Raglan even if they are ultra vires or contravene

Raglan's instructions 8

Appendix 2—Sample Index of Authorities

Index of Authorities

A. Treaties and Conventions

Convention on the High Seas 1958, Apr. 29, 1958, 450 U. N. T. S. 82 6,9,11

Convention on the Territorial Sea and Contiguous Zone 1958, 29 Apr. 1958, 516 U. N. T. S. 205 11

United Nations Convention on the Law of the Sea 1982, 10 Dec. 1982, 1833 U. N. T. S. 3
.... 6,7,11,19

B. United Nations Resolutions and Other Documents

Declaration on the Inadmissibility of Intervention in the Domestic Affairs of States, GA Res. 2131 (XX) 1965
.... 6

International Law Commission, Draft Articles on the Responsibility of State for Internationally Wrongful Acts, UN Doc. A/CN. 4/L. 602/Rev. 1 (2001) 1,2,3,7,10,16

International Law Commission Report for the Commission's Fifty-fifth Session (2004) 5

C. International Cases and Arbitral Decisions

Corfu Channel Case (*UK v. Albania*) (Merits), ICJ Rep. 1949 .... 4, 25

Factory at Chorzów (*Claim for Indemnity*) Case (*Germany v. Poland*) (Merits), PCIJ Ser. A, No. 17, 1928
.... 10

Gabčíkovo-Nagymaros Project Case (*Hungary v. Slovakia*), ICJ Rep. 1997 .... 7, 8

Lotus Case (*France v. Turkey*), PCIJ Ser. A, No. 10, 1927 6

Military and Paramilitary Activities in and Against Nicaragua Case (*Nicaragua v. USA*), ICJ Rep. 1986 ... 5

Neer, 4 R. I. A. A. 60 (U. S. -Mex. 1926) 17

Nottebohm Case (*Liechtenstein v. Guatemala*), ICJ Rep. 1955 .... 6, 10

Rainbow Warrior (N. Z. v. Fr.) 10 R. I. A. A. 217 (1990) 25

D. Municipal Cases and Laws

Container Corp. of America v. Franchise Tax Board, 463 US 159, 103 S. Ct. 2933, 77 L. Ed. 2d 545 (1983)
.... 13

Street v. Corr. Corp. of Am., 102 F. 3d (6th Cir., 1996) 2

E. Treatises and Other Books

L. Alexander, Navigational Restrictions Within the New Los Context (1986) 18

H. Grotius, The Freedom of the Seas (trans. by R. Magoffin, 1916) 18

A. de Hoogh, Obligation Erga Omnes and International Crimes (1996) ·················· 17

F. Journal Articles

O. Akiba, International Law of the Sea: The Legality of Canadian Seizure of the Spanish Trawler (Estai), 37 Nat. Res. J'l (1997) ·················· 7

A. Laursen, The Use of Force and (the State of) Necessity, 37 Vand. JTL 2004 ·················· 8

Van Zwanenberg, Interference with Ships on the High Seas, 10 ICLQ 1961 ·················· 7

Appendix 3—Two Sample Prayers for Relief

Prayer for Relief

Appollonia respectfully requests this Honourable Court to adjudge and declare that:

(a) Raglan is responsible for the attack and the wreck of *The Mairi Maru* and all consequences thereof by virtue of (i) the acts of Thomas Good, which are imputable to Raglan and (ii) its failure to respond appropriately to unlawful activities in its archipelagic waters.

(b) Raglan is responsible for the loss of *The Mairi Maru* and its cargo because Raglan's scuttling of the vessel was illegal and, therefore, Raglan owes compensation to Appollonia on behalf of its citizens who suffered direct financial and other losses.

(c) Raglan does not have standing to seek compensation for economic losses resulting from acts that occurred wholly outside of its territorial waters and exclusive economic zone.

(d) Appollonia did not violate any obligations owed to Raglan under international law in transporting MOX through the waters of the Raglanian Archipelago.

Conclusion and Prayer for Relief

For the foregoing reasons, the Kingdom of Raglan, the Respondent, respectfully prays that this Honorable Court:

1) DECLARE Raglan is not responsible for the attack on the Mairi Maru and owes no compensation to Appollonia for any injury resulting therefrom.

2) DECLARE Raglan's act of scuttling the Mairi Maru was in accordance with international law.

3) DECLARE Appollonia had violated international law by transporting MOX through Raglan's archipelagic waters without prior notification or consent of Raglan.

4) ORDER Appollonia to pay compensation to Raglan for the cost of its decontamination efforts and for the loss suffered by its ecotourism and sport fishing industries.

Using Jessup Skills in Your Legal Career

▶ 1. Introduction

Most students who compete in the Jessup will go on to practice law, either in a law firm, corporation, government or the nonprofit sector. Others will pursue a career in academia. Whatever your career choice, your participation in the Jessup will provide you with a set of skills and experiences that will be of great value to your future practice. This remains true even for those students whose practice does not involve public international law, and for those students who do not become litigators. The skills demanded and developed by the Jessup are cross-disciplinary and essential to all lawyers, whether practicing mergers and acquisitions in a large international law firm, immigration law at a small boutique practice or as a government lawyer working on health care legislation.

Like any single course or activity in law school, the Jessup cannot fully prepare you for the professional practice of law. However, students who compete in the Jessup emerge with abilities and experiences that give them a distinct advantage over those who have not. This is particularly true for those competitors from countries and jurisdictions where moot court is not part of the traditional law school curriculum.

The purpose of this section of the Jessup Guide is to help students identify the skills learned while competing in the Jessup and illustrate how these skills will be beneficial throughout their careers.

▶ 2. Skills Needed for a Successful Legal Career

Lawyers are, first and foremost, problem solvers. Clients, be they corporations, individuals, foundations or governments, come to lawyers with a specific legal problem and expect a solution.

Solutions may come in the form of a simple "yes" or "no" answer, or may involve a lengthy legal analysis and long-term plan of action. But, in all circumstances, a lawyer is expected to communicate a clear, understandable and legally sustainable answer to the client's specific problem. Lawyers are also expected to be creative and imaginative in the generation of ideas, especially when a legal problem has no obvious or decisive solution (not an uncommon experience in law practice). Lawyers must exercise good judgment and be prudent in every recommendation he or she makes.

A lawyer cannot be a useful problem solver or idea generator if he or she cannot effectively communicate ideas and solutions in writing and orally. Detailed knowledge of the law is essential, but without excellent written and oral communication skills, legal knowledge will not be useful to a client.

The vast majority of lawyers will work with other lawyers in a team, the size of which can vary anywhere from two to two hundred. Relationships in such teams demand flexibility and willingness to play either a supporting or leadership role, depending on the circumstances. Lawyers are constantly interacting with opposing counsel, clients, judges, government officials and counterparties. A lawyer must be able to work with others in a collegial and professional manner towards a common goal of providing a client the best possible advice or approach to a particular problem.

Finally, a lawyer is expected to work hard. Because the implications of improper legal advice can have serious consequences, lawyers simply cannot afford to be lazy with their work. They must expend maximum efforts to provide the solution the client wants and needs. At the same time, lawyers do not have unlimited time in which to think about the facts and the law. Accordingly, lawyers must be efficient with their tasks, focusing on the issues that are most relevant and setting aside those which are unimportant. The ability to prioritize and distinguish between important and unimportant issues requires sound judgment.

The above abilities—problem solving, idea generation, creativity, sound judgment, effective written and oral communication, team work, ability to prioritize—are all skills that the Jessup is intended to foster in law students. Each particular phase of the Jessup Competition, starting from the day the Compromis is released until competitors shake hands with opponents after their final oral round, demands and develops each of these skills.

A. Fact Analysis

The first section of the Jessup Guide is entitled "Working with the Compromis". It is no coincidence that a discussion of how to read and analyze the facts set out in the Compromis comes before the section on how to conduct international law research ("Researching International Law"). Gathering and understanding the facts of a case, transaction or other legal situation is the critical first step for any lawyer before substantive legal research can begin. Lawyers who start to develop legal theories without first assessing the available facts are doing their clients and themselves a disservice.

The Jessup Compromis is a complicated fact pattern that is purposely designed to include both important and unimportant factual details ("unimportant" in this context usually means a fact that is not essential to the relevant legal analysis). As described above, a good lawyer has the judgment to distinguish between important and unimportant facts, and can prioritize the important facts in the overall context of the legal analysis. A good lawyer can also recognize the value in a seemingly unimportant fact. Jessup competitors are expected to do the same.

Of course, in real world legal practice, the facts are never as self-contained as they are in the Jessup Compromis. And young lawyers are often tasked with legal research projects that are far removed from the facts of a particular matter (either because they are unknown at the time, or the legal issues to be researched can be analyzed without reference to the facts). Nevertheless, Jessup judges are always impressed with those competitors who are able to focus on the important factual details and use even seemingly obscure facts to support their legal arguments. This is an important exercise that will yield benefits when it comes to undertaking fact gathering and analysis in your legal career.

B. Legal Research

Young lawyers spend many hours conducting research of both primary (case law, codes, legislation) and secondary (treatises, articles) sources. The ability to conduct legal research effectively and efficiently is crucial. Lawyers are not only expected to find and understand the relevant legal authorities, they are also expected to find such authorities within a limited amount of time.

As the Jessup Guide section on "Researching International Law" points out, conducting research in public international law is somewhat unique because of the disparate sources of law. Nonetheless, Jessup competitors have the experience of setting out a research action plan, identifying the hierarchy of legal sources, conducting systematic and intensive legal research in a limited period of time and distinguishing the most important legal authorities from less important sources. These are essential skills for young lawyers regardless of the subject area of law being researched.

Furthermore, those Jessup students who take advantage of the free electronic legal database passwords distributed annually by the International Law Students Association ("ILSA") are also exposed to what is now an established method of legal research. For those competitors from countries that do not have regular access to such legal databases, knowledge of the basic search techniques is an advantage when applying for a job as a young lawyer.

C. Legal Writing

Most lawyers spend a significant portion of their time writing memoranda, letters, e-mails, legal briefs, etc. As noted above, in-depth knowledge of the facts and law are of little value if a lawyer cannot communicate effectively in writing. Legal writing must be clear, concise, precise and understandable to the readers. Any written work product, whether it is a brief to the highest court in the land or an explanatory e-mail to another lawyer, must be well-organized and presented logically. As all students may discover during the Jessup Competition, legal writing is an ongoing process that requires regular reassessment of assumptions and refocusing of the inquiry, as well as constant editing and revision.

The Jessup is obviously focused on written advocacy, i.e., a submission designed to convince the court of the correctness of your case. This is obviously helpful to those students interested in a litigation career, either before national courts and administrative bodies or before international courts and arbitration tribunals. Jessup competitors will be pleasantly surprised to see how similar the Jessup rule requirements and style of written memorials are to other types of written advocacy submissions.

But the legal writing skills developed during the Jessup are relevant for all areas of legal practice. Of course, the purpose and method of writing a memorial is different than drafting a commercial contract or a client memorandum, but they involve the common goal of conveying information in a clear, precise, logical and understandable fashion. Regardless of your career choice, you will find the Jessup writing process to be of great value.

D. Oral Advocacy

The Jessup is clearly invaluable experience for those students who pursue a career as an advocate before domestic and international courts and tribunals. Indeed, many Jessup alumni report that the grilling by judges during the Competition was more challenging (and rewarding) than what they usually experience before real judges and arbitrators. Oral argument at the Jessup is great practice for real world advocacy because the goals are the same: to answer questions, clarify confusion and satisfy doubt in the minds of the judges, reinforce the key arguments in the written submissions and to effectively demonstrate to the court that your position is legally well-supported and preferable to the position of the other side.

But even those students who do not choose a career in litigation will come to realize the importance of effective oral communication. All lawyers, regardless of practice area, are called upon to give presentations, explain a client's position to opposing counsel, negotiate with counterparties and participate in conference calls. In so doing, a lawyer must be confident and able to clearly express their ideas in a manner appropriate for the audience. Effective public speaking takes many years to master, but the Jessup is a formidable stage in the development of those skills.

Teams from more than 80 countries worldwide participate in the Jessup and many of the students are not native English speakers. The fact that many Jessup competitors are speaking in their non-native language makes the public speaking element of the Jessup all the more impressive.

E. Time and People Management

Jessup competitors around the world share the experience of intense interaction with their teammates and coaches while trying to balance other commitments, both academic and personal ones. Law practice is no different. Lawyers are constantly juggling assignments, court appearances, meetings, drafting, appointments and travels. Those who are able to manage such conflicts with as little stress as possible are usually the most effective lawyers, and they also tend to be the happiest. Jessup competitors who are able to effectively balance the incredibly demanding memorial drafting and oral pleading practice schedule with their other schoolwork, as well as their personal lives, will be well placed to do the same in a professional legal environment.

Managing people is also a critical part of law practice. Lawyers often work in teams, but also have constant interaction with legal assistants, secretaries and service providers (e.g., couriers, photocopy and binding, court clerks, etc.). Convincing people to willingly cooperate and perform their required tasks within a tight deadline is not always easy, especially when stress levels are high. Jessup competitors have been exposed to the reality of working in a small team with a single goal (i.e., drafting a good memorial and winning oral pleading rounds), as well as having to deal with librarians, professors and fellow students while preparing for the Competition. This is very similar to the experience many will have in their professional environments.

F. Professionalism

Some competitors find the Jessup rules of behavior (both written and oral) peculiar and overly formal, such as addressing judges as "Your Excellency", immediately asking the president for extra time once time has expired and never speaking at the counsel table. However, proper respect and deference shown to the court and to one's adversaries is an essential part of building the integrity and effectiveness of the legal system, and is indispensible to building one's personal image as a professional lawyer.

At first glance, this may seem like an insignificant skill set for a legal career, but it should not be underestimated. Jessup competitors will be surprised at the lack of professionalism amongst some lawyers, even at the highest levels of private and public practice. Breaches of etiquette and bad behavior not only brings the general image of lawyers into disrepute, but such behavior usually ends up having negative consequences for the client that the lawyer is supposed to be helping. Similarly, Jessup competitors will find themselves penalized if proper respect is not shown to the judges, fellow competitors and volunteers at the competition venue.

This makes it all the more important for Jessup competitors to maintain the practice of decorum and civility that the Competition demands. By learning to treat judges and your opponents with respect, even when in vigorous disagreement, Jessup competitors are taking an important step towards cultivating an image of professionalism.

G. Cultural Awareness and International Experience

In a globalized world, lawyers are increasingly called upon to deal with cases and transactions with significant cross-border issues and ramifications. But many lawyers feel uncomfortable when dealing with opposing counsel, clients or counterparties from other countries. Jessup competitors have a big advantage in this respect. Not only does the subject area of the Jessup—public international law—facilitate international peace and cooperation, but the format of the entire Competition is geared to foster cultural understanding amongst students and judges from dozens of countries. This is an invaluable experience for lawyers whose practice requires interaction with foreign parties.

H. Substantive Knowledge of International Law

Most Jessup competitors will never have the honor of appearing before the real International Court of

Justice. But this does not mean the deep knowledge of international law developed by Jessup competitors will go to waste. Opportunities to practice international law abound in government foreign ministries, the United Nations, international organizations (e.g., World Bank), and nongovernmental organizations (especially those focused on international human rights). Public international law is also increasingly important in cross-border disputes and transactions involving corporations, so there are now greater opportunities for Jessup alumni to put their knowledge of international law to good use in private law firm practice. International trade law, sovereign immunity, economic sanctions, export control regimes, foreign corrupt practices, international environmental regulations and foreign investment treaty arbitration are all sub-areas of public international law that are increasingly important to corporations.

▶ 3. Conclusion

As a tool of legal education, there are few experiences that rival the Jessup. What is also unique about the Competition is how it reflects real world law practice in so many ways. Those competitors that put in requisite time and efforts to the Competition will be better prepared for professional law practice than their peers who did not compete in the Jessup.

Sample Predictive Memorandum

SAMPLE PREDICTIVE MEMORANDUM

MEMORANDUM

TO: Joe Smith
FROM: Legal Intern
DATE: November 17, 2012
CASE: Luke Baird v. Betsy Schmidt; file number 0928-78
RE: Internet jurisdiction; motion to dismiss due to lack of minimum contacts

QUESTION PRESENTED

Luke Baird, an Illinois resident, has field a complaint against Betsy Schmidt in the Northern District of Illinois alleging defamation through a posting on lovehimorleavehim.com. In the posting, Schmidt accused Baird of conducting an extramarital affair while on business trips. The posting was forwarded via e-mail to Baird's wife and employer in Illinois. By posting the accusation, has Schmidt established sufficient minimum contracts with Illinois such that the court may exercise personal jurisdiction over her?

BRIEF ANSWER

Probably yes. Under the Due Process Clause as interpreted by the Supreme Court and the Seventh Circuit, a non-resident defendant establishes minimum contacts with a forum by committing an (a) intentional act which is (b) expressly aimed at the forum and (c) causes harm, the brunt of which is suffered—and which the defendant knows is likely to be suffered—in the forum. Schmidt's intentional posting of the statements is not in dispute and she expressly aimed her actions at the forum by referencing Illinois in her posting, identifying Baird's Illinois employers, and inciting readers to contact Baird's wife. The court will presume that the harm has accrued in Illinois since that is where Baird resides. Because Schmidt knew that Baird lived and worked in Illinois and refused to remove the posting, she knew or should have known that her actions would likely harm Baird in Illinois. Thus, the court will likely find that Schmidt established minimum contacts with Illinois such that it is entitled to exercise personal jurisdiction over her.

FACTS

On May 24th, 2012, Defendant Betsy Schmidt ("Schmidt"), a California resident, posted an anonymous profile page about Illinois resident Plaintiff Luke Baird ("Baird") on the lovehimorleavehim.com website. Compl. ¶14; Schmidt Aff. ¶18; Baird Ex. A. Lovehimorleavehim.com, Inc. ("Lovehimorleavehim"), an online "community for truth in dating", provides a forum for users to post comments about the truthfulness of personal dating profiles located on other websites. Compl. ¶6. Schmidt's posting—which included Baird's photograph, full name, and "perfectmatch.com" username of "drlove"—referred to Baird as a "lying cheating bastard", and accused him of conducting an affair with Schmidt while he was engaged to another woman. Baird Ex. A. In addition to its account of Baird's infidelity to his then-fianeé and current wife, Schmidt's posting also described Baird's questionable business practices of using research grants from his post-doctoral fellowship at the University of Chicago to fund trips taken with Schmidt. Id. According to Schmidt, she created the posting on lovehimorleavehim.com in order to "alert other women to [Baird's] lies". Schmidt Aff. ¶17.

None of the material events referenced in Schmidt's posting occurred in Illinois. See id. at ¶7-12; Baird Ex. A. Schmidt and Baird first met during elementary school in California, Schmidt Aff. ¶1, and during the course of their affair, they only spent time together in California and Washington, id. at ¶7,11-12. Nevertheless, the posting did mention Baird's wife, Denise, by name along with Denise's employment at the Latin School in Chicago. Baird Ex. A. Schmidt wrote, "I hope someone lets her know about him …" Id. The posting also described Baird's employment as a post-doctoral fellow at the University of Chicago, id., while listing Illinois, California, Maryland and Washington as the posting's relevant locations, id. Schmidt claims that she selected these locations because they were the locations that Baird himself had listed on his perfectmatch.com profile. Schmidt Aff. ¶19.

Lovehimorleavehim is a Delaware corporation with its principal place of business in Menlo Park, California. Compl. ¶3. Although the website is accessible worldwide, users may search the profile pages on the website by their listed geographic locations. Id. at ¶17. At least 200 of the profile pages located on lovehimorleavehim.com feature individuals located in Illinois. Id. at ¶7. The website, which averages 300,000 visitors per day, id. at ¶8, allow users to create and post profile pages, respond publicly to profiles, and to email the poster directly. id. at ¶19.

After Schmidt created and submitted the profile page on lovehimorleavehim.com, she e-mailed a hyperlink to the page to five friends, none of whom lived in Illinois. Schmidt Aff. ¶23. Schmidt did not ask any of her friends to forward the hyperlink to anyone else, but someone did forward the link to Baird's wife in Illinois and to Baird's supervisors at the University of Chicago. Compl. ¶22,26. As a result, Baird has experienced harm to both his marriage and his career. See id. at ¶ 25,27-28. He has been forced to move out of the home he once shared with his wife. Id. at ¶ 24. In addition, Baird's supervisors at the University of Chicago have commenced an investigation into his business expenses, place him on unpaid leave, and refused to serve as references for his nation-wide job search. Id. at ¶ 27-28. Baird has now filed suit in the Northern District of Illinois alleging that Schmidt's profile page constitutes defamation under Illinois law. See Compl. ¶ 31. Schmidt contacted us asking for advice, and she is hoping to pursue a motion to dismiss the case for lack of personal jurisdiction.

DISCUSSION

The court will probably find that Schmidt established minimum contacts with Illinois sufficient for the court to assert specific personal jurisdiction over her. A federal court may exert personal jurisdiction over Schmidt only if Illinois state courts may do so. See Fed. R. Civ. P. 4(k)(1)(A). Under Illinois's long-arm statute, Illinois state courts may "exercise jurisdiction on any ... basis ... permitted by the Illinois Constitution and the Constitution of the United States". 735 Ill. Comp. Stat. 5/2-209(c) (2012). The Seventh Circuit has interpreted this catch-all provision as authorizing jurisdiction to the extent allowed by the United States Constitution. See Hyatt Int'l Corp. v. Coco, 302 F. 3d 707,714-15 (7th Cir. 2002). Thus, it is sufficient to evaluate whether the exercise of personal jurisdiction over Schmidt would comport with the Due Process Clause of the Fourteenth Amendment. In International Shoe Co. Washington, 326 U. S. 310 (1945), the Supreme Court held that Due Process requires that a defendant establish certain "minimum contacts" with the forum before a court may assert specific personal jurisdiction over the defendant.

The Supreme Court applied International Shoe's minimum contacts doctrine to a defamation suit in Calder v. Jones 465_U. S. 783 (1984). In Calder, a California actress brought suit in California against a writer of a national magazine based in Florida. The Court held that personal jurisdiction was proper because of the "effects" in California of the writer's Florida conduct. See id. at 789. The Seventh Circuit's interpretations of Calder in Wallace v. Herron, 778 F. 2d 391 (7th Cir. 1985), Indianapolis Colts v. Metro Baltimore Football Club, L.P., 34 F. 3d 410 (7th Cir. 1994), and Janmark, Inc. v. Reidy, 132 F. 3d 1200 (7th Cir. 1997) are somewhat ill-defined and potentially conflicting. However, the Northern District of Illinois has read into the Seventh Circuit's holdings an implicit Calder "effects test", suggesting that the court will likely apply all three prongs of the test to Schmidt's case. In order to satisfy the Calder effects test, a defendant must: (i) commit intentional tortious actions; (ii) expressly aimed at Illinois; (iii) which cause harm to the plaintiff in Illinois that the defendant knows is likely to be suffered in Illinois. See Euromarket Designs, Inc. v. Crate & Barrel Ltd., 96 F. Supp. 2d 824, 835(N. D. Ill. 2000)

This memo will first discuss the Northern District of Illinois's interpretation of Seventh Circuit precedent applying the Calder effects test. This memo will then argue that because Schmidt intentionally posted the allegedly defamatory statements, the first prong of the effect test is not in dispute. It will then show that Schmidt's actions were expressly aimed at Illinois. Finally, the memo will demonstrate that Schmidt knew or should have known that Baird was likely to suffer personal and professional harm in Illinois as a proximate result of her actions. Thus, the court will probably find that Schmidt established minimum contracts with Illinois such that the exercise of personal jurisdiction over her is proper.

▶ I . **The Northern District of Illinois has interpreted potentially inconsistent Seventh Circuit precedent as requiring a defendant to satisfy all three prongs of the Calder effects test.**

The "[r]elevant jurisprudence of the Seventh Circuit has not been consistent in the verbiage used to determine personal jurisdiction". Caterpillar Inc. v. Miskin Scraper Works, Inc. , 256 F. Supp. 2d 849, 851 (C. D. ILL. 2003). Strikingly, the Seventh Circuit's most recent application of Calder appeared to forsake the "express aiming" prong of the effects test. See Janmark, 132 F. 3d at 1202. In Janmark, the court found that the exercise of personal jurisdiction in Illinois over a non-resident defendant was proper on the basis of a single telephone call made by the defendant in California to one of the Illinois plaintiff's customers in New Jersey. See id. Because the defendant's call allegedly caused the New Jersey customer to cancel his purchase of miniature shopping carts from the plaintiff, the court held that the "injury"—and thus the international tort—had "occurred" in Illinois. See id. Finding the location of the injury dispositive, the court wrote, "there can be no serious doubt after Calder that the state in which the victim of a tort suffers the injury may entertain a suit against the accused tortfeasor." Id. Thus, the Janmark court appeared to interpret Calder so broadly that virtually any tort causing harm to an Illinois plaintiff would justify personal jurisdiction over the defendant.

However, the Janmark court did not explicitly overrule Seventh Circuit precedent, and the Northern District of Illinois has not adopted Janmark's broad interpretation of Calder. The Seventh Circuit had previously rejected the assertion that a victim's place of injury by itself can serve as a sufficient basis for the exercise of personal jurisdiction over a non-resident tortfeasor. See Wallace 778 F. 2d at 394 ("[w]e do not believe the Supreme Court, in Calder, was saying that any plaintiff may hale any defendant into court in the plaintiffs home state. Where the defendant has no contacts, merely by asserting that the defendant has committed an intentional tort against the plaintiff").

In Indianapolis Colts, the court refused to base its finding of personal jurisdiction solely on a showing that the injurious "effects" of the defendant's alleged infringement of the plaintiffs trademark occurred in the forum state. 34 F. 3d at 412. Rather than rest on "so austere a conception" of personal jurisdiction, the court held that the defendant Baltimore Colts football team could be forced to defend itself against the plaintiff's suit in Indiana because "the defendant had done *more than* brought about an injury to an interest located in a particular state". Id. (emphasis added). Not only had the defendant harmed the plaintiff in Indiana by infringing its trademark, but also the defendant had "'entered' the state" through its nationwide television broadcasts of Baltimore Colts football games. Id.

On its face, the "entry" requirement of Indianapolis Colts appears to conflict with Janmark's unqualified assertion that anyone who intentionally cause a tortious injury in Illinois is amenable to suit there. See Caterpillar, 256 F. Supp. 2d at 851-52 (describing the tension between Janmark and Indianapolis Colts). However, since Janmark, district courts in the Seventh Circuit have resolved this linguistic discrepancy by equating the "entry" requirement of Indianapolis Colts with "express aiming". See, e. g., id. at 852; Richter v. INSTAR Enters. Int'l, 594 F. Supp. 2d 1000, 1010 (N. D. Ill. 2009); Nerds on Call, Inc. V. Nerds on Call, Inc., 598 F. Supp. 2d 913, 917, 919 (S. D. Ind. 2008).

In other words, regardless of whether it is characterized as "entry" into the forum state or as "intentional and purposeful tortious conduct ... calculated to cause injury in the forum state", Caterpillar, 256 F. Supp. 2d at 851, there must be some "express aiming" at the forum state—in addition to mere "effects" suffered by a resident of the forum—in order for a court to assert personal jurisdiction over a non-resident tortfeasor. See id. Thus, despite the varying language used, courts in the Northern District of Illinois have all adopted some version of the traditional three-factor "effects test".

▶ **II . Schmidt's posting satisfies each prong of the Calder effects test.**

A. Schmidt intentionally posted the online profile

In Illinois, under the effects test, personal jurisdiction over a nonresident defendant first requires that the defendant commit "intentional tortious actions". Euromarket, 96 F. Supp. 2d at 835. Defamation is an intentional tort. See Calder, 465 U. S. at 789-90. Schmidt does not dispute that she intentionally posted the statements. See Schmidt Aff. ¶ 18. Additionally, in judging the motion to dismiss, the court will resolve any conflicts in the affidavits in the plaintiffs favor. RAR, Inc. V. Turner Diesel. Ltd., 107 F. 3d 1272, 1275 (7th Cir. 1997). Thus, the court will accept as true Baird's allegations of defamation and hold hat Schmidt has satisfied the first prong of the test.

B. Schmidt "expressly aimed" the posting at Illinois

Under Illinois law, the second prong of the effects test requires that a defendant "expressly aim" her actions at Illinois. Euromarket, 96 F. Supp. 2d at 835. In assessing whether a defendant has "expressly aimed" her tortious activity at the forum state, courts determine whether the forum state is the focal point of the activity, such that the alleged defamatory statements involve conduct, people, and events in the forum.

See. e. g. , Jackson v. Cal. Newspapers P'ship, 406 F. Supp. 2d 893, 897 (N. D. ILL. 2005). In Jackson, the court refused to exercise jurisdiction over a defendant newspaper publisher on the basis of an online article that allegedly defamed multi-sport professional athlete Vincent E. ("Bo") Jackson. The defendant's article on the "dangers of steroid abuse"—which mentioned that Jackson had lost his hip as a result of his use of anabolic steroids—was deemed insufficient to confer personal jurisdiction because "the defendants did not contact Illinois sources, did not focus the story on Illinois or any event that occurred in Illinois, and did not know that the plaintiff resided in Illinois". Jackson, 406 F. Supp. 2d at 896.

Other courts have similarly declined to find jurisdiction on the basis of defamatory articles where the forum state was not the "focal point of the article". See, e.g., Revell v. Lidov, 317 F. 3d 467, 473 (5th Cir. 2002) (holding that the court lacked jurisdiction over non-resident defendants in Texas where the defendants' allegedly defamatory online posting contain[ed] no reference to Texas, nor … to the Texas-activities of [the plaintiff]); see also Young v. New Haven Advocate, 315 F. 3d 256, 263 (4th Cir. 2002) (refusing to exercise jurisdiction over defendants in Virginia where the focus of the defendants' allegedly libelous online articles was Connecticut).

Courts are much more likely to find express aiming when the defendant's online posting focus on the forum and individuals within the forum. See, e.g., State Farm Fire & Casualty Co. V. Miraglia, 2007 U. S. Dist. LXIS 75712 (N. D. Tex. Oct.. 11, 2007). In Miraglia, the court held that the exercise of personal jurisdiction in Texas was proper on the basis of allegedly defamatory comments about a Texas company that the defendant had posted on an Internet bulletin board operated by Yahoo. com. Id. at*4. According to the court, the defendant's comments were "expressly aimed" at Texas, given that the postings (a) "often referred specifically to … Texas locations", and (b) "specifically named" individuals whom the defendant "knew to be Texas residents". Id.

The fact that Schmidt's posting did not rely on Illinois sources or describe events that occurred in Illinois does not mean that Illinois was any less the "focal point" of her posting. In Zidon v. Pickrell, 344 F. Supp. 2d 624(D. N. D. 2004), a North Dakota resident brought suit against his former girlfriend, alleging that the ex-girlfriend had defamed him via postings on a website that she had created. Although the website neither drew its content from North Dakota sources nor discussed events that had transpired in North Dakota, the website did contain specific references to the plaintiff's North Dakota residence, the plaintiff's employment in North Dakota, and the plaintiff's family members in North Dakota. On the basis of these facts, the court concluded that the exercise of jurisdiction over the defendant was proper in North Dakota, since the defendant had "particularly and directly targeted North Dakota with her Web site". See Zidon, 344 F. Supp. 2d at 631-32.

Schmidt exhibited a similar intent to "particularly and directly target" Illinois with her posting on lovehimorleavehim.com. Like the postings in Miraglia and Zidon, Schmidt's profile page makes clear that

Illinois was the "focal point" of her statements. Schmidt's entire profile page was exclusively concerned with the conduct and reputation of an Illinois resident. See Baird Ex. A. Moreover, Schmidt's profile page mentioned numerous Illinois persons and places in addition to Baird, including the University of Chicago (Baird's employer in Illinois), Baird's wife (a resident of Illinois), and the Latin School (Baird's wife's employer in Illinois). See Baird Ex. A. Schmidt also listed Illinois as one of the relevant locations for her posting, id., and users may search the profile pages on the website by their listed geographic locations, Compl. at ¶ 17. Finally, Schmidt arguably encouraged readers to contact Baird's wife by writing, "I hope someone lets her know about him ..." See Baird Ex. A. By making numerous references to Illinois persons and places and by identifying Illinois as one of the profile page's relevant locations, Schmidt did more than target an Illinois resident; she aimed her conduct expressly at Illinois such that Illinois was the focal point of her statements.

C. Schmidt caused foreseeable harm to Baird in Illinois.

i. Baird felt the brunt of the harm caused by Schmidt's posting in Illinois.

In Illinois, to satisfy the third prong of the effects test, a defendant must cause harm to the plaintiff in Illinois that the defendant knows is likely to be suffered in Illinois. Euromarket, 96 F. Supp. 2d at 835. The court in Jackson found that the brunt of the harm from the allegations of steroid use did not occur in Jackson's home state because he had a national reputation. See 406 F. Supp. 2d at 896. The Jackson court distinguished Calder, noting that "because the entertainment industry of which [Jones] was a part was centered in California, she experienced the most severe harm in California". Id. Other jurisdictions have found that the brunt of the damage done to a plaintiff's personal (as opposed to professional) reputation occurs where she resides. See e.g., Zidon, 344 F. Supp. 2d at 632.

Baird specifically alleges that Schmidt's actions have caused him harm in Illinois by damaging his reputation, causing emotional distress, and impairing his earning capacity, see Compl. ¶ 35-37, allegations that the court will accept as true. Though Baird is seeking jobs nationally, has taken grants from foundations and the federal government, and has traveled frequently for business, Compl. ¶ 10-11, Schmidt Aff. ¶ 6, Schmidt will have difficulty convincing the court that Baird has a national reputation analogous to that of Jackson, who was a well-known professional athlete. However, even if the court accepts Schmidt's argument, Baird has nevertheless experienced "the most severe harm" in the forum where he lives and works. Baird's career and marriage are centered in Illinois. See Compl. ¶ 10. Because of the fallout from the posting, his wife forced him to move out of his Illinois home, Compl. ¶ 24; and his Illinois employer suspended him without pay, Compl. ¶ 27. The court will thus likely find that the primary effects of Schmidt's posting were felt in Illinois even if Schmidt's statements did harm Baird's job prospects across the country.

ii. Schmidt should have foreseen that Baird would be harmed in Illinois

Most likely, the court's determination of whether or not Schmidt should have known that Baird was likely to suffer harm in Illinois will closely relate to the extent to which Schmidt expressly aimed her actions at Illinois. In Calder, the Court found that because the libelous story focused on the actress's professional conduct in California, the writer "knew that the brunt of that injury would be felt by [Jones] in the State in which she lives and works ..." Calder, 465 U. S. at 784. Similarly, Schmidt knew about, and therefore focused her posting on, Baird's professional and personal misconduct in Illinois. See Baird Ex. A. She also emailed the posting to friends, Schmidt Aff. ¶ 23, increasing the likelihood that someone might contact Baird's wife and employer. Furthermore, upon learning of the posting, Baird alleges that he explicitly asked Schmidt to remove it from the website and she refused. Compl. ¶ 23. At that point, Schmidt could not have doubted the harm that she was causing. Because she knew Baird lived and worked in Illinois, and because she directed her posting at Illinois, she should have foreseen that Baird would likely suffer harm in Illinois.

CONCLUSION

The court will likely find that Schmidt's posting on lovehimorleavehim.com established minimum contacts with Illinois. By intentionally creating an "Illinois-tagged" profile page on a website searchable by geographic location, and by making specific references to several Illinois persons and places throughout her page, Schmidt "expressly aimed" her conduct at Illinois such that Illinois was the "focal point" of her tortious activities. Schmidt's profile page caused Baird to suffer harm in Illinois, and Schmidt knew that the effects of her profile page would be felt primarily in Illinois. Schmidt's posting thus satisfies the criteria for "minimum contacts" under Calder as interpreted by the Seventh Circuit and the Northern District of Illinois.

Sample Record

SAMPLE RECORD: *BELL-WESLEY V. O'TOOLE*

SUPERIOR COURT FOR THE STATE OF AMES

REBECCA AND SCOTT BELL-WESLEY,
    Plaintiffs,
v.
DR. STEPHEN O'TOOLE,
    Defendant.

CIVIL ACTION 96-2004
COMPLAINT

JURISDICTION

1. Plaintiffs Rebecca and Scott Bell-Wesley are a married couple residing in the State of Ames.

2. Defendant Stephen O'Toole is a medical doctor who resides and has his medical office in the State of Ames.

CAUSES OF ACTION

3. Plaintiff Scott Bell-Wesley is an architect, under employment of the City of Holmes, City Planning Department.

4. Plaintiff Rebecca Bell-Wesley is an attorney, practicing with the Office of the Attorney General of the state of Ames, in the City of Holmes.

5. Prior to January 4, 2011, Plaintiff Rebecca Bell-Wesley had given birth to three deformed children, each of whom had died within six months after birth. Defendant O'Toole had informed Plaintiffs that there was a seventy-five percent chance that any child they conceived would suffer and die from the same congenital deformity.

6. Plaintiffs chose to lead a childless lifestyle by procuring a sterilization operation.

7. On Octorber 16, 2008, Defendant performed a vasectomy on Plaintiff Scott Bell-Wesley for the

purpose of preventing conception and birth of a child.

8. Defendant O'Toole was solely responsible for the performance of said operation, and for Plaintiff's post-operative care.

9. Plaintiffs were advised by Defendant that the operation would not render Plaintiff Scott Bell-Wesley sterile immediately, and that an alternative means of birth control should be used by Plaintiffs until ten weeks after the opration.

10. Plaintiffs used an alternate method of birth control for three months after Scott Bell-Wesley's vasectomy.

11. Plaintiffs were futher informed by Defendant O'Toole that a sperm count would have to be performed twelve to fourteen weeks after the operation in order to confirm the success of the operation.

12. Plaintiff Scott Bell-Wesley returned to the office of Defendant O'Toole on January 8, 2009, at which time the Defendant performed a sperm count and informed Plaintiffs that Mr. Bell-Wesley was sterile.

13. Defendant O'Toole determined that Plaintiff Rebecca Bell-Wesley was pregnant on April 20, 2010.

14. Plaintiff Rebecca Bell-Wesley gave birth to Frank Michael Bell on January 4, 2011.

15. Plaintiff Scott Bell-Wesley is the biological father of Frank Michael Bell.

16. Defendant's separate acts of negligence were the proximate causes of the injury suffered by Plaintiffs.

17. Plaintiffs were injured by the birth of their unplanned child.

18. Defendant's negligence has denied Plaintiffs their constitutionally protected right of self-determination in matters of childbearing.

19. Plaintiffs have incurred mental, physical, and financial injuries as a result of the conception and birth of their child, for which Defendant is liable.

REMEDY

Wherefore, Plaintiffs pray the Court for the following relief:

20. That Defendant be held liable for the cost of Scott Bell-Wesley's vasectomy, including his medical expenses, his pain and suffering, and Rebecca's loss of consortium during her recuperation period, in the amount of $10,000.

21. That Defendant be held liable for the medical expenses and pain and suffering caused by Rebecca Bell-Wesley's pregacy and for Rebecca Bell-Wesley's loss of consortium during the last part of her pregnancy, in the amount of $15,000.

22. That Defendant be held liable to Plaintiff Rebecca Bell-Wesley for the medical expenses and pain suffering caused by her giving birth to Frank Michael Bell, in the amount of $25,000.

23. That Defendant be held liable to Plaintiffs for their emotional trauma caused by the conception and birth of an unplanned and unwanted child and for the additional emotional trauma resulting from Plaintiff's

reasonable expectation that the child would suffer from a congenital deformity, in the amount of $100,000.

24. That Defendant be held liable to Plaintiffs for lost earnings incurred as a result of Rebecca Bell-Wesley's pregnancy and the birth and care of their child, in the amount of $16,000.

25. That Defendant be held liable to Plaintiffs for injury to Plaintiffs' lifestyle, which is impacted financially by the care and rearing of their child, and for their loss of control over their leisure hours, in the amount of $250,000 (See Exhibit A, attached).

26. That Defendant be held liable to Plaintiffs for the financial and emotional cost of rearing their child, in the amount of $350,000.

Plaintiffs further pray that the Court order any additional measure of damages as would be just, and that provision for attorney's fees be made.

Respectfully submitted,
Scott and Rebecca Bell-Wesley
by their attorney
Jane E. Harvey
Jane E. Harvey
Llewellyn, Murray&Silber
325 North Bridge Road
Holmes, Ames

Dated: January 16, 2011

EXHIBIT A (in part)

From the 2010 annual report by the Department of Health and Human Services, Washington, D.C.:

The cost of raising a child, outside of possibly purchasing a home, is the single greatest investment a family will make. Current projections, stipulating that theirs is virtually no limit on what a couple may invest, indicate that the very minimum parents will spend bringing a child up to majority will be $200,000. This figure includes the basic costs of housing, feeding, and clothing the child, as well as the minimum costs of maintaining his/her health up to age eighteen. Addition of even several moderately priced extras—early professional child care, private schooling, college, allowances, for serious illness—can push the cost of childrearing beyond $300,000. And these figures do not yet even contemplate the emotional costs of a raising a child.

SUPERIOR COURT FOR THE STATE OF AMES

REBECCA AND SCOTT BELL-WESLEY,
Plaintiffs,
v.
DR. STEPHEN O'TOOLE,
Defendant.

CIVIL ACTION 96-2004
DEFENDANT'S ANSWER

1. Defendant admits the allegations in Paragraphs 1—5 of Plaintiffs' Complaint.
2. Defendant denies the allegations in Paragraph 6 of Plaintiffs' Complaint.
3. Defendant admits the allegations in Paragraphs 7—14 of Plaintiffs' Complaint.
4. Defendant is without sufficient information to respond to Paragraph 15 of Plaintiffs' Complaint.
5. Defendant denies the allegations in Paragraphs 16-26 of Plaintiffs' Complaint.

FIRST AFFIRMATIVE DEFENSE

6. Plaintiffs assumed the risk of possible failure of the sterilization procedure.
7. Since even perfectly performed vasectomies are not successful in all cases, Plaintiffs assumed the risk of failure of the operation, whether resulting from negligence or regrowth.
8. Since the social value of sterilization operations is so high, society has imposed this assumption of risk or waiver of recovery rights for those engaging in a procedure which cannot yet be made 100% effective, regardless of whether negligence was involved.

SECOND AFFIRMATIVE DEFENSE

9. Defendant was not neligent in his operative or post-operative procedures with Plaintiff Scott Bell-Wesley.
10. Plaintiff Scott Bell-Wesley suffered a tubal regrowth which was a statistical failure of the procedure not caused by Defendant's negligence.

THIRD AFFIRMATIVE DEFENSE

11. The birth of a child is always a benefit and a blessing which outweigh any financial costs, as well as any pain and suffering incurred during pregnancy.
12. Where the parents' express purpose in procuring a vasectomy was to prevent the birth of a deformed child, the birth to the parents of a healthy child caused them no injury.
13. Therefore, Plaintiffs did not suffer any damages and Defendant is not liable to Plaintiffs.

FOURTH AFFIRMATIVE DEFENSE

14. Broad social policies prohibit the awarding of child rearing damages in actions for wrongful pregnancy.
15. Therefore, Plaintiffs are not entitled to any damages for the cost of raising their child.

FIFTH AFFIRMATIVE DEFENSE

16. Plaintiffs have failed to mitigate the damages claimed in Paragraph 23 of their Complaint by refusing, as they have in the past, to undergo amniocentesis, a safe, simple test conducted early in the pregnancy, which would have determined that the child being carried was normal and healthy.

17. Plaintiffs have further failed to mitigate the damages in that they have not offered their unwanted, unplanned child up for adoption.

Respectfully submitted,

Dr. Stephen O'Toole

by their attorney

D. Nathan Neuville

D. Nathan Neuville

Ericson, Swanson and Moses

1977 Pond Ave.

Holmes, Ames

TRIAL RECORD (Parts have been omitted)
(REBECCA = REBECCA BELL-WESLEY)

COUNSEL: Mrs. Bell-Wesley, what happened in the months of following the presumably successful sterilization procedure?

REBECCA: Well, shortly after Scott's vasectomy I accepted an offer from the Attorney General to become one of his First Assistant Attorneys General.

COUNSEL: Are there many of these First Assistant Attorneys General?

REBECCA: Oh, no. Just a handful—no more than four or five, each located in a different city in Ames.

COUNSEL: I see, and are you more involved in this new position than in your prior position?

REBECCA: Yes, various department heads reported to me. I also had considerable discretion over the policies promulgated by our office, as well as identification of our litigation goals and authorization of compromises and settlements.

COUNSEL: You say "had". Are you no longer in this position?

REBECCA: It's not clear. I have taken a six-month leave of absence, so I should return to work sometime in May. In the meantime, many things could happen. The Attorney General's Office is a political office, you know.

COUNSEL: Was your position as First Assistant Attorneys General obtained by political appointment?

REBECCA: No, the Attorney General usually only bothers himself with hiring or bringing in his own first assistants and department chiefs. I was hired out of law school by a department chief at the time.

COUNSEL: And what was your salary change upon acceptance of your most recent position?

REBECCA: It went from $64,000 per year to $80,000.

SUPERIOR COURT FOR THE STATE OF AMES

REBECCA AND SCOTT BELL-WESLEY, Plaintiffs, v. DR. STEPHEN O'TOOLE, Defendant.	CIVIL ACTION 96-2004 FINDING OF FACT AND CONCLUSIONS OF LAW

FINDINGS OF FACT

1. Plaintiffs made a conscious decision to avoid the possibility of the conception and birth of a child. The motive for this decision was their fear of having a deformed child.

2. In furtherance of this decision, Plaintiff Scott Bell-Wesley obtained a vasectomy from Dr. O'Toole on October 16, 2008.

3. Expert testimony showed that Defendant failed to sever properly the tubes of the vas deferens, and the Plaintiff Scott Bell-Wesley was never rendered sterile.

4. Defendant negligently performed a sperm count and informed Plaintiffs that Scott Bell-Wesley had been rendered sterile on January 8, 2009.

5. Defendant is a gerneral practitioner medical doctor who has performed vasectomies in his office over the past few years.

6. Plaintiff Rebecca Bell-Wesley conceived a child and bore that child, Frank Michale Bell, on January 4, 2011.

7. Plaintiff Scott Bell-Wesley has been established as the biological father. The pregnancy and childbirth were normal and without complications, except that they were unplanned; Frank Michale Bell was born healthy and has remained so.

8. Plaintiffs declined to absort the child on moral grounds, and have declined to give the child up for adoption for personal reasons.

9. Plaintiffs' lifestyle has changed dramatically since the birth of the child.

10. Both parents have lost, and will continue to lose, time and wages in their chosen careers as a result of caring for the child.

11. Both parents profess a deep love for their child even though they bring the present action.

12. Expert testimony established that amniocentesis would have revealed that the fetus was not deformed and was in fact in good health.

CONCLUSIONS OF LAW

1. Defendant Dr. Stephen O'Toole negligently performed a vasectomy on Plaintiff Scott Bell-Wesley on October 16, 2008. The vasectomy was unsuccessful.

2. Defendant O'Toole negligently performed a sperm count on January 8, 2009, informed Plaintiffs that the operation was successful, and told them that Scott Bell-Wesley had been rendered sterile.

3. The conception and birth of Plaintiffs' child would not have resulted had the operation been successful.

4. Plaintiffs have stated a cause of action for negligence.

5. Plaintiffs' damages are limited to the out-of-pocket costs, pain and suffering, emotional trauma, lost earnings and loss of consortium associated with Scott Bell-Wesley's vasectomy and Rebecca Bell-Wesley's pregnancy. A reasonable award for these damages is $100,000.

6. Damages are not awardable for the costs associated with rearing a healthy child, because the benefits of a healthy child always outweigh any attendant costs.

DATED: May 13, 2011

NANCY LLEWESTEIN
NANCY LLEWESTEIN
Ames Superior Court Judge

SUPERIOR COURT OPINION

Llewenstein, J.

In this bench trial, the Court is faced with a difficult problem involving not only the rights of individuals, but also numerous social and systemic considerations. It is apparent that Scott Bell-Wesley's sterilization operation was performed negligently. Not only was the operation itself ineffective, but also the Defendant was subsequently negligently in performing a sperm count on Plaintiff Scott Bell-Wesley and in informing the Bell-Wesleys that, on the basis of this test, Mr. Bell-Wesley had been rendered sterile.

Plaintiffs allege that the birth of a healthy son must somehow be compensated by the Defendant. The idea that a child would grow up being supported by someone other than his parents by virtue of the fact that his parents did not plan for or want him is extremely disturbing. The very real inability to assign a dollar amount to such an injury is exceeded only by the harm which such an award could do to families and individuals in our society. Perhaps I am old-fashioned, but I believe people are still filled with mystery, joy and inspiration at the birth of a new human life. In this case, where the Plaintiffs' prior conceptions resulted in the births and tragic deaths of three congenitally deformed infants, the birth to them of a healthy child is truly a blessing. The bebefits of a healthy child clearly outweigh any and all costs associated with raising the child.

Scott Bell-Wesley's vasectomy was improperly performed and the post-operative care he received was inadequate. The defendant is liable for his improper medical treatment, and therefore, damages of $100,000 are awarded to Plaintiffs. However, Ames will not join the ranks of jurisdictions recognizing child-rearing costs as an element of damages in a wrongful pregnancy action. The benefits of a healthy child always outweigh any attendant costs or burdens. This case is not different.

SUPERIOR COURT FOR THE STATE OF AMES

REBECCA AND SCOTT BELL-WESLEY,
Plaintiffs,
v.
DR. STEPHEN O'TOOLE,
Defendant.

CIVIL ACTION 96-2004
JUDGMENT

JUDGMENT OF TRIAL COURT

The issues in the above action have duly been heard by this Court, and this Court have made and filed its findings of fact and conclusions of law on May 13, 2011. It is, therefore, ORDERED, ADJUDGED, AND DECREED, that judgment be entered for Plaintiffs as to Defendant's acts of negligence and Plaintiffs be awarded $100,000 in damages.

DATED: May 20, 2011

John James
Clerk of Court

SUPERIOR COURT FOR THE STATE OF AMES

REBECCA AND SCOTT BELL-WESLEY,
Plaintiffs,
v.
DR. STEPHEN O'TOOLE,
Defendant.

CIVIL ACTION 96-2004
NOTICE OF APPEAL

Notice is hereby given that Petitioners, Rebecca and Scott Bell-Wesley, appeal to the Court of Appeals for the State of Ames (N. E. Division) from the final judgment entered in this action on the 20th day of May, 2011.

Dated: May 21, 2011

Jane E. Harvey
Jane E. Harvey
Attorney for Appellants
Llewellyn, Murray & Silber
325 North Bridge Road
Holmes, Ames

SUPERIOR COURT FOR THE STATE OF AMES

REBECCA AND SCOTT BELL-WESLEY,
Plaintiffs,
v.
DR. STEPHEN O'TOOLE,
Defendant.

CIVIL ACTION 96-2004
STIPULATION OF THE RECORD

It is hereby stipulated by the attorneys for the respective parties in the above-named action that the following shall constitute the transcript of the record on appeal.

1. Pleadings before the Superior Court of the State of Ames:
   a. Summons (omitted)
   b. Complaint
   c. Exhibit A
   d. Return of Services (omitted)
   e. Answer
   f. Affidavit of Service (omitted)
2. Trial Record
3. Findings of Fact and Conclusions of Law
4. Opinion of the Superior Court of the State of Ames
5. Judgment of the Superior Court of the State of Ames
6. Notice of Appeal
7. This Designation

COURT OF APPEALS FOR THE STATE OF AMES
(N. E. DIVISION)

REBECCA AND SCOTT BELL-WESLEY,

Plaintiffs,

v.

DR. STEPHEN O'TOOLE,

Defendant.

Sittings Below:
Judge Llewenstein
CIVIL ACTION 96-2004

OPINION AFFIRMING THE TRIAL COURT'S DECISIONS OF LAW

Syllabus: This case arises out of facts centering around the birth of a child …

…

The Plaintiffs' appeal in this case must be rejected by this Court. We do so largely on the same grounds that led Judge Llewenstein to reject them in the first instance. While we will explain ourselves at length below, we do not wish to imply that our discussion intimates anything but agreement with Judge Llewenstein's views …

COURT OF APPEALS FOR THE STATE OF AMES
(N. E. DIVISION)

REBECCA AND SCOTT BELL-WESLEY,

Plaintiffs,

v.

DR. STEPHEN O'TOOLE,

Defendant.

CIVIL ACTION 96-2004
NOTICE OF APPEAL

Notice is hereby given that Petitioners, Rebecca and Scott Bell-wesley, petition for certiorari the Superme Court of the State of Ames, from the decision of the Court of Appeals for the State of Ames (N. E. Division) in this action on the 13th day of July, 2011.

Dated: July 21, 2011

Jane E. Harvey

Jane E. Harvey

Attorney for Appellants

Llewellyn, Murray & Silber

325 North Bridge Road

Holmes, Ames

IN THE AMES SUPREME COURT

REBECCA AND SCOTT BELL-WESLEY,	Sitting Below:
Petitioners,	Judge Trimble
v.	Judge Lule
DR. STEPHEN O'TOOLE,	Judge Haentgens
Respondent.	CIVIL ACTION 96-2004

GRANT OF CERTIORARI

This Court hereby grants certiorari on the following issue in the case of Bell-wesley v. O'Toole:

Whether the cost of raising a healthy child should properly be included as an element of damages in a wrongful pregnancy action.

Assume that no arguable issue exists concerning:

1. Plaintiffs' timeliness in bringing the action under the relevant statute of limitations.

2. Defendant's negligence in performing the operation and in performing the sperm count upon which he relied in informing Plaintiffs that Scott Bell-wesley was sterile.

3. The actual amount of damages as a goal upon appeal. Quantification and award of each element is determined upon remand; the issue then is whether the court should recognize each type of damage as recoverable.

Appendix E — Sample Appellant Brief

SAMPLE APPELLANT BRIEF: *BELL-WESLEY V. O'TOOLE*

IN THE SUPREME COURT OF THE STATE OF AMES

CIVIL ACTION NO. 96-2004

SCOTT AND RECECCA BELL-WESLEY, PLAINTIFFS-APPELLANTS

V.

STEPHEN O'TOOLE, DEFENDANT-APPELLEE

BRIEF FOR THE PLAINTIFFS-APPELLANTS

Jane E. Harvey
Attorney for the Plaintiffs-Appellants
Llewellyn, Murray& Silber
325 North Bridge Road
Holmes, Ames

TABLE OF CONTENTS

TABLE OF CONTENTS i
TABLE OF AUTHORITIES ii
PRELIMINARY STATEMENT 1
QUESTION PRESENTED 1
STATEMENT OF FACTS 2
SUMMARY OF THE ARGUMENT 4
ARGUMENT 5
  I. STANTARD OF REVIEW 5
  II. THE SUPERIOR ERRED BY REFUSING TO FULLY COMPENSATE THE BELL-WESLEYS FOR ALL FORESEEABLE DAMAGES RESULTING FROM SCOTT'S NEGLIGENT STERILIZATION, INCLUDING THE COSTS OF HAVING AND RAISING THEIR CHILD 5
    A. The Bell-Wesleys Should Recover Damages for All of Their Injuries, Including the Costs of Raising Their Son, Because Such Damages Are Reasonable and Foreseeable, and Thus Subject to Recovery Under Standard Tort Law Principles 5
    B. Policy Considerations Requires that Injuries to Scott and Rebecca Be Compensated Fully like those in Any Other Negligence Case 7
  III. ALTERNATIVELY, IF THIS COURT WILL NOT AWARD FULL DAMAGES, THIS COURT SHOULD AWARD DAMAGES FOR THE COSTS OF RAISING FRANK BELL-WESLEY OFFSET BY THE BENEFIT OF HAVING HIM 10
CONCLUSION 11

TABLE OF AUTHORITIES

CASES   **Page(s)**

Burke v. Rivo, 551 N. E. 2d 1 (Mass. 1990) 7,9,10,11
Custodio v. Bauer, 59 Cal. Rptr. 463 (Cal Ct. App. 1967) 6
Kingsbury v Smith, 442 A. 2d 1003 (N. H. 1982) 8
Lovelace Med. Ctr. v. Mendez, 805 P. 2d 603 (N. M. 1991) 5,6,8
Marciniak v. Lundborg, 450 N. W. 2d 243 (Wis. 1989) 5,6,9
Ochs v. Borrelli, 445 A. 2d 883 (Conn. 1982) 10
Provencio v. Wenrich, 261 P. 3d 1089 (N. M. 2011) 7
Sherlock v. Stillwater Clinic, 260 N. W. 2d 169 (Minn. 1977) 10,11
Univ. Of Ariz. Health Sciences Ctr. v. Sup. Ct., 667 P. 2d 1294 (Ariz. 1983) 10
Zehr v. Haugen, 871 P. 2d 1006 (Or. 1994) 6,9

OTHER AUTHORITIES

Michael T. Murtaugh, Wrongful Birth: The Courts' Dilemma in Determining a Remedy for a Blessed Event, 27 Pace L. Rev. 241 (2007) ·· 7

Restatement (Second) of Torts ·· 10

W. Page Keeton et al., Prosser and Keeton on the Law of the Torts (5th ed. 1984) ············ 5

PRELIMINARY STATEMENT

Following Stephen O'Toole's negligent performance of a vasectomy on Scott Bell-Wesley, Scott and his wife, Rebecca, conceived and gave birth to their son, Frank. The Bell-Wesleys sued O'Toole in the Superior Court for the State of Ames, seeking damages for his negligence, which resulted in their unplanned pregnancy and the unexpected birth of their son. R. at 1-2. Following a bench trial, the Superior Court determined that O'Toole had acted negligently when he botched Mr. Bell-Wesley's vasectomy and follow-up testing, and the court awarded the Bell-Wesleys damages to compensate them for their medical expenses, pain and suffering, and loss of consortium. R. at 12-15. Notwithstanding this finding of negligence, the Superior Court declined to award the Bell-Wesleys all reasonable and foreseeable damages stemming from the vasectomy that O'Toole negligently performed. Specifically, the Court refused to compensate the Bell-Wesleys for the financial burden associated with raising their son. R. at 14. The Bell-Wesleys appealed the Superior Court's denial of full damages to the Court of Appeals for the State of Ames. R. at 16, and the Court of Appeals also declined to require that O'Toole pay full damages, including the reasonable costs of the son's upbringing, R. at 18. The Bell-Wesleys petitioned this Court for further review. R. at 19. This Court granted certiorari to determine whether the Bell-Wesleys can recover the costs of raising their son to majority. R. at 20.

QUESTION PRESENTED

O'Toole negligently performed a vasectomy and follow-up testing on Scott Bell-Wesley. As a result of O'Toole's negligence, the Bell-Wesleys unexpectedly conceived and gave birth to a son, incurring the costs of his delivery and upbringing. Under fundamental tort law principles, individuals are liable for all injuries flowing naturally and foreseeable from their negligence. Should O'Toole be held liable for the full result of his negligence, including the extensive costs associated with raising a child?

STATEMENT OF FACTS

Scott Bell-Wesley is an architect with the Holmes City Planning Department, and his wife, Rebecca, is an attorney in the Attorney General's Office of the State of Ames. R. at 1,9. The Bell-Wesleys made a conscious decision to forego having children. R. at 1. They made this difficult decision after they previously had given birth to three children, all of whom tragically died within six months of birth due to a genetic congenital disorder. Id. Their doctor, Defendant-Appellee Stephen O'Toole, advised the Bell-Wesleys that there was a seventy-five percent chance that any future child they conceived would suffer from the same lethal congenital disorder. Id. Based on O'Toole's advice and their fear of bringing another ill child into the world, the Bell-Wesleys chose to remain childless. R. at 1,11. They did not adopt. See id. Instead, they devoted their lives to each other and to their careers. See R. at 3,9.

In order to guarantee the lifestyle they had chosen and to guard against the risk of delivering a fourth sick child, the Bell-Wesleys asked O'Toole to perform a vasectomy on Scott on October 16,2008. R. at 1. O'Toole botched the procedure and failed to sever the tubes of Scott's vas deferens properly, leaving Scott capable of fathering another child. R. at 11. O'Toole then compounded his surgical error by improperly testing Scott Bell-Wesley's sperm count. Id. Based on the results of this test, O'Toole informed the Bell-Wesley family that he had successfully sterilized Scott. R. at 2,11. O'Toole was incorrect, and the Bell-Wesleys remained unaware that Scott was still fertile. R. at 2,11.

Shortly after Scott's vascectomy in 2008, and based on the choices she and Scott had made about their lifestyle, Rebecca accepted a promotion to First Assistant Attorney General of the State of Ames. R at 9. Her salary increased from $64,000 to $80,000 per year. R. at 10. The Bell-Wesleys also resumed marital relations after O'Toole informed them that the vasectomy had been a success. R. at 2.

In April 2010, Rebecca and Scott Bell-Wesley discovered that they were pregnant again. R. at 2. Even though the Bell-Wesleys feared that their unborn child would suffer the same fate as their three deceased children, they decided not to terminate the pregnancy on moral grounds. R. at 11-12. They also decided not to undergo amniocentesis, which the Court concluded would have revealed that the Bell-Wesleys' son was healthy. R. at 12. On January 4, 2011, Rebecca gave birth to a healthy baby boy, Frank Michael. R. at 2.

The Superior Court found that O'Toole was negligent. R. at 12. The court determined that he negligently performed Scott's vasectomy and negligently performed a sperm count test on Scott, leaving the Bell-Wesleys unaware that they could conceive a child. Id. The court further determined that the Bell-Wesleys' child would not have been born but for O'Toole's negligent treatment of Scott Bell-Wesley. Id. As a result of O'Toole's negligent acts, the Court held that he was liable to the Bell-Wesley family and ordered him to pay $100,000 to cover the Bell-Wesleys' out-of-pocket medical costs, pain and suffering, lost earnings, and loss of consorium. R. at 13. None of these decisions are challenged on appeal.

The Superior Court, however, decided not to award the Bell-Wesleys damages for the costs associated with raising their son to adulthood. While the Bell-Wesleys obviously love their son deeply, R. at 12, his conception and birth have nonetheless caused them severe emotional, physical and financial harm, R. at 2. Their son's unexpected birh has forced the Bell-Wesleys to alter their lives dramatically. R. at 12. Both parents have lost, and continue to lose, time and wages from their careers in order to care for their child. Id. Rebecca's leave of absence in connection with the pregnancy has also jeopardized her job. R. at 8. The financial and emotional costs of raising Frank present the Bell-Wesleys with a formidable buden. In fact, the record shows that the very minimum that most parents will spend to raise a child is $200,000. R. at 5. Even though the Court found that "Scott Bell-Wesley's vasectomy was improperly performed and the post-operative care he received was inadequate", the Court refuesed to compensate the Bell-Wesleys for the extensive financial costs associated with raising their son. R. at 14. The Bell-Wesleys appeal this decision. R. at 16,19.

SUMMARY OF THE ARGUMENT

The fundamental tort goals of deterrence and fairness require that O'Toole pay for the reasonably foreseeable damages he caused when he negligently performed Scott Bell-Wesley's vasectomy and subsequent sperm count. This Court should seek to place the Bell-Wesleys in the same position they would have been in had O'Toole performed Scott Bell-Wesley's vasectomy or follow-up testing correctly. Their damage award shoud reflect the pain and suffering, emotional trauma, lost earnings, costs of raising their son, Frank, and the sacrifice of their chosen lifestyle. The trial court's insistence that a child's birth is always a costless blessing is without merit or any factual basis and disregards the purpose and structure of tort law.

Should this Court not award the Bell-Wesleys full damages for policy reasons, this Court shoud nevertheless apply an alternative rule adopted by some jurisdictions and award damages for the costs of raising Frank offset by the benefits of having him. Although the emotional benefits the Bell-Wesleys receive from parenthood are of an entirely different kind than the financial injuries and pain and suffering inflicted on them by O'Toole's negligence, this rule presents the most just and reasonable alternative to full compensation.

ARGUMENT

I. STANDARD OF REVIEW

Whether the Bell-Wesley family can recover the full cost of raising a healthy child as an element of damages in a wrongful pregnancy action is a question of law and is thus reviewed *de novo*. See Lovelace Med. Ctr. V. Mendez, 805 P. 2d 603,614 (N. M. 1991)

II. THE SUPERIOR COURT ERRED BY REFUSING TO FULLY COMPENSATE THE BELL-WESLEYS FOR ALL FORESEEABLE DAMAGES RESULTING FROM SCOTT'S NEGLIGENT STERILIZATION, INCLUDING THE COSTS OF HAVING AND RAISING THEIR CHILD.

A. The Bell-Wesleys Should Recover Damages for All of Their Injuries, Including the Costs of Raising Their Son, Because Such Damages Are Reasonable and Foreseeable and Thus Subject to Recovery Under Standard Tort Law Principles.

This Court should overturn the denial of the Bell-Wesleys' claim for compensation for the expense of raising their unplanned child because the Superior Court's refusal to award plaintiffs all foreseeable damages—as is the standard in tort cases—was erroneous. The general rule in tort cases is that "a person has an obligation to exercise reasonable care so as to not cause foreseeable harm to another". Marciniak v. Lundborg, 450 N. W. 2d 243,245 (Wis. 1989) (citation omitted) (holding that costs of raising child to majority may be recovered by parents as damages for negligently performed sterilization procedure). Under this rule, individuals are held liable for all injuries flowing naturally and foreseeably from their negligence. See W. Page Keeton et al., Prosser and Keeton on the Law of Torts 43 (5th ed. 1984) (describing theories of liability for negligence). This rule applies equally to tort cases such as these—so-called wrongful pregnancy or wrongful conception cases. As one court explained, "[w]here the purpose of the physician's actions is to prevent conception through sterilization, and the physician's actions are performed negligently, traditional principles of tort law require that the physician be held legally responsible for the sonsequences which have in fact occurred."

Marciniak, 450 N.W. 2d at 248. Here, the Superior Court found that O'Toole was negligent when he botched Scott Bell-Wesley's vasectomy and follow-up sperm court. R. at 12. The Superior Court also concluded that O'Toole's failed procedure resulted in the birth of the Bell-Wesleys's son. Id. None of these factual findings are challenged on appeal. Accordingly, under the basic rules governing damages in torts cases, included cases such as these, the Superior Court should have awarded the Bell-Wesleys all foreseeable damages associated with Frank's birth. The Superior Court, in contravention of the standard rules governing tort cases, failed to do so when it declined to award the Bell-Wesley family *all* reasonably foreseeable damages resulting from O'Toole's negligence, and this decision was legal error.

The Superioer Court should have awarded the Bell-Wesleys damages that included the costs of raising Frank Bell-Wesley to majority, because such damages are "foreseeable". In wrongful pregnancy cases, courts have determined that foreseeable damages include the costs of having and raising an unexpected child. Marciniak, 450 N.W. 2d at 248. This is because the obvious consequences of a botched vasectomy include the conception and birth of an unplanned child and the associated costs of raising that child. See id. at 245 ("We therefore conclude that the parents of a healthy child may recover the costs of raising the child from a physician who negligently perfroms a sterilization."); Custodio v. Bauer, 59 Cal. Rptr. 463,476 (Cal Ct. App. 1967) (nothing that recoverable damages included the cost of the unsuccessful operation, mental, physical and nervous pain and suffering during pregnancy, and costs of rearing the child); Zehr v. Haugen, 871 P. 2d 1006, 1011-13 (Or. 1994) (commenting that "expenses of raising the child and providing for the child's college education" are recoverable in cases "based on defendant physician's alleged failure to perform a tubal ligation"); Lovelace, 805 P. 2d at 612 (recognizing that doctor who performed negligent sterilization can be required to pay "damages in the form of the reasonable expense to raise [later born child] to maturity"); Provencio v. Wenrich, 261 P. 3d 1089 (N.M 2011) (to similar effect); see also Michael T. Murtaugh, Wrongful Birth: The Courts' Dilemma in Determining a Remedy for a Blessed Event, 27 Pace L. Rev. 241, 300-03 (2007) (arguing that courts should focus on the intent of the plaintiffs in undergoing a vascetomy, and should award costs for rearing a child to those motivated by non-economic reasons).

Just like the plaintiffs in Marciniak, Custodio, Zehr, Lovelace and Provencio, the Bell-Wesleys have sustained serious physical, financial, and emotional injuries as a result of O'Toole's negligent sterilization and follow-up testing, and they are entitled to recover all foreseeable damages, including the cost of raising Frank. The Superior Court's failure to award damages for child-raising has left the couple uncompensated for significant economic harms, namely the estimated $200,000 it will cost to raise Frank to maturity. See R. at 5. The costs of raising Frank are a direct financial injury to the parents, no different in immediate effect than the medical expenses resulting from the wrongful conception and birth of a child. Therefore, under the normal rules of damages in tort cases, which require that plaintiffs receive *all* foreseeable damages, the Bell-Wesleys should recover for the costs of rearing Frank.

B. Policy Considerations Require that Injuries to Scott and Rebecca be Compensated Fully like Those in Any Other Negligence Case.

The Superior Court erred in rejecting the Bell-Wesleys' claim for child rearing damages as a matter of public policy, because public policy counsels that the Court should allow plaintiffs to recover full damages that reasonably flow from negligent sterilization procedures, including the cost of child care. Where a couple elects not to have children, it should be presumed as a matter of policy that the birth of child would not benefit them. See Burke v. Rivo, 551 N. E. 2d 1,4 (Mass. 1990). As the Burke court explained, "[t]he very fact that a person has sought medical intervention to prevent him or her from having a child demonstrates that, for that person, the benefits of parenthood did not outweigh the burdens, economic and otherwise, of having a child." Id. ; see also Lovelace, 805 P. 2d at 612-13("an interest to be protected in this stting is the parents' desire to safeguard the financial security of their family").

Although the Bell-Wesleys love their son greatly, Frank's conception and birth substantially injured the Bell-Wesleys' physical, emotional and financial well-being. The couple's decision to undergo a vasectomy demonstrated that they rejected any benefits of procreation. The Bell-Wesleys assessed their opportunities and resources and radically altered the goals of their marriage. They decided to devoted more time to each other and their careers, only to have their expectations shattered as a result of O'Toole's negligence. While they could have adopted children, the Bell-Wesleys instead chose to pursue a childless lifestyle, recognizing that parenthood entails numerous costs, burdens and responsibilties that may outweigh its attendant joys. Here, however, the Court substituted its own value judgment for that of the Bell-Wesleys and ignored the legitimate economic damages suffered by the Bell-Wesleys that are routinely recognized by the law of torts and courts in several other jurisdicitions.

Furthermore, the Superior Court's decision not to award full damages to the Bell-Wesleys contravenes the fundamental tort law policy in favor of fully deterring negligent behavior. Full recovery by wrongful pregnancy claimants is necessary to deter negligence in performing vasectomies and post-operative care. See Kingsbury v. Smith, 442 A. 2d 1003, 1005 (N. H. 1982)(stating that failure to recognize wrongful birth claims would lower the standard of professional conduct and expertise in the area of family planning). Faced with a blameworthy defendant, O'Toole, and his innocent victims, the Bell-Wesleys, this Court does society a disservice by granting immunity to the tortfeasor and leaving his victims uncompensated. Negligent physicians like O'Toole must not be allowed to escape the consequences of their carelessness. Thus, courts must assess doctors for the full costs of their malfeasance in order to provide adequate incentives for safe, effective medical procedures.

In addition, the recognition of the Bell-Wesleys' claim will not result in psychological harm to Frank if he discovers that he was unplanned. The public record of this case is already replete with references to Frank being unplanned—a fact that will not change depending on what damages are awarded. Furthermore, even if damages make a difference, Frank could easily be protected from this unlikely event by keeping the names of those involved in this action confidential. If anything, Frank's psychological well-being dictates a full recovery because any recovery by the Bell-Wesleys will inure to Frank's emotional benefit. It will relieve the economic pressure of raising an unexpected child and permit the parents to concentrate on giving the child the love and care he needs. See, e.g., Burke,551 N. E. 2d at 4-5; Marciniak, 450N. W. 2d at 246 ("We do not perceive that the [plaintiffs]) in bringing this suit are in any way disparaging the value of their child's life. They are, to the contrary, attempting to enhance it"). Accordingly, concern for Frank's psychological harm does not support denying the Bell-Wesleys's full compensation.

Nor, as argued by O'Toole below, are damages too speculative in this case. Childrearing costs can be estimated satisfactorily using data availble from the government and other sources, see R. at 5, and Courts have previously accepted these estimates. See Marciniak, 450 N. W. 2d at 247 (nothing in negligent sterilization case, "[j]uries are frequently called on to answer damage questions that are far less predictable than those presented here"); see also Zehr, 871 P. 2d at 1012 (holding that damages for child rearing are "not, as a matter of law, too speculative to permit recovery"). Accordingly, this Court should award the Bell-Wesleys damages for all of their injuries, including the costs of raising their son.

III. ALTERNATIVELY, IF THIS COURT WILL NOT AWARD FULL DAMAGES, IT SHOULD AWARD DAMAGES FOR THE COSTS OF RAISING FRANK BELL-WESLEY OFFSET OF THE BENEFIT OF HAVING HIM.

If this Court is unwilling to award full damages, the Court should alternatively award damages to the Bell-Wesleys for the costs of raising theirson, offset loy the benefits the Bell-Wesleys derive from having a son. This rule is consistent with the tort law's goal of deterrence and fair compensation for injuries, and it has been applied by a number of jurisdictions to avoid a situation where a plaintiff is unable to recover the costs associated with caring for a child born as a result of a negligent sterilization procedure. See, e.g., Univ. of Ariz. Health Sciences Ctr. V Sup. Ct. , 677 P. 2d 1294,1299 (Ariz. 1983); Ochs v. Borrelli, 445 A. 2d 883 ,886 (Conn. 1982); Sherlock v. Stillwater Clinic, 260 N. W. 2d 169, 175- 176 (Minn. 1977). The rule requires the court to subtract the estimated benefit of the child to the parents from their recovery.

See, e.g., Burke, 551 N. E. 2d at 5. This approach also conforms with the Restatement (Second) of Torts, which states:

When the defendant's tortious conduct has caused harm to the plaintiff or to his property and in so doing has conferred a special benefit to the interest of the plaintiff that was harmed, the value of the benefit conferred is considered in mitigation of damages, to the extent that this is equitable.

§ 920 (1979); see also Ochs, 445 A. 2d at 886 (citing the restatement to this effect).

In a similar failed vasectomy case, the Minnesota Superme Court ruled that a husband and wife were entitled to recovery for the costs of raising an unwanted child minus "the value of the child's aid, comfort and society". Sherlock, 260 N. W. 2d at 176. Similarly, the Massachusetts Supreme Judicial Court ruled that a woman could recover for the costs of raising a healthy but unwanted child, offset by the estimated benefit of the child, after a doctor negligently performed a sterilization procedure. Burke, 511 N. E. 2d at 6. While that court's ruling was a limited to those failed sterilizations that were originally obtained for financial or economic reasons, the important policy considerations underlying the court's ruling also apply to situations in which a sterilization is obtained for non-economic reasons and the family makes substantial financial decisions based on that choice.

Cases like Sherlock and Burke are analogous to the situation here, where an unplanned birth resulted from a botched sterilization procedure. Applying the same reasoning here, this Court could credit any benefits of having a child against the Bell-Wesley family's substantial financial loss when determining appropriate damages. Although the emotional benefits the Bell-Wesleys receive through the joys of parenthood are of an entirely different nature and kind than the financial injuries and the pain and suffering inflicted on them by O'Toole's negligence, this rule has the advantage of providing something closer to full and fair remuneration to the plaintiffs. This is essential because the Bell-Wesleys' deep love for their son does not negate the fact that his birth was unplanned. The Bell-Wesleys' affection for Frank will not provide them with the resources to cover his expenses, nor will it replace the time and energy diverted from their careers. Therefore, in the event that this Court finds the birth of an unwanted child after a negligent sterilization a benefit, it should apply the offset rule from Sherlock and Burke, and remind this case for determination of the costs shouldered by the Bell-Wesleys as a result of raising their son and the benefits derived from his birth.

CONCLUSION

O'Toole's repeated negligence caused the Bell-Wesleys's substantial physical, financial and emotional injuries that were left uncompensated by the Superior Court. Therefore, this Court should reverse the judgment of the Superior Court and Court of Appeals of the State of Ames and award full recovery to the Bell-Wesleys.

Respectfully Submitted,

Jane E. Harvey

Jane E. Harvey

Attorney for the Plaintiffs-Appellants

Appendix F — Sample Appellee Brief

SAMPLE APPELLEE BRIEF: *BELL-WESLEY V. O'TOOLE*

IN THE SUPREME COURT OF THE STATE OF AMES

CIVIL ACTION NO. 96-2004

SCOTT AND REBECCA BELL-WESLEY, PLAINTIFFS-APPELLANTS

V.

STEPHEN O'TOOLE, DEFENDANT-APPELLEE

BRIEF FOR THE DEFENDANT-APPELLEE

D. Nathan Neuville
Attorney for the Defendant-Appellee
Ericson, Swanson and Moses
1977 Yvonne Ave.
Smith, Ames

TABLE OF CONTENTS

TABLE OF CONTENTS i
TABLE OF AUTHORITIES ii
PRELIMINIARY STATEMENT 1
QUESTION PRESENTED 1
STATEMENT OF THE FACTS 1
SUMMARY OF THE ARGUMENT 3
STANDARD OF REVIEW 3
ARGUMENT 4

I. THE COURT SHOULD NOT AWARD THE APPELLANTS DAMAGES FOR THE COSTS OF RASING THEIR NORMAL, HEALTHY SON TO MAJORITY

   A. Frank's Birth Did Not Injure the Appellants Because Giving Birth to a Healthy Child Cannot Be an "Injury" 4

   B. Even if the Birth of Appellants' Son Constitutes an "Injury", Frank's Birth Did Not Cause a Compensable Economic Injury to the Bell-Wesleys Because They Sought Sterilization for Purely Non-Economic Reasons 7

II. THIS COURT SHOULD NOT ADOPT A RULE THAT OFFSETS THE APPELLANTS' DAMAGES BY THE BENEFITS OF A CHILD BECAUSE SUCH BENEFITS CANNOT BE QUANTIFIED 8

III. EVEN IF THE APPELLANTS' OFFSET RULE APPLIES, THE EMOTIONAL BENEFITS THE BELL-WESLEYS WILL RECEIVE FROM THEIR SON OUTWEIGH THEIR FINANCIAL COSTS 9

CONCLUSION 10

TABLE OF AUTHORITIES

CASES   **Page(s)**

Boone v. Mullendore, 416 So. 2d 718 (Ala. 1982) 5, 8
Burke v. Rivo, 551 N. E. 2d 1 (Mass. 1990) 7
Chaffee v. Seslar, 786 N. E. 2d 705 (Ind. 2003) 4, 8
Cockrum v. Baumgartner, 447 N. E. 2d 385 (Ill. 1983) 8
Girdley v. Coats, 825 S. W. 2d 295 (Mo. 1992) 5, 6
Hartke v. McKelway, 526 F. Supp. 97 (D. D. C. 1981), aff'd 707 F. 2d 1544 (D. C. Cir. 1983), cert. denied 464 U. S. 983 (1983) 7
Hitzemann v. Adam, 518 N. W. 2d 102 (Neb. 1994) 5, 6

McKernan v. Aasheim, 687 P. 2d 850 (Wash. 1984) ·· 5, 6
Ochs v. Borelli, 445 A. 2d 883 (Conn. 1982) ·· 8
Pub. Health Trust v. Brown, 388 So. 2d 1084 (Fla. App. 1980) ································ 9
Rieck v. Medical Protective Co., 219 N. W. 2d 242 (Wis. 1974) ·························· 5, 6
Sherlock v. Stillwater Clinic, 260 N. W. 2d 169 (Minn. 1977) ···························· 3, 9
Terrell v. Garcia, 496 S. W. 2d 124 (Texas Civ. App. 1973) ······························ 5, 8
Univ. of Ariz. Health Sciences Ctr. v. Sup. Ct., 667 P. 2d 1294 (Ariz. 1983) ·············· 9

OTHER AUTHORITIES

Judy S. Loitherstein, Towards Full Recovery—The Future of Damages Awards in Wrongful Pregnancy Cases, 25 Suffolk U. L. Rev. 735 (1991) ··· 4

PRELIMINARY STATEMENT

Appellants Rebecca and Scott Bell-Wesley brought suit in the Superior Court of the State of Ames against Dr. Stephen O'Toole, an established Ames physician, seeking damages for the birth of a healthy, normal child following an unsuccessful sterilization. R. at 1-4. The Appellants sought at trial to obtain approximately $766,000 in damages, including $250,000 for injury to their lifestyle and $350,000 for the financial and emotional costs of raising their son Frank. R. at 3. The Superior Court found that Mr. Bell-Wesley's vasectomy, which was performed by Dr. O'Toole, was unsuccessful. R. at 11, 12. As a result, the Superior Court awarded the Bell-Wesleys damages for their out-of-pocket costs, pain and suffering, and loss of consortium incident to the vasectomy. R. at 13. The Superior Court refused to award the Bell-Wesleys damages for the costs of raising their son, holding that the benefits they received from their healthy, normal child obviously outweighed the costs of rearing him. R. at 14. The Court of Appeals for the State of Ames affirmed. R. at 18. The Bell-Wesleys now appeal the lower courts' decisions.

QUESTION PRESENTED

Plaintiff-Appellants Rebecca and Scott Bell-Wesley sought sterilization for non-economic reasons. After performing an unsuccessful vasectomy, Defendant-Appellee Dr. Stephen O'Toole mistakenly informed Scott Bell-Wesley he was sterile. Appellants thereafter conceived and gave birth to a healthy, normal son, Frank. Should the Appellants' damages be limited to the costs associated with the sterilization procedure and pregnancy?

STATEMENT OF THE FACTS

The Appellants are a successful professional couple residing in Holmes, Ames. R. at 1. Scott Bell-Wesley is an architect and Rebecca Bell-Wesley is an Assistant Attorney General for the State of Ames. R. at 1. On three occasions before the January 2011 birth of their son, the Appellants attempted to start a family. R. at 1. Each time, however, Ms. Bell-Wesley gave birth to a sick infant that died within six months due to a fatal congenital abnormality. R. at 1. Dr. O'Toole accurately informed the Appellants that there was a seventy-five percent chance that any child they conceived would suffer from the same abnormality. R. at 1. For the sole purpose of avoiding the conception of another sick child, the Appellants decided to have Mr. Bell-Wesley sterilized. R. at 7.

On October 16, 2008, Dr. O'Toole performed a vasectomy on Mr. Bell-Wesley. R. at 1, 11. The surgery was not successful. R. at 1-2. After a follow-up sperm count test, Dr. O'Toole mistakenly informed Mr. Bell-Wesley that he was sterile. R. at 2. Eighteen months after the vasectomy, Ms. Bell-Wesley discovered that she was pregnant. R. at 2. On January 4, 2011, the Bell-Wesleys gave birth to a healthy, normal son, Frank. R. at 11-12. The Appellants have continued to raise Frank and have declined to put him up for adoption. R. at 12.

On January 16, 2011, the Bell-Wesleys filed suit against Dr. O'Toole. R. at 2. After a bench trial, the Superior Court held Dr. O'Toole liable and awarded the Bell-Wesleys $100,000 for their out-of-pocket costs, pain and suffering, and loss of consortium. R. at 13. The Court, however, declined to award the $350,000 in damages that the Bell-Wesleys sought to compensate them for raising a normal, healthy son because the Bell-Wesleys, who for many years tried to have a child, obviously benefited from their son's birth. R at 14. Dissatisfied with the amount of damages they had been awarded, the Bell-Wesleys appealed. R. at 16. The Court of Appeals affirmed the Superior Court decision, agreeing that the Bell-Wesleys could not recover damages relating to child-rearing costs because the benefits of having a healthy child obviously outweigh any supposed burdens. R. at 18. Seeking a different result, the Bell-Wesleys appealed the decision to this Court. R. at 19.

SUMMARY OF THE ARGUMENT

This Court should affirm both lower courts' decisions that the Appellants' damages are limited to the out-of-pocket costs, pain and suffering, and loss of consortium incident to the vasectomy. Their damages should not include the costs of raising their healthy, normal son to maturity. The Appellants sought sterilization for non-economic reasons. Therefore, they have not sustained an injury from Frank's birth. Moreover, awarding the full costs of raising Frank to majority will harm his mental health, discourage doctors from performing needed sterilizations, and grant a windfall to the Appellants.

This Court should also decline to adopt a rule that would offset the Appellants' claimed damages by the benefits of having a healthy son because courts cannot, and should not, quantify the benefits of a child. Attempting to monetize the benefit enjoyed by the Appellants in Frank's existence demeans his life. However, even if this Court adopts this alternative rule, the emotional benefits the Appellants will receive from Frank far outweigh the costs associated with his parenting.

STANDARD OF REVIEW

While this court reviews issues of law *de novo*, it must defer to the trial court's findings of fact. See

Sherlock v. Stillwater Clinic, 260 N. W. 2d 169, 172 (Minn. 1977) (deferring to trial court determination of facts to support a negligence decision).

ARGUMENT

I. THE COURT SHOULD NOT AWARD THE APPELLANTS DAMAGES FOR THE COSTS OF RAISING THEIR NORMAL HEALTHY SON TO MAJORITY

A. Frank's Birth Did Not Injure the Appellants Because Giving Birth to a Healthy Child Cannot Be an "Injury".

Because the benefits of a healthy child outweigh any attendant costs or burdens, the costs of raising a healthy child can never be an element of damages in a so-called "wrongful pregnancy" action. The Superior Court correctly joined the vast majority of jurisdictions in adopting a bright line rule prohibiting plaintiffs from recovering the "ordinary costs of raising and educating a normal, healthy child conceived following an allegedly negligent sterilization procedure". Chaffee v. Seslar, 786 N. E. 2d 705, 708 (Ind. 2003) (cataloguing the thirty-one states refusing to allow damages for child-rearing expenses associated with raising a healthy child). Many jurisdictions currently limit recovery in wrongful pregnancy cases to child-bearing costs. See Judy S. Loitherstein, Towards Full Recovery—The Future of Damages Awards in Wrongful Pregnancy Cases, 25 Suffolk U. L. Rev. 735 (1991). For three reasons, this Court should follow suit and adopt a rule that precludes awarding the child-raising damages the Bell-Wesleys seek.

First, this Court should affirm the Superior Court's decision that Frank's birth—like the birth of any healthy child—cannot be described as a compensable "harm". Recognizing that "life … cannot be an injury in the legal sense", a majority of courts have held that the birth of a healthy child does not damage that child's parents. See Chaffee, 786 N. E. 2d at 708 (declining as a matter of policy to award damages for the costs of raising a child). Although raising an unplanned child may be costly, "human life is presumptively invaluable", id., and the "intangible benefits [of raising a child], while impossible to value in dollars and cents are undoubtedly the things that make life worthwhile". See Terrell v. Garcia, 496 S. W. 2d 124, 128 (Texas Civ. App. 1973) (holding, in a negligent sterilization case, that the benefits accruing from parenthood outweigh damages accruing from the birth of a healthy child); Rieck v. Medical Protective Co., 219 N. W. 2d 242, 244-245 (Wis. 1974) (recognizing that children contribute "to the welfare and well-being of the family and parents" and refusing to allow child-raising costs because that would create "a new category of surrogate parent"). Simply put, "[t]he birth of a healthy child, and the joy and pride in rearing that child, are benefits on which no price tag can be placed." Boone v. Mullendore, 416 So. 2d 718, 722 (Ala. 1982) (citation omitted). The result here should be no different: the underlying policy rationale—that human life can never constitute a harm—applies equally to Frank. Although his birth was unplanned, Frank's life is invaluable, both to himself and to his parents. Consistent with this rationale, the Superior Court correctly determined that Frank's birth did not "harm" the Appellants.

Second, this court should adopt the majority rule because it is impossible for the Appellants to prove—or any fact finder accurately to project—future damages for child-rearing costs. See Hitzemann v. Adam, 518 N. W. 2d 102, 107 (Neb. 1994) (refusing to award child-rearing costs in wrongful pregnancy case in part because costs are speculative and difficult to assess). For example, in Girdley v. Coats, 825 S. W2d 295, 298 (Mo. 1992), the Supreme Court of Missouri rejected a claim for child-raising damages because "[t]he costs of child rearing—and especially education—are necessarily speculative". See also Mckernan v. Aasheim, 687 P. 2d 850, 853 (Wash. 1984) (declining to recognize damages for raising healthy child because of "the speculative nature of the damages ... and the possibility of fraudulent claims"). The Appellants contend that general tort principles dictate Dr. O'Toole's accountability for all "reasonable" and "foreseeable" damages; however, the Appellants do not provide any ready means of calculating these supposed damages. This is because no fact finder can foretell the actual costs of raising, educating, feeding, and clothing Frank for the next eighteen years. Although the Appellants offer a government report excerpt that approximates the average cost of raising a child to maturity, see R. at 5, this off-the-rack estimate is just that. This report, not specific to Frank, underscores the impossibility of estimating Appellants' claimed damages in this case. Instead, the rule developed in cases like Girdley, McKernan and Hitzemann, all of which rejected child-rearing damages as too speculative, is the only practical result. Accordingly, the Court should reject the Appellants' efforts to recover speculative damages for raising their son.

Third, this Court should reject the Appellants' attempt to recover for costs of raising Frank because such damages are disproportionate to the supposed harm of having a healthy child. The Appellants argue that the deterrence goal of tort law demands physician accountability for their full damages. However, where—as here—the recovery they seek is grossly out of proportion with Dr. O'Toole's culpability, the goal of deterrence is ill-severed. See Johnson, 540 N. E. 2d at 1370 (adopting limited damages rule in wrongful pregnancy suit on public policy grounds); Rieck, 219 N. W. 2d at 244-245 (precluding recovery for birth of unwanted child because of excessive burden on physicians, nothing that such a recovery "would be wholly out of proportion to the culpability involved, and that the allowance of recovery would place too unreasonable a burden upon physicians").

The costs of raising Frank to adulthood, estimated by the Appellants at over $350,000, R. at 3, are astronomical in comparison to those involved in a vasectomy, a low-cost, out-patient operation performed in the doctor's own office. The Superior Court's award of substantial damages for the prenatal period, coupled with the injury to Dr. O'Toole's professional reputation, together serve tort law's goal of deterrence. To go beyond the trial court's award and assess liability grossly disproportionate to Dr. O'Toole's negligence would result in the practice of defensive medicine and increased sterilization costs. Physicians will likely pass these costs on to their patients by charging greater fees for sterilization, denying a socially valuable, low-cost family planning option to patients. Consistent with these considerations, the Court should affirm the Superior

Court's decision rejecting the Appellants' claim for damages for raising Frank.

B. Even if the Birth of Appellants' Son Constitutes an "Injury," Frank's Birth Did Not Cause a Compensable Economic Injury to the Bell-Wesleys because They Sought Sterilization for Purely No-Economic Reasons.

This Court should affirm the Superior Court's holding that the Appellants should not obtain full child-rearing costs as damages because they sought sterilization for non-economic reasons and were thus not financially damaged. Courts do not award full child-rearing costs where the parents, like the Appellants, sought sterilization for eugenic or therapeutic reasons. See, e.g., Burke v. Rivo, 551 N. E. 2d 1, 6 (Mass. 1990) (stating that where the purpose of sterilization was therapeutic, parents should not recover child-rearing costs). Instead, courts award damages for the pre-natal period only. In Hartke v. McKelway, 526 F. Supp. 97, 99 (D. D. C. 1981), aff'd 707 F. 2d 1544 (D. C. Cir. 1983), cert. denied 464 U. S. 983 (1983), for example, the plaintiff had suffered an ectopic pregnancy. Fearing that another pregnancy might be fatal, she obtained a tubal litigation. Id. However, her sterilization was unsuccessful and she later gave birth to a healthy child. Id. Because Mrs. Hartke sought her sterilization for therapeutic reasons only, the court limited her damages to pre-natal period. Hartke, 526 F. Supp. at 105.

Here, the Appellants, like the plaintiff in Hartke, yearned for a healthy child like Frank. Before Frank's birth, the Appellants had tried to start a family three times, only to see each attempt result in the birth of a sick child who died in infancy. R. at 1. The Appellants abandoned their hopes of having a family only when Dr. O'Toole informed them that it was highly probable that any child they conceived would suffer the same fatal congenital illness. Mr. Bell-Wesley, like Ms. Hartke, pursued surgical sterilization solely to avoid the birth of another deformed child, not to avoid the costs associated with raising child. R. at 11. Thus, the Appellants escaped the injury they sought to avoid. This Court, therefore, should limit their damages accordingly.

II. THIS COURT SHOULD NOT ADOPT A RULE THAT OFFSETS THE APPELLANTS' DAMAGES BY THE BENEFITS OF A CHILD BECAUSE SUCH BENEFITS CANNOT BE QUANTIFIED

This Court should also reject the Appellants' invitation to apply a "benefits rule" that discounts their alleged damages for child rearing by the benefits they enjoy from raising their son, because the benefits received from raising that child can never be weighed against the costs of raising that child. Although a small handful of jurisdictions have adopted such a rule to offset awards of child-rearing damages, see, e.g., Ochs v. Borelli, 445 A. 2d 883 (Conn. 1982); Chaffee, 786 N. E. 2d at 708 (nothing three jurisdictions that apply this rule in negligent sterilization cases), most jurisdictions have rejected this rule because it would "invite speculative and ethically questionable assessments of damages that in the long run would cause a great emotional impact on the child, its siblings and the parents". Boone, 416 So. 2d at 722. Indeed, as noted above, most courts have recognized that human life is invaluable, and thus not subject to monetary quantification. See, e.g., Chaffee, 786 N. E. 2d at 706, 708 (holding that "damages for an allegedly negligent sterilization procedure may not include the costs of raising a subsequently conceived normal, healthy child" because "all human life is presumptively invaluable"); Cockrum v. Baumgartner, 447 N. E. 2d 385, 388-389 (Ill. 1983); Terrell v. Garcia, 496 S. W. 2d 124, 128 (Tex. Ct. App. 1973), cert. denied, 415 U. S. 297 (1974).

Put differently, under the Appellants' proposal, the "harm" to parents alleging wrongful pregnancy and seeking full child-rearing costs is the financial suffering, while the "benefit" is the lifelong relationship with a child. Because this benefit is not quantifiable, the two cannot be compared as a matter of law. See Johnson, 540 N. E. 2d 1370. Here, the result is no different. Frank's life is invaluable and should not be subject to monetization. Accordingly, the Court should not award child-rearing damages to the Appellants, even if such damages are offset by the benefits of having a child.

III. EVEN IF THE APPELLANTS' OFFSET RULE APPLIES, THE EMOTIONAL BENEFITS THE BELL-WESLEYS WILL RECEIVE FROM THEIR SON OUTWEIGH THEIR FINANCIAL COSTS

Even if the Court were to apply the Appellants' proposed damages offset rule, their demonstrated desire for a healthy child requires a holding that the benefits predominate in this case and that damages should not be awarded for the claimed child-rearing costs. In applying this rule, the Court looks to reasons for sterilization as well as the benefits enjoyed by the plaintiff due to raising his or her child, and where those benefits outweigh the claimed harms, damages requests necessarily fail. See Sherlock, 260 N. W. 2d at 176. In other words, the equitable principle embodied in the proposed offset rule requires that the plaintiff's damages be offset by the value of the child's aid, comfort and society, which will benefit the parents for the duration of their lives. Id.

Courts regard the reason parents sought sterilization as the most telling evidence of whether, on balance, the child's birth actually damages the couple. See Univ. of Ariz. Health Sciences Ctr. v. Sup. Ct., 667 P. 2d 1294, 1300 (Ariz. 1983) (observing that where the reason for sterilization was fear of a genetic defect, the birth of a healthy baby is likely to be a "blessing" rather than a "damage"). Courts also consider the parents' subsequent conduct, such as whether they put the child up for adoption. See Pub. Health Trust v. Brown, 388 So. 2d 1084, 1086 (Fla. App. 1980) (nothing that the failure to place the child up for adoption indicates that the parents are benefited by keeping the child).

Here, the evidence overwhelmingly suggests that the Appellants benefit tremendously from their son. They have declined to put Frank up for adoption, R. at 8, demonstrating their awareness of Frank's substantial benefits. Moreover, the Appellants sought sterilization for non-economic reasons. When the Appellants conceived each of their three deceased children, they determined that the joys of parenthood exceeded the emotional and financial costs of pregnancy, birth and child-rearing. Nothing indicates that the Appellants altered this evaluation; they sought sterilization solely because they feared the birth of a fourth sick child. R. at 8. As such, the birth of Frank—a normal, healthy son—has not economically damaged the Appellants. Thus, the Appellants' own evaluation of the costs and benefits of parenthood, evident from their repeated attempts to have a healthy child, demonstrates that Frank's birth was, on balance, a benefit to them. Even should this Court apply the Appellants' proposed damages offset rule, therefore, it should determine as a matter of law that Frank's benefits outweigh any supposed harm suffered by the Appellants and deny any damages for child-rearing.

CONCLUSION

For the foregoing reasons, the judgments of the Superior Court and the Court of Appeals should be affirmed.

Respectfully submitted,

D. Nathan Neuville

D. Nathan Neuville

Attorney for the Defendant-Appellee

Bibliography

Alisha, Sekoshi & Joshua Sekoshi. *Introduction to Advocacy*. St. Paul: Foundation Press, 2013.
Alcaraz, Enrique & Brian Hughes. *Legal Translation Explained*. Manchester: St. Jerome Publishing, 2002.
Cao, Deborah: *Translating Law*. Clevedon: Multilingual Matters Ltd, 2007.
Cohen, M. L. & Kent C. Olson. *Legal Research*. West/Thomson, 2000.
Edwards, L. H. *Legal Writing: Process, Analysis and Organization*. Aspen Publishers, Inc., 2002.
Garner, B. A. *Black's Law Dictionary*. West, 2009.
Neumann, Richard K. *Legal Reasoning and Legal Writing*. Aspen Publishers, Inc., 2001.
Schiess, Wayne. *Better Legal Writing*. William S. Hein & Co., Inc., 2005.
陈庆柏. 涉外经济法律英语(第3版). 北京:法律出版社,2007.
陈忠诚. 法窗译话. 北京:中国对外翻译出版公司,1992.
陈忠诚. 法苑译谭. 北京:中国法制出版社,2000.
[德]黛布拉·李,[美]查尔斯·霍尔,[土]玛莎·赫尔利. 美国法律英语——在法律语境中使用语言(学生用书). 北京:世界图书出版公司,2006.
[美]德沃斯基. 法律英文写作的第一本书. 江崇源、林懿萱译. 北京:北京大学出版社,2006.
傅伟良. 英文合同写作指要. 北京:商务印书馆国际有限公司,2002.
何美欢. 论当代中国的普通法教育(第二版). 北京:中国政法大学出版社,2011.
何美欢. 理想的专业法学教育. 北京:中国政法大学出版社,2011.
何主宇. 最新法律专业英语. 北京:机械工业出版社,2003.

李克兴,张新红. 法律文本与法律翻译. 北京:中国对外翻译出版公司,2004.
林利芝. 法学英文攻略. 台北:新学林出版股份有限公司,2004.
陆文慧. 法律翻译——从实践出发. 北京:法律出版社,2004.
[美]吕立山(Robert Lewis). 合同与法律咨询文书制作技能. 北京:法律出版社,2007.
[美]史蒂文·瑞斯. 美国律师手记. 王文蔚译. 南京:江苏教育出版社,2006.
孙万彪. 英汉法律翻译教程. 上海:上海外语教育出版社,2003.
孙万彪. 汉英法律翻译教程. 上海:上海外语教育出版社,2004.
陶博. 法律英语:中英双语法律文书制作. 上海:复旦大学出版社,2004.
薛华业. 通用英文合约解释. 香港:万里书店有限公司,1985.